T0354810

"Nadine is a very authentic story teller ... amplifying the voices of society with its diverse and complex makeup while focusing on the human side of what happened during the 18 days in Tahrir during the revolution! It's a smooth enjoyable insightful and moving read that sheds light on various perspectives through a neutral inclusive narrative."

—Amr El Tobgy

"Nadine illustrates the stories with authenticity and compassion. They are diverse but all part of the society, Nadine made a big effort to bring them to light. Her language is both simple and rich."

—Mona Samy

Tahrir Voices

18 ORDINARY EGYPTIANS IN 18 EXTRAORDINARY DAYS

NADINE MOUSSA

authorHOUSE®

AuthorHouse™
1663 Liberty Drive
Bloomington, IN 47403
www.authorhouse.com
Phone: 1 (800) 839-8640

Edited by Nada ElAttar, Nermin Serhan and Dominique Phohleli
Illustrations by Yasser Gaessa

Published by AuthorHouse 12/22/2018

ISBN: 978-1-5246-5645-4 (sc)
ISBN: 978-1-5246-5644-7 (e)

Print information available on the last page.

This book is printed on acid-free paper.

To all Egyptian martyrs, men, women and children, we will forever remember you and to you we all owe our hope for a better future. To all the families of the martyrs, may you live to see a better tomorrow, may you find peace and may you never feel that their sacrifice was in vain.

To my little precious gems, Khaled and Zeyad, thank you for your patience and interest in my dream of this book. To my husband, Tarek thank you for your patience and understanding in sacrificing our family evenings for me to spend time on this book. May my time invested in this book be worthwhile.

DISCLAIMER

The personal stories, perspectives and recounted incidents in this book are strictly those of the respective characters. Whenever possible, validation of incidents is indicated, however the stories are subjective and highly personal narratives. The author, the editor and the publisher, therefore, make no claims on the accuracy of the validity of these stories and personal points of view. Also, please note that all exchange rates mentioned refer to the rate at the time of the interview.

TABLE OF CONTENTS

Part 4: The Others

* *I have changed names in accordance with the request of interviewed people featured in these chapters*

ACKNOWLEDGMENTS

This book would never have made it onto ink and paper had it not been for the many people who believed in my vision and helped me realize my dream.

I would like to thank my husband's college friend, Gilles Urvoy for inspiring me with buying the voice recorder to assist me in pursuing my dream of writing. Little did I know that it would be instrumental in pursuing this book.

I am indebted to my dear childhood friend Rana Jaward who has helped me in formulating the concept of my book and Rana Harouny who has helped me in the move from essay writing to non-fiction writing. I deeply appreciate my childhood friend, Tchaiko Omawale, and my dear friends Pauline Adams, Cindy Thompson and Yasmine Shafie for giving me valuable feedback on my writing.

I would like to thank my mother, Laila Ibrahim, and my father, Mohamed Abdel-Salam, for helping me in translating some terms and proofreading a couple of chapters. I would like to thank my mother-in-law and my father-in-law who babysat while I interviewed characters. I know this has been hard for my husband, Tarek Zaki thank you for believing that this book was worth your sacrifice. I want to thank my two gems, Khaled and Zeyad, who despite their young age somehow understood the importance of my book and were always keen to know my progress.

My dear brothers, Mustafa and Kareem Moussa, who have always encouraged me to follow my dreams, preaching that everything is possible and supported me in pursuing my book. They are my drive, for my underlying urge that Egypt will become a better place where my brothers will reconsider reconsider visiting and maybe even living in.

I have reverted to several professors in the journey of this book who I would like to thank; Dr. Gehad Ouda, Dr. Malak Rouchdy, Dr. Samia Mehrez and Dr. Radwa Ashour for helping me in visualizing and conceptualizing my book.

I am very grateful for the help of Sheikh Faisal Eid Mohamed from Al Azhar University who patiently validated and provided me with the verse number of quoted verses of the Quran or Hadiths.

Among the most difficult aspects of this book was finding interesting characters and I was lucky as dozens of dear friends and acquaintances willingly helped me. Among them are Nadine Sinno, Lamia, Yasmina Abou Youssef, Randa Haggag, Amr El Tobgy, Zeyad El Tahawy, Marwa Sharaf ElDin, Dr. Bassem Youssef, Nadia Abou El Magd, Sarah El Deeb, Khaled Sharkawi, Nelly El Zayat, Amal El Garhy, Heba Labib, Amira El Borolossy, Yehia El Alaily, Ehab Kamel, Mohamed Elwy, and Aya Elwy.

I would like to thank Dalia Abdel Moniem for introducing me to Monique Hiller who edited two initial chapters.

I would like to thank all the people who generously gave me their time and have not featured in my book. The late Ghada Abdel Azeem may she rest in peace, Nevine Mansour, Khaled Sharkawi, AbdelKarim Mardini, Mohamed Atwa, Shoukry Fouad, Samer Atallah, Yasmine Shafie, Mohamed and Ahmed Elwy, and Salma Nyazi.

I would like to thank, Mohamed Ali Moussa, who wrote the legal proxy, which characters signed and who gave me legal advice.

I would like to thank all the amazing men, women, and children who believed in my idea and never tired of my continuous questioning, calling and prying into their minds. You have all inspired me in your own way.

I would like to thank my good friend Mahitab Marzouk, for her valuable feedback on my first edition.

I would like to thank my best friend from university, Amr El Tobgy, who has been always encouraging me to follow my dream and helped me in defining my personal branding.

I would like to thank Nermin Serhan for editing and validating information and translating words.

Our children went to the same nursery in Kenya, years have gone and we stayed in touch. I would like to thank Dominique Hartney Phohleli for your encouragement and your fresh eyes in the final editing, all the way from her home in South Africa.

Last but not least, I cannot describe how much I am indebted to my old jogging friend, Nada ElAttar, who was the first to edit this book and helped me take my writing to another level. I could not have done this without you. Thank you for your patience and dedication and for believing in this book.

"When you talk you are only repeating what you already know
But when you listen you may learn something new"
Dalai Lama

INTRODUCTION

"What lies behind us
And what lies before us
Are tiny matters
Compared to what lies within us"
Ralph Waldo Emerson

What Drew me to the Revolution?

It was as if we were living in the dark ages. On Friday, January 28, 2011, all main forms of communication, internet and mobiles, were abruptly severed. I felt dismay and shock at what seemed to be a desperate attempt by the ancien regime to restore their upper hand by clearly displaying their indomitable power. However, this display of power backfired, as many men and women resented having their right to communicate unceremoniously halted. It certainly annoyed me and encouraged my underlying urge to join the demonstrations but my husband, Tarek, refused. Like many households, our differences in opinion really rocked our boat. Tarek could not entertain the concept of me voluntarily participating in protests that escalated into violent clashes with the audacious security forces resulting in injuries and casualties. I resented my predicament as every cell in my body was urging me to be out there showing my support demanding, bread, freedom, and social justice. In the end, my maternal instincts prevailed over any other urge. However, my need to do something in some way or another persisted.

The government restored mobile communications on the morning of the 29th and Internet a few days later. I managed to call my dear friend, Randa Haggag, to check on her. She was among the activists in Tahrir Square, and I hold her in high esteem as she risked her life for a better Egypt. While she was actively demonstrating, I felt small in her shadow as I was not able to do the same, but my desire to contribute became even more pressing. While talking to Randa, the idea of documenting and writing the stories of some protestors and activists who unknowingly conceived this revolution, was born.

I was genuinely intrigued and keen to understand the positions of both the revolutionary and the anti-revolutionary. This book is a humble multifaceted attempt to canvass the wide range of participants' and observers' perspectives and motives which made this revolution so fascinating— capturing the attention of the world and cementing it firmly in the annals of this country's and world history.

Those eighteen days in 2011 inspired me more than any other personal, national or international event before. I felt involved, attentive and extremely emotional. I was very proud of my brave compatriots on the streets, risking and losing their lives. Their meaningful chants and heartfelt songs echoed throughout the nation. Within hours, I was crying profusely, angry at the ancien regime (the old regime). Like many others, I was on an adrenaline-packed rollercoaster ride experiencing and witnessing extreme emotions.

Never will I forget the night of Friday January 28 when I stayed up on vigil, anxious and afraid due to the grand escapade whereby thousands of convicts escaped or were released from nearby prisons creating chaos and dismay. I could not sleep, paralyzed by fear. I was ready to jump at any trespasser to protect my children and kept an iron bar, from my husband's weight set, by my side, in case anyone dared attack my family or me. Tarek also had one iron bar with him. We moved with these makeshift weapons around the house, on full alert.

When I spoke with my friends and family, I realized that this was a phenomenon shared with everyone. We were all completely immersed in the political situation and scared, but people had different views and some were extreme, polar opposites cloaked in a thick cloud of intolerance. It was disturbing to see the virtual world of Facebook turning into a fighting ground. Friends quarreling about who is right and who is wrong, each with their varying perspectives. Disrespect brewed and grew. Some stopped being friends because of their different standpoints and some family members stopped speaking to each other. This I just could not bring myself to understand, and perhaps much of the general dismay maybe attributed to rampant online cursing. Language is a pivotal foundation to the mindset of any people. Egyptians need to tone down the cursing epidemic to regain societal values.

I believe that my dear parents brought me up as an open-minded individual who is fully aware of her upbringing and morals, tolerant of others regardless of their views, race, origin, faith, gender, and age amongst other factors. Yet, in their old age they have grown intolerant themselves. When differences arise, one can argue and debate but in the end if the differences persist then we can agree to disagree. Would you agree? Is it truly necessary that we part ways? Can we not convey our message without cursing and hurting one another and breaking ties? Can we not celebrate our diversity? Can we bring up our children to tolerate differences? Is there room to implant tolerance within the fabrics of the educational system?

The events of the January 2011 revolution were intense for all Egyptians. The incidents that unraveled during the revolution depicted the universal struggle between perceived good and evil. Those for the revolt and those against it. It was a period filled with different feelings ranging from hope to fear, anger and happiness, rejoicing and mourning, unity and discord, faith and doubt, clarity and rhetoric, optimism and pessimism, humor and tragedy all delicately intertwined; a rollercoaster of emotions. Egyptian people have captured the awe of the world persistently on headlines. This roller coaster of emotions has inspired me and captured the attention of so many people the world over, evident by the high media coverage on countless satellite channels during this historic insurgence.

Points of View

The people I selected to feature in the book are a very simple reflection of Egyptian society, but by no means a comprehensive representative sample. I have met male and female activists, anti-revolutionary women – feloul (members or supporters of the old regime), an activist doctor, a victim who lost his eye, and a widow who lost her love. I interviewed a police officer, a former member of the ruling party, a military conscript and a former Jihadist imprisoned under the Mubarak regime. Among the characters in this book is a Coptic lawyer, a journalist, a former member of Ikhwan (the Muslim Brotherhood), a woman from Upper Egypt with no formal education and a self-educated woman referred to in the traditional manner as Um or mother followed by her eldest child's name along with her twelve-year-old son. Overall, by December 2013 I had interviewed thirty-nine people, recorded sixty-eight hours of tape, which I have translated, transcribed, rewritten, and validated by the characters over a period of thirty-one months.

In the past, I was always ashamed of the e-mails and social media posts circulating, mocking images that belittled and undermined Egypt. 'Only in Egypt' posts including sarcasm like spelling mistakes or mistaken signs or absurd literal translations. But during this revolution, Egyptians regained their long lost pride and dignity. History was in the making and it needed documentation. This book is an attempt to document the voices of eighteen ordinary Egyptian men and women from different ages, perspectives and experiences.

When our children grow up they need to understand what the feloul were thinking when they supported former President Mubarak. What Hezb el kanaba which literally means the couch party, a term created by Ezzat Amin, director, actor, and author of a book called "Hezb El Kanaba", to refer to the people who criticized the revolutionaries and wanted security and stability.

Our future generations should know how events unfolded from a mere demonstration to a full-scale nationwide revolution. They should be able to imagine what their fathers, mothers, uncles, aunts, brothers and sisters were facing when they risked their valuable lives and demonstrated or when they opted to stay in their homes attentively following the events on television over long sleepless nights clouded by fear and uncertainty. Our children should in the very least have the chance to read this book and think critically in order to reach a better understanding of their past, present and future.

The eighteen stories presented in this book will attempt to shed some light on key pressing questions. Not many Egyptians are active enough to try to ask why or honestly try to understand the viewpoints of others. They quickly judge and stereotype 'the other', assuming they are wrong and overbearingly confident that they themselves are right. Egyptians need to imagine being 'the other', putting themselves in the other's shoes to see their view point, their lens and even attempt to empathetically feel their social situation before drawing conclusions. I invite Egyptians to listen to those eighteen voices without judgment. Try to understand their opinions, try to respect and tolerate them even though you may differ. I invite all non-Egyptians to live through these eighteen authentic Egyptian voices for a better understanding of Egypt and Egyptians. Many Egyptians, like many humans, procrastinate and lack the inherent drive to move away from their own circle of comfort to other circles. They ultimately fall into the silent yet powerful majority, who repeatedly underestimate their importance.

Initially, there were many questions prickling my mind as I ventured into this book project. What drove activists onto the streets, risking their lives? Why are anti-revolutionaries adamantly against this change? How did an innocent victim lose his eye forever but not his faith? Why did a civilian dream of dying a martyr? Why is the ancien regime against liberalism? What were the former ruling party's thoughts about the blatant corruption? Why did they allow corruption? How did the media portray the truth to the public? Why is the Ikhwan (Muslim Brotherhood), so worried about opening up? What are the shortcomings of the current legal system? What was the police officer thinking when violence erupted? Why doesn't the police officer quit his job? How are those who are uneducated interpreting the revolution? Why does the army seemingly believe that Egypt is not ready for democracy? The book will attempt to tackle these questions but not necessarily answer all of them.

The stories of these ordinary individual voices touch the surface of what Emerson refers to as "what lies within us". The characters in this book are real people whose bona fide journeys shed light onto the basic issues that Egypt is facing and what they perceive to be the proper trajectory for reform. They are real people who will share how and where the system has failed them and will also shed light on their perception of the future of Egypt. Is it dark like the depressive dungeons at South Africa's notorious prison "Robben Island"? Is it bright like the dazzling sun on the hot vast Sahara Desert? Is it dark and grey like the aftermath of a deadly devastating tornado? Is it colorful like the rainbow over the crisp blue skies?

In addition to depicting the characters' attitudes towards the revolution, this book will also tell the story of how some changed their views over the course of time or how their perspectives were reinforced over time.

Lastly, I came across this quote; it surely rang a bell with me. "The highest form of ignorance is when you reject something you don't know anything about." Wayne Dyer. Open your minds, listen to what these people have to say, recognize their needs and understand their concerns, build bridges where we agree and let us move forward. After emphatically listening and reading, if we still reject certain ideas it will be from a deeper understanding and not blindly listening to hearsay. We can agree to disagree. Let information and understanding enlighten us to become better individuals, better humans, better Egyptians carving a brighter future for one of the most ancient civilization on earth. Let us evolve from an intolerant society that shuns and curses differences to a tolerant society that celebrates and respects diversity.

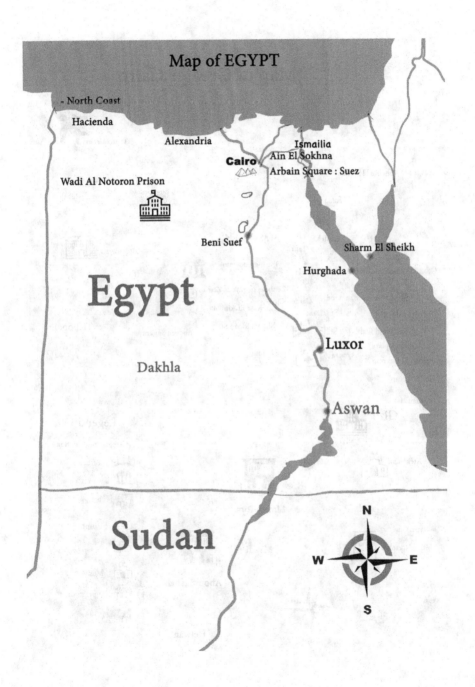

Map of EGYPT

- North Coast

Hacienda

Alexandria

Ismailia
Ain El Sokhna
Cairo
Arbain Square : Suez

Wadi Al Notoron Prison

Beni Suef

Sharm El Sheikh

Hurghada

Egypt

Luxor

Dakhla

Aswan

Sudan

N
W E
S

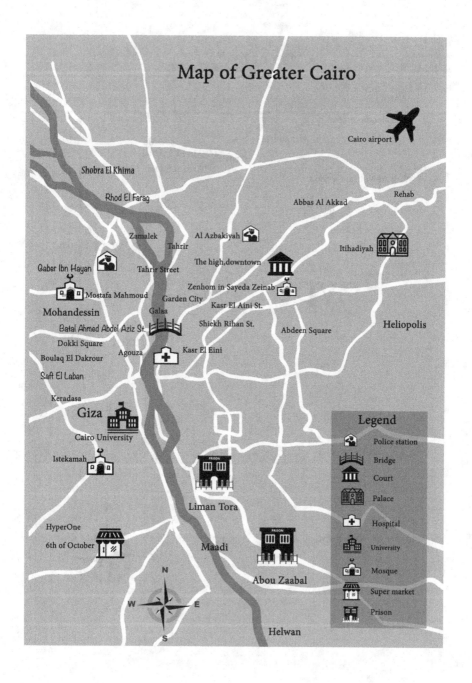

TIMELINE OF EGYPTIAN REVOLUTION

6 June 2010
Death of Khaled Said in Alexandria caused a surge of outrage at the inhumane police treatment of Egyptians.
7 December 2010
Rigging of parliamentary elections led to NDP flagrant win of 98% of the seats.
17 December 2010
Mohamed Bouzaizi set himself on fire in an act of despair that sparked the Tunisian revolution and the wave of insurgency in the Arab world known as the 'Arab Spring".
31 December 2010
Attack on All Saints Church in Alexandria led to elevated patriotism against terrorism.
14 January 2011
Overthrow of Tunisian President Zein Al Abedeen causing hope in the Arab world against despotism.
25 January 2011: The Day of Revolt.
Egyptian youth in the thousands protest, on Police Day, the inhumane methods of the police. Nationwide protests in Suez, Cairo, Alexandria, El Mahalla El Kobra and Aswan.
26 January 2011
Protests continued and were violent in Suez.
27 January 2011
The Muslim Brotherhood declared its support for the protests and Mohamed El Baradei returned to Egypt. Protests, violence, and arrests took place.
28 January 2011: Friday of Anger.
Thousands took to the streets protesting the handling of peaceful protestors by the police and the blatant severance of mobile and internet communication. Key Muslim Brotherhood figures arrested including Essam El Erian and Mohamed Morsi, between the night of 27 and the early morning hours of 28. Port Said, Beni Suef, Mansoura and Manufiya joined the wave of anger. The National Democratic Party, NDP headquarters was set on fire in Cairo within the vicinity of Tahrir square.
The army mobilized and a curfew was announced. A chain of prison breakouts and torching of several police stations dominated the evening.
29 January 2011

Many foreigners evacuated. Civilian checkpoints set up guard in neighborhoods to compensate for the police's conspicuous withdrawal. New government was instated under Prime Minister Ahmed Shafik.

30 January 2011

Chaos subdued as the army mobilized further and civilian checkpoints controlled residential areas.

31 January 2011

President Mubarak announced Head of intelligence Omar Suleiman as vice president. The ministry of interior, to save face, reinstated the old slogan "The Police Serve the People."

1 February 2011: March of the Millions.

President Mubarak announced constitutional amendments and that he would not run for fifth term.

2 February 2011: Camel Battle

Internet connections resumed. Mubarak supporters and thugs employed by the ruling National Democratic Party members rode camels and horses along with many others on foot, attacked the protestors in Tahrir leaving causalities and many wounded.

3 February 2011

Violence, injuries casualties and arrests continued.

4 February 2011: Friday of Departure.

Several protests across cities in Egypt clearly displayed the growing discontent with the violence.

5 February 2011

Minister of Interior Habib El Adly placed under house arrest.

6 February 2011: Sunday of Martyrs.

Tahrir witnessed a somber martyr funeral. Muslim Brotherhood met Vice President Omar Suleiman and negotiated a covert deal.

7 February 2011

Wael Ghoniem administrator of the Facebook page 'We are all Khaled Said' released after 12 days in police custody. Wael appeared on Dream TV with Mona El Shazly in an emotional interview that ended with him crying for the innocent lives lost and his abrupt termination of the interview.

8 February 2011

Tahrir and other main squares saw bigger crowds, some believe due to the emotional interview with Wael Ghoniem the evening before.

9 February 2011

Labor unions went on strike demanding higher wages and better conditions. Violence and clashes persisted.

10 February 2011

Lawyers and physicians marched to Tahrir. Growing anticipation with rumors that the president was about to step down. However, President Mubarak appeared in his last televised speech disappointing the public as he stated he would remain in office another six months while transferring his power to the vice-president. Frustrated protestors took off their shoes waving them in the air in an act of anger and disrespect.

11 February 2011 Friday of Departure.

Disappointment with the last speech led to escalated protests nationwide. President Mubarak and his family left the palace to Sharm El Sheikh. Vice President Omar Suleimen announced at 6pm in just thirty seconds that the President had stepped down and handed over the power to the Supreme Council of Armed Forces. Egyptians partied like never before, all night long.

12 February 2011: Clean up.

The following morning witnessed huge efforts by Egyptians to clean up Tahrir. By the afternoon, it was spotless.

19 March 2011: Constitutional referendum

The first electoral experience that included mass voluntary participation in decades. During the referendum on changes to Mubarak's constitution, the Islamist propaganda machine lobbied that 'yes' voters would go to heaven and the 'no' voters would go to hell. The changes were accepted.

October 2011: Maspero massacre

Protestors angry at the demolition of a church in Upper Egypt marched to Maspero, the national state television building, for a peaceful sit-in. Soldiers attacked the protestors resulting in the deaths of many, most of whom were Christians.

1 February 2012: Port Said stadium riot

Soccer match between Al Ahly and Al Masry ended with people from the stalls of Al Masry fans attacking Al Ahly fans in a bloody battle leaving many dead and scores injured.

June 2012: Presidential Elections

Eleven presidential nominees ran in the election. The run off was between two polar candidates: former minister of aviation, General Ahmed Shafik, and head of the Muslim Brotherhood, Mohamed Morsi. Mohamed Morsi barely won the vote, and took office on June 30, 2012.

August 2012: Soldiers in Sinai

Militants targeted government officials in Sinai, leading to insurgence of violence. During Ramadan, fourteen soldiers brutally killed at sunset.

Constitutional declaration

On November 22, 2012, President Morsi issued a constitutional declaration granting him sweeping power to ensure that the judiciary would not declare the Islamist led constitution as illegitimate. In December the second constitutional referendum took place with a yes vote.

Itihadiya violence

The provocative declaration led to massive protests and bloodshed in front of the presidential palace where the supporters of President Morsi attacked the opposition, tortured, injured and even killed a few.

Tamarod

With the parliament suspended and no legal entity that could check the executive decisions, young Egyptians took matters into their own hands. A movement called Tamarod, which means 'rebellion', was born, demanding early presidential elections. They announced ambitious targets concerning the number of signatures they intended to collect to give legitimacy to their request.

30 June 2013

The largest protest in Egypt's history demanded that President Morsi step down. Atmosphere was electric with wary fear that the growing impatience of the Islamists with the opposition would lead to larger scale repetition of the 'Itihadiya' incidents.

3 July 2013

The military feared such civil confrontation and unrest so General Sisi announced on July 3 the ousting of the president, suspension of the constitution and early presidential elections and the appointment of the head of the constitutional court, Adly Mansour, as temporary president.

14 August 2013

Outraged with the ousting of President Morsi, his supporters held a sit-in at Rabaa Al Adawiya and Al Nahda squares. After several warnings that the crowds needed to disperse due to the grave inconvenience to both neighborhoods, bloody clashes between supporters of ousted President Morsi and the police took place.

Constitutional committee

A more liberal constitutional committee came into place granting more human rights. The third constitutional referendum took place with majority voting yes to the new constitution.

Presidential Elections 2014

After 11 nominations in 2013, the elections of 2014 had only two nominees running for President: General Abdel Fatah ElSisi and Hamdeen Sabahy. Sisi won a landslide victory with 96.7% of the vote.

PART I

The Seeds

"They remembered a million useless things…but all the relevant facts were outside the range of their vision. They were like the ant, which can see small objects but not large ones."
George Orwell

" "

CHAPTER 1

Fallen Fundamentalist

"Islam began as something strange and it will return to something strange as it began, so glad tidings for the strangers." Prophet Mohamed, PBUH

After my Ikhwan contact got cold feet about this project, I eagerly searched for another person to interview. Coincidentally, at the time, we were painting our house and I asked the painter if he knew anyone from the Muslim Brotherhood. He got me in touch with one of his neighbors, Mohamed, who prefers not to disclose his full name. We met in a simple café called Mandy Cafeteria, on the banks of Mansouria Canal in Kerdasa. He voluntarily came prepared with documents proving his imprisonment. That did indeed impress me. We met on Monday December 3, 2012.

Early Affiliation

He keeps a dark long beard and prefers to wear a *galabeya* (traditional countryside clothing) in the village, but elsewhere he wears trousers and a shirt. His kind face masks a horrible experience. Mohamed was born on April 10 1977, in Kerdasa, Giza. His father is a retired government employee of the Social Affairs Ministry, and his mother is a homemaker. He studied in neighborhood public schools and then went on to study history at Cairo University. During the summer holidays, Mohamed worked as a painter or gardener to help his family. Early on, right after his freshman year in university his life took an unexpected direction.

When he was in high school at the tender age of sixteen, two of his uncles introduced him to *Ikhwan* (The Muslim Brotherhood). Their apparent intention was to familiarize their nephew with *ahkam* (theological rules) like how to pray, how to perform ablutions and how to be *taher* (pure). One of Mohamed's cousins was also a member. Whilst in secondary school, Mohamed enrolled in complimentary Islamic

2

lessons at his mosque, a service provided by the *Ikhwan*. In return, *Ikhwan* expected Mohamed to adopt pious humble behavior, namely praying regularly, respecting others, encouraging mutual respect and taking care of the poor. He attended these lessons for around three to four years. The classes were divided into small groups of four or five, which they called, *ousar* (families) and each was led by an older member. The purpose of these "families" was to support the advancement of their members; religiously, culturally, mentally and even physically through sports. The overall vision or aim was that these *ousar* would benefit society as a whole.

During the Mubarak era, authorities suppressed religious groups and groups that adopted political agendas to combat tyranny. Mohamed joined another group called *Gama'at Al Jihad Al Islamiya*, which he believes, was an offshoot of *Ikhwan*. He was not officially a member of the group but affiliated to them religiously if not politically. He had moved on to *Al Jihad* because he felt they had a more aggressive stance and demand for change than *Ikhwan*; a stance that he deemed necessary. Moreover, this group delved more into Islam than *Ikhwan*. *Al Jihad* instilled in its followers a notion that strongly implicated the old *nizam* (regime) as a religiously and politically illegitimate party that is unable and unworthy of ruling Egypt due to its endemic injustice and corruption. The simple fact that national expenditure lacked proper control and surveillance undermined the regime.

Potential recruits attended lessons about the Holy *Quran* and *hadith* recital, which elaborated how a Muslim needs to treat himself, his family and *Allah* (God). Lessons also covered politics, economics, culture and sports. There was no artillery training among the children. Only the *nokhba* (elite), when they were adults and had reached a level of maturity the group deemed sufficient, underwent military training. Mohamed was involved with the group for around three years, after which his destiny took a very bad turn. He was never an actual militant and was never interested in becoming one.

Police Crackdown
During the parliamentary elections at the end of 1995, police wanted one of Mohamed's uncles, who had been acquainted with suspects in the assassination attempt of the former Prime Minister Atef Sedki. *Amn Elmarkazi* (Central Security Forces) arrested two of Mohamed's uncles on November 26, 1995. It was a heavy operation wherein armored police trucks and even army tanks blocked most entrances to the village of Kerdasa, along with the Mansouria, and Marryoutia roads. Police conducted massive, haphazard and indiscriminate arrests of whoever did not have his ID handy. Some were arrested simply because a police officer decided he did not like them. There were also targeted arrests for those suspected of being involved in the assassination, those who knew the suspects, and those who were members of *Gama'at Al Jihad Al Islamiya* or who were members of similar Islamic groups. Around

eight hundred and fifty people were arrested in this wave of crackdowns. They were detained at an *Amn Elmarkazi* (Central Security) camp, on the Cairo - Alexandria desert road. The authorities transferred a few of the detainees to the state security offices in Gaber Ibn Hayan and Lazoughli streets and at Nasr City where they were questioned about their links to the *Gama'a*. This hunt persisted until 1997. Some of the people arrested managed to escape and lived on the run for some fifteen months while *Amn Elmarkazi* searched for them like hawks. Many of those detainees had not committed any crimes, but state security wanted them due to their affiliation to the Islamist movement. Two of those detainees, Aly and Youssef, were relatives of Mohamed and he allowed them to stay in his house for a night or two. After March 1997, informants reported that some of the former detainees were returning to Kerdasa village and to their homes. The second wave of crackdowns resulted. It did not occur to Mohamed that he was committing a crime when he gave shelter to the two detainees. The way he saw it, he was helping brothers. This was just a humane gesture towards innocent men.

It was a cold night; Mohamed and his brother were at their home. Suddenly they heard very loud banging on the ironclad main door. Police used very derogatory words demanding that the brothers open the door; vulgar and dirty terms. Mohamed was dumbstruck and quickly jumped outside the window with his brother, running away from their home, and seeking shelter on the roof for a couple of hours. From the roof, they saw armored police cars and police officers carrying machine guns. It was a frightening sight. Mohamed never expected such a thing to happen, as he had not committed any crime.

The following day a messenger went to their mother's uncle explaining that authorities only wanted to question Ahmed, Mohamed's younger brother, who was just fifteen at the time. His mother yielded to her uncle and Ahmed accompanied his great uncle to *Amn Eldawla* (State Security). Unsatisfied, the police also demanded to see Mohamed, who went to *Amn Eldawla* with his great uncle on March 12, 1997. Their mother and great uncle were under the impression that it was a simple questioning, after which the two boys would return home, considering their young age and perceived innocence. It never crossed their minds that the two brothers were in jeopardy. *Amn Eldawla* detained Mohamed and his brother Ahmed and during a specially arranged night shift, the prosecution presented their case to the General Prosecutor. It was around two or three in the morning. Mohamed believed that the tyrannical regime did what it pleased, unheeding to any political ideology it confronted.

The two brothers were surprised when officers moved them from Kerdasa station to Gaber Ibn Hayan. Mohamed later discovered that prior to his and Ahmed's arrest, police had caught and interrogated their escaped relatives. During questioning, their relatives mentioned that they had spent a couple of nights at Mohamed and Ahmed's family home. Consequently, the police arrested the two brothers. During the ensuing investigation, the brothers mentioned that they attended lessons organized by the *Gama'a*. They recited the *Quran* and read a book about *el share'a* (Theology), and *Hadiths* (sayings of the prophet). Lessons were not solely about religion. Some lessons included football and other group sports. None of their activities was a threat to the ruling government.

Torture

Ironically, the first few days in police custody are called *tashreefa*, which means honoring ceremony. For forty-five days, the police officers ran the investigation in a manner that cannot be described as civilized. Mohamed was insulted, beaten and tortured in the nude. His private organs and all sensitive organs: the mouth, the tongue, ears and the nose suffered assault. The police electrocuted these organs and beat him. The most painful was the electrocution. Police officers slapped Mohamed and beat him with guns and rods, kicked him, drenched him with cold water, and forced him to kneel. Some days the police officers hung him upside down by his feet, which led Mohamed to lose his balance and even his consciousness. Other days, officers hung him by his hands and at others times by both his hands and feet, as if Mohamed was a piece of meat. Sometimes the officers shoved him like a swing to make him feel sick. There was a feeling being conveyed that these prisoners were not human beings deserving of respect and dignity. Mohamed believes that if they were animals the officers would have treated them better. He was a survivor of physical and psychological torture.

Mohamed's cell could take about five prisoners but the police packed it with some twenty prisoners or so, all crammed into a room that was one meter and a half by three meters, less than five square meters. There was not enough space for all to sleep, so they took turns; some would stand, while some sat and others slept. There were no beds. They slept on the bed sheets and blankets that smelled worse than the dirty cold floors. The toilet was inside the same cell with a persistent stomach-wrenching stench. The cell was suffocating with no windows and no ventilation. Torture took place above their cell and the screams drilled into their bones.

For these first forty-five days, prison guards blindfolded Mohamed and his cellmates. Even in blindfold, Mohamed was able to identify whose voice was crying out in excruciating pain. Guards blindfolded, handcuffed and tied the prisoners upside down, all in an effort to cripple them physically and psychologically. Whenever the guards finished torturing one prisoner, they shoved him into the cell, forcing him to fall on top of the other prisoners, often causing injuries. There were about three rooms overfilled with inmates. At the time, Mohamed and his brother Ahmed remained together, deriving some warm comfort from their companionship.

One may attribute the sadistic use of torture by the police to the hunger for power, as Orwell wrote in 1984 in a conversation between the guard and Winston, the prisoner:
"How does one man assert his power over another, Winston?"
Winston thought. "By making him suffer" he said.
"Exactly...Power is in inflicting pain and humiliation."[1]

Mohamed heard from his fellow inmates that three people under investigation were tortured by *Amn Eldawla*: Sheikh Mahmoud, Brother Ali and Brother Nabil. It was said that Brother Nabil had died because of gunshot wounds in the hospital at Leman Tora prison. Brother Ali had been sleeping in the ward one night when reportedly, someone injected him with an unknown liquid and the following morning he was found dead. The prison doctor had not prescribed any injections. These stories are hearsay from Mohamed's fellow convicts admitted to the hospital ward. He heard the voices growing quieter and meeker until the guards silenced a few of these voices forever. Mohamed gathers that since these men did not cede to accusations and did not provide any important information, the officers decided that that they were useless and simply got rid of them. This is his theory. As was customary during the Mubarak era, media claimed the convicts had died in conflict.

Rumor had it that Sheikh Mahmoud had been removed from Lazoughli and en route on the Cairo Alexandria desert road, was shot dead with two bullets. The media, however, said, that officers killed him during a fight at the same location. According to Mohamed, these men simply died because they belonged to the *Gama'at Al Jihad Al Islamiya,* and he even believes the court never officially convicted them of any crimes. Law must govern security forces where sentences, whether life imprisonment or death sentence, are executed based on proof and conviction and not on the personalization of justice; the latter can never be 'justice'.

While Mohamed recounted these disturbing details of memories in prison to me, the azan (call for prayer) called for zohr (noon) prayer. He had three hours in which to pray. Mohamed, however, is very devout and pious, and therefore adheres to the preference of praying gama'a (collective or group prayer) at the mosque, rather than praying anywhere within the three-hour period. We remained silent during the azan. Normally I say a prayer upon hearing azan and then continue talking, but that day I felt that Mohamed would want to stay quiet. Mohamed excused himself to go to the mosque and perform the prayers for about twenty minutes. He offered me tea and breakfast; I gratefully declined the latter as I had had mine early in the morning.

After the forty-five days of interrogation and torture, once again guards took Mohamed and Ahmed, conspicuously in the middle of the night, to the general prosecutor's office. Prior to appearing before the prosecutor, guards gave the inmates clean clothes, brushed their hair, and placed hoods over their faces, ensuring they could not see or be seen by the public. Mohamed believes that the general prosecutor was in reality a disguised national security officer as he felt the prosecutor did not prevent or try to protect the prisoners from psychological torture by the police back in 1997, or such abuses as allocating a mere one pound per day per head for food. The officers would let the prisoners practice what they should say in front of the prosecution and many just obeyed out of fear of more torture. Police recorded the coerced confessions of the prisoners. If a prisoner dared to speak the truth or even demand his right to an attorney, the guards would detain him in a cell below the prosecutor's office and repeat the interrogation, cursing him and subjecting him to physical torture. The prisoner would once more be presented to the general prosecutor and coerced into a fabricated confession and denied defense, just to the liking of national security.

Due to the pain and screams from the torture Mohamed saw and heard, he opted to confess to crimes he did not commit in despair and desperation, hoping to stay alive. He confessed that he attended the religious lessons and played sports with members of the *Gama'a* and was aware that certain Jihadists were planning attacks. In reality, Mohamed was clueless as to any such attacks or missions. One inmate served fifteen years due to having a name similar to a wanted Islamist. The *Gama'a*, remaining silent during the plight of their members, did not have the contacts or the ability to fight for Mohamed's release.

Guilty Conviction
The guards moved prisoners who were young and minimally involved in any offenses to *Tora* prison near Maadi. Juvenile prison was only for criminal offences and not political prisoners. Mohamed recalls a young boy called Ayman who was imprisoned by the police at the age of ten, alongside adult political prisoners. The convicts who committed more serious offenses were imprisoned in a high-security section of Tora known as *Akrab* (Scorpion). Once they arrived, they were welcomed with a round of beatings and torture. Guards dragged members of the group on their stomachs for some fifty meters. Officers used their big boots to kick the prisoners in the head, face and chest, demeaning the prisoners and sadistically enjoying inflicting indignity upon them. In this welcome procedure, the guards bruised Mohamed's knee and arms. He stayed in this prison until the date of his hearing in front of the general prosecutor. One morning, Mohamed and his fellow inmates were presented to a hearing at the military court for *geneyat* (felonies). The trial, which took place in 1997, was referred to by its sequential case number. At the time, the lawyers who were defending their case were candid in managing their clients' expectations.

Apparently, the prosecution had built the felonies case upon the intention of the defendants rather than their actions. *During the Mubarak era, under the emergency law it was common practice for civilians to receive military trials, wherein they had no right to appeal. Human Rights organizations have raised concerns about this practice; however, even after the revolution, civilians continue to face military trails. According to Ahdaf Soueif in 2012, "Six thousand two hundred and thirty-five young non-military people are serving military sentences now. Another twelve thousand and twenty-five are carrying suspended sentences."[2]*

Most of the accused denied all the charges, as many of them were fabricated. On August 17, 1997, Mohamed and his friends attended their final sentencing hearing where the Judge charged them with reviving the *Jihad* organization in Egypt. The hearing had lasted for around two months at Hekstep, an area located on the Cairo Ismailia road. Lawyers defended each of the accused who appeared before the court. The crime was almost uniform: affiliation to an illegal group. Another crime was abetting felonies like attempted assassination. The court found many of the accused guilty, some in absentia, as they were abroad. Their charges included attempting to overthrow the ruling regime and thwarting the nation's interests. The accused were all Egyptians, from all across the country. Some were from the districts of Naheya and Badrasheen in the capital, and some were from Luxor, Aswan and Sharkiya. Others from Kerdasa. In total, eighty-seven men were accused and sentenced to imprisonment.

Mohamed's sentence was three years. Others received five years. Guards segregated the prisoners according to the duration of their sentence. Mohamed was transferred to Abou Zaabel prison. Since Mohamed had been imprisoned during his interrogation and sentencing for some six months, this period was considered part of the three-year sentence, so at the time he had a remaining two and half years to serve. Upon arriving at prison, guards blindfolded Mohamed and told him to strip naked for them to search him. Guards gave him very rough and spiky overalls. As usual, the welcome committee or *tashreefa* tortured Mohamed with wooden batons and electrocution. Once the guards removed his blindfold and Mohamed set eyes on his cell, he felt as if he was inside his grave. The walls of the coffin-like cell were some fifty centimeters thick, with a small window for ventilation. A heavy iron door ensured that the cell was sealed shut. It had a small window for ventilation some forty centimeters by sixty centimeters. He was lucky to have his brother's company for most of the duration of his imprisonment in cell number 14.

Cell No. 14

Mohamed saw prisoners bearing clear physical marks of torture. In some cases, the prisoners had severe calcium deficiency due to the cold floors and lack of proper nutrition, and in one case a prisoner almost became paralyzed. Malnutrition and dehydration were rampant with limited food portions and nutritional variety. Mohamed's portion consisted of three loaves of *baladi* bread, *foul* (fava beans), or lentils. The foul had weevils swimming on the surface. His food contained unpalatable green weeds, which grow next to vegetables. For lunch, they had foul or lentils with sticky rice that looked like dough. Their water source was the Ismailia stream. Due to the surrounding factories alongside the riverbank, the water was polluted with a thin film of oil on its surface. The inmates sometimes used their undergarments as a filter before drinking from this water, which left black particles and oil staining the cloth, impossible to wash without detergent. The prisoners were so under-nourished and suffering from lack of calcium that emaciation was normal. Some of his neighboring inmates were desperate to the extent that they scraped lime from the walls, dissolved it in some water and drank it in order to compensate their bodies with some form of calcium. His neighbors who were imprisoned over a longer period, had convulsions and they suffered extreme pain in their legs.

For around six months, the prison chef denied the prisoners salt in their cooked food. Meat and eggs were a rarity and the security officers selected the best from this rare supply, leaving the worst for the inmates. Moreover, the meat served was mainly fat, but with no other option, they ate this food to survive.

There was no room for cleanliness in prison. They had no soap or detergents to bathe themselves or clean their cells. These, seemingly, were considered luxuries. To make matters worse, the cell did not have toilets. This was worse than the one at the draconian *Amn Eldawla* (state security). Each cell had two buckets: one for water and the other for defecation and urination. Once per day guards allowed prisoners access to the main bathroom, where there was fresh water and a place to dispose of the excrement. Imagine the stench. There was no disinfectant to wash the buckets, leaving microbes, fungus, bacteria, and viruses to infest and multiply. The one bucket of water per cell was used for multiple purposes including drinking, maintaining personal hygiene and washing utensils. The wardens served prisoners' meals in utensils inside the cells. The inmates used that same bucket of water to wash their prison overalls and then they left them close to the window to air out. Their clothes were mostly damp when they wore them, as there was not enough space to hang all their clothes. Circumstances were abhorrent.

The beatings and the blindfolding were haphazard and purely irrational. One time, a senior officer was passing by Mohamed's cell and for some unknown reason the officer demanded that Mohamed be removed and receive a beating.

The inmates had their heads and beards shaved intentionally to distort their appearance. Sometimes even their eyebrows were shaven off. Dismally, even their hair and facial hair were tools for further personal humiliation. As for personal hygiene, it simply did not exist.

A few inmates developed kidney failure during their imprisonment. During the first three years, Mohamed knew three prisoners who could not withstand these dire circumstances and died; two brothers from Fayoum and another person from Kalioubiya. The former from intestinal tuberculosis and the latter who died in hospital. Mohamed's cell was sandwiched between those of the two brothers. Mohamed perceived that a nurse, not a doctor, usually prescribed painkillers and antibiotics but nothing more.

During this time, the warden prohibited any visitors officially or unofficially, including during the trial period. The prison authorities visited the prison for regular inspections. If a cell had extra blankets, or containers or trousers or jackets, authorities withdrew them. The warden would punish an inmate if he found a booklet with one of the parts of the Holy *Quran* or the complete *Quran* in the cell. He confiscated Mohamed's extra blankets and forced him to sleep directly on the humid, reeking ceramic floor. Sometimes when he slept on blankets, the floor would actually soak the blankets with humidity, as the prison was built on agricultural land. The warden forbade inmates from keeping any personal belongings. Mohamed recalls when an officer intentionally dropped the *Quran* to the ground and stepped on it; blatant heresy. So-called Muslims trampled upon the inmates' possessions, clothes, food, *Quran* and whatever else.

Mohamed draws a parallel between the political universe and the prison universe. The first victims of the Islamist political scene outside were all the political fundamentalist prisoners inside. Before he was sentenced, he recalls an official telling him that a member of the Islamic Group *Al Gama'a Al Islamiya* was advocating a non-violent initiative, which was being used to pressure prisoners. During his court hearing in 1997 and while he was in *Tora*, investigative police dogs were unleashed on the prisoners and bit and bruised them, inflicting pain and humiliation on the inmates in a grotesquely inhumane manner. When the terrorist attack on tourists took place in Luxor in 1998, Mohamed was at Leman Abou Zaabal. Mohamed recalls how, when Habib El Adly replaced Hassan El Alfy as Minister of Interior, the prisoners automatically received a beating.

Mohamed stayed at Abou Zaabel for thirty months. When ten inmates from Kerdasa including Mohamed and his brother had completed their sentence, they went to the military court to confirm the termination of their time. The court, however, denied them release and extended their sentences without an actual hearing. The court papers stated that Mohamed upon his release from prison rejoined the *Jihadists* activists and hence he was re-arrested and imprisoned. But in reality, none of this happened. *Amn Eldawla* imprisoned them once more at Gaber Ibn Hayan. The officer in charge was new (replacing the initial officer in charge) and welcomed the group with the usual cold shower of cursing. Shortly after, security transferred them to Leman Abou Zaabal high security prison for detainees, where the guards did not permit *Quran* recital or any loud noises. For instance, when an inmate heard the *azan* (the call for prayers) outside the prison and proceeded with a recital of the *azan* within the jail, the guards would angrily ask him, "Why are you calling for prayers?" and give him a beating. Mohamed believes it was a war on Islam. These guards claimed to be Muslims but Mohamed questions their faith if they beat someone for possessing the *Quran* or calling for prayers.

Whenever an officer entered a cell all prisoners were expected to stand alert, facing the wall. The cells were bigger than in the previous prison. They measured four by six meters and had bathrooms, an upgrade from the previous cells. Suitable for ten to fifteen inmates, most days there were twenty-five prisoners sharing one cell. Ventilation was almost non-existent. In the summer, it reached such a horrible extent that there were cases of suffocation due to the large numbers of prisoners in a closed off space and not enough oxygen to breathe. Drops of humidity dripped over the wall. Given the atmosphere of the cell, water vapor was a constant factor accentuated by the humidity from the floors, walls and body temperatures.

At Leman Abou Zaabel, the warden delivered food in plastic bags and there were no plates or utensils so Mohamed and other inmates had no choice but to eat their food off the ground like dogs. This treatment reflected the political situation; when that improved the treatment of prisoners consequently improved. Mohamed stayed in this prison the remainder of his indefinitely extended sentence, except for the final month before his release. Here the warden allowed visits by his family in a room partitioned by fences. Gradually, with the slow improvement of conditions, his parents could send him textbooks and the Holy *Quran*, which had to go through censorship first at state security, followed by another check by a social worker. Authorities did not allow all books, only those deemed academic reading material.

Many inmates celebrated the attacks of September 11, 2001 as a victory against American capitalism or more specifically the world order under American leadership. A little before this the prison authorities allowed inmates to grow their beards. While he was in university, Mohamed had a small beard.

Spite
Mohamed felt that his religion was the reason behind his incarceration. His imprisonment never dented his faith and he continued to practice Islam diligently.

During Ramadan, almost all Muslims fast throughout the sacred month, from before sunrise until sunset. Mohamed continued to fast during his time in prison despite the fact that the food he ate had more dust and small particles covering it more than usual in Ramadan. Mohamed's cellmates used to retell their own stories, laughing at funny incidents, in an effort to live normally. Amongst them, they had plenty of stories to share.

After a pleasant evening sharing anecdotes, the next morning the officers would look at them with spite, annoyed at the fact that the prisoners had been laughing the night before in their 'party', and so the officers beat them up. This also happened even if the gathering was for *Quran* recital. Some inmates knew contacts in the security apparatus that allowed food to enter or even visits inside the office of state security within the prison. However, a security guard warned an inmate he favored, not to share his food with the others. Against all odds, the inmates would use the worn torn threads from the blankets as a cord between the cells to send small pieces of food across to one another. They tied blankets to the bars and the inmates hurled the food across some six meters to the neighboring cell. It was a simple touching gesture; they were sharing the same plight and delights. If state security came to realize that an inmate defied orders by sharing his food, a security official would beat his legs with elastic rods called *donok*.

With the passing of the months, the warden allowed inmates around twenty minutes per day in the sunlight to air their blankets, dry their laundry and catch some fresh air. Those brief minutes had a wondrous effect on their morale. They walked in a small area some six meters by twenty meters. During this time, they could use the bathroom's running water to wash up or wash their utensils and empty their waste. For a limited period, the warden allowed food from outside the prison, which their families willingly provided. In reality, Mohamed's mother sent him food all the time, however, he often did not get to enjoy eating it. It was normal that by the time an inmate received his food, the guards would have already eaten most of it, leaving him just the wings of a goose and some pieces of fruit. When his mother came to leave food for her sons the guards mistreated her, cursed her and left her stranded for hours. She used to arrive early in the morning, and return home late at night. The warden allowed family visits twice a week, but in reality, the frequency depended on the family's economic standing, as transport and food required a budget. During those visits, Mohamed had the chance to talk to his uncle who was also an inmate in a separate part of the prison. Visitors and families crowded the visiting room. During the visits, Mohamed could not touch his mother as an iron fence divided the room. He missed her touch and soothing hug. He had been a teenager when authorities took him from his mother's care and denied him her irreplaceable love.

With the passing of time, the warden softened and allowed inmates to socialize, eat and pray together. They even cooked in the courtyard after creating a sort of outdoor kitchen. They built an oven, which accommodated baking for some three hundred inmates. They set up a small garden in the courtyard. One prisoner attempted to escape, and was caught outside the prison but within the military barracks. This backfired on all inmates as the warden further tightened the conditions overnight after they had been relaxed. Unfortunately, after the attempted escape, the guards destroyed both the garden and the kitchen. Mohamed felt hopeless, as it seemed that conditions had returned to the unbearable starting point.

Mohamed was a prisoner for ten years. Although his sentence was only three years, the court kept extending his sentence without a hearing. Mohamed presented appeals. When his lawyer presented his case to prosecution he never appeared in court and was returned to prison on the same day. Towards the end of his time, prison conditions improved. His family presented appeals claiming the innocence of their son and requesting his release. Meanwhile, Mohamed was transferred from the prison to state security.

Lost Trust

Among the visitors were state security officials, one of whom unexpectedly apologized to Mohamed and his fellow inmates from the same case for their unjustified lengthy imprisonment. The official even promised a swift release for Mohamed and his group. This apology by the official was a psychological victory for Mohamed, bringing him gratification. After all, the warden attempted to coerce him into declaring that the *ancien regime* was legitimate and that the opposition had no right to undermine it, and Mohamed had not ceded. He could not accept the legitimacy of an illegitimate and unqualified regime when it came to politics and religion. In his mind, this apology was a great achievement on the road to legitimacy.

During his last days in prison, the warden gave instructions to Mohamed on how to live post his sentence in a passive way, intentionally deluding any notions of personal growth. The regime advocated against any active community participation, be it political, social, or religious, to ensure the desired status, which was aloof and non-influential. He was not supposed to invite other Muslims to pray and in general, he had to mind his own business. These requests angered Mohamed but he kept it to himself. His case was presented to a couple of officials, who seemed to be speaking a foreign language, so outrageous were their claims. Mohamed had never held a firearm or entered the army, and was innocent of any violence.

An officer said, "Some of your colleagues are initiating a call against violence. It will be wise to meet and join them."

Mohamed said, "I have never been violent in the first place to meet them. I had trusted the *Gama'at al Jihad* (Jihad Group), and look what happened to me. I trusted the police who summoned me for allegedly a mere five minutes and I ended up imprisoned for ten years. I have lost my trust in both the *Gama'a* and in the police."
After moments of silence the officer said, "You refer to the ruler as an atheist?"
Mohamed said, "Yes I do."
Officer said, "Why? Does he stop people from going to the mosque?"
Mohamed said, "Yes he does. In Kerdasa, the mosque is open before and after each prayer then its doors are closed." (This changed after the January 25 revolution.)
Officer said, "Why did you come to my office?"
Mohamed said, "I did not. You summoned me."
The officer said, "Then please leave." Mohamed had clearly annoyed the officer.

Prior to his release, Mohamed was gradually pressured to sever all ties with *Gama'at al Jihad* and to give his compliance to police authorities henceforth. In other words, they wanted him to spy for state security. Mohamed is glad that nothing caused him to waver in his conviction not to sign documents condemning violence.

His brother was transferred to Wadi el Natroun prison on the Cairo Alexandria desert road around January 2007. This was the first time the two brothers were separated during their imprisonment. Mohamed felt a big void and was very lonely as his brother had always been there, and they had carried the weight of their ordeal together.

Most of the inmates outright rejected any sort of reconciliation with the government; in their mind and often in reality, they had not committed a crime in the first place. Moreover, most of those who signed this anti-violence pact were imprisoned, which undermined the credibility of the pact, given the reputed torture and forced accusations. The warden granted extra privileges to the inmates who signed the anti-violence pact: access to a radio, pens, family visits without any barriers and transfer to better cells. As for Mohamed, he could not give up his beliefs for material benefits. His peace of mind was more important than any worldly matter.

The court sentenced one of Mohamed's uncles to fifteen years in *Al Akrab,* a high security prison at Tora. His other uncle was exonerated. An officer tried to convince Mohamed to comply with the anti-violence pact so that he may be reunited with his brother and uncle. During one of their family visits, they talked and his uncle advised him not to meet the officer in the first place, and to reject the pact completely. Ultimately, none from his case were released before 2007, reconciliation or not. It was all talk and no action. The only exceptions were people who were exceptionally sick with kidney failure or other disease.

Same but Different

The Islamist groups had different approaches to challenging the regime. The various Islamist groups included *Ikhwan, Salafists, Al Gama'a Al Islamiyya* and *Gama'at al Jihad*. Islamic groups whether society considers them fundamentalist, or not, in Mohamed's opinion are legitimate, unlike the illegitimate old *nizam*, regime. The Islamist groups were not going to budge from their position, as their policy is legitimate. Armed or military operations, coup d'états, or guerrilla warfare is the approach of *Gama'at al Jihad*. *Ikhwan* believe change will only come about in a completely peaceful manner with society as a base and with its backing. *Ikhwan during Morsi's era have been accused of violent actions. Al Gama'a Al Islamiyya* like *Jihad* has an inclination to individual assassinations of officers or investigators. They were also outspoken against the prime minister or the ministry of interior. *Salafism* is based on the study of Islam with all its references and as such is more dogmatic in its ideology than *Ikhwan*. The *Salafist* advocate obedience to the ruler. The movement, *Tala' el Fatah*, (Vanguards of the Conquest), found it necessary to plan a hastened military coup that failed, causing around one thousand arrests in the 1990's.

Authorities had a network of undercover men spying and surveying each mosque, interested in who grew his beard, who the *Imam* was, who gave lessons, who hung out together after the prayers, and other such things. Mohamed learnt that authorities maltreated some of his friends, who communicated with each other after being released. It did not happen to him personally.

Mohamed only sat the exams for the first term of his first year in university, before his imprisonment. Later, in prison, the warden allowed him to sit for further examinations on three occasions. He sat the exams of the second term of the first year of university, at Tora prison in 1997. This happened once, and he did not sit for any other exams for almost ten years until 2006. His parents brought him textbooks on several occasions. Cairo University had suggested that each college would have exams in a specific prison and the inmates would travel accordingly. However, prison authorities refused the plan and the university refused to send its professors to several prisons to administer the tests. Prison authorities allowed an inmate called Ashraf to sit exams by court order, but state security overruled the order, displaying the authority's invincibility.

The third and final time Mohamed sat for an exam, he was transferred to *Tora* prison to sit for the second term exams for the history department of the college of arts. He met inmates from Sinai prison. While he was waiting for the exam, the warden summoned him and informed him of his planned release based on an appeal. Because of this change in events, he did not sit for the exam. Mohamed was escorted to state security, at the 10.5-kilometer point on the Cairo- Alex desert road.

There an officer said, "Mohamed you will be released soon but you need to report with state security once per week."

Mohamed was happily reunited with his brother, who had arrived a day earlier. Their stay dragged on lasting around nine days.

Mohamed said, "It seems they have tricked us and will not be sending us home. I will sleep for a couple of hours. Wake me up in two hours so I can return home."

A little less than an hour into his nap, guards awakened Mohamed in the cell and his joke became his reality. At one in the morning, the guards called out their names and shortly afterwards the warden released them. They were joyous at this astonishing, surreal turn of events.

As Mandela rightly said, "It is said that no one truly knows a nation until one has been inside its jails. A nation should not be judged by how it treats its highest citizens, but it's lowest ones- and South Africa treated its imprisoned African citizens like animals."[3] *From Mohamed's personal account of prison above, it may be argued that Egypt is not very far from South Africa.*

Freedom

After ten years of being imprisoned, Mohamed was freed at two in the morning of May 27, 2007, released on the Cairo Alexandria road. He took his few clothes and books and returned home a man, having left a teenager. He was saddened to return home without his younger brother. His family and neighbors felt hopeful and viewed Mohamed's release as a symbol that authorities would release all the wrongfully arrested. As predicted, two months later, authorities released Ahmed after an appeal. His parents were jubilant beyond description, while reacquainting themselves with their grown sons.

The security crackdown imprisoned almost all members of *Gama'at Al Jihad Al Islamiya*. When the prison released Mohamed, he realized that the organizers were all imprisoned. He could only recognize some people who simply accepted its ideology. He informally met some of the old members in mosques.

Against Injustice

On January 25 2011, bloggers planned protests to denounce inhumane and torturous methods of the police against civilians and the blatant human rights abuses. Many Egyptians hoped for a change in the regime but did not know if matters were going to be aggravated or the status quo maintained. Around three years after his release, thirty-three-year old Mohamed opened a small grocery store in his neighborhood. Due to his experience as a political prisoner, his customers asked him for updates and his opinion on the current political turmoil. He asked them to be patient as events unfolded. With the escalated security reaction and the death of protestors, it turned out that the police were ill-equipped to handle such great numbers of protestors, and Mohamed started believing that change was close.

A neighbor asked, "What do we do?"

Mohamed replied, "Participate with the people."

Despite their urge to protest, Mohamed and Ahmed respected their parents' wishes and did not participate in the protests. Two teenagers - Hossam and Youssef – from the village had died in the protests and Mohamed's parents did not want their sons in harm's way after their ten years of imprisonment. They had sacrificed enough in their lifetime. Mohamed's younger brother Ahmed, however, could not resist, and participated once without their parents' knowledge.

According to what Mohamed heard, police left the prisons on January 28, 2011 and the sergeant told inmates, "The officers left, do what you can." The inmates feared dying behind walls with no food and hence they improvised using ropes, barrels and whatever else to open the doors, and escaped.

The second speech by former President Mubarak affected many Egyptians on an emotional level, that rung in empathy and sympathy with some, unlike the first speech. Personally, Mohamed was unaffected given the grave injustices he witnessed; however, the speech influenced his parents. The following day witnessed the attack on the protestors that ultimately changed the position of Egyptians one hundred and eighty degrees. Mohamed believed that since Mubarak was starting to cede demands, it could mean only one thing: the path to the end of Mubarak's era.

During the revolution, Mohamed continued operating his grocery shop. He followed Al Jazeera channel as his main source of information. He was in a state of despair with state channels and newspapers, which were far from being independent, let alone ethical. This drove Mohamed, along with many other Egyptians, to boycott state media.

Ikhwan do not have a militia. Many of their members practice self-defense but that does not mean they are armed men ready to fight. Mohamed cannot say how many people in his neighborhood are *Ikhwan* but they are numerous, however the Islamic political affiliation is clearly dominant. They preach religion advocating punctual prayers. Many view the late entry of *Ikhwan* in the revolution as a black spot in its history. Although individual members participated independently, as an organization they joined the activists on January 28, 2011. Mohamed still did not participate.

On Dec 27, 2009 Alaa Al-Asawany wisely wrote, "The interests of the regime in Egypt have truly become contrary to the interests of the Egyptian people."[4] *This disconnect was reflected in the prevalent injustice throughout the country* as depicted by the injustices police committed against Mohamed and Egyptian society as a whole. He believes that for trust to rebuild between the people and the police, the latter need to withstand the effects of the policies under the old *nizam*. Only when the police base their actions on justice can the people regain trust in the force. The police force needs to clearly define and set the nature of dealings between themselves and the people, with a clear code of conduct which respects human beings and the law. Will they deliver on the slogan that the police serve the people? Will the police serve the regime? Egypt needs law enforcement based on the principle of equality, be it a minister or civilian in question.

During the presidential elections, Mohamed abstained from the first round of votes as he felt that ambiguity cloaked the elections. He feared rigging. Moreover, with the disqualifaction of his preferred candidate Sheikh Hazem Abu Ismail, a hard-liner *Salafist* lawyer and political leader, because his mother held a Green Card, Mohamed lost interest in any presidential candidate. He felt the elections were a masquerade controlled by a director who determines the hero based on his preference. In Mohamed's view, none of the candidates was good enough, and the Islamic candidates were the best of the worst. Nonetheless, in the runoff he voted for Mohamed Morsi. Mohamed was wary as Morsi went back on his word when he announced that he would run for presidential elections even though earlier he mentioned he would not.

Mohamed, an Islamist, did not vote for Islamist presidential candidates in the first round as he believes you need to doubt individuals or institutes before giving them your vote of confidence. Until this date, many people are afraid of *Ikhwan*. Mohamed envisions that *Ikhwan* may imprison Islamists who opposed them if the brotherhood suspected them of favoring their own kind; they would do anything to further advance their objectives to maintain power. But he believes Islamists would never kill. Mohamed realizes that his theory is far-fetched but this reflects the extent to which he doubts everything, since in politics everything is possible. As the old regime was founded on corruption, it subsequently left civilians mistrusting the state. There was no other choice for Mohamed but to vote for Morsi, as he could never choose the old regime. Even though Ahmed Shafik was not the regime, he surely was its son, a branch of the same tree.

From Mohamed's viewpoint, January 25 was a revolution and not a coup d'état; a revolution that rose against injustice. A revolution in the name of all of those Egyptians who sleep each night on an empty stomach, repressed and discriminated against.

Fundamentalist

Mohamed believes that the principles of the army are not Islamic, and that any institution built on a colonialist base is secular and hence not Islamic. Anything not Islamic that conflicts with Islamic *Sharia'a* (theology) by default is unacceptable for Mohamed. During the revolution, the army was neutral. If the army had taken sides, it would have led the soldiers into a dark tunnel whether they sided with the protestors or backed the old regime. *This prophecy materialized when the army sided with the people after Egyptians flooded the streets on June 30, 2013 demanding an end to President Morsi's term.* The road of direct confrontation, had it been taken, would have set the army and the police against each other, as the police are the right arm of the old regime. With the long lasting rivalry, Mohamed foresaw a civil war between the two power hungry Machiavellian institutes, the army and the police. The people were hoping that the army would side with the people rather than take its neutral stand. However, as some believe, the army did slightly slant towards the people in this struggle.

Mohamed got married in 2008 and has two children, a girl age four and a boy age two. Mohamed is busy with his family obligations and does not have time for political or religious affiliations. Categorized as a former convict without a bachelor's degree, his chances of employment are almost obsolete and he needs to find creative and sustainable self-employment. He is no longer running the grocery store. Currently he is in the process of establishing a wholesale business supplying food items to small groceries, restaurants and cafés in his vicinity. With the economic recession tightly gripping the country, Mohamed has had to supplement his income by working as a laborer painting buildings or trading in chicken stock.

Mohamed has an extreme perception of the west and the Ottomans' influence on Egypt. This is a clear example of how people view and define corruption differently, which therefore leads to a difference in how they define good and bad. Mohamed believes Mohamed Ali corrupted Egypt when essentially a descendant of the Ottoman rule borrowed secular, scientific, freemason ideas from the west and implanted them in Egypt. In his eyes, all the subsequent laws and systems are a corrupt and harmful remnant of a bad base and hence Egypt has all the problems it is facing today. For Mohamed, it is impossible to reform the regime as the seeds of the tree were corrupt, which ensures the tree will reap the corruption.

Mohamed refers to Christians as *Nassara* (Nazarites) and has normal commercial and social relations with them. He believes that the *ancien regime* instigated religious strife to instill sympathy with the state and ensure its existence as the protector of Christians. If Egypt becomes a true Islamic State, the Christians will enjoy more rights than they do under a secular state. *Sayedna* Amr Ibn El A'as stood up for injustice committed against a Christian by his own son who had abused his power, as Amr Ibn El A'as believed that any injustice is injustice regardless of creed or religion. Christians who are able to pay a tax – for under Sharia'a law non-Muslims pay a tax for not being Muslim – the state will excuse and treat well. If an unfortunate man was caught stealing he will not have his hand cut off as he was in need, Islam is a religion of mercy.

Women are more than half the community. Islam gave women many rights and defined their duties. Mohamed refers to *hadith* and the *Quran*, which he interprets that the wives of the prophet should only leave their homes when necessary and must obey their husbands. The role of women in the home is the basis of the whole society. The husband's role is to be the breadwinner, occupied with his work and only supervising the household. It is the role of the wife to raise the children well and manage the house, and when the husband returns, for him to see his children dressed well and his meal ready. If the wife falls short in her duties, then society becomes handicapped. A woman only works outside the home if it is financially necessary or if she has to provide for herself, as long as her work is suitable; that is, a job that does not require physical contact with men and is not physically demanding or strenuous.

Ambiguous Future

Mohamed is optimistic about Egypt's future and urges Egyptians to be patient in order to reap the fruits of the revolution. Military rule has been the name of the game since 1952 and it will take time to establish civilian rule and erase the corruption that has spread over all levels of Egyptian society like an aggressive cancer. For improvements to filter in, people need to be patient and need to change, just as they were patient with all the corruption and injustice that became the norm. Individuals need to change for the better and try to positively influence others to change for the better as well. There will be a transitional period plagued by ambiguity before we can see the horizon and vision becomes clear. Unfortunately, the old regime left Egypt, not at the starting point, but below it. It needs to climb out of this hole just to reach ground zero, where it can start building the house in proper order. This climb will take time.

To kick-start these improvements in institutes, a process of cleansing must take place. The government must properly select the key leadership positions that would ensure the success of this crucial and strategic move. Just as the president selects the best candidate for ministerial positions, the same must happen for all the state institutes. This cleansing process must be followed by a two-fold strategy, bottom up after appointing the right caliber on the top. It is worth noting that if the top fails in the process, reform will never take place, and the leader should reform but not oppress.

Mohamed views the controversial constitutional declaration, which undermined the integrity and raised questions about the intentions of *Ikhwan*, as a 'necessary evil'. State television and print are infested with views that are opposed to the ruling *Ikhwan*. *Ikhwan* have the right to appoint the government from within its ranks as the President and his Freedom and Justice Party, the political wing of the *Ikhwan*, won the elections and the majority of seats in parliament. If opposition parties are invited to join the government, then that is fine; and if they do not, they cannot complain. In Mohamed's understanding, in any democracy, the winning party appoints the government and he believes that the public needs to understand that. *Democracy is a new, misunderstood concept for Egyptians as in United States democracy the majority of the government comes into office via election with only the cabinet and Supreme Court judges appointed.* The future situation of Egypt is bleak and needs a cohesive government to deal with it. Mohamed defends the presidential decree issued in November 2012, which placed President Morsi's decisions above the law, as he believes it was necessary to navigate the critical steps on the road to democracy. The decree was meant to safeguard the imminent dissolution of the consultative council and the constitutional committee, as the parliament and the court had already been dissolved.

Mohamed did not read the constitution; he is concerned with the few articles that refer to Islam and not so much the rest. For him, so long as the administrative clauses do not conflict with *Sharia'a* he has no issue. For instance, he would have preferred a ban on alcohol in Egypt. Lowering the marriage age of women from eighteen to sixteen is not a problem so long as the doctors endorse the marriage. He sees no problem as long as a doctor announces whether or not someone's body is ready for marriage and actually examines the man and the woman. This would be in addition to the parents' acceptance and acknowledgment that the bride and groom are mentally mature for the marriage.

When it comes to *Ikhwan*, Mohamed believes the people need to be patient with them as it is their first experience as rulers, at a level of 'Kindergarten (KG1) politics' in all its dealings nationally, regionally and internationally. The emphasis needs to be on the national level, which requires a lot of reform and building, and in his view, the international scene is much easier to handle. Egyptians need to realize that *Ikhwan* are men of honor, not thieves like the old regime, and like all humans, they will make mistakes. Mohamed believes that whatever efforts the ruling *Ikhwan* will make, the people will notice.

Before leaving, Mohamed insisted on inviting my parent's driver and me not only for tea, but also for a lunch of grilled chicken, pigeon and saffron rice. He was very hospitable and the food was very tasty. It was my first time eating poultry that was seasoned and stored underground, which gives it a rich and savory flavor.

Coup

Mohamed feels that the National Salvation Front is not patriotic, as Dr. Mohamed Baradei and Hamdeen Sabahy were both offered positions in the government after the presidential elections and they both declined. In his mind, the intelligence units worked against the ousted President by releasing figures from the old regime from jail like former President Mubarak and Ahmed Ezz. *In other words, the counter-revolution has succeeded in drowning the revolution.*

Even though Mohamed did not participate in the 2011 revolution, his parents allowed him to participate in Islamist-led protests only months after the historic 18 days in January 2011. Demonstrations demanded that *Sharia* become the base of the Egyptian state before the presidential elections. With President Morsi's rule threatened, Mohamed's parents gave him the green light to join the protests at Rabaa Square at Madinet Nasr, and Nahda Square at Giza. When he finally joined the crowds, Mohamed felt the love and patriotism, and the notable absence of self-interest.

Mohamed believes the base for democracy is the ballot box wherein *Tamarod* was not a democratic process, and that just as the people elected the president, the people should have ousted him via a democratic process like a referendum. In Mohamed's opinion, June 30, 2013 was a military coup and not a revolution, which is in contradiction with freedom and democracy. Mohamed doubts the numbers quoted by the BBC, as the number of people on the streets is difficult to quantify. Ousted President Morsi ceded to change the government and to changes in the constitution after a huge turnout of people on June 30. Before General Sisi demanded these changes, however it was too little too late for the people on the streets. Mohamed did not see any weapons at the sit-ins he attended - the most he saw were small cutlery knives and wooden rods, for self-defense.

Political analyst Amr Hamzawy: "Not a single society which transitioned from autocracy to democracy got it right in the first elections. Look at what happened in Eastern European countries, you had communists assembling and coming back."[5] He predicted well as Egypt ousted its first democratically elected President just a year after being sworn into office. Allow me to interrupt this narrative with an update on the current situation in Egypt. On June 30, 2013, millions and millions of Egyptians have taken to the streets withdrawing confidence in the ousted President Morsi and Ikhwan. On July 24, Egyptians flocked to the streets in what was reputed to be the biggest protest the world has ever seen to delegate the Egyptian army to deal with 'terrorism'. Weeks later the police started the crackdown on those so-called 'peaceful protestors' discovering coffins filled with artillery and weapons. It started early on August 14 and culminated with the largest number of deaths throughout that same day. Unfortunately, Mohamed's prediction that the

Egyptian people will see the efforts that the Ikhwan will make to improve the country did not come to fruition. However, in Mohamed's view improvement did take place. Egypt's foreign policy became independent from international pressures. However, all internal and external stakeholders worked to ensure that President Morsi failed, with the frequent electricity cuts and the sudden appearance of the dam being built in Ethiopia in 2011. *Egypt opposes the building of this dam as it claims it will negatively affect the water quota from the Nile River.*

Affairs will not change as long as the law is working in favor of the ruling regime and not the people. Change will occur, for example, when media stops broadcasting lies, or at least conflicting stories. For instance, reporting the death of the 25 soldiers in Sinai in August 2013. In some versions of the story, they had finished their conscription. In others, they were going on holiday or had just finished holidays. In his view, the army has totally lost its popularity with its people. Baradei resigned his post, as there was an agreement that Qatar was going to mediate before the forced dispersal of the protests. Katatny, a key member of Freedom and Justice Party and former Speaker of Parliament, promised a release, and this agreement simply was not kept, according to Mohamed. In September 2013, security officers barricaded Kerdasa and arrested many of its inhabitants. Mohamed knows the police arrested some of his friends who had never even participated in protests. He hopes that the General Prosecution proves his friends' innocence. He stayed put at his home during the crackdown. Again, his 10 years in prison and all the torture and hardship he faced have made him shy away from or at least minimize his involvement in such events.

The court decision to ban the *Ikhwan* organization had taken place before this and was never truly implemented as the ban drove them into underground mode. Mohamed sees that Egypt, the mother, is going through a very difficult and lengthy delivery but expects a healthy baby; however, it is unclear as to whether or not the mother will survive. In his mind, it will take a minimum of three years.

Mohamed believes Egypt needs major reform to cleanse it from corrupt institutes and thoughts, and refers to a hadith by Prophet Mohamed, PBUH that says, "Islam began as something strange and it will return to something strange as it began, so glad tidings to the strangers." (Book 1 Hadith 270) He then adds a continuation of the Hadith, documented by Ibn Maja and found only in Salafi sources asking about the meaning of 'strangers', "It was said, "Who are those strangers, Messenger of Allah?" He said, Those who reform what people have corrupted or those who reform the people who are corrupting."

CHAPTER 2

Struggling Society

"What nation, at whose ignorance nations have laughed"
Al Mutanabi

I wanted to meet a typical khemar (long loose veil usually reaching below the waist) clad Egyptian mother, of the kind that introduces themselves in the traditional way as 'Um' followed by the name of her eldest son. I also felt the need to record a child's take on the revolution as Egypt has a very young population with over thirty percent under the age of fifteen. I remember watching Ali and Um Ali on ONTV one time and both of them impressed me. Coincidently, the following day I was talking to my aunt's husband, Elwy Mohamed, about the people I am seeking for this book and he told me he could get me in touch with Um Ali, whom he had met at Tahrir. I called Um Ali and she readily agreed. The first time around, we could not meet, as Ali had a high fever and the second time we met at Hyper One at Cilantro Café in the afternoon of Tuesday July 3, 2012. This chapter will cover Um Ali's point of view and the following one recounts that of Ali.

Will Power

Her name is Sabah Fawaz Ibrahim, the Arabic word *sabah* means morning. Sabah is a proud fifty-year-old homemaker. She is a short, medium-built woman with a wide waistline who wears a *khemar*. Sabah has a genuine smile and eyeglasses cover her kind, dark brown eyes. She is a simple woman who strikes one with her positive disposition. *In Egyptian communities like Sabah's, where hardship is a daily way of life, overweight women are traditionally perceived as showing signs of good fortune and health.*

On December 26, 1962, Sabah was born in the district of Boulaq El Dakrour, one of Egypt's largest informal settlements, located south of the capital. Her father was originally from Souhag, South of Cairo. He was a construction worker, mostly hired as a day laborer, struggling to make ends meet. Sabah's mother was a homemaker. Her family was very old-fashioned, conservative and did not believe that girls should be educated. Education was for boys, so Sabah never went to school. It was not a financial decision but rather one based on socially ingrained gender discrimination. Sabah was very jealous of her brothers, who attended school and later went onto university. She used to sit next to them while they studied, and taught herself how to read and write through what may be called second-hand reading and writing. She definitely likes to boast about her pure willpower to learn, and indeed it is impressive that she taught herself these skills. Her brothers sometimes helped her and at other times, she intruded on their private lessons, ardently seeking to learn. Sabah has sent her daughter to school, breaking the restraints of the society that sought to keep her from studying.

Sabah believes that the role of women in society is equal to that of men, if not more important. Society defines men and women as partners in life and hence roles should not be separated and defined per se. Whether the woman works outside or just works in the house, she is an integral part of society. Since the days of the Pharaohs and the days of the Prophet, Peace be Upon Him (PBUH)[6], it was clear that God created men and women as equal partners in society. Decisions should not be based on gender, but on qualifications, in order to eliminate discrimination. Actually, women can be more qualified than men in several fields.

Sabah, like many Egyptian girls was a victim of female genital mutilation (FGM) at the age of nine. She will never forget the pain. As per common practice, a doctor did not carry out the procedure. Her daughter, Sarah, is fifteen years old and Sabah has refused to mutilate her daughter as she has learned that it is a custom reeking of ignorance and has nothing to do with religion. Thanks to her readings, *Um Ali* has been able to climb out of the grave of ignorance. Out of her circle, many families have decided to stop the practice known as 'circumcision' (but that is actually FGM), which dates back to the times of Pharaohs. In the past, families followed customs and traditions diligently but now, science and knowledge are slowly influencing traditions.

Marriage

In 1995, Sabah got married to her neighbor, Mohamed Ali, *unconventionally late at the age of 33 since at that time women married in their early twenties in Egypt.* A year after Mohamed and Sabah got married they moved into a small apartment at an informal rural area called *Saft El Laban* in *Giza.* They lived in a small two-bedroom apartment with a living room, bathroom and kitchen where they stayed for fourteen years. *Saft El Laban can be viewed as the more favorable representation of Egypt's struggling society that lives below the poverty line, having access to utilities only briefly.* Electricity is connected but water only runs for around an hour or two a day. Fortunately, they have sanitation/sewage pipes. Water comes at dawn and before seven in the morning, the water company shuts the main tap. Some days there is no running water at all. *Um Ali* tries to do all the housework during those early morning hours and the rest of the day, bottles and buckets of water are used for daily needs. If they miss the dawn shower, Sabah and her family take their showers using a pail and bucket. *According to Ahram online, this area did not have access to water for around 6 weeks during the hot month of August, which coincided with Ramadan of 2012. Um Ali* recalls this great inconvenience vividly.

Sabah's first-born, Fatma, died at the age of one due to breathing difficulties, as they could not afford treatment. A year after their loss, Sabah and her husband were blessed with their second daughter, Sarah, in 1997, followed by their son, Ali, in 2000. After that she had and lost her a fourth child, Hagar, who was born prematurely and died while in an incubator. *In Egypt, traditionally a mother is called the mother of her eldest son's name, in Sabah's case, Um Ali, which means the mother of Ali. I will refer to Sabah as Um Ali in the rest of the chapter and her husband as Abu Ali, which means the father of Ali.*

In a traditional patriarchal society, the man is the provider for the family. *Abu Ali* provided for his siblings and his direct family. When he was younger, he used to repair shoes, which required him to sit for hours on cold ceramic floors. His health became fragile and eventually he suffered from bone erosion, better known as osteoporosis, wherein his bones withered like those of an older man despite the fact that he was only forty. It became difficult for Mohamed to stand on his feet and he could no longer provide for his family. In 2007, *Um Ali* went on welfare due to her husband's indisposition. *Um Ali's* mother and father-in-law passed away and her brothers-in-law contribute to her family's welfare by covering their household expenses. One of *Abu Ali's* brothers is a public employee and another owns a shoe shop. *Um Ali* cannot leave her husband for long periods of time, as he needs someone to help him go to the toilet. This makes it difficult for her to earn a living.

Eviction

Um Ali has personally witnessed injustice and suppression. The small apartment that they moved into in 1996 had indefinite rent control in the contract. The long-established law fixes rent over years regardless of time and inflation, favorable to the tenant but unfair to the owner. In 2010, a lawyer bought the building and amended their new contract adding the word "*moshahra*" (notice) to it and the year 2002. Apparently, this word, added to the contract in this particular year negates the previous standing contract and all the rights it had guaranteed according to the new rent law that now specifies the rent and the duration of the contract. This play on the contracts permitted the landowner to ask the tenant to leave if he refused to pay the increase in rent; a move previously unheard of.

The shrewd landowner said, "I am going to increase the rent from one hundred pounds per month to three hundred pounds per month, with a contract that covers fifty-nine years."
Um Ali replied, "We have a valid contract at one hundred pounds per month. Besides, we cannot afford three hundred pounds rent."
The landowner said, "Forget this old contract. I am capable of evicting you."
To which *Um Ali* replied, "Have mercy on us, can't you see my husband's condition."

The landowner stuck to his word and heartlessly kicked her and her family out of their apartment and onto the streets of Giza in 2010. It was injustice as the landowner blatantly abused *Um Ali's* inability to hire a lawyer to defend their rights in court. Ali and Sarah cried when they left their home, which was filled with memories. However, although Ali was sad, he had faith in God.

Um Ali had lived in the apartment for fourteen years and was apprehensive, worried and hurt from how cruel and unfair life can be. Her neighbors gathered three thousand pounds for them - around four hundred and thirty dollars at the time - the amount needed to rent a new apartment. *Um Ali* could have resorted to violence to secure her rights but she never condones violence, and wants the law to secure her rights. She vouches that nonviolent struggle is the best strategy. *Martin Luther King also believed this as he wrote, "He who lives by the sword will perish by the sword."*[7] It is because of this defeat of right by might that *Um Ali* is convinced that those who were treated unjustly have more of a drive to stand up against injustice; something which has shaped her future.

Um Ali presented several requests and statements, at police stations and even the general prosecutor's office, seeking justice concerning what her previous landlord had done. In *Um Ali's* view, authorities never even considered her request, but simply tossed it out. She never stood a chance.

Mother of the Square

Um Ali noticed that the demonstrators were demanding bread, justice, equality and human dignity, as well asserting a minimum and maximum wage. It was not a revolution; it was a stand, an *Intifada* (uprising), protesting the injustice and suppression exercised by the ministry of interior. *Um Ali* recalls groups of people discussing their demands for reform; nobody was talking about overthrowing the government. No one imagined that a revolution was unfolding. Repeatedly, protestors were drenched with the water hoses, forcing them to disperse. Despite this, shortly after the police hosed them down, they regrouped. *Amn Elmarkazi* (the central security forces), beat protestors, even dragging a few on the ground.

This Friday, January 25 2011, was the birth of the revolution, which, in *Um Ali's* view, is continuing, and far from over. Media had clearly depicted that police in Cairo withdrew on the night of January 28. However, *Um Ali* recalls the police beating protestors in front of *Azbakia* police station the day after, on January 29. This discrepency between what was reported and what was really happening, makes her question the credibility of media.

Um Ali developed a special bond with the protestors. They named her 'the Mother of Revolutionaries' or 'the Mother of the Square' and she in return, refers to them as her 'January children'; To this day, they continue to call and check on her.

On the Friday of Anger, January 28 2011, one of her 'January children' described to *Um Ali* an incident on the Kasr El Nil Bridge. A sniper shot an activist who fell on the asphalt. Her 'child' threw himself on the victim who was reciting the *shehada* (a Muslim prayer said before dying, specifying that there is no God but one God and that Mohamed is his prophet). In the middle of this moment, her 'child' managed to record a video of the dying man with his mobile and later showed it to *Um Ali*; a video she will never forget.

Usually the Friday *zohr* (noon) prayers are broadcast live from one of the mosques, but on January 28, it was a pre-recorded prayer. This scared *Um Ali* as it was very awkward. Among the unusual state news broadcasts, was an announcement that Israel had mobilized warships heading to Egyptian shores. To *Um Ali*, this was an example of the questionable news being broadcast by the media. She was scared, thinking, "Is Egypt in danger? Where are we heading?" However, she bravely stood her ground in Tahrir.

ElMidan
Um Ali likes to refer to Tahrir as the *Midan* (the square), *similar to Egyptian novelist Ahdaf Seouif, "The Midan has been our Holy Grail for forty years."*[8] During the eighteen days in Tahrir, *Um Ali* felt as if she was outside Egypt and she liked everything about it. It was perfect. It was heaven. There was nothing negative, and the atmosphere was completely charged with positive energy. *Um Ali* is very proud of the fact that not one single act of sexual harassment took place in that time. *That was unusual with Egypt's track record of endemic sexual harassment.* No ideology was propagated in Tahrir, all Egyptians were united. *Ikhwan, Salafi,* liberals were all one voice. Everyone was proud to state that he or she is Egyptian, period. Protestors genuinely cared for one another, distributed food generously and kept the *Midan* clean. There was no selfishness.

Um Ali shared a loaf of bread with a complete stranger and they drank water from the same bottle. After the ludicrous rumor spread that protestors ate free KFC meals, she remembers a parked car close by Tahrir from which a man unloaded free yogurt. The man, a Christian, had bought it. With people anxious and scared, many refused to take the generously offered yogurt. *Um Ali* found this man in tears saying, "I swear, I am Egyptian. I am not a foreigner. I brought food, the only way I can help. I am too old to participate in the protest." In response, many went to his car and took the free yogurt. Other times, an old woman would bring a vegetarian dish called *koskhari*, a traditional Egyptian dish made of rice and lentils, and on other days, stuffed vegetables were provided. Food varied, and supplies were inconsistent.

Um Ali did not like it when President Mubarak implied in his speeches that the protestors in Tahrir were foreigners intending to ruin the nation, as it was simply not true. *Um Ali* calls the second speech, '*khetab al nahnaha*' (speech of sobs), as former President Mubarak seemed to be tearful, and ultimately gained the sympathy of many Egyptians. However, President Mubarak's tears did not move *Um Ali* as she believed with certainty that he would not change. At the time the *rayees* (president) was eighty-three years old. How could one expect him to change? No matter how much he cried, the bloodshed was still fresh, and tears would not and could never wash away the blood. If matters had not escalated on February 2, *Um Ali* speculates that the people staying in their homes would have gone to Tahrir to convince the protestors to return home and let the *rayees* finish his term. President Mubarak's supporters believed people should respect him due to his old age, period. He had given his word that he would not run for office again and would only complete his remaining six months in office. Households were split between those pro-Mubarak and those who were pro-revolution. The president's speech did not win over those at Tahrir, as they were relentless in perusing their goal. Slogans like this one accurately reflected this sentiment: "*Mesh hanemshy howa yemshy*" (We are not leaving; he is leaving).

Anxious, *Um Ali* slept intermittently for three days. Shortly after the second speech, she and her family went home to take their long overdue shower and have a much-needed change of clothes. Before sleeping, *Um Ali* turned on the television. The first national channel was broadcasting a telephone interception during a televised interview with Safwat El Sherif, former Secretary General of NDP (National Democratic Party). *Um Ali* recalls El Sherif saying something like, "Why are you focusing on Tahrir square? Tomorrow you will see many people supporting the President in a march starting from Mostafa Mohamoud Mosque. He has many supporters."

At this moment, *Um Ali* instinctively felt that a confrontation was imminent. When she went to bed that night, she was edgy and slept restlessly with one eye open. After a couple of hours, she woke herself and her children to return to the square. All entrances into Tahrir were sealed and so *Um Ali* and her children could only enter through Kasr El Aini Street. Back at Tahrir, she shared her premonition with her fellow protestors and they informed her that others had warned them. True to that warning, the following day, February 2 2011, men entered Tahrir armed with knives and swords, passing through Mostafa Mahmoud square.

Unbelievable Strength

Um Ali did not sense any difference between men and women. They were all human beings, and they were all Egyptians. *Um Ali* will never forget February 2, the day when the boys and men selflessly and courageously secured the safety of the girls and women at Tahrir. That was the only time she sensed a difference between men and women; when the men took the front rows in defense while the women converged in the center, the furthest they could be from the attack.

The women also played their part, helping the men to break the sidewalks into small pieces and handed them stones to throw at the assailants. *Um Ali* carried the stones inside her *khemar*. Women helped carry the wounded to the makeshift hospital. Several doctors did not leave the square, caring and attending for the wounded men and women. The women helped make way for the ambulances to carry the seriously wounded to nearby hospitals.

Um Ali bravely stood up to defend the *Midan*. She remembers the sharp clanging sound of the iron that the protestors used to call for reinforcements at that front. It was the first time *Um Ali* heard the term 'Molotov cocktail.' A flying Molotov bomb thrown from the roof of a nearby building, hit a man, setting him on fire. *Um Ali* recalls another man who used his own jacket and a blanket in an attempt to extinguish the fire.

An old tall man in his seventies managed, on his own, to struggle with three men on horses and managed to bring them down, *Um Ali* recalls. Ali and *Um Ali* watched in awe. The old man only fell to the ground when the camel hit him on his chest. *Um Ali* remembers this same old man used to bend down and kiss the youth pleading that nobody leaves Tahrir on February 12. He had a vision that the activists would have achieved a lot more if they stayed put for another week.

She later saw an online video showing a high-ranking member of the military above the national museum pointing at the tents where the activists were camping. That sight reminded *Um Ali* of a verse from Quran, "They plot and plan, and *Allah* too plans; but the best of planners is *Allah*." *(Quran Al Anfal 8:30)*. Although they were few in number and unarmed, they were able to defend themselves and stay inside the symbolic Midan Al Tahrir. The activists were the victors against the armed *baltegeya* (thugs). Many died or were wounded on this unforgettable day. Some assailants were arrested. Eventually, the protestors were able to secure Tahrir square and restored calm, but the anger was exploding.

Solidarity

After the attack on the protestors, more people joined Tahrir to protest the violence and bloodshed. The Friday of Departure, February 4 2011 witnessed masses of people swarming the main squares in Egypt: Cairo, Port Said, Suez, Alexandria and Ismailiya where marchers moved in awesome unity to the main squares. The protestors in Cairo divided; some stayed at Tahrir and others went to Itihadiyah Palace.

It did not occur to *Um Ali* that she should feel fearful, and she never thought of taking her children to a safer place. The courage of the protestors strengthened and inspired her. When she found that a protestor, Atef, was shot dead and was lying in the street in a pool of his own blood after protecting and defending her and her family, she knew that leaving to safety was not an option for her. There was no going back, only moving forward.

Some of the youth would go outside Tahrir to a nearby café, to watch the news and return to inform the rest. The Supreme Council of the Armed Forces (SCAF) met twice during those eighteen days, abnormally, without former President Mubarak, who was the head of SCAF. That certainly was a significant absence, to say the least. It was among the signs, in *Um Ali's* mind, that the end was near.

In her opinion, if the army had truly protected the revolution, then they should have prevented the assailants from entering into peaceful Tahrir, or at least stood as a barrier between them and the square. She questions the army's position as 'the protector of the revolution'. From whom did they protect it? Protestors were sitting at Tahrir, peacefully and unarmed, while armed men riding camels and horses entered the square along with men on foot attacking the revolutionaries. The men were armed with swords, broken pieces of ceramics, whips and chains. *Um Ali* cannot forgive the army as they actually made way for the assailants to enter Tahrir and from that day on, she suspected army involvement at the level of Supreme Council of the Armed Forces, at least.

Climax

At the figurative Midan alTahrir, meaning Liberation Square in Arabic, *Um Ali* hoped that Egypt would change and turn into a genuine democratic state where injustice disappears. It was a dream to imagine that President Mubarak would abdicate his position, the first step in the journey towards liberation-Tahrir. Nobody dared during the former era to walk in the street calling for the downfall of the president. Already, this was a great achievement that merited extreme joy. The *ancien regime* is like a tumour that has been removed by a surgeon, but not before the cancer has managed to spread. Similarly, the people succeeded in removing former President Mubarak, but the the influencers still remained. The people were overjoyed as the tumor was removed, heedless that the cancer was still present.

As weeks and months passed, protestors faced the bitter reality that nothing had changed besides that first incredible step. It was as if the people still trained in the same camp, and were still confined within its walls and yet, were unable to exit. It was a reality shock for *Um Ali*. She was saddened that the momentum of the sit-in was lost and yet remained optimistic.

Anti-climax

The *old nizam* is not just the president it was the whole state including SCAF. When *Um Ali* chanted to end military rule, she did not mean just SCAF but army control over all the state institutes. *Um Ali* wants to see all the major institutes run by civilians and not the military. The army needs its sole occupation to be with the security of Egypt. Many retired generals are assigned to run state institutes and this is ironic, as it contradicts the concept of retirement and belittles the concept of equal opportunity, in *Um Ali's* opinion. She is tireless; she has participated in most demonstrations since the revolution.

During the eighteen days, *Ikhwan* were partners in the revolution like all Egyptians. But after those days, they referred to activists as treasonous, abandoning the noble cause that everyone stood up for, in order to reap the benefits solely for *Ikhwan*. This upset *Um Ali*, and activists share this feeling of betrayal. *Um Ali* believes that no revolution transpires in a mere eighteen days; it is still incomplete. She recalls that *Ikhwan* called their members to leave the square, claiming that they had achieved the impossible.

After the celebrations, differences arose amongst the protestors with many leaving Tahrir feeling their mission accomplished and others staying put at the *Midan* as it was only one met demand out of many. Elderly protestors like *Um Ali* understood that it was not wise to have all the playing cards in the hands of the army and specifically SCAF, to which President Mubarak handed power.

Third Party

Um Ali despises preferential treatment as was the case of the accused, former President Mubarak, who was relocated several times from the prison to the military hospital at Maadi. Regular prisoners almost never relocate to hospitals outside the hospital ward of the prison.

Courts are viewed as the hands of God on earth hence must be impartial and just. *Um Ali* is not satisfied with the sentence which Mubarak was serving (at the time of the interview he had been given a life sentence that was later overturned). Prophet Mohamed PBUH said, "If Fatima (his daughter) stole, then Mohamed would cut her hand." President Mubarak and his sons are no better than Fatima and *Um Ali* believed the judge should be trying him for high treason and sentencing him accordingly. The court hearings for the lawsuit against the former president were postponed several times. *Um Ali* cannot help but hold comparisons between the treatment of the former *rayees* received during his lawsuit and a professor who was awaiting trial. One was flown in and out of court in a helicopter and enjoying five-star hospital treatment at the state's expense, while the other, Dr. Hind, lay handcuffed to a hospital bed for fighting for her rights and country. She could never understand how a respectable doctor ended handcuffed to a hospital bed! *Um Ali* is baffled. Ideally, revolutionary courts render justice and swift sentences, but this was not destined in Egypt. The people who destroyed the papers at *Amn Eldawla*, (state security), in *Um Ali's* opinion, deserved the death sentence.

Um Ali views the military as having two facets, SCAF and the army. She believes SCAF, with their position as mere observers, only protected themselves and the *ancien regime* while the army protected the nation's interests. This while, in Tunisia, the army mobilized and protected the civilians and the revolution against the police force. Military police, Special Forces 777 and *Amn Eldawla* are all accused of firing at civilians. Initially, on Friday 28, *Um Ali* bet that the army would not fire against civilians as the army is for the people and not for the regime. Until July 2012, the army had not played any significant role in the revolution. The counter-revolution or the mysterious 'third party' is SCAF, in *Um Ali's* view. *This concept of third party can be referred to as Orwellian as it resembles Orwell's portrayal as the scapegoat Snowflake in <u>Animal Farm</u> and again in <u>1984</u> as the enemy Eurasia. In the former, whenever something went wrong the blame automatically and unquestionably hung upon Snowflake[9]. Similarly, in Egypt, people always place the blame on the mysterious third party.*

The police and the army have never been on good terms but with the revolution, it is not clear if they have ignored their differences to unite against the insurgency or not. *Um Ali* does not doubt that the police fired at civilians and does not believe their official statements, as she herself had seen them fire. She does not buy the theory of the 'third party' as Egypt is a state with several security organizations and no party could infiltrate that defense unless known and approved. She believes the 'third party' is a creation of the *ancien regime* to maintain the balance of power as it had been prior to the revolution.

Dramatic Irony

Um Ali boycotted the presidential elections in 2012, not accepting anything while the country is under military rule. She wrote a banner, "I refuse presidential elections under military rule and I refuse the writing of a constitution under the military rule." Nonetheless, *Um Ali* views the fact that Ahmed Shafik failed the presidential elections as a clear indication that the revolution had succeeded, since Shafik was the prime minister appointed during the revolution.

The constitution needs to represent the eighty-two million Egyptians with all their differences and sects. Egypt has constitutional experts who foreign countries consulted during the drafting of their constitutions. *Um Ali* questions the government's failure to consult these experts on the constitution of their own country. Why do foreign countries appreciate Egyptian experts whereas the Egyptian government overlooks them? *Um Ali* believes the constitution must be revolutionary, reflecting all the demands of the people that took to the streets on January 25, 2011. The Supreme Council of the Armed Forces, SCAF, must not control the constitution. *Um Ali* lobbied for ten days on the street for the rejection of the constitution but due to alleged rigging, it has passed. The Islamist constitution gives the military more power than the 1971 constitution, as she sees it; it guarantees the military's status as a state within the state, which she compares to Afghanistan. *Um Ali* refers to article 198 of the 2012 constitution, which upholds the military's right to trial civilians in military courts, should civilians trespass on military sites. This same article exists in the 2014 constitution.

Um Ali quotes a sarcastic proverb by Al Mutanabi, "You nation, at whose ignorance nations have laughed." *Um Ali* wonders how a Prime Minister forced to resign via popular protest reached the run off for the presidential elections. She wonders at how ignorant Egyptians are to live such a dramatic irony. Although she boycotted the elections, *Um Ali* volunteered to observe the presidential elections and saw many men and women voting for Shafik out of sheer fear of *Ikhwan*.

Based on the 2012 presidential elections, it is clear that Egyptians are ready for democracy. A law intending to ostracize Ahmed Shafik was revoked. Nonetheless the people themselves excluded him in the ballot. Ignorance is not an excuse to delay democracy, as the late Omar Suleiman said. *Um Ali* believes the educated segment of Egyptians has been able to raise awareness and educate the illiterate segment.

Um Ali is hopeful and feels that everything is for the best and she hopes that their stand at Tahrir amongst so many other Egyptians will secure other families against injustices, like eviction from their rightfully rented apartment she and her family had experienced.

Living Harmoniously

Um Ali recalls that as a girl she lived in a building with two Christian families in a caring neighborly relationship. She remembers them being embarrassed to eat in front of them during Ramadan, out of respect to their fasting and the holy month. She happily entered Churches at their weddings, celebrating their joy.

At *Saft El Laban*, their neighborhood, Muslims and Christians live peacefully and harmoniously together. *Um Ali* explains that Egypt is like a pigeon with two wings, if one wing is broken then the pigeon cannot fly, the two wings represent the two faiths. Egypt is a nation that embraces all its citizens. Each citizen has his rights and obligations regardless of his or her faith. All Egyptians are partners in this nation and no one party should take more or fewer rights than the other should. This is equality. *Um Ali* says, "Our country belongs to us all."

Um Ali believes that attacks on Churches were the strategy of the *ancien regime* to instill strife and disturbances in society, to distract people from the plagued political arena. During the presidential elections, the *ancien regime* tried to propagate that Christians voted and supported Ahmed Shafik, portraying him as their candidate. However, she knows Christians who voted for other candidates like Hamdeen Sabahy, and Abdel Meniem Abou El Fotouh.

Assaults

After the revolution, during the events at the cabinet building incident, *Um Ali* recalls an incident where she saw a woman struggling to carry a wounded, bleeding man on her back and moving him away from the army, who were about to surround him. It was an incredible act of bravery and strength, which moved *Um Ali*. One of her 'January children' called Mourdy was assaulted by the army who tore his clothes, dragged him on the ground, stole his mobile, camera and wallet and inhumanely electrocuted him and throwing away his body when he was on the verge of death.

At the *Abbasiya* blood bath, *Um Ali* and her children stood very close to the army tank and *Um Ali* pulled her daughter to get her out of harm's way. Sarah was not afraid.

Sarah said, "Our brothers have died. We cannot run away. We must stand strong."

Negativity crawled onto Tahrir after March 2011 when *Ikhwan* appeared to want the fast track to achieve their ambitions and interests, as was demonstrated in their parliamentary and *shoura* (Upper house of parliament) elections. *They reached a crossroads where Islamists and activists who once were united against Mubarak, parted ways.* The vision for Egypt was different in the eyes of the revolutionaries and Islamists.

Misgiving

Um Ali does not trust *Ikhwan* and is against them, based on their history. She recalls that the founder of *Ikhwan*, Hassan El Bana, accepted a scholarship from the British, including a promise from the King of Egypt that he guaranteed him a parliamentary seat. However, when the King had a change of heart, Bana turned against him and resorted to violence and bloodshed that he sanctioned, advocating that ends justify the means. In 2011, they betrayed the revolution even before Mubarak actually stepped down. On February 9, *Ikhwan*, represented by El Beltagy, agreed to meet with the late Vice President Omar Suleiman and made an agreement that *Ikhwan* were advocating that the protesting was enough, and everyone should go home while President Mubarak finished his six months in office. *Um Ali* considers this the first betrayal of the revolution by *Ikhwan*.

As months have passed, *Um Ali* has been reading between the lines. El Beltagy said in some slip of the tongue that if protestors chanting against President Morsi did not pull their act together, then there would be another attack such as the infamous camel attack, referring to the deadly February 2, 2011 attack, which turned the tide against the *ancien regime*. *Um Ali* gathered from this statement that *Ikhwan* were the ones behind the attack and not former NDP, National Democratic Party, as perceived. *It is a possibility, yet unproven by the court.*

Um Ali has realized that people inside the *Midan* have a different viewpoint to those who were outside by default. Another suspicious fact that *Um Ali* ponders that the escaped Morsi, was able to make a telephone call to Jazeera when all the mobiles were not operating. Why did he have access to a satellite phone? How could Morsi have escaped from a prison at Wadi El Natroun, a desolate hillside? Which families that live there helped Morsi escape, as he has claimed?

Um Ali denies the statement by Ahmed Shafik and Omar Sulieman that the *Ikhwan* killed protestors; she is ready to testify in court that it is not true. However, *Ikhwan* abandoned Tahrir for a short while after they held talks with the late vice president around February 9. She finds this to be a betrayal. Moreover, the *ancien regime* have repeatedly used *Ikhwan* to attain objectives and then discarded them, which justifies her distrust.

The parliament failed to live up to the expectations of the revolution, as there was only one good law that came out of it. According to this law, a working woman who is the sole bread winner of her household, would be entitled to some form of pension whether she is divorced, widowed, or if her husband is disabled as in the case of *Um Ali*. The government supports them with around one hundred and twenty pounds per month, less than twenty dollars (at the time of the interview). However, *Um Ali*

36

does not know how to claim it. Finally, there was one law that addresses struggling society. The minimum income her family needs is one thousand five hundred pounds to cover, rent, school, food, and clothes.

During President Morsi's speech at Tahrir, he announced that he would have full presidential powers denouncing the SCAF's complementary constitutional declaration. However, the following day he was sworn into office at the Constitutional Court. The President's actions contradicted his words; one day, denouncing constitutional declaration and the next day sworn into office at the Constitutional Court. After the presidential elections, *Um Ali* found it was still too early to judge and she wanted to give them the benefit of the doubt. However, by January 2013, it was clear in *Um Ali's* mind that either President Morsi should leave office, or he should face charges. Better still, the court should release former President Mubarak, as the former is much worse than the latter, to her dismay. Egyptians need to be patient. Activists are similar to *Hezb el Kanaba* as they both want stability. Activists shed their blood in the hope of a better Egypt. They seek stability based upon the valid revolutionary demands. She cannot accept stability when the minimum and maximum wages are still not in effect. How can there be stability when thousands and thousands of families are eating from the garbage? *Um Ali* is not deceived. She rejects illusionary stability.

ONTV, a local television channel, contacted Ali's mother via an activist, Nazly, as they wanted to talk to women who participated in the revolution, and Ali tagged along. *Um Ali* presented a picture of a school exam to Reem Magued, the TV host in June 2012. Among the questions in the final exams of the third year of secondary school was an essay asking how the army saved a Nile ferryboat and how the army protected the revolution. Ali's sister, Sarah, was obliged to answer a question that imposed on her an opinion, inhibiting her freedom of opinion or expression. If she answered differently, she risked losing points in her final exam and indeed, she failed.

Future
The irony is that Egypt is the mother of civilizations and yet today, it is not living in a civilized state. Egypt is filled with riches, but *Um Ali* believes that other countries, and not Egyptians, enjoy this fortune while the country neglects the unfortunate who are overwhelmed by tragedies. In 2008, a rockslide demolished buildings in a place below the Moqattam hill called *Doweiqa*, east of Central Cairo, killing seventeen, trapping hundreds under rubble, and leaving dozens of families homeless. *According to the blog called "Egyptian Chronicles" by Zeinobia, Moqattam is formed from limestone and therefore does not hold against water. The area should not be inhabited. Authorities however, ignored the advice of geologists.*

Um Ali sees a bright future for Egypt where it will evolve to shine as one of the great nations in the world once the revolution continues and succeeds in attaining its demands. The revolution must reap its fruits. The activists will succeed when they win the elections and a substantial portion of parliamentary seats; for instance, forty percent of young revolutionaries should become politicians. These revolutionaries would succeed in destroying corruption. Elders, however, are not leaving any possibility for this to happen, as they do not want change or reform. *Um Ali* is of the opinion that a revolutionary does not believe in democracy and laws, as a revolution is a short-lived state of emergency where the law is suspended.

After the first one hundred days of President Morsi's rule, while protesting in September 2012, *Um Ali* demonstrated her creativity. While she was protesting the Islamist led constitution, she came out with lyrics and rapped them on the street. I was very surprised and happy to watch her.[10] She wore a black galabeya and blue *khemar* as she rapped these verses, which rhyme in Arabic:
"Morsi Beh Morsi Beh, a kilo of tomato is for seven pounds,
Morsi ya Morsi ya Morsi, justice or leave the chair,
Morsi ya Morsi ya Morsi, freedom or leave the chair,
the *nahda* (renaissance) project we have not seen…
those who are asking what is new? Everyday a new martyr perishes.
Raise, raise and raise your voice.
They want the revolution to die. I am not afraid like the past.
The revolution is in every place.
The voice of the revolution is rising, rising.
The voice of the revolution will not die."

Um Ali says, "Don't despair, the revolution is continuing." Activists should not raise their hopes on *Ikhwan* as history has proven that *Ikhwan* are not revolutionaries. Activists need to unite and depend on themselves and be patient. The revolution needs a long endurance strategy. The only hope for Egypt is that its people become aware. In 2011, people rebuked *Um Ali* for joining the protestors. However, two years later, more people have changed heart and support her. *Um Ali* has doubts and worries as to how Egyptians will reach this awareness. State TV is still the propaganda machine of the regime just like during Mubarak's era. Egypt 25 is the channel that propagates *Ikhwan* policy. She is disappointed that the Azhar radio station is airing less Quran and is now politicized, distracted from spreading the words of Islam. She hopes Egyptians will eventually live in dignity. *Um Ali* is an optimist but also a realist as she predicts that more bloodshed and violence will infest the country before all attain dignity. She cannot bet on the army as she initially holds them accountable for handing the reigns of the country to *Ikhwan*.

Third Wave

Um Ali participated in the *Tamarod* campaign and collected signatures as she found it a means to overrule Islamic fascism. She camped in front of the palace with her son until the military announced the good news of overthrowing President Morsi.

Um Ali classifies the Egyptian revolution into three waves. The first was January 2011; the second was November 2011 at Mohamed Mahmoud Street; and *Tamarod* ushered in the third wave in July 2013. For her the revolution continues. Now from the point of view of *Hezb El Kanaba* who have become the newly initiated activists, July 2013 is a new revolution. It was a revolution and not a military coup, as in her definition in a coup the military makes the move and not the people.

The new 2013 government is weak and made up of old people. She hopes revolutionaries will win a substantial portion of the seats in the future. After *Ikhwan* won the parliamentary elections, they said that legitimacy is in the parliament, and not Tahrir. *Um Ali* finds it ironic as it was Tahrir that gave *Ikhwan* the golden chance to win the majority of seats in the parliament, in the first place.

If Field Marshal Sisi runs for President, she will certainly not vote for him, she says. She made up a creative chant, "*Yaskot kul man khan, askar, feloul, Ikhwan*" which means, "Down to all traitors, military, *feloul* and Muslim brotherhood."

The revolution is an idea that cannot die. Egyptians rose against President Mubarak, the Godfather. The army protected the *rayees* as they lashed out at the people with the demeaning virginity tests and the bloody street war at Mohamed Mahmoud Street. In her mind, it is apparent that a deal took place between the army and *Ikhwan* for power sharing. For her the army, *Ikhwan* and *feloul* all have blood on their hands. She boycotted the constitutional referendums in 2012 and 2014, as they were both illegitimate, for protecting military superiority and allowing civilians to face military courts.

Um Ali's husband passed away at the end of 2014 leaving a void in her life, and yet opening an opportunity for her to start working. She was no longer tied down by the need to assist her late husband.

Um Ali represents a typical Egyptian homemaker struggling in society who ventured to Tahrir in hope for a better tomorrow and until today, she is still waiting for the better tomorrow.

CHAPTER 3

Candid Child

"A revolution is not a bed of roses. A revolution is a struggle between the future and the past." Fidel Castro

Egypt has a very young population, with over thirty percent under the age of fifteen. Therefore, I felt the need to record a child's take on the revolution. I remember watching Ali and Um Ali on ONTV once and both of them impressed me. Coincidently, the following day I was talking to my aunt's husband, Elwy Mohamed, about the people I am seeking for this book and he told me he could get me in touch with Um Ali, whom he had met at Tahrir. I called Um Ali and she readily agreed. The first time around, we could not meet, as Ali was sick with a high fever. Our second try succeeded and we met at Hyper One at Cilantro Café in the afternoon of Tuesday, July 3, 2012 on the same day that I met his mother, interviewed in Chapter 2.

Little Man

He was wearing black trousers and a bright orange shirt. Thin and of average height, he is around one meter and fifty centimeters tall, with vivid brown eyes and brown hair. He leaves the impression that he is a quiet, obedient boy, and his eyes shine with intelligence. Ali was eleven and a half years old at the time of the interview.

Ali Mohamed Ali was born on February 19, 2000 in Cairo. Ali's father, *Abu Ali*, used to work in a shoe shop at Ateba, in Central Cairo, but currently he is bedridden. *Abu Ali* has been indisposed for a long time, for around nine years now. Ali's mother, *Um Ali*, is a homemaker. Ali has an older sister, Sarah, who is thirteen years old and attends an all-girls public school. Sarah does not know many verses of the Quran by heart, unlike Ali who knows thirteen of the thirty parts of the Quran. Ali started learning the Quran at the tender age of five. *Ali and his sister did not enjoy the benefits of attending pre-school, which Egyptians perceive as a luxury and not a foundation stage, partially because many cannot afford it.* At the age of seven, he enrolled in a public primary school and obtained a certificate from *Azhar. The school system is supervised by the Azhar, one of the first universities in the world, and a chief center of Islamic learning.*

Ali enjoyed listening to his father when it came to politics. *Abu Ali* is very politically inclined and enjoys political discussions. When he was single, he was a member of the *Wafd* party. When Ali grows up, he wants to study political science and economics.

Ali helps his mother by running errands and buying groceries, while his sister helps with the household chores. He also helps in the house if needed. Ali has a progressive opinion, as he believes boys and girls play the same role in society and their only difference is physical. Ali even perceives that women should enter the army and fight in wars, disregarding the stereotype that women are weak. God has created humans not man and woman. *This thinking is not common in Egyptian patriarchal society.*

Initial Doubts

A day prior to the pre-announced demonstrations, *Um Ali* and Ali came to learn about the scheduled protest against the oppression of the people by the police officers. The first day of the protests, Ali and his family stayed at home, glued to the television screen to watch the news. His mother sensed that the national state TV was not portraying the reality of the situation on the street. The media claimed the protestors were youth who want to destroy the country. Ali and his parents did not sense that from the coverage of other channels. *Um Ali* never expected violence to reach such levels but she was proud that the youth persevered.

That night, while watching the news they talked about the events.
Ali said, "Dad! Mom! There is a protest called for tomorrow in Tahrir and Imbaba. One of the planned marches will start from Imbaba to Tahrir." Imbaba to Tahrir is around five metro stops.
Abu Ali said, "Yes I have heard about it too."
Um Ali said, "If the protest is a genuine rising against injustice, then we should go and stand with them so that we can voice our request for justice."
Abu Ali said, "If they are funded by foreigners with the intent of destroying the country we will stand up against them to protect Egypt".
On January 26, Ali and his family packed a small bag and camped in Tahrir.

Tahrir Camp

Ali was wary when walking into the square, expecting that he and his family would be beaten and forced to leave. Inside the square, tear gas, rods, bird pellets, and rifle shots pervaded the scene. Nevertheless, at Tahrir, his doubts evaporated and he was certain that they were doing the right thing. That night some people managed to sleep within the square, whilst others slept on the sidewalks; Ali slept on the street. Without tents or blankets, the night was very cold and his bones ached. Witnessing the protests was Ali's initiation into politics.

Throughout the 18 days, *Abu Ali* would accompany them some of the time and on other days, his daughter or son who took turns to take care of him to assure that they could both join the protests. On other occasions, Ali's aunt or neighbor took care of his father.

On the night of January 27, central security forces, mobilized to try to force the protestors to leave *Tahrir* after sunset. Following this assault, Ali and his family packed their belongings and returned to their simple home. However, the family's will was not broken, but rather strengthened as they returned fully charged on the Friday of Anger, January 28, 2011. Ali joined the demonstrations as he knew and believed that the *ancien regime* was corrupt, and did not guarantee security.

Ali moved back and forth, avoiding the security officers. Eventually, he was able to enter the square with his family where they camped until March 3. At Tahrir, Ali heard from people that fighting was underway across the governorates and that police fired live bullets at the peaceful protestors. Suez started the wave of protests, ahead of Cairo, and witnessed the withdrawal of security forces before the capital.

The more the President ignored the demands of the people, the more he buried himself in his own grave as the demands of the protestors escalated. By Friday January 28, people had already voiced their demand that the regime should fall. A simple yet life-altering demand that has changed the course of Egypt's history forever. On that Friday morning, the government cut off mobile phones and internet lines in preparation for a street war. Ali considers this to be among the unintelligent moves the *ancien regime* made, as although it meant to curtail the street movement, it backfired, provoking more people who originally were not revolutionary, to protest.

The *ancien regime* was unbelievably callous, belittling the masses and placing itself at a point of no return. The old government's handling of the matter led to increased flocks of protestors from around five thousand to twenty thousand, then thirty thousand at Tahrir square *(Foreign Policy Magazine puts the smallest estimate of the number of protesters in Tahrir during the 18-day sit in at "more than quarter of a million").* The numbers kept growing. In his second speech, former President Mubarak addressed Egyptians, giving his people an ultimatum "to choose between chaos and stability." Ali resented this limiting choice as most protestors did, and believed that Mubarak's reign was over. He did not believe that chaos would prevail.

Ali was confident that Egyptians could protect themselves by themselves and still overthrow the dictator. Former President Mubarak stated that civilians had the right to protest peacefully, but did not have the right to vandalize any property. Ali viewed this as propaganda, as security officers assaulted protestors even when no violence or vandalism took place.

Ali used to sleep on nothing more than a plastic sheet and a bed sheet on the sidewalk. Sticks and sheets of plastic material were used to set up tents. During the nights, gunshots echoed against the buildings with rampant fighting underway. Filled with anxiety and suspense, Ali did not get much sleep. During the cold winter nights, a fire was lit to keep warm. Sitting next to one another covered by the blankets, they were able to feel warm despite the chilly temperature. Ali remembers that somehow the teargas kept them warm during the various sit ins. Some days it was raining, and one day it was pouring particularly heavily.

There were days that would pass and they would have nothing to eat; sometimes up to three days, but they neither felt the cold nor the hunger as they were filled with excitement, fighting for their freedom. Other days they would ration among them whatever people generously distributed at Tahrir. Bread sticks were distributed and sometimes they ate bread and jam or processed cheese or falafel. All levels of society were trying to help the protestors in their impossible mission. Ali used the toilets at Omar Makram mosque or the nearby restaurants.

Heaven-Like

Ali felt overwhelming love and equality. The true Egypt, in Midan alTahrir that he deemed to be heaven on earth. It was indescribable. Protestors genuinely feared for one another and if violence erupted, men thought of the women and girls before their own safety. The one thing he did not like was the few street vendors who sided against the protestors during police attacks during those utopian days. However, overall, Ali was thrilled that protestors were united in vision, acting as if one hand.

Demonstrators talked, cleaned, sang patriotic songs such as those by the late Sheikh Imam. They chanted, slept, and ate together. They were beautiful days. Among the lyrics were 'the brave are brave and the cowards are cowards.' *Ali fondly reminisced about the songs, which rings a bell with what Martin Luther King said, "In a sense the freedom songs are the soul of the movement."[11] Sheikh Imam's lyrics among other songs personified the soul of Tahrir.*

The second speech by former President Mubarak had an emotional tone that triggered the soft spot of many Egyptians. However, right after it, matters rapidly slipped out of the regime's hands. This led to divisions within the protestors at Tahrir and all over the country. Some believed Mubarak was genuine and called onto everyone to leave Tahrir, whereas others did not believe him and insisted that protestors should hold their ground. Ali agreed with the latter and wanted to continue to participate in the sit-in, as he believed that Mubarak should resign. After what had taken place, it was impossible to go back to the Mubarak era.

Ali believes that God blinded former President Mubarak, leading him to act unwisely by sending out men to beat up protestors in Tahrir. It was God's will that early on, the intentions of President Mubarak revealed themselves and the hearts of people changed, uniting them and joining them in harmony. Many Egyptians wanted the former President to step down and were not willing to wait another day, week or even month with him in office.

Bloodshed

On February 2, *baltegeya* (thugs) assaulted the protestors. Ali had heard that the ruling National Democratic Party gathered these men from Imbaba. The party summoned the *baltegeya* whenever they needed to mobilize, especially during the various elections in the past. The army allowed these thugs to enter the square, and for this reason Ali believes that President Mubarak, as the senior commanding officer of the Egyptian army, was accountable for the attack. With the passing of time, he has not changed his view. On the contrary, he even doubts that *Amn Eldawla* (state security), and *Mokhabarat* (intelligence), were behind the attack, and doubts the Muslim Brotherhood.

Ali was inside the square during the attack behind the front lines. He helped as much as he could, by breaking stones or helping out in the makeshift hospital. Ali would throw large stones hard on the ground shattering them into small rocks. He carried the stones inside his t-shirt or within his arms. Unbelievably, he was not afraid.

Ali remembers fighting with all his strength as he felt the undying urgency to protect the square; otherwise, he felt he would have been destined for a gruesome death. The assailants were armed with whips and knives while the protestors defended themselves with small rocks. Because a few of the assailants were riding camels and horses into the square, the media called this day the Camel Attack. Ali recalls seeing men carrying a traffic light and he could not believe their strength as they actually threw the heavy metal post at the men on camel and horseback. The weight of the traffic light succeeded in making a few horses and camels fall to the ground, and the protestors beat the fallen riders.

Ali will never forget the sight of a child whose eye was bleeding and he recalls a moving brief conversation with his treating doctor at the makeshift hospital.

The doctor said, "Drink this juice."

The child replied, "How can I drink juice when children are dying?"

After humbly declining the juice and patching up his eye, the child ventured out into the square where a bullet hit him in the head, killing him. This boy refused to drink juice in solidarity with the innocent lives only to join them a short while later.

Solidarity

After February 2, more Egyptians started to support the peaceful activists and many joined Tahrir in protest at the violence and bloodshed. The vision became clearer for all. It was almost a consensus that attacking peaceful protestors was a taboo. Friday of Departure, February 4, witnessed floods of people swarming the main roundabouts in Egypt: Cairo, Port Said, Suez, Alexandria and Ismailiya where marchers moved in awesome unity to the main squares. The protestors in Cairo divided. Some stayed at Tahrir, while others went to Itihadiyah palace.

It is strange that when Ali saw someone fall down wounded, rather than getting scared, his perseverance increased. He was a child, little shy of becoming a teenager, who saw unspeakable bloodshed. *One wonders how this will affect Ali when he grows up into a mature man. Will he become a disturbed man? Will he be a wise man who matured too young?*

His mother is his role model in many ways; she is a very brave and pious woman. Seeing death, she is no longer afraid of it. Like mother like child, Ali and his sister, Sarah, were not afraid of dying. They never asked their mother to go home and they never complained that they had had enough. Apparently, the violation they felt during their eviction, gave them momentum and a sense of purpose in the fight against injustice.

Climax

Friday February 11 was 'the Friday of Stepping Down'. Ali joined the march from Tahrir to Itihadiyah Palace in Heliopolis. Upon returning to Tahrir, Ali and others watched the TV at a café on the sidewalk of Talat Harb Street close to the square. Omar Suleiman appeared on state television after *maghreb* (sunset) prayers, announcing that President Mubarak has stepped down. Happiness is an understatement of how Ali felt on this evening. He was euphoric, like the majority of Egyptians. Former President Mubarak finally succumbed to the demands of the people.

The climax resulted in people cheering and jumping with joy that President Mubarak was no longer the president. A dream had come true. As the night got colder and darker, more and more people swarmed into Tahrir, which was packed until four in the morning. It was a phenomenal sight. At daybreak, many proud Egyptians took to cleaning Tahrir and painting its sidewalks. It was big scale volunteer process and was finished by midday on Saturday. Blankets folded, tents dismantled and personal affairs were packed. *A new dawn was breaking and Egyptians were overexcited.*

Few children accompanied their parents at Tahrir during those eighteen days. Ali believes that if he does not plan for a better future, he will remain in the vicious cycle of poverty forever. The role of children in society is to help build their future by whatever possible means. There is no doubt that adults have a bigger responsibility to build the future of their children. Ali is optimistic about his own future but believes he can only define it partially, while the bigger portion is determined by the state of the government and the country. The upcoming president and his policies will be fundamental in judging if Ali's future will be better under the new era or the old era. Ali will try, on his own, to shape his own future but success is something that God grants.

Anti-climax

After February 11 2011, there were maybe a handful of tents remaining at Tahrir. Almost everybody left the square but Ali and his family continued in the sit-in along with some protestors who withstood the attacks on February 2. The Brotherhood was among the groups who withdrew and their members were vocal about the necessity that people leave the square. Ali did not leave the square, because he understood that a regime is not merely its president. Things were not clear and simple. Just because Mubarak abdicated his position, it did not mean that the revolution was over and had accomplished its demands. There were many other unmet legitimate demands, which Ali believed in, and hence he continued his sit in at Tahrir. Ali and his family stayed at Tahrir until March 3, 2011 when the army changed its policy and used excessive physical force to remove and drag the protestors from the square. It was the first time Ali saw the army fire at civilians. Two days later the police and military police physically removed the protestors. Since then, events have been unfolding one by one and things have been rapidly going downhill.

Ali is popular among the revolutionary youth who call him and check on him frequently by phone. Ali frequently connects to the internet, where he reads information about organized marches and protests and informs his mother, so that they could join along with his sister and occasionally his father. Ali and *Um Ali* have participated in almost every protest, march and sit-in since the revolution. Ali would attend school and join the demonstration afterwards.

In Ali's view, the revolution was incomplete and hence one could not judge if it had succeeded or failed. The revolution was still at its infancy, partially successful and certainly continuing. The mere fact that a strong counter-revolution had been in full fledge was a sign, along with the lack of security, and the smear campaigns against protestors –indicating that it was a force to reckon with. Ali was not happy with the turn of events after the revolution, as the people he thought were protecting the revolution actually betrayed it. These would be the army and Brotherhood, who accused protestors of being thugs, and *feloul* through their newly elected ruling party. The Brotherhood were just like former President Mubarak.

Somehow Neutral

Until July 2012, the army had not proven where it stands, in Ali's view. To Ali the army is separated into two segments, the army as a body and the Supreme Council of the Armed Forces (SCAF), as the head of this body. He cannot judge whether the army had protected the *ancien regime* or the revolution; however, he believes that SCAF had clearly protected the *ancien regime,* and continues to safeguard it. The army itself as a body, however, seems neutral. There are a few incidents Ali recalls where the Military Police fired machine guns at civilians, but he does not perceive them as the army. He is not satisfied with this neutral position, as he perceives that the primary role of the army is to protect its people; the people are the country and by default, the army needs to side with the people. Simply, without the people there is no country. At this stage, he cannot generalize that the army has protected the revolution.

Ali perceives a rivalry amongst the ranks of the army and police who have despised one another for many years now. The army sometimes basks in the glory of the state, with good treatment, insurance and benefits, unlike the police. The army at the time of the interview is well loved and respected by the people, unlike the detested police. However, Ali believes that at times of danger, the police and the army will unite temporarily and foes will become friends. Similarly, Ali compares them to the religious parties of *Salafists* and *Ikhwan*. Ali compares the army with the *Salafist* clear straightforward agenda of radical Islam, and the police, Ali compares to *Ikhwan*. *The latter, people perceive as Dr. Jekyll and Mr. Hyde showing a clear case of 'split personality'.*

There is a clear difference between the two. While *Ikhwan* are politicians and not religious clerks, the *Salafists* are religious clerks and not politicians. In fact, only recently did the latter enter the political scene, after having previously spoken against mixing religion with politics. After the revolution, however, *Salafists* had a change of heart. *Salafists* only endorsed the former presidential nominee of the Brotherhood Mohamed Morsi so that Ahmed Shafik, former prime minister, would not win the presidential election race. *It was popularly referred to as "squeezing a lemon" to indicate the bitter choice.* Many revolutionaries did the same, and many later regretted it after the polemical presidential decree in December 2012.

Pro Boycotting

If the revolution succeeds, then Egypt has a bright future, like Turkey. But if it fails, Ali cannot predict its future. It is ambiguously opaque; nobody can know what it will be like.

If Ali was eighteen years old and had the right to vote at the presidential elections in 2012, he would have boycotted the elections, as he believes it was rigged. It is obvious to Ali that it was democratic masquerade that the voters played along with, simply because most Egyptians voted for either Mohamed Morsi or Ahmed Shafik. Both ended in the runoff. In the first round, over five million voted for Morsi and another five million voted for Shafik. Ali is baffled that Egypt with a population of ninety million has only fifty million who are eligible voters. During the elections, the majority of the voters abstained or boycotted. He thinks that boycotting was the right choice, and that those who voted are the cause of the state of loss prevalent in Egypt.

Like many Egyptians, Ali on the one hand did not want Shafik to win as he represents the supporters of the *ancien regime*. On the other hand, he did not want Morsi to win, as the Brotherhood had helped to exhaust the revolution. Ali believes that *Ikhwan* have obscurely betrayed the revolution. When asked questions, they do not answer directly but carry you to the conclusion, which the secret society wants to establish. For instance, before the revolution, they held a clear stand viewing bank interest as *haram* (sinful). However, after the revolution, it became acceptable to them. *Ikhwan* base their ideology on opportunistic interest and not on truth. Ali believes one can convince *feloul* much easier than members of *Ikhwan* as the latter are unfalteringly fixated on their views and positions.

Mixing Religion and Politics

Muslims and Christians are brothers and sisters in Egypt and have lived in harmony for centuries. However, there are evil people who light the match and throw it in the hay every now and then, striking fires, which creates the impression that religious strife exists. Ali thinks some Egyptians unwittingly help ignite this fire, as has been demonstrated with the use of religion in the political arena. Recently, for example, in a mosque at Alexandria, a Sheikh preached politics rather than religion in his sermons. This led to a violent outbreak in early 2013.

Ali believes that Islam should not mix in the dirty game of politics. Politics in the modern day is not the same as in old days of Prophet Mohamed (PBUH) when politics were more or less 'clean' and decent during the time when atheism prevailed. Today, politics has mutated into a deceiving, dirty apparatus that is unbecoming of religion. In defining the state, Ali advocates a civilian state with reference to *Sharia* law, not one that adopts *Sharia* law. If Egypt implemented *Sharia* law, cutthroat competition would ensue among the Islamic schools as to which interpretation of *Sharia* will prevail. Will it be the *Salafi*, *Ikhwan*, *Sufi* or *Al Azhar* School? The scene would dismally reflect an attitude of "I am right and he is wrong". Ali is against the mixing of religion and politics because of this threat that, if realized, will force each religion to set up parties and lead to differentiation and separation within the political scene. Ali has many times argued futilely with his pro-*Ikhwan* grandmother, who supports a political party based on religion.

Violence Continues

Ali and his family were fortunate that they all walked away from Tahrir unharmed. Khaled is a friend Ali met at Tahrir, who got hurt in almost every violent incident, starting with the 'Friday of Anger' in January, Mohamed Mahmoud street war in November 2011, council of ministers in December 2011, and Abbasiya incident in front of the ministry of defense in July 2012. Ali believes that the Brotherhood instigated the killings in November 2011 as they hurled rocks at the police so that the police would fire back. At Abbasiya, the first line of infantry so to speak was the army and the police were the second line. Even at Abbasiya, Ali recalls that the Brotherhood attracted protestors then withdrew, leaving the protesters exposed to their attackers. Throughout these incidents, Khaled, his friend, suffered injuries in his head, his eye, his arms, his leg and some twenty shots at his back. Khaled was lucky, as the ceramic chip, which injured his eye in Abbasiya, did not blind him. Assailants threw pieces of broken ceramics and stones supplied by a ceramic factory from rooftops and Khaled received a blow to his head. Khaled was standing with his friend, Ossama.
Ossama said, 'What happened?"
Khaled, clueless replied with another question, 'What?'
Suddenly Khaled felt something warm trickle down his head and from his mouth. Instinctively he placed his hand on his head and then looked at it and saw that it was bloody. Panic-gripped Ossama helped Khaled get to the makeshift hospital to attend to his head wound. Despite all his wounds, Khaled who is a strong youth, in his twenties, has regained his health and made a full recovery.

Ali will never forget the snipers stationed above the *Mogamaa El Tahrir* governmental building, during the council of minister incident, where a thirteen-year-old boy was shot in the head and killed in front of Ali. The bloody flesh of his brain scattered some seventeen meters away from his body. After the sniper killed the boy, he provokingly stood up on the roof waving his weapon as if saying; I am up here, unafraid, displaying no remorse or regret. Not one ounce of regret. Ali asks, is this not cold-blooded murder?

Differences

In Egypt, people lack the culture of freedom of expression and this clearly reflected on the political and social fronts. Egyptians are not able to respect the opinion of the other. On the contrary, they will shout at each and fight verbally. *Most recently, the fight turned violent at Itihadiya Palace in December 2012 amongst supporters of the President and opposition, concerning the presidential decree granting President Morsi sweeping powers.*

The plan to disunite Egyptians has succeeded and is guaranteed to shatter this ephemeral unity. The ruling elite realized that the unity demonstrated at Tahrir and many other squares across Egypt will threaten them and hence authorities attempt to obliterate the danger with the classic divide and conquer approach. Instead of respecting 'the other', Egyptians detest people with a viewpoint different from their own, and do not listen to one another. *This intolerance in 2011 was towards feloul and in 2013 was towards the Brotherhood and Islamists with only two types of labeling: the good and the bad.*

Most of Ali's friends are not involved in the revolution. Those who are, are split amongst the Brotherhood, *feloul, hezb el kanaba,* and one revolutionary. His friends and extended family are like the various colors of the rainbows reflecting Egyptian society. Ali defines *hezb el kanaba* as people who want and expect their demands to be met without getting up from their comfortable living room couch and they are willing to follow whoever rules. However, Ali knows that to achieve security and freedom, one must strive for it. *His words are in line with what Martin Luther King wrote, "Freedom is never voluntarily granted by the oppressor. It must be demanded by the oppressed."*[12] Security has been the overarching demand of the majority of Egyptians who agreed with the constitutional referendum in March 2011, but Ali questions the existence of the promised security.

Ali is frank when he states that the shortcoming of the activists after the revolution was that their focus was on the weaknesses of the Brotherhood, ignoring their own mistakes. Activists can never achieve anything by blaming, as per Egyptian saying: 'hanging the clothes hanger on the Brotherhood', who, in turn utilized the mistakes of the activists to their own advantage. Activists were distant from the streets and the people, while the Brotherhood have been able to win ground, big time, due to their widespread social work.

Education Mishap
In his young political mind, the pressing sectors of society that need addressing, reform or even rebuilding are justice, military, media, the ministry of interior, and education. Without cleansing these institutions, affairs will never settle. There are three political forces stirring matters in the state; the administrative, legislative and the judiciary. The three forces need to be separated and placed on equal footing to establish proper checks and balances.

Being a student, Ali explains why he is not satisfied with the education he is receiving. This education is just a matter of the student gaining a certificate and not any knowledge and development. The government teaches the students what they want them to know only. Ali gets into trouble at school because he is vocal about his political opinion. One day, Ali disagreed with his teacher in class while discussing the political scene. He resented and refused the teacher's view that activists were hooligans. Only one of his teachers is a revolutionary like him, and whenever he gets into trouble, he resorts to her to defend him. Ali is referred to as *thawragy* or 'revolutionary'. At school, if he disobeys the teacher he would be hit with a stick or hose on his palm. At his sister's school, the teacher would ask any student who misbehaves, to take off his shoes and lie on a desk while the teacher hits the soles of his feet. His mother confronts the administration about the abuse, herself a clear activist against any form and sort of violence anywhere.

Ali cannot afford private tutoring to complement the classes at school however; he participates in in-class groups of ten students outside the school hours, with an additional cost of around four hundred pounds, almost sixty dollars, for Ali alone. He takes around four days of lessons in three out of the eighteen subjects in his curriculum. Ali feels that the teachers are concerned that students answer the questions and complete their homework, regardless of how they reply and what they understand. The curriculum is built upon memorizing and not understanding. Like in any institute, Ali has met good teachers and bad teachers. Ali's school has both boys and girls. Each class has around forty students.

Ali attends *Al Azhar El Sharif Saft El Laban School* but wants to change schools. He feels that *Al Azhar* no longer produces great thinkers and scientists as in the distant past, during the time of Colonel Ahmed Orabi, the rebellious army general and nationalist in the nineteenth century. Ali believes that *AlAzhar's* main purpose is to earn money, rather than spread the message of Islam and hence, the quality of students has dropped. As much as he wanted to, he could not change schools in 2013 due to a complicated bureaucratic process.

The most important sector that needs complete attention and increased funding is education sector. If Egypt addresses education properly, the country would take a gigantic leap forward. Education in Egypt is peripheral. In the past, teachers were respected as they explained various topics to students. Unfortunately, today the curriculum is designed to be memorized rather than explained. Education is dependent on private tutoring, exhausting the child's mind. Egyptians do not want ignorance, they seek knowledge. *Unfortunately, the education system fails to deliver on knowledge. Moreover, it leaves no time for children to play and for their imagination to grow.*

Future

In July 2012, Ali could perceive form the actions of the Brotherhood that they were driving the nation backwards. However, Ali still considers the possibility that in the future, they will strive for progress. At the time, the Brotherhood were only concerned with the ballot boxes and trying to win seats. If the people voted for the revolution, Ali is certain it would collapse, as ballots by default lead to divisions and once divided, the revolution would fail. What made the revolution succeed was the unity of the Egyptian people during those eighteen days. Ali is fond of the two republics as depicted by satirist Bassem Youssef: the *Ikhwan* republic and the non-*Ikhwan* republic, where the citizens of each view things very differently. In November 2013, the TV network canceled a popular satirist show, a clear act of suppressing freedom of expression. Ali believes Bassem should not be held responsible if his audience misunderstands his message.

The ministry of interior should not be a tool of torture. In the era of the Muslim Brotherhood, torture still took place at the conspicuous *'gabal el ahmar'* which means red hill and the high security prison, *Tora*. The kidnapping of protestors also persisted. Ali noticed that the metro stations around the square frequently had their lights switched off, which facilitates kidnapping. The tear gas used in 2013 was not like that used in 2011, and vinegar and Pepsi no longer relieved the burning sensation. Ali could feel the tear gas 'burning his skin'. The canisters were lighter and did not sink like the old ones, and once thrust it kept spinning around, dispatching the CS gas. The police should be there to protect civilians from criminals. Media should not be placating the regime but should be objective in covering the stories in a way that opens the minds of the viewers, not framing opinions. It should invite critical thinking. Television channels should be a means for education and learning.

The revolutionary cries for bread were not just meant literally. It also symbolized state services covering good education and health care services. President Morsi's government had recently set a quota for subsidized bread limiting the daily ration to three loaves of bread per individual, causing an outcry among the majority of Egyptians facing hardships every day. Moreover, the size of the loaf has significantly shrunk.

Ali finds it difficult to judge the future well. However, he remains optimistic. He cannot understand the stubbornness of the Brotherhood during the violent outbreak in December 2012 in front of the presidential palace, as in his opinion, violence begets more violence. Violence against protestors will win more Egyptians to the ranks of the protestors, as the violence is clearly unfair and unjustified. Violence can never be the solution, or it would have worked for Mubarak or Tantawi. Ali humorously compares the two presidents, Mubarak ignoring the people by saying "*khalihom yetsalou*" (let them have fun) and Morsi's speeches paralyzing people, or "*yetshalou*". The two Arabic words are very similar, with a difference of just one letter that gives two completely different meanings. When it comes to the army, Ali believes they can do something helpful but he cannot depend on it. Ali is not concerned with the rumors about the Brotherhood having a militia, as another militia could be born if needed.

Two Years Plus Later

Tamarod started out as a good idea but evolved into supporting the expected nomination of General Sisi as President. This contradicted the revolutionary demands of a civilian rule. Ali camped out at *Itihadiyah Palace* from June 30 to July 3 when the military announced the ousting of President Morsi in response to the millions who took to the streets. The numbers were greater than January 2011. Ali chose to camp at the palace because it was symbolic of demand that the president has to step down.

When the army called for the people to take to the streets again on July 26 2013 to give the green light for fighting terrorism, Ali declined. He simply could not sanction the killing of another human being, as the killer could at any stage, turn his gun at Ali himself. Nonetheless, Ali supported the clearing of the sit-ins held by the supporters of the ousted President although he maintained that this dispersion should not be violent or bloody.

Ali believes the new 2013 government is crippled, and has failed to bring about any change. For Ali, the ministry of interior has yet again returned to the notorious practices during the last period of President Mubarak's era, under Minister Habib El Adly. Fifty people who are mainly *feloul* and military supporters, not activists, are cooking up the constitution. It therefore seems to him that military superiority is guaranteed. The new regime has retreated to the dark days of suppression and injustice, worse even than Mubarak's regime. Ali hopes that a real revolution will take place to correct this dramatic detour, with more people taking to the streets than on June 30, 2013.

While other people were anticipating the New Year, 2014, Ali was very anxious about his father's health, as he had suffered a hemorrhage. *Abu Ali* passed away on December 30, 2013 leaving Ali lost without his revered father. Ali cried most of the time and could not focus on studying for his midterm exams early in January.

Ali represents a large proportion of the Egyptian young population. The perceptive minds of these youth brighten the future and give many Egyptians hope that tomorrow will be better. I was thrilled to watch Ali coincidently on YouTube, sharing his candid opinion on why the 2013 constitution was illegitimate[13].

CHAPTER 4

Desperate Despair

"And when you look long into the abyss, the abyss also looks back at you."
Nietzsche's Beyond Good and Evil

My friend, Marwa Sharaf ElDin, got me in touch with Bassem Youssef, a heart surgeon who came into fame after the revolution with the huge success of his satirical political show called B+ on You Tube and later "Al Barnameg", which means 'The Program' on satellite television. Bassem got me in touch with Aly, a fellow staff member at the same hospital. When I called Aly to set up an appointment he was readily available and we met at Costa Coffee at Gamaat El Dowal Street in Mohandeseen on Sunday October 2, 2011.

His Love of Heart Surgery

He is a tall, well-built man with a bald head. Conscience of his weight, he is trying to shed some kilograms. He has big brown eyes and wears eyeglasses. Often when he talks, he looks at one above his glasses. He felt very depressed when he turned thirty years old, realizing that age was creeping up on him. His name is Dr. Aly Ghoneim and he was born on May 30, 1981 at Giza. He had a conservative French education at the College de la Saint Famille (College des Peres Jésuite). He is staff member in the Cardio-Thoracic Surgery Department at Kasr El Aini Hospital. It is the biggest research and teaching hospital in Egypt that provides free treatment to the public, and is equipped with modern medical equipment sometimes better than private hospitals. *Aly smokes, and I have always found it ironic how doctors smoke although they are fully aware of the health threats.*

Aly does not believe that there are any issues between Muslims and Christian. The only difference he would sense in school was when the religion classes separated them. He, a Muslim, attended the mass at the Church. Aly recalls one time a fellow

Christian Copt was stirring anti-Muslim sentiments, and fellow Copts chastised him for his twisted thoughts. His Coptic friends went to Mosques with them. Once a supervisor saw them inside the Mosque, and to avoid any trouble, the Christian friends joined their Muslim friends in prayers. Muslims and Christians have lived peacefully since the days of Amr Ibn El Ass in 640. He recalls the religious tension in Egypt created during the Sadat era, which flourished under Mubarak. The regime used it as a decoy to distract and divide people whenever they deemed necessary.

Both of Aly's parents are over sixty years old and had careers in engineering. His father used to have a consulting office and his mother is a university professor. For over five years now, they always watch the talk show host Mona El Shazly and criticize the desperate state of the nation.

Aly is a proud and independent young man, who unlike many Egyptian men, does not depend on his parents' financial help. Hence, he lives like most of the middle class, independently struggling to make ends meet. Doctors do not have an easy life in Egypt, as many might perceive. He is personally suffering due to the low salary scheme, as is the case in all government institutes in Egypt. Aly is bewildered by this state of affairs. He went by the book; he attained 98 percent in his high school diploma with excellent honorary notes and was among the top one hundred students out of his graduating class of one thousand eight hundred medical students. And yet, he struggles to cope financially.

He selected one of the best specialties and succeeded in proving his skills. He is now assisting a renowned surgeon and two other professors. Currently he is preparing his Doctorate, in heart surgery. Without a doubt, heart surgery is the love of Aly's life.

Around two years ago, he married Amira, his college sweetheart, who he had met in an emergency room when she was an intern. With his meager salary, he could not afford an engagement ring. He decided to take a bank loan to buy a diamond, repaying it in installments. *Many Egyptian men get financial help from their parents when they get married but Aly preferred not to.* He is a proud father of young baby girl, Jamila.

Les Misérables

Aly sees the suffering amongst the low paid wage earners or the unemployed, struggling to keep their cherished family members alive, particularly at Kasr Al Aini hospital and the Abou-el-Reesh hospital for children. Children with congenital heart disease require open-heart surgery and need to wait for their turn among one thousand eight hundred other children. They have two hundred and fifty kids on the urgent care list, requiring an operation within a week, but the doctors are fully aware that they are only capable of operating on ten kids per week! What will happen to the two hundred and forty? He has told mothers and fathers, on many occasions, that their son or daughter will have to die, as they cannot afford the operation. Aly has witnessed plenty of sorrow and pain in his life. The worst ever, a situation that breaks his heart, is to see and hear the sorrow and pain of a mother losing her beloved child, unable to save him or her for financial reasons. The screams and tears are so deep when they are alive but destined to die, and the mother cannot do anything to save her child's life.

Aly cannot really dissociate himself from the stark reality that causes strains between him and his friends who are against the revolution. One of his friends admires former President Hosni Mubarak; Aly believes his friend is disconnected from reality. How can he perceive the president as a good person? How can he be fighting for him to maintain power with all the wrongs in Egyptian society? Caliph Omar Ibn Al Khatab was worried that God would ask him about the state of an animal on Judgment Day, let alone a human being.

Given the conditions of the country and the difficulty in improving the standard of living, how could a man who lived at a *dawar* (farmer's dwelling) in the village of Kafr El-Meselha, get a golden opportunity to join the Egyptian Military Academy and grow in its hierarchy till he became the top man in office? Former President Mubarak comes from an unfortunate little village where people barely have enough to eat, and, as he grew older, he left it to join the army, and apparently never looked back. With his humble upbringing, one would think he would have a better understanding of the real state of Egypt. Instead, he allowed his own people to be buried further in dirt and mud. Aly holds former President Mubarak personally responsible for the sorrowful state of the nation. A state he likes to call "Les Misérables", after the French novel, especially as he came from a shantytown, and saw how people lived and still live. How could he forget? How could he be so ruthless and so disconnected as to worsen the state of education and health to the present day levels? Aly is filled with hatred towards him, but is powerless and can only vent his anger by talking to his inner circle of friends and family.

Silent Majority

When the going gets tough, people need to join forces, stand up together and shout aloud that they have rights. People are not dogs, maltreated in such an inhumane merciless manner where the value of human life is cheap. Even dogs deserve humane treatment. Aly feels his humanity has withered over time as he witnesses the unfair, crude loss of life brought forth by a decaying healthcare system infested with malpractice. With Aly's '*la vida loca*,' he is not living well in Egypt, as his humanity and sanity struggle with the dire situation he sees at work, which contrasts so sharply with his own lifestyle. This leaves him feeling uneasy and troubled.

Aly finds it difficult to understand the silent majority. His friends who are living a good life, question his need for change in the country when he personally lives a privileged life. They have not seen what he has seen: how the unfortunate men and women are treated, how difficult their lives are. The former ruling elite must abdicate their power; they have failed their people tremendously. *They forgot the purpose of their rule, as Thomas Moore writes: "Why do you suppose they made you king in the first place? ... Not for your benefit, but for theirs. They meant you to devote your energies to making their lives more comfortable, and protecting them from injustice. So your job is to see that they are all right, not that you are- just as a shepherd's job, strictly speaking, is to feed his sheep, not himself"*[4] *This applies to all forms of rulers.*

Once, while Aly was talking to his silent, passive friends, he wished that one day he would go to protest in front of a ministry and get killed, so that they would wake up; as surely they would not be the same if their best friend is killed. He argues that they should not wait until someone close to their hearts dies for them to change; they need to wake up and change on their own initiative.

Over the weekend Aly would shut off from his medical life and spend it at Hacienda Bay, an affluent summer compound on the Mediterranean coast, with his rich friends. They would discuss things like the latest Hummer model or an upcoming soccer match between Real Madrid and Barcelona, which they wanted to attend. Come the start of the working week, he could be confronted with the death of a patient from a simple appendicitis. Aly hates his double life.

Aly is willing to die fighting for a noble cause, to achieve a better nation where the standards of living are acceptable. We are all mortals, and we will all die eventually, but Aly prefers to die a sudden quick death. Death comes in a second, without any introductions, and God will be the judge of lives: What have you done in your life? What are your good deeds and your bad deeds? He cannot understand how most people are blinded and tightly gripped with worldly possessions, especially as they will all be lost in a second, when death finally knocks on their door.

Aly has frequently worked in the emergency unit at the hospital and has come across death many times, to the extent that he claims he can smell death. Sometimes a patient is stable but Aly smells death and in a second he sees the patient's eyes are blank and suddenly he flat-lines. Dying is a terrifying moment, a time of leaving all that is known behind and being alone. If one lives his life and never forgets that his moment is always imminent, then one would live better. The definition of Islam is surrender. Devout Muslims preach and practice this attitude, where faith of the pious transcends worldly possessions. Therefore, devout Muslims are ready for death whenever it comes. Aly loves his wife and his daughter and wants the best for them.

He has faith that if his time has come, God will provide for them through other means, and that he is merely one of God's many instruments.

Victims of Torture

Sometime in 2005, after midnight, Aly was inside the operating room when suddenly there was loud banging on the doors. Five daunting officers wearing khakis entered forcibly into the operating room.

Aly said, "You are not allowed to cross the red line as the surgery room is sterile and you are contaminating the environment. Please go out and I will follow you."

The officer said, "We are looking for a neurosurgeon."

Aly excused himself from surgery and as they led him to the resuscitating room Aly thought that one of their colleagues must have been injured. He was wrong. In the room, he saw a young boy of about sixteen years old who had sustained injuries all over his body.

Aly asked, "What happened to him?"

One of the officers replied sarcastically, "Its normal doc. He was hit by a car or fell from a height. Just work it out."

Aly's senior whispered to him, "Be quiet, these are security people and the patient is a convict."

During his examination of the patient, Aly noticed his burnt genitalia. There were several cigarette burn marks on his body, evidence of the rumored torture practice of the police. The boy was hit with a *shoum* (thick stick) until he hemorrhaged, and the officers decided to bring him to the hospital to save him, or more likely, to document his death. Aly later discovered that the boy was the brother of the suicide bomber who had jumped off the bridge while detonating a bomb at the district of Al Azhar in April 2005. The brother was admitted to hospital care for three days, before he died. The following day, the first page of *al-Ahram* newspaper reported his death, stating he had suffered severe depression in prison, to the extent that he banged his own head on the walls until he died. Sadly, the father had envisioned this danger after his older son's suicide bombing and tried to flee with his younger son to Libya, but was stopped and arrested by police. For any other newspaper reader, the story would not draw attention. But Aly knew the deceased and the circumstances surrounding his death, and could not help but feel sickened and frustrated at how the truth was being distorted and buried in a pile of lies.

Aly recalls meeting a convict in the past, with an abnormal edema and swelling in his face. When asked what happened, the convict stated quite seriously that he had fallen down the stairs while the police officer standing next to him laughed. He had been beaten so badly by the police that he resembled an alien in a sci-fi movie.

Aly recounts that he once saw Ayman Nour, former presidential candidate, lying on the cold ceramic floor of the hospital in his underwear, gritting his teeth in excruciating pain.

Aly recollects another incident involving state security abuses. There was a twenty-six-year old bearded student at Al Azhar University by the name of Abdou. Abdou had undergone open-heart surgery and had a prosthetic aortic valve installed. He suffered rheumatic fever. By an unfortunate twist of fate, at university he once was seated next to the main suspect of the Al Azhar bombing, and was therefore wrongfully accused of being complicit in the crime, and imprisoned. As Abdou lives with a prosthetic valve, he is required to live in a clean environment to avoid infections and complications. Any infection in the blood would stop the valve from functioning and would require another surgery. While at the ward, not surprisingly, Abdou caught an infection due to the prison environment. Aly checked on him on the eighth floor of the hospital usually reserved for prisoners requiring medical attention. The floor sealed by security wardens guarding big metal gates. Abdou was in a critical condition, needing urgent surgery within two or three days. His scheduled operation on Saturday morning would need transferring across the street from the ward to the hospital, but Aly knew that the guards would delay bringing him in, and the operation would need to be re-scheduled. To avoid this happening, he demanded that Abdou be admitted into hospital on Friday night. By nine on the Friday night, Abdou had not appeared, and the ward was not answering their phone.

Aly went across to see what was holding up his patient and found a security officer in his air conditioned office, equipped with an LCD screen and decoder, watching the world cup games live.
Aly said, "Where is Abdou my patient? He is late."
Security officer said, "Abdou is not my responsibility, he is the responsibility of *Amn Eldawla* (State security)."
Aly politely replied, "Please call *Amn Eldawla*."
Aly sensed that State Security was intentionally neglecting this patient so that he would die.
He spoke to someone from *Amn Eldawla* over the phone. "If my patient, Abdou, does not get transferred within two hours, I will personally report you to the head of the hospital. Your apparent negligence is an attempt to let him die."

Exactly fifteen minutes later, a big armored car accompanied by Special Forces transferred the young boy in his wheel chair to the hospital. The following morning the operation was successful. Abdou called Aly after the revolution and informed him of his long overdue release. He is an example of an arrest and imprisonment without any trial or sentence. While imprisoned Abdou had undergone two open-heart surgeries and he contracted Hepatitis C.

Despair

One of Aly's surgeon friends was newly married and a proud new father of a baby boy. The new father was distraught at his baby's diagnosis with a rare congenital heart disease that required surgery unavailable in Egypt. Aly and his friend made all the arrangements and were about to fly the baby boy to Italy for the surgery, when the child suffered from a cardiac arrest and died. The baby died twenty-five days old, on January 25, 2011, the same day the revolution had started. The father did everything he could but it was destiny. Aly could not help but wonder about fathers who do not even have those contacts, let alone the means to fly their children abroad for medical care. What would they do? How did they manage alone?

Aly lost faith and hope in the system many times, as he witnessed the brutality of life that faces regular Egyptian families. Aly has strong faith that God almighty wants Egypt to become a better nation and hence he perceives that when the people protested, God destined it. Humans are mere instruments and tools that God has created for destiny to unfold. Humans, who have ruled and ruled unfairly, must answer to the Almighty. Injustice and devilry is omnipresent. There are times when God chooses to show his power. The Egyptian revolution, in Aly's point of view, is one such glorious manifestation.

Former President Mubarak was a tyrant who did as he pleased with the nation, and so did his family. It was a Machiavellian oligarchy, where the president, the military and the business tycoons ruled the nation, accumulating riches while the masses grew poorer. Civilians could not think about politics as they were too busy struggling to provide for their families. If President Mubarak had been more intuned to the sentiments of his people and responded quickly and sincerely to their desires, matters could have turned out differently. He could have been a public hero rather than a villain. Aly believes that God blinded him to reality so that he would meet a different destiny.

Aly is realistic in thinking that suffering will continue, or even worsen in the future, but he is optimistic as he has faith that at certain times and certain places, the morally right will prevail over the immoral. Aly is confident that eventually, the state of Egypt will be ameliorated and the suffering eliminated. Every person needs to play his role in serving our country, but we all need to have awareness that we are doing the right thing with no overshadowing doubts. Aly encourages civilians to throw away their passive roles and their seclusion within their homes and to get out on the streets and actively contribute in whichever way they can.

Making Ends Meet

In 2011, Kasr El Aini hospital, in an example of true democratic process, held elections for dean of the faculty. Of the seventeen candidates that stood, Dr. Hussein won the position. At the time, the fifty-two-year old surgeon was among the best of his class, dedicated to teaching and operating at the hospital. His own father had also been the dean, and previously head of surgery. His mother was a head of internal medicine. Hussein sacrificed his life for the sake of teaching, providing free lessons in the auditorium daily at 7 in the morning. Dr. Hussein helped Aly in getting his paperwork ready for his current fellowship in Montreal. Dr. Hussein was the only candidate for the Dean's position whom Aly believed in and trusted to have good intentions. The other sixteen candidates he believed, wanted the prestigious title to further their own names and fortunes, or the honor, or the high salary of a quarter of a million pounds per month, a little less than forty-one thousand dollars. The dean's salary is a good example of the gigantic gap between the haves and the have-nots. Aly's salary at the time of our interview was fixed at only one thousand pounds, less than one hundred and seventy dollars per month. He is forced to work outside the hospital to earn additional income to support his family.

Aly's ideal job would be to work full time in one medical center that is equipped with proper facilities. He would like to have time to conduct studies, do research, and meet his patients before and after operations and be able to follow up on cases after six months, among other things. He works day by day, case by case, and this means that his income is not steady. Aly wishes he had a decent fixed income and could sleep at night knowing that if he breaks his hand or has any other ailment, he would still have a source of income. If he were to be injured, or need bed rest for a month, his income would cease to exist. Aly compares himself to a cab driver, despite his high educational achievements. He is not seeking to make a big salary, just a decent one that will allow him to study and do research while he continues to practice medicine. Very few doctors in Egypt spend sufficient time on research. Aly loves his work; the sound of the ventilator, the operating theatre, his tools, and even the ghastly sight of blood. For him to have the peace of mind that enables him to perform miracles on the operating table, he needs to know that when his daughter reaches school age he can afford to send her to one of the best schools in Cairo. It is a mere dream, given the current pay structure and social security benefits at hospitals.

Many days, Aly gets so desperate that he looks at his wife, Amira, and tells her it is time to immigrate. The double life he lives within two extremely different societies in one country is tearing him apart. Among the elite, death befalls while one is sick in bed. The family mourns, and they arrange the burial, funeral and have little concern about finances as they usually have more than one breadwinner in the family or substantial savings. On the other hand, the less fortunate in society would ponder on where to bury the deceased, whether or not they will be able to afford the funeral services and how they will make ends meet as the deceased was the sole provider. The latter is the reality for the majority of Egyptians.

Beyond Hope

Before the revolution, Aly was already aiming to immigrate. With a fifty-year lag in medical technology in Egypt, there are many surgical procedures that are not performed, which he wants exposure to. In the past years, he had been trying to finalize his USMLE, the medical equivalency in the USA so that he could work there. Aly has already finished the Canadian equivalency. Unfortunately, his country has nothing more to offer his ambition and talent.

For Aly, Kasr El Aini Teaching Hospital is a representative symbol of the state of Egypt. Renewal and renovation of the hospital will follow once Egypt is reformed and saved from from the rampant corruption that exists. Once this takes place, the country can arise from the dark alleys of illiteracy to the bright skyscrapers of knowledge. Aly believes that existing infrastructure needs to be demolished and rebuilt from scratch with the proper blueprints, in order for reform to take place. Frequently, Aly says to himself in despair, "It is hopeless!"

Aly never believed in the rallying power of protests given the evidence of the past, like during the protests in the industrial city of Mahala in 2008. He thought, "If they continue for a whole year, nothing will ever be achieved." He knew that Egypt had fallen into a deep abyss of despair. No hiker could ever scale that terrain. He hoped to escape a suffocating fate by simply flying away. The Egyptian people have long forgotten the ability to be positive and proactive and have stagnated like a swamp. Only a miracle can change Egypt.

Heavenly Helping Hand

A miracle certainly unfolded, revealing itself in the unity of the Egyptian people during the revolution. It was as if a heavenly force was moving human instruments to take a stand as a united force for the good of all Egyptians. Dr. Aly felt that the revolution was not the work of mortal men but rather, some form of divine intervention. Aly is confident that former President Mubarak will have an untimely end, given that the old *nizam* (regime) he led was unjust, rotten and corrupt. He feels that this would be retributive justice; God's revenge against the disbeliever who abused the blessings bestowed upon them. It is unnatural that a bunch of young people manage to take down *Amn Eldawla*, which has a wealth of force and people knowledge. In his view, the security apparatus is trained to protect the *rayees* (literally meaning chief, but popularly used to refer to the president), with at least two million capable and programmed heads to defend the interests of the regime, and dismally, not the law. Aly draws a comparison to a fed and trained bulldog who is conditioned to protect its provider and taught how to fight fiercely in the ring. If one day a burglar comes to rob his owner, the dog would be unleashed to ravish the trespasser. However, when that day comes, the bulldog unexpectedly runs away and deserts his caregiver. In reality, the state security did just that on the eve of the 'Friday of Anger'. The people called for change and angels supported them, so it seems.

It all started after January 17, 2011 when Mohamed Bouazizi set himself on fire in Tunisia as a police officer withdrew his business license, disastrously and abruptly cutting off his income. She also slapped him, which showed why a lot of the consequence was about dignity. Henceforth, the Tunisian revolution fast tracked and in so doing, inspired many Arabs throughout the region. In Egypt, the inspiration manifested itself on January 25, when various young male and female activists on Facebook pages and videos, circulated on You Tube, called for protests. Aly checked the 'We are all Khaled Said' Facebook page before the January 25 to get information on the announced location of the protest. Aly supported this initiative, as when it came to the political theatre, he had reached his tipping point and was displaying meltdowns where he lost his manners and cursed uncontrollably.

Curious to Participate
Aly was involved with the revolution on two fronts. The first front was as an Egyptian young man fed up with the old *nizam* who could not see any signs of hope, especially with his gruesome experience at Kasr El Aini Hospital. The second front was as a surgeon attending to the wounded that overwhelmed the field hospital.

Late on the cold dark night of January 25, Aly and two of his friends decided to go check out Tahrir, as they had heard there were skirmishes taking place and they were in neighboring affluent district of Zamalek. Their sentiments were not revolutionary; they were just bored curious young men seeking something interesting. They crossed the bridge and saw real action. He saw an unbelievable number of police officers clad in black and a good number of protestors. The atmosphere was friendly as he heard the police officers pleading with the activists to return to their homes and abandon the sit-in.
A police officer said, "We all go home tonight, and return to protest tomorrow morning."

The officer was surely kidding, as the police were distant from the revolutionary fervor. Aly noticed that the police officer looked decent, like one of his friends; these were not aliens, but fellow Egyptian brothers. Police just follow strict orders. During Aly's military service, the first form of punishment in the army was called *tekdeer* (to make the soldiers miserable), making soldiers stand still holding their caps against their chests with their chins for up to an hour. A notch worse would be when his superior would order him to don his backpack and stay standing for an hour.

Aly remembers his experience as a soldier for one year after university. How he had observed the very low intelligence of the soldiers. For over sixty years, the country has been ruled by a military that unfortunately does not reflect the brilliant minds of Egyptian society. There was always a line up to exercise. Many times Aly would pass the lineup and his *soul* (lieutenant) would shout: "Soldier, where are you?" If Aly replied with a sentence longer than five words, the lieutenant would not understand, and just command: "Go to your place, soldier!" Aly views the army as one of the most corrupt institutes in the country. The army would demand their requirements from the national budget without any budget proposal or discussion to secure its funds. The ministry of interior would follow suit with a similar lion's share or a little less. The balance of the budget gets distributed to the not so important sectors, in the eyes of the deep security state, like health, education, justice and others.

On that first day, Aly heard slogans demanding civil rights, but nothing about *"eskat al nizam"* (down with the regime), as has been claimed. Just after midnight, he heard a scream, *"Edrab!"*, "Attack!" The police had been given the command to bombard the demonstrators with tear gas shells. He felt engulfed by a black cloud of officers, closing in on the group. The police gave orders to evacuate the roundabout, as Wednesday was a working day. The protestors had abandoned their idea of retiring to their homes earlier, in retaliation to police brutality. Aly saw plenty of police cars and sensed that the police, who actually left an open space through which the protestors could escape, outnumbered the protestors. They ran for their lives and the first day of protest ended with the successful dispersion of the crowds.

Aly returned home and eagerly switched on the news channel, only to hear that members of the *Ikhwan* (Muslim Brotherhood) were protesting and looting shops. Aly did not buy into the state media deceit, as he had seen the people with his own eyes. No looting was taking place. He joined the protest in the afternoons of the following two days, going straight after finishing work in the nearby Kasr El Aini hospital. On Thursday January 27 2011, the number of protestors was significant. Among Aly's thirteen childhood friends, only four participated in the demonstrations. The other nine represented the passive silent majority. Those nine spent January 25 at a pool party in one of the exclusive suburban compounds, playing Wii and enjoying good food and company. Even after the revolution, the complacent silent majority would like everything to go back to normal.

On Thursday, word of mouth was spreading that the internet and all forms of communication was expected to be shut down on Friday January 28, in an attempt to thwart the pre-announced revolution on the internet. Protesters were to gather in all main roundabouts in the governorates of Cairo, Giza, Suez, Mansoura, Alexandria and Aswan. This provoked Aly and his friends to action. For him it was a dream come true that Egyptians were being transformed from complacent individuals to assertive, loud citizens capable of standing up publicly for their rights and say 'No' to their oppressor. He agreed with his friends to meet on Friday January 28 at noon, in front of a *shawarma* restaurant on Syria St. They planned to pray the *Zohar* (noon) prayers at Mostafa Mahmoud Mosque and then observe how the day would unfold. They agreed that regardless of whether or not they were able to talk on the telephone, they would meet at noon. Disruptions in communication were not going to stop them. Aly woke up earlier than usual on that Friday because of the excitement he felt. The phones were working then, and he was able to call his friend Youssef and confirm their meeting at noon. After they hung up, the internet and mobile networks intentionally crashed. His wife was pregnant at the time. Amira completely supported Aly, and understood his desire and need to participate in the demonstrations. Unusually, his parents, who are overly protective of their son, also backed him up and prayed for God to protect him.

Day of Action

At noon they met as agreed and walked together to the mosque, arriving before the sermon. Aly looked around and saw men and women, Copts and Muslims. Eye contact exchanged between strangers sufficed to transmit the feeling of a unified purpose. They shared a common drive; they intended to claim their lost rights, fed up with the downtrodden state of Egypt. He was disappointed with the Sheikh that preached the Friday sermon, who was advocating obedience to the ruler as the proper attitude mentioned in the Quran (4:59), indicating that Muslims need to obey God, the Prophet and those in charge. But the preacher forgot to mention that this condition applies as long as the latter obey God's will. Before the sermon began, state security members encircled the prayers with a disturbing cordon. Aly started to feel anxious for the first and last time during the revolution. He was thinking, "What will they do to us?" Quickly the numbers of the men in black grew to three lines of them, and Aly feared that he was about to be captured and arrested. Aly and his friends came prepared with masks that they bought from pharmacies, vinegar bottles and headscarves, and all the necessary protective measures against the anticipated tear gas assault by the police. It was clear they were not just pious Muslims performing the Friday prayers. Aly looked at his friends and saw their growing discomfort at their situation in their eyes. After prayers had finished, he remembers a young, light bearded man wearing a tight T-shirt and a scarf in the colors of the Palestinian flag around his neck, suddenly jumping and shouting *"al shaab yoreed esqat al nezam"* (the people want to topple the regime). His chant was a catalyst that ignited the masses to chant loudly and forcibly.

After prayers, the number of people walking in the neighboring streets was unprecedented. The overwhelming crowds diminished the three lines of police officers. Before prayers, they seemed intimidating, but after the prayers, the police were lost in the sea of people. Their sheer numbers broke the cordon eventually, and Aly felt himself moving with the momentum of the crowd, chanting the famous *"eish, horeyaha, adalah egtamaeya"* (bread, freedom, social equality). He saw people watching from overlooking balconies and he waved at them, calling out, *"Ya ahalena endamou elena"* (our families, come join us). The crowds moved along the long Gamaat El Dowal St and moved to Batal Ahmed Abdel Aziz St. He looked behind him and saw the horizon of people stretching as far as the eye could see. While Aly was walking, he recognized some women from Gezira club. What he found amazing was their high social status; they were classy people who had the means to live a good life, wearing Burberry and Ralph Lauren polo shirts. And yet, they were on the streets demanding a better living for all Egyptians. The fortunate became so suffocated, incapable of breathing, for the sorrows of the unfortunate, that they shouted on their behalf. *Usually, people who revolt are the downtrodden social class who cannot afford living, as Moore said in* <u>Utopia</u>*. "As for the theory that peace is best preserved by keeping the people poor, it's completely contradicted by the facts. Beggars are by far the most quarrelsome section of community. Who is more likely to start a revolution than a man who is discontented with his present living conditions? Who could have a stronger impulse to turn everything upside down in the hope of personal profit, than a man who'd got nothing to lose?"* [15] *In Egypt, the elite took to the streets preempting the masses, in an outcry against the dire poverty in the country.*

Onslaught of Tear Gas

Aly kept walking all the way to Dokki and under a bridge he turned left into Tahrir Street, which leads to the symbolic Tahrir square, its name literally meaning Liberation Square. He sensed that a confrontation was going to take place at Galaa Square, as there were plenty of police blocking the small bridge crossing over the Nile. Aly and his friends agreed that if they separated they would meet at the cinema on Tahrir Street. Aly was probably in the third row of protesters confronting the police. He felt scared. When he looked at his friends Mena and Nazli, and a nearby old woman, their facial expressions and their physical expressions of defiance, replaced his fear with anger. These brave women saw the cops and wanted to charge forward. Nobody was going to stop them. There was something indescribable in the air on this Friday of Anger. Aly tells his friends who missed that Friday that they would never really understand how phenomenal it was. There was a sense of safety, not in the physical sense, but in the moral sense. They were one hundred percent on the right track; there was no shadow of a doubt that he was assisting justified anarchy. He wanted to attract attention to the inhuman plight of Egyptians.

The first row of protestors held hands, raising them up in the air, chanting *"Selmeya! Selmeya!"* (Peaceful, Peaceful) Aly recalls that the police officers and their cars were so overwhelming in numbers that it seemed impossible that the protestors would be able to cross them and march towards Tahrir square. He felt that the protestors were holding the police in contempt for their growing unpopularity due to the torture and abuse of the emergency law that they practiced. Clearly, the police's unpopularity was growing. Before the protestors reached the police by some three hundred meters, the latter fired canisters of tear gas at them. Aly used his masks and the vinegar, but nothing really helped the overpowering burning sensation that the gas ignited. People from behind were pushing forward, and so the protestors collided with the police. Things happened so quickly Menna fell down. Aly helped her up and handed her to Raouf, his friend. Seconds later, Aly heard some people calling for a doctor; quickly he responded and found out that a forty-eight-year old man had fallen on the asphalt, with very weak pulse. He had no medical tools with him, just his bare hands, and a dying man was lying across the street. Aly believes that the man suffered from either a diabetic coma, or a heart attack. He could not do anything for him, and thousands of men and women surrounded them. All Aly could do was hold the dying man's hand reassuringly and ask him to recite the *shahada* (a prayer recited by a dying Muslim declaring allegiance to God and that there is only one God), which he did. He died while holding Aly's hand.

That day, Aly also saw an old woman with a bleeding head injury, possibly caused by a rock. She simply placed a Band-Aid on it and continued walking, resilient and unstoppable. He and his friend Youssef walked with the crowds. Aly saw a colleague from the hospital called Adham, walking in the crowds wearing a professional mask and gloves, carrying two buckets of water. He would hold the hurled tear gas canisters he managed to get his hands on, and sink them in the water to deactivate them. Adham's resourceful thinking impressed Aly. Around this time, a canister fell next to Aly's feet. He could not see or feel anything for around thirty minutes and had great difficulty breathing, as he is asthmatic. He hung onto Youssef and moved wherever his friend went, as Aly literally could not open his eyes, which were burning like fire. Darkness enveloped him. When he was able to open his eyes about thirty minutes later he noticed that he was sitting next to a kiosk, and an old woman and a young girl were helping him with Pepsi and vinegar to soothe his eyes. The kiosk owner was distributing free cartons of bottled water. It was a strong sign of solidarity from the kiosk owner, with the men and women who took to the streets saying 'no' to the state of living in Egypt. It seemed to Aly as if the kiosk owner was protecting something sacred.

Aly separated from his friends. Some charged forward, stuck in the battle on the Galaa Bridge, while others rested with Aly. In the midst of the struggle, the police stopped firing tear gas as the wind was blowing the gas back at them. Nature had defeated *Amn Eldawla*. Protestors had room to run away from the gas, but the police could neither run nor fall back into the crowds. Aly saw them falling, one by one, into the cloud of smoke. The police were desperately trapped. Aly recalls clearly seeing a lieutenant ordering his officers to set their cars on fire and then ran away, in a futile attempt to frame the protestors. He walked on Tahrir Street and found several police officers running.

Coincidently, Aly came across two of his colleagues from the hospital, Hossam and Rasha, in a car.
Rasha said, "Aly what are you doing here?"
Aly said, "My friends and I are saying it is enough already."
Rasha said, "There is a crisis at Kasr El Aini hospital, you are needed there. Get in the car."
Aly quickly complied rode off in the car.

Chaos at the Hospital

Once he arrived at the hospital, Aly was shocked at how it was filled with patients, literally lying on the ground, as the number of the wounded was much greater than the capacity of the hospital. It was an unprecedented sight. Because of the overwhelming cases, there was a lack of communication between the head nurse and the senior doctors. They were at a loss as to which procedures to follow for patients. It was pandemonium. To make matters worse, the hospital did not have sufficient sterile medical tools. Five patients with gunshot wounds needed operations and required underwater seals, which would drain coagulated blood from the bullets. The patients urgently needed intercostal tubes, or within a few minutes, they would die. The blood would collect and compress, leaving the patients unable to breathe. Aly decided that it was worth the risk of infecting the patients with HIV or Hepatitis, rather than losing them completely, and so he went ahead and did the procedures with the unsterile medical tools. The patients may not be infected but if they were, they would still be able to live for some time. For surgeons it is highly taboo to conduct a procedure on a patient with unsterile equipment. It simply is not done. Aly compares it to walking naked in the street. However, this was an emergency under extenuating circumstances, and they really had no choice.

A couple of hours later, Aly went to check on the newer section of the hospital across the street, known as the French Kasr. There were around six or seven men who were sniped at Tahrir square, and suffered gunshot wounds in the head by live ammunition. All these men had been taking pictures using cameras or their mobiles and hence were targeted by the snipers. Anybody trying to save a target, was also shot at by snipers. They targeted three locations of the body: head, neck and chest, all of which left their victims with a low chance of survival. These were clearly well trained and well-positioned snipers. Aly does not believe the rumors that these snipers were foreigners. There is a police station at the entrance of the hospital where patients specify what accident they were involved in prior to entering the hospital for treatment, and from these reports, he saw evidence that they were shot while taking pictures.

One of the young victims, a twenty-one year-old, was in the intensive care unit after open-heart surgery. He had been shot in the back and the bullet caused damage to his spine, rendering him a paraplegic and unable to breathe on his own. Aly will never forget how on Saturday morning this patient told Aly, 'I am not sad, I am very happy even though my life is over. I just pray that I will never regret this." The patient died a few days later.

Aly took photos of all the victims and martyrs and posted them on his Facebook page, including the injuries suffered, the surgery required, and how the injuries occured. Some patients were worried when Aly asked for permission to video record them. There was a woman who was shot in her spine as she was taking her son home from the hospital. She stayed in the intensive care unit for many days, declining any interviews, let alone recordings.

Aly believes that the senior management of Kasr El Aini is corrupt. He believes they conspired with security and allowed police to use their ambulances to transport weapons into Tahrir to be used against civilians as well as *baltegeya* (thugs) to attack the protestors. They used the ambulances to block Kasr El Aini Street, cutting off access to the Liberation Square. The security did not even permit access to medication. Employees of the hospital were paid to check cars and not allow medicine and food into the square. They were armed with knives, *senag* (small swords) and *shoum* (thick sticks). Only cars without supplies were allowed to pass.

Winds of Change

On Friday night, Aly went to check on his wife at their home in Mohandeseen. The following morning, he and his friends met at the square in front of the Opera House. He remembers his Facebook status: "Things won't be the same anymore." Saturday was a funeral procession for all the fallen martyrs. He remembers seeing around five thousand men in procession with four bodies towards Omar Makram Mosque to pray on their souls, and another funeral procession from Imbaba. Once blood spilled, things could not be the same; Egyptians truly cherish life. It was not just another day that will pass by and be forgotten. It will never be forgotten.

Aly thinks the reason behind the success of the revolution is '*endemam el kotlah lel nokhba*,' the majority joining forces with the elite. On Saturday January 29, the masses joined the educated elite, forming a strong peaceful unity that succeeded eventually in overthrowing the dictator. Protestors did not resort to violence unless personally attacked. *Martin Luther King vehemently believed in nonviolence. He said,*

"Nonviolent resistance when planned and positive in action could work effectively even under totalitarian regimes"[16]

Aly will never forget the You Tube video with a young Egyptian man who stood defiantly in front of the big police van[17]. He was fearless and did not budge as the van approached him. At that moment, he was stronger than the van and its driver, as his courage was magnificent. It was on the Kasr El Aini Street. Onlookers called him *'al ragel'* (the man), encouraging him until eventually, more men stood beside him. His sheer willpower briefly stopped the car. He was peaceful, and his faith and belief were contagiously inspiring, inspiring the awe of onlookers.

More Bloodshed

More people were hurt at Tahrir, and doctors helped the victims in a make shift hospital on Mohamed Mahmoud Street. Aly went to Tahrir as a revolutionary. He helped victims at the hospital, where he was better equipped than at the square. The hospital was in close proximity to all the casualties and the victims. This 'hospital' became equipped with almost everything.

Aly was talking with one of his professors, Dr. Sayed.

Aly asked, "Is there anything missing we can provide?"

Dr. Sayed said, "A suction machine, and I have managed with the donations and sent one already." This machine is usually used in the resuscitation room.

The number of deaths on Friday 28 and Saturday 29 of January 2011 was unbelievable. Aly is confident that the official death toll can be easily multiplied by two to reach the true figure. Aly recalls the deadly train accident in 2002 when he was in his fourth year of medical school. A passenger train traveling from Cairo to Luxor caught fire from an exploded cooking gas cylinder. The fire raged on for two hours before the train conductor realized what was happening and stopped the train, but it was too late. At that point, there were officially three hundred and eighty-three people burnt to ashes. However, the real number of casualties exceeded one thousand. It was the biggest disaster in Egypt since the 1973 war. Unfortunately, Egyptians do not trust official figures, as repeatedly they have been understated. The compensation paid to the family of each of the victims of the fire was around four hundred pounds, less than sixty dollars. Aly could not help but wonder how the value of human life could be cheaper than that of a sheep, which costs around one thousand five hundred pounds (around two hundred and twenty dollars).

Back to Tahrir square, where *baltegeya* attacked police stations and set them ablaze. Police officers killed them in alleys and severed their heads from their bodies, hanging them out for the public to view. This is immoral, but Aly finds it necessary in order for people to ask, "Why did this happen?" Some people believe that protests bring a dramatic halt to the economy, which he cannot deny. But people were were protesting because there were wrong policies in the first place. They protested against civilians placed on military trails, to demand the lifting of the emergency law, and to insist on an end to military rule.

After President Mubarak's humbugging second speech, most Egyptians were divided between those sympathizing with the former President, and those persisting with the demand that he leave. The army announced that the Supreme Council of Armed Forces was in a continuous session, and would always stand by the people. Aly's friend Raouf, passed by him and they took a taxi to Tahrir. On the way, they listened to the news on the radio, which stated that a key Islamic leader had announced after Mubarak's speech, that protesting now would be *haram* (a sin).

Aly went to the Mubarak supporters' protest at Mostafa Mahmoud Square to observe, because he believes that one must see both sides in order to decide which path to take. Dr. Aly saw the late Sheikh Al Sharawi on television, a cleric known for his wisdom and moderate views. On his deathbed the sheikh said, "If you saw a struggle between two rights then you are mistaken, as there is only one right. If you are right then don't worry, because it's the right that will win at the end ....always ....as there can never be a conflict between two correct parties." Aly quotes the Quran, "Nay, We hurl the Truth against falsehood, and it knocks out its brain and behold, falsehood doth perish! Ah! Woe be to you for the (false) things ye ascribe (to us)" (21:18). The right will always prevail over the wrong. No matter how widespread evil and corruption is, and no matter how complicated scenarios play out, truth will find its own way to the surface.

Desperate Limbo

Aly visited Tahrir square on many Fridays. He has no political affiliation and has no interest in politics, as it is not his cup of tea. Each person needs to focus on his or her own domain, for the productivity cycle to gain and maintain momentum.

Hossam Badrawy, former Secretary General of the NDP (National Democratic Party), announced that former President Mubarak was going to step down. Cheers and celebrations were loud in the streets. Aly was so thrilled that he celebrated prematurely, until he heard the final speech, in which Mubarak announced that he had appointed a vice president to run the country, keeping certain critical powers with *rayees* Mubarak. He saw men and women suffering heart attacks in shock, in Tahrir. Others lost consciousness in disbelief. Protestors demonstrated their anger by removing their shoes and waving them in the air in a depiction of hitting the former President, a sign of utmost disrespect in Egyptian culture.

The following morning, on Friday February 11, Aly woke up beyond despair. He had lost every molecule of hope in his body. Then he heard the army's statement guaranteeing that all the demands of the protestors would be met. Aly sat on the ground in Tahrir playing with sand and pebbles, feeling in limbo. Even though he lost hope, he persisted in the sit in.

Breathtaking Day

After the *Maghreb* (sunset) prayers, Aly heard people screaming in excitement that the former president had stepped down. This was not the first time people said it, but in previous times it had turned out to be a rumor. Aly only believed it when he saw a man running with his laptop open, broadcasting on the Jazeera channel the breaking news with the vice president's speech. It was by far the best moment in his life. He shouted loudly "*Allah Akbar*," (God is Great) and "*Erfaa rasak enta masry*," (Lift your head up for you are an Egyptian)' along with others. He was jumping, leaping, dancing and cheering from six in the evening until two in the morning, without feeling time. The popular saying, "Life is not measured by the breaths we take, but by the moments that take our breath away," summarizes the happiest, most breathtaking day of his life. Aly teased his friends who did not join in the celebrations.

During these celebrations, Aly felt as if his soul was elevated up into the sky, along with the martyrs and the prophets. It was out of this world. Once at home alone, as his wife was in America at the time, Aly switched on the television and watched all the moving songs with visuals of the brave martyrs. Aly is not an emotional man and usually never cries. He did not cry when his grandmother died, or when his brother had cancer. But that night, he cried, for hours. He cried over the cherished lives that were lost. In the thirty years of his life, the martyrs were the purest people he witnessed. Some were very close to his circle. One of his wife's colleagues died on January 28, 2011. One moment he had been with his friends in Tahrir Street, and the next, he was lying on the ground, dead, on the Galaa Bridge. Aly had been standing close by, and it so easily could have been him. It is very cruel and heartless for men and women to die while demanding their human rights. The most precious thing in this world is human life, and yet so many lives were lost on the streets. It was very painful, especially for the mothers of the martyrs. He cannot understand how the mothers were holding up with their sons or daughters unjustly killed.

After the euphoria of the revolution, his target changed to achieving temporary medical exposure in North America, with the aim of returning to Egypt to benefit his country, hoping the circumstances will improve during his absence. He has faith that when the time is right, a good opportunity will arise.

Ignorance and Immorality

Egypt had a golden chance to start on the right track after the revolution, but missed this opportunity due to ignorance. The danger of the prevailing ignorance was demonstrated when the results of the constitutional referendum in March 2011 came out, with almost eighty percent agreeing with the changes. Many of the voters chose 'yes' as they were brainwashed into thinking that they were good Muslims for doing so, and that 'no' represented the Christians and the disbelievers. Others voted 'yes' for stability. Aly voted 'no' along with the enlightened minority. Aly ironically observes that six months after the vote, neither Islam nor stability dominates. There is a very dangerous segment of society, which can be termed as the 'educated ignorant', who finished secondary school and yet are not able to read and write, who vote according to the visual signs on the ballot. Public schools have around eighty students per class and students are obliged to take private sessions with the teacher to pass the exam.

Taha Hussein is a great Egyptian writer and intellect who came up with a famous motto, "Education is like the air we breathe and the water we drink." When Taha was Minister of Education, he introduced free education to all. Little had he envisioned what poor standards the public education system would reach. Around forty-eight percent of Egyptians cannot read or write. Egyptians are very pious and religious people. However, they have lost faith and belief in their own capabilities and abilities, and in the process, have lost their morals. Aly perceives that the uneducated are mainly the ones opposed to the revolution, incapable of understanding current or world affairs, let alone reading the newspapers and making sense of news. Moreover, the remaining fifty-two percent who are supposedly educated, are not truly educated in all senses of the word, as they were not taught how to understand, but what to memorize, completely off the trajectory that Hussein had designed. Aly has low expectations and sees Egyptians as buried in ignorance. He respects the law of nature and the saying: "Answer a fool according to his folly."

Aly asks how we expect people to react when a tyrant ruled Egyptians for over thirty years, giving them no free will, no rights, no healthcare, no education, no food, and no income. The *ancien regime* succeeded in destroying Egyptians who, as a result, currently have no sense of morality.

Aly cannot believe how the *baltegeya* attacked and killed protestors on Wednesday February 2, 2011. But how can he blame an ignorant thug whom the system created, a man desperate for money to the point at which he is driven to kill? That day neurosurgeons were overwhelmed by all the head traumas resulting from the violent assaults.

Aly views Egypt as being plagued by the evil triangle of ignorance, poverty and disease. At *Kasr El Aini hospital*, he has treated patients representing the average Egyptian citizens who are very poor, very sick and lacking knowledge. Aly believes that to view the real Egypt there are three key locations: Kasr Al Aini hospital, the army, and prisons. *This chapter sheds some light about Kasr Al Aini Hospital and in the book, characters will share their experiences in the army (Chapter 15) and in the prisons (Chapter 1).*

Trauma

Trauma replaced euphoria in November 2011. Aly joined the wave of protests at Mohamed Mahmoud Street. What he witnessed was truly traumatizing - *coming from a cardiac surgeon, one should not lightly dismiss this*. Aly went with three of his friends, and he cannot forget the sight of blood everywhere. He saw girls shot dead, Sheikh Imad Effat from *Azhar* who tried to be a peacemaker, shot dead. *Ironically and prophetically, his email address, according to Egypt Independant, was 'shaheed_elazhari', which means El Azhar martyr.* By midnight, Aly was scared, as there were few people on the street, and so many dead. He decided to distract himself by checking on the makeshift hospital, which was a disaster when it comes to hygiene and medical standards.

After his firsthand experience of the horror at the makeshift hospital in November 2011, Dr. Aly lost all hope. He reconsidered the state of Egypt and wanted out. He remembers a man boldly stating that the harassed girl whose clothes were torn and was dragged on the street, deserved such treatment, and so were the fire fighter and an eight-year-old who were shot dead. Things cannot change as long as the morals of the people are missing and, sadly, many people are clueless and unaware.

Aly now holds the conviction that many Egyptians are inherently bad people and will never change. During the run-off presidential elections in 2012, Aly wrote on his ballot, "This ballot is the death certificate of Egypt, there is always a third choice," absolutely rejecting the polarized two options in front of him. Aly was saddened by how *Ikhwan* tarnished the reputation of Islam, focusing on the superficial surface, rather than the genuine core of Islam. There is an Arabic saying, 'When does a nation reach its worst? When its imbeciles rule it,' that holds significance for Aly.

Aly recalls that during the November bloodshed, Katatny, the *Ikhwan* speaker of parliament, was applauding the ministry of interior for their handling of the protestors. Aly cannot but wonder how the roles have been reversed, the change of fate. As the Arabic proverb says, "As you chastise you will be chastised." In 2013, many *Ikhwan* were killed.

In Aly's mind, *Ikhwan* and the military both need to be removed from the political equation, as each is dirtier than the other. Egypt deserves a third choice. A frustrated Aly says, 'we deserve a third choice.' It cannot be either military rule or political Islam.

The revolution had brought hope to Aly that Egypt could improve, and that the morally right would prevail. However, in April 2012, he was once again filled with despair at the situation, as the counter-revolution had succeeded in wiping out the revolution. He is one hundred percent pessimistic about the future and is heartbroken to admit that those pure martyrs had died in vain. It has been worthless, and the situation is chaotic. He had a heated debate with some surgeons who were excited that Omar Suleiman, the former head of intelligence, had nominated himself for president. The surgeons wanted to support his candidacy. Aly was once more shocked at the level of ignorance. They were keen to replace an autocratic leader with his key right hand man, who is very likely to create yet another autocratic tyranny. *Aly's feelings resemble those of the Old Woman in Voltaire's 'Candide'. The Old Woman said, "For is there anything more stupid than to be eager to go on carrying a burden which one would gladly throw away, to loathe one's very being and yet to hold it fast, to fondle the snake that devours us until it has eaten our hearts away?"*[18] Egyptian society is sick, with highly educated individuals who are not knowledgeable, even ignorant, and incapable of discussing differences in a civil manner. *Will they let the snake 'eat their hearts away?'*

Aly has followed his dream and is currently working at a hospital in Canada. He moved to Montreal in September 2012 on his own. He attained a fellowship at a Canadian hospital and is literally starting his career from scratch, in a respectable, well reputed hospital where everyone respects each other and human life is valued. Canadians are people who work productively, respect one another and their laws, and have no room for hatred. Aly's wife Amira and their daughter, have moved to Washington State in the USA in order for Amira to finish her medical certificate. In the last few months, Aly has realized how far back Egyptian medical practice is, having stopped progressing at the 70's or 80's. In Egypt, medicine is mainly malpractice.

Aly cannot continue to see any more pain and death in Egypt, and hopes that he is able to continue working and living abroad. He has abandoned his initial plans of returning to Egypt. When we talked in November 2012, Aly was hurting at the heartless death of the fifty children at Assiut, when their school bus collided with a train. He was mad at the manner in which people on Facebook were using this tragedy to attack *Ikhwan*, without talking about the children and their families. What has happened to morals? Where has morality gone? Where is humanity? Egyptians have lost their ethics, claiming piety but in reality having forgotten about the afterlife.

Over Two Years Later

Aly continues to feel endless despair, as no change on the ground has taken place in Egypt. It seems the country was driven into a dead end, with no promising solution on the horizon. In 2013, Egypt is trapped in a vicious cycle of violence and blaming the other, rejecting differences rather than accepting them.

Tamarod was a brilliant idea brought forward by young non-partisan activists that the public embraced in millions, including Aly. The army and the *ancien regime* certainly endorsed it. After its success in collecting millions of proxies demanding early presidential elections, Aly questions why they announced the creation of a political party. It seems to Aly, that all parties are corrupt. The political scene is a hazy place where one cannot distinguish between what is right and what is wrong. In Aly's view, Dr. Baradei was the soul of the revolution. But after he resigned his post in the new government, Aly is baffled at how he 'left the fight' and he has lost trust in Dr. Baradei, along with the revolution.

On June 30, 2013, Aly joined Egyptians in Montreal supporting the *Tamarod* initiative. In his opinion, July 3, 2013 was a bigger revolution than January 25, 2011. He cannot understand how people may refer to 2013 as a coup and not 2011; both were revolutions supported by the military. Simply put, nothing major will happen in Egypt without military backing and blessing. However, if General Sisi runs for presidency, then it is no longer a revolution. Aly imagines that the General will manage the National Security due to the terrorism the country is attempting to overcome, leaving the government to the president. As for the controversial July 26, 2013 when General Sisi implored Egyptians to flock to the streets, delegating the army to deal with terrorism, Aly did not think it was necessary, except to prove to the western media that this was not a *coup d'état*.

Aly surely still feels in limbo, with Egypt facing the peak in a triangle of damage. Egyptians simply see any form of competition, like the national soccer matches between Ahly and Zamalek clubs, as a contest of winners and as losers; the good and the bad, forgetting that there is a little bit of good and bad inside every one of us. The difference is how we manage the conflicting forces. Egyptians have succumbed to the bad in them, forgetting the good.

PART II

The Turmoil

"The greatest glory in living lies not in never falling,
but in rising every time we fall"
Nelson Mandela

CHAPTER 5

Suez the Spark

"If the people one day will to live then destiny must respond and the night must disappear and the chain must break." Aboul-Qacem Echebbi

The friend of my brother's sister-in-law got me in touch with a journalist, Sarah El Deeb, who suggested I meet an activist from Suez; the catalyst of the revolution. I refer to him in this chapter as Mahmoud, as he was uncomfortable signing a formal proxy. Fortunately, he had a meeting in Cairo so we met at Maadi City Center in a café on Monday October 1, 2012. During the interview, he got a call informing him that the meeting he had traveled for was postponed, which was annoying for him. However, it was my luck that he had come, so that we could meet in person rather than over Skype.

Proud Patriot

Usually you never see him clean-shaven. Mahmoud has a goatee and is stout with average height, wears glasses and is almost bald. Mahmoud was born in *Sharkiya* on February 1, 1973 during the war, just before the victory. His family is originally from Suez. His parents witnessed the wars with Israel in 1967 and 1973, which led them to move from Suez to the Sharkiya governorate in 1967, where it was safer, being further away from the borders. He is the only one among his brothers and sisters who was not born in Suez, which upsets him, as he is very loyal to his governorate.

After the war in 1974, his family moved back to their hometown. His father was a manager at the Ministry of Education in Suez and his mother a school headmistress in Mahmoud's primary school. He went to the most well-known public schools in Suez. Mahmoud studied Hospitality and Tourism at Port Said University. His family consists of people with diverse specialties; from an archeologist, to an engineer, to a pediatrician. He embarked on a career in the hotel industry.

During university and in the period he was waiting for his military service to begin, Mahmoud underwent training at various hotels. Once he enlisted in the military, the army stationed him in *Ismailia* for a year, during which time he experienced a completely different facet of life, very distant to his comfortable civilian world. He had no choice but to follow orders and obey instructions in tasks he despised. His experience was interesting, exposing him to men from different backgrounds, governorates and mentalities. The military was a good transition from the comfort of a teenage life, in which his parents gave him pocket money, to his working life where he was financially independent. Mahmoud did not have a choice in selecting his vacation days. He believes the rigidity of the military service was beneficial in forming his adulthood. The conscription is a patriotic duty for any man who loves Egypt and Mahmoud is very patriotic. *His mobile phone's ringtone is set to a patriotic song "Ya Baladi…Ya Baladi…ana bahebek ya Baladi," which means (my country…my country, I love you my country) and another time "ya Habibti ya Masr" (my beloved Egypt).*

Mahmoud tested the waters in tourism for a few years before moving into the fast food business in Ein El Sokhna, and has been working in this industry for thirteen years. His wife, Marwa, works in the administration of a petroleum company. He currently lives in Suez with his wife and three children.

The Catalyst

According to Wikipedia, some online activists refer to Suez as Egypt's Sidi Bou Said, the instigating city of the Tunisian revolution. Mahmoud recalls that unrest started in Suez before the rest of Egypt on January 21, with small-scale protest in front of the government offices, which ended by nightfall. On January 25, a few days later, Mahmoud spent most of the day at home. In the evening, he went to check on one of his restaurants and found the streets blocked. He could hear the sounds of police firing tear gas canisters. He managed to take a detour and reach the restaurant, where he parked his car. The main street was cordoned off with the heavy presence of *Amn Elmarkazi*, (Central Security forces). Curious to know what the commotion was about, he stopped a passerby.
Mahmoud said, "What is happening?"
Passerby said, "There are protests. Three have been killed."

It was very strange, as the Suez area was not accustomed to protests, let alone killings, with the exception of wartime. Mahmoud knew that things would not be the same with the shedding of blood. Some of the inhabitants of Suez are originally from Upper Egypt and are famous for their manliness, pride and high self-esteem. The people of Suez are vengeful and famous for their aggressive nature. Police vans drenched protestors with hoses of water to pressurize the crowds to disperse.

Mahmoud recalls that the first man to fall was Mostafa Ragab, who had stopped at a café before heading to his shift. A bullet killed Mostafa after he left the café around seven in the evening. Mostafa had no interests or activities in the political realm and he came from a very simple family, but none-the-less it was his last living day. Mahmoud visited Mostafa's family and was dismayed to discover that the martyr's mother had kidney failure and is a widow with three daughters, and that her late son was the one providing for them. Mahmoud wonders who will provide for the late Mostafa's family.

At the Morgue

By ten the following morning, January 26, the families of the men who were killed were waiting in front of the morgue surrounded by a crowd, morbidly waiting to receive the bodies of their loved ones and proceed with the funeral. They were struggling to come to terms with their sudden loss. The head of police refused to hand the bodies over to the families, fearing that a procession would take place, further fueling people's anger at the senseless deaths. This was a grave misjudgment on the part of the morgue security personnel. After all, the father of one of the deceased just wanted to honor his son and bury him as soon as possible. *In Islam, it is favorable to bury the body as soon as possible after death, following a ritual cleansing, wrapping and prayer.* Meanwhile, reportedly, the head of police, whose relative was among the deceased, discreetly moved the body, exiting from the rear of the building into a big police van, to go and bury him. Once the parents waiting in the front of the building discovered that the police had released a body while they stood waiting until six in the evening to recieve the bodies of their children, their feeling of loss and mourning mixed with rage and anger at the denied right to prompt access to their beloved deceased. It was like throwing gas on fire. This blatant differential treatment changed something forever. This was the spark that ignited the revolution in Suez.

Violence erupted; rocks and Molotov cocktails were hurled. Shortly thereafter protestors moved to Police Station Number Forty, which is located in a popular district.

Fire in the Police Station

On the cataclysmic Friday of Anger, January 28 2011, crowds of people marched through the streets in protest, heading to the main governorate office. Chants demanded the resignation of President Mubarak and the governor of Suez. Protestors did not want to set the governorate building on fire as they were against acts of vandalism.

While Mahmoud was protesting in front of the municipality, he was surprised to hear that the police station in the neighborhood of Al Arbain was broken into around two in the afternoon, culminating with the escape of prisoners. It had been set on fire. This is where the real fighting happened and lasted from noon until four or five in the morning on a daily basis. Civilians assaulted, restrained and beat many officers. Mahmoud believes that people wanted revenge for previous police behaviour; unlawful framing of people for crimes they did not commit, and for abuse and torture inflicted on civilians. They jumped at this window of opportunity and struck back.

The crowds moved from Al Arbain station to the Suez police station. Mahmoud recalls that around eighteen died at the Suez police station. It was a gut-wrenching, heart-breaking, bloody day. *Amn Elmarkazi* officers fired indiscriminately. Things were rapidly getting out of control.

Mahmoud believes that the police officers did not sleep for around three days. Reinforcements came from neighboring Ismailia and Port Said, but they were no match for the number of people from Suez. Mahmoud estimates that there were between twenty and thirty thousand protestors. Women, old and young, participated in the revolution, though they were a few among the sea of men. The police put pressure on the people of Suez by confiscating many licenses, cars and motorbikes. There was a feeling of forceful suppression and the people suffocated with the police's arrogance.

Near Death

The first life to be lost on January 28 was a man who happened to be standing next to Mahmoud, near to the Suez Police Station. It could so easily have been Mahmoud who lost his life in that moment. He was part of a funeral procession making its way from a nearby mosque towards the governate building. Heedless, the police fired upon the mourners with tear gas and rifles. Mahmoud quickly ran, taking cover behind the trunk of a tree and bracing himself for death. He will never forget the deafening sound of bullets hitting the tree trunk, or the pungent smell of tear gas or the burning sensation in his eyes. It was like being in a war zone. The whole scene was strange and surreal. Many of the souls lost that day were innocent bystanders. Among the martyrs was a school headmaster who had parked his car next to a mosque on his way to pray the *Maghreb* prayers (sunset) when he was shot dead by a bullet that hit him in his back. Another man watched the turmoil from his balcony and died from a seemingly random shot. There was a man behind a shop counter who received a shot in the head. All night the police and protestors were provoking each other, as the protestors attempted to break into the station. Mahmoud saw low-ranking policemen firing their machine guns being photographed, contrary to official statements by the ministry of interior, saying that police were not armed.

After a while, the suffocating teargas made Mahmoud almost faint. He was helped to a friend's nearby home and after around an hour, he was feeling better. Night had fallen and he went to secure his restaurant. The windows were broken but nothing stolen, although hooligans had been looting many stores. It was complete chaos. Mahmoud believes the police received orders to withdraw from the streets. The army mobilized on Friday evening, and arrived at Suez by dawn.

The army stationed units to secure key public establishments. When they showed up close to his restaurant, Mahmoud talked to the Lieutenant and asked him to keep an eye on his store while he went home to sleep. This was at around four in the morning. Mahmoud slept restlessly, tossing and turning for a few hours. Later that morning, he returned to the shop and decided to safeguard the store by stacking bricks or rocks infront of broken windows. It was impossible to find any repairman willing to come out at this tumultuous time.

Social Bonding

On January 29, with the rampant lawlessness, neighbors gathered to establish civilian checkpoints and take security measures into their own hands. The police, at this point, were absent. Mahmoud recounts that Sheikh Hafez organized this initiative; he was among the civilian activists who protected Suez against an Israeli tank invasion during the October war. Some men met with Sheikh Hafez at the Mosque of Martyrs and agreed to summon men via the loud speakers of the mosques. The army's role was that of a spectator to all the skirmishes, as their sole aim was to safeguard strategic public property. Civilian men stood armed, on full alert. Some had licensed handguns, others had knives or rods and any instrument that could serve as a weapon. It is common to find licensed guns in this area, as those whose origins are from Upper Egypt but live in Suez, find it a question of honor to be armed.

Mahmoud recorded a televised telephone interview with Al Jazeera channel on January 29 with Dina Samak. In the interview, it was evident that Mahmoud's voice was hoarse and faint from all the shouting, chanting and protesting. He described the creation of the civilian checkpoints as a happy moment, uniting the people to protect private and public property. The civilians ensured that all roads were blocked; cars and people were checked for weapons and if found, they were confiscated and handed over to the army. During this period, civilians also retrieved a stolen ambulance. Although the times were tense, these checkpoints brought people together. Neighbors bonded, or were even introduced to each other for the first time. It was a rare display of bonding and unity that Mahmoud feels is unlikely to re-occur.

Before the revolution, social interaction was minimal, with each household immersed in its daily life. If a neighbor was facing difficult times, the regular response was, "It's none of our business. Let each one focus on his business." *This is not the traditional way relationships are conducted amongst neighbors in the Middle East. Things have changed dramatically this last century as people have become less community focused and more individualistic.* Mahmoud appreciated the closeness between neighbors which these checkpoints brought forth. The community spent two weeks from January 29 until February 11 together, while guarding their homes. It was an awesome sign of unity, as they were all hand in hand. After the revolution, these men would reminisce of those pleasant yet anxious days, that they perceived as good times. Some nights they would share pumpkin seeds to pass the time, and on other nights share tea from a thermos.

During this time, Mahmoud had the chance to talk to people and understand their views; those who supported the revolution and those who were against it. One of the greatest things about the Egyptian people is that during tough times they unite.

Mahmoud claims that the spirit at Al Arbain Square at Suez was better than the utopian Tahrir spirit during those eighteen days. People maintained high morals and a greatly tolerant mentality. If someone threw a paper on the ground, the person behind him or her would pick it up and throw it in the garbage; it was unbelievable teamwork. Al Arbain Square was very organized with different tents marked to indicate their functions. It was a great feat to organize such huge number of people, without a leader, and maintain proper facilities in an open roundabout.

Bourgeoisie

Mahmoud is an activist who whole-heartedly participated during the protests. The revolution displayed the sense of awakening among the rich who felt responsible to stand up for the endless suffering of the less fortunate. The rich took to the streets on behalf of the unfortunate class who were not demanding their rights, because they are simply overwhelmed with the everyday plight of survival. Morals have been shaken up and self-realization has come about, with Egyptian people admitting to having lost their good morals, and the dire need to regain them. In Mahmoud's view, the people who created this revolution are the best-educated and most decent two million Egyptians: the true, educated, patriotic elite who in reality, are not facing any financial crunch. Protestors were the cream of society, those who went to the top-notch universities like the American University in Cairo, who lived in villas, whose fathers were diplomats and other elite professions, who could afford to travel. They felt Egypt's honor compromised and its role in the world peripheral. In reality, the state was deteriorating at a frightful pace.

The well-to-do had no choice but to voice their despair. It was not a matter of rich or poor, but a matter of a decaying society that had to be shaken and nurtured. Moreover, these protestors were not the class of people facing the horrendous failure of the institutions and the grave problems of society. *They were living a good life, but did not like the state which Egypt had fallen into. They wanted Egypt to rise to its previous glorious days. So the Egyptians rose to the occasion and as Marx rightly stated, "The bourgeoisie, historically, has played a most revolutionary part."*[19]

The rich, like the poor, are eating food that is bloated with fertilizers and hormones that cause cancer. Everyone is inhaling the lead infested air filled with carbon monoxide from burning garbage and rice hay. Everyone is using running water that is not properly treated. Some claim that those who drink it suffer from kidney failure, which has become a recent phenomenon in Egypt. Years back, all Egyptians, rich and poor, drank tap water and kidneys were mostly fine. The well to do, despite their wealth, are not living a good life if they cannot provide their kids an environment that is free of pollution at all levels.

Before the revolution Mahmoud was a simple civilian who was apathetic and had nothing to do with politics. He did not have an opinion. His activism initiated him into the world of politics.

Unexpectedly

Mahmoud will never forget this incident. He cannot recall which day after the Friday of Anger but it was after the *zohr* (noon) prayers. Mahmoud was marching in a protest when he suddenly saw his mother standing on the sidewalk in tears. Mahmoud, surprised to see her there, quickly walked to her and embraced her.
Um Mahmoud said, "What does he want? We have grown old now, let the youth live. He must go. We are over, we are going to die."

Mahmoud was greatly moved to see his mother supporting the protestors and he could not help but cry at her her heartfelt words. At nearly seventy years old, Mahmoud's mother is relatively fragile. He feared for her welfare and so, took her back home. His father, at seventy-six years old, was in poor health. While he could not physically participate in the protests, morally he supported his son and the activists.

Mahmoud's mother was initially afraid and rejected the protests, beckoning her children to return home.
Um Mahmoud said, "This is enough Mahmoud. Come back home for your kids' sake. Aren't you afraid for your children?"
Mahmoud said, "No I am not afraid."

At the time of transcribing and writing this chapter, it is the second anniversary of the revolution, and I cannot help but feel a strong déjà vu, as Suez is witnessing yet again a round of violence alongside Port Said and Ismailia. The court sentenced 21 men from Port Said to death for accusations of being involved in the stadium massacre that took place on February 2, 2012 where Ahly football fans were attacked, brutally killed and thrown off the stadium bleachers. The unrest has led President Morsi to put into effect a state of emergency and curfew in those three governorates.

Mubarak Helped the Revolution

Mahmoud believes that what made this revolution succeed were the infamous speeches by former President Mubarak during the eighteen days. Nobody ever imagined that Mubarak would leave office alive. Public opinion expected him to stay president until his natural death or assassination. It was beyond imagination that he would step down. All the concessions he made were not real actions, but more of an anesthetic. Protestors were adamant that the President should go, and they were not going to budge until he quit. In a huge sign of disrespect, they waved their shoes in the air. How could a President go back to office when his people waved shoes at him? His image was tarnished and he lost the respect of the people. When he appointed the late head of intelligence Omar Suleiman as vice president, the selection met with more grunts from the protestors. Mahmoud explains that Mubarak probably imagined that his speeches would appease a wave of protest that would eventually die down. However, Mubarak could not have been more wrong, for without a doubt, his speeches provoked the people more than it appeased them.

After the second speech, many people sympathized with Mubarak and were willing to let him stay in office for six months. However, this revolution was God-protected, as Mahmoud says, as the following day witnessed the assault on the protestors. Mahmoud never liked Mubarak; who ever sees the same president all his life? He compares the former *rayees* (chief) to Ramesses II who ruled Egypt for sixty-six years. Mahmoud believes that the *feloul* (remnants of the old regime) were behind the attacks on February 2, and has not changed his opinion over the course of the years. If the attacks had succeeded in the arrest of the protestors and clearing off the square, it would have stamped and extinguished the revolution's spark. However, the attacks on the protestors did not succeed.

Writing History

On February 11, 2011, a day after the disappointing final speech of former President Mubarak, Mahmoud was participating in street protests from morning until late afternoon. While having lunch at his home he watched a bulletin announcing that the president would address the nation. Protestors in Cairo were heading to the Itihadiya presidential palace. Filled with anticipation at the announced speech, he called his sister who was in Cairo.

Mahmoud said, "Where are you?"

His sister replied, "We are on the way to the palace. It's either us or him."

Mahmoud was following the news on television and the internet, and at the time his restaurant was closed. Breaking news interrupted a TV broadcast with the historic announcement from the vice president. He could not believe his ears; he had to hear it a couple of times to make sure he had heard correctly. *It lasted thirty seconds, and yet, poetically ended a thirty-year rule of a Pharaoh. It was sweet, poetic justice.* Mahmoud ran to his balcony, shouting 'God is great!' A dream had come true. Contemplating the invincible power of the people, strong enough to overthrow the president, Mahmoud felt a surge of adrenaline and his heart raced. Mahmoud believes that if President Mubarak had not left office, the police would have tracked down the protestors to arrest or kill them. He is very proud that he was part of the revolution and that he was not afraid. During the 18 days, he could not help but fearfully ponder what would happen if the revolution failed; what would follow; what would happen to him. This commonly shared fear is probably one of the reasons why the revolution was on the right track. The revolution has not yet succeeded; it is still on the path.

Mahmoud took his daughter to the streets to celebrate, proudly waving the Egyptian flag and celebrating the end of Mubarak's regime. At the Al Arbain Square where the late Mostafa Ragab was shot dead, strangers were hugging each other, overwhelmed with joy. The square is referred to as *Meedan Al Shouhada* (the Martyrs' square) since the revolution. Previously it was called *Sidi Al Arbain*. For the first time in his life, Mahmoud felt he was witnessing something he could recount to his grandchildren one day. It was historic. Mahmoud recalls the war stories his mother and father told him that essentially are a piece of history. Before the revolution, Mahmoud felt that he had nothing to be proud of or to remember and share. Now, Mahmoud has witnessed and participated in the history of Egypt, a rare and treasured moment. His children and grandchildren will hear his stories and read this book; they will know what happened, something to value and have pride in. Those who did not participate in the revolution have missed something very big, which history will never replicate.

Left Too Soon

Mahmoud does not doubt that the biggest mistake the activists made was to leave Tahrir square on February 12, as they failed to read the political scene thoroughly. Former President Mubarak handed over the country to SCAF, the Supreme Council of Armed Forces, which is far from the activists' coveted civilian rule. Mahmoud criticizes the activists; they should have stayed at the square until the military handed over power to a civilian presidential council. They should have started with a new constitution followed by elections, as preached by Dr. Baradei, the key opposition figure. The *ancien regime* still exists with all its institutions; the people successfully removed only its head, the president.

All sorts of security organizations, intelligence, *Amn Eldawla* and investigators started to survey Tahrir like hawks, circling and looking for prey. *Baltegeya* started visiting the famous square and reports of cases of sexual harassment arose. *As the country spun into a backward political process, sowing discontent and disunity, the outcome became inevitable; as Martin Luther King wrote, "When creative statesmanship wanes irrational militarism increases"*[20] Henceforth, Tahrir changed for the worse and was no longer utopia. Mahmoud does not doubt that the ensuing events were part of the bigger plan to exhaust the revolution and quell its spirit. Mahmoud believes that media played a key role in reflecting and emphasizing this negative image. The plan was to make the Egyptians grow to hate the revolution, which had brought them nothing; they were still unemployed – actually more people were laid off post the revolution, still living an undignified life, and to make matters worse, with no security and an increase in rampant robberies.

Mahmoud believes that the revolution continues in the hearts of the people, though many are despondent. During the eighteen days, Egyptians theatrically displayed their best values. But after February 11, 2011, the pitfall of the revolution revealed the worst parts of Egyptians. Egyptians are selfish opportunists who believe that his or her view is right, hence, he or she is better than the "other" is. This revolution is God-like. Mahmoud feels that each time it drives off course by cunning attempts to exhaust it, some heavenly act occurs, making the revolution stand strong again.

Mahmoud noticed that after February 11, new faces participated in the protests so that they would get a feel for those 18 days they missed. It was like some form of 'revolutionary tourism.' There were many incidences like this after Mubarak stepped down. Many families went to take pictures at the world renowned Tahrir square, and even tourists came to visit it. The civilized Egyptians who peacefully toppled the dictator had impressed the world. Egyptians started to love being Egyptian, after a long period of embarrassment and hatred towards their own country. Hearing the national anthem after Mubarak stepped down, Mahmoud felt differently now. He felt proud. Seeing the flag waving in the wind drew immense feelings of pride in Mahmoud, feelings that were otherwise absent.

Selfishness
Egyptians are very emotional people, and are not bloodthirsty. Egypt's history going back over 400 centuries, has helped it withstand the turbulent days of the revolution, as the Egyptian genes immersed in ancient civilization resurfaced during those eighteen days. Yet over time Egyptians, have changed for the worse to their own detriment.

When Mahmoud travels abroad, he realizes the stark reality of how truly mismanaged and how plunged in injustice Egypt has become. Egyptians are disrespected and treated like third class citizens. Mahmoud blames this on the leader; if the leader were strong and good then subsequently all Egyptians would command trust and good treatment. If their fellow Egyptians do not respect them, why would foreigners? He is dismayed at how adults act. He refers to incidences such as adults allowing their small children to sit on their laps while driving as examples of irresponsibility and carelessnes that is rampant in Egyptian society.

The *ancien regime* succeeded in killing Egyptian gallantry; however, this revolution has awakened it from the dead. There was a time when, if girls were harassed in their neighborhoods, the community would have treated it as a scandal. Things have changed to an extent that it has become normal and acceptable for a neighbor to sweet talk the girl next door. Now, if a woman is harassed in front of a man, he would simply turn and walk away, undisturbed and unmoved. Gone are the days were men were filled with honor, pride, bravery and chivalry.

Mahmoud sees that the media has played a role in the change of attitude and the popular "I, I, I" phenomenon soaked in selfishness has taken over. Fortunate people have become concerned with their homes and holidays, oblivious to other people's lack of ability to merely survive and feed their families. Society became self-involved to the extent that a man would fear informing his own brother that he bought real estate, thinking that his very own blood would get jealous. The old *nizam* (regime) succeeded in getting each family so grossly involved in earning its own living, that it ignored all other aspects of society, most importantly, politics and social responsibility.

A large proportion of Egyptians are illiterate and uneducated, making it all the more difficult to take the leap from the self-centeredness to communalism. The youth are manipulated and molded into being passive, selfish adults. The education system is a dire failure. Mahmoud is saddened when his daughter, who goes to primary school, carries a school bag filled with books that Mahmoud feels are heavier than her own weight. A bag heavy with books that don't teach anything is a useless burden. Private lessons have become a necessity at such a young age given the fact that many classroom teachers are under-paid and ineffective. The educational institution needs to be set up from scratch.

Past Wars

In Suez, things were different from Cairo, as the general public took control when the police left the city on January 28, 2011. Banks and shops closed, and many found themselves in difficulty without access to cash. Curfew in Suez was as early as 3pm.

The Third Army in Suez played a very admirable role. The army and the people of Suez are very close, as they have witnessed wars together. The people of Suez stood beside the army during the war against the enemy over the course of history. They share blood and therefore have a special bond. The British forces tried to invade Suez in 1956. On October 24, 1973 had it not been for the joint efforts of the army and the people of Suez, the Israelis could have reached Cairo. Mahmoud recounts that the army, who were in short supply of artillery, was about to surrender. Had it not been for the support of the civilians, the enemy tanks would have reached beyond Suez. Among the old slogans echoed in the streets of Suez is, "Suez is the people and the army," echoing the unfaltering partnership between the army and the people who played an integral, complementary role for each other. During the war, the people of Suez were the ones who fed the army. Mahmoud recalls his mother wholeheartedly cooking and feeding troops. The army at the time did not have sufficient funds and needed the support. Due to their geographic location and their natural disposition, the people of Suez are prone to sacrifice, as history has witnessed.

Mahmoud remembers that as a boy, he could see damaged Israeli tanks across the city. The remnants of the war stayed in place for many years, including the rabble of knocked down buildings. His family was forced to abandon their home, and rented a place in the city of Zagazig, Sharkiya governorate, away from the dangers of war. The worst experience is being forced to leave one's home and belongings. Moving to Zagazig, Mahmoud's family felt like beggars seeking a new life. *While recounting his childhood memories of the ugly war, Mahmoud had tears in his eyes. I had not noticed at first, so I carried on asking him when all this happened. He was silent and that is when I noticed the tears behind his glasses as he recalled this traumatic period of his life. I felt embarrassed that I had asked him this sensitive question. His voice faltered, and it took him a moment to gather himself.* People were forced to leave their homes in Suez, Ismalia and Port Said, and migrated all over Egypt.

Mahmoud says that the cities at the war front have always defended Egypt. However, they have never received their due share of the national budget or development projects. The irony is that Suez is the richest governorate in Egypt with the Suez Canal, petroleum, factories, and sea docks. And yet, the infrastructure does not reflect this wealth. Suez is getting peripheral treatment, with bad roads and polluted water; around 40% of the people of Suez suffer from kidney failure. Throughout Mubarak's rule, Mahmoud does not recall that the President ever visited Suez. He feels discrimination towards the people of Suez, despite their sacrifices for the country. The Third Army treated the people of Suez with respect. Nobody was beaten, and just twelve were arrested but later released. The activists and the army were continuously in touch, throughout periods of communication and periods of conflict and tension. Mahmoud saw pictures that showed a different ball game in

Cairo, with the military police beating and dragging civilians. General Sedky, head of the Third Army, dealt with matters in Suez in a very dignified manner and now is chief of staff at the army. Mahmoud differentiates between the Supreme Council of the Armed Forces, and the Third Army, which is the army division covering Suez and mid to South of Sinai.

Power Struggle

After the famous eighteen days succeeded in getting the president out of office, the power struggle commenced. Mahmoud describes people who made their first appearances in the protests, as though they landed by parachutes onto the revolution, and hijacked it. History has shown that intellects and wise men create revolutions and the mobs carry it out, while the social climbers are the ones who reap its benefits. *Shabab* led the revolution, the young men and women of Egypt, many of whom died or were wounded. Power grabbers came onto the theatre, sucking the power and the game changed into a power struggle.

After the parliamentary elections, the political scene sidelined the liberals as *Ikhwan* and *Salafists* won the majority of the seats. A couple of months after the unpopular run-off between Shafik and Morsi with the latter winning, the top military junta suddenly retired after sixteen soldiers were killed in Sinai, in August 2012. *It is not clear if the decision was an outcome of the killings or not.* Nobody could have foreseen all these unlikely outcomes. Mahmoud notices that it is clear that the revolutionary power is a direly scattered force. Each party dreams of having a part of the cake, however, they are all clueless to the fact that there is no cake to share. Sadly, people may describe Egypt as torn to pieces. Parties are only concerned with party interests and not the nation's interest. Mahmoud analyzes this to be the reason controversial candidate Shafik actually entered the run-off, as the liberal elite love themselves, and failed to create coalitions. Mahmoud says, "The one who loves his country must sacrifice for the sake of his country." Politicians must place personal and party interests on a back shelf. Unfortunately, this has not happened. Mahmoud refers to this selfishness as an endemic 'Mubarak's virus' in Egyptian society.

Liberal activists have reverted to the media as their main vehicle for communication, invited as speakers on several talk shows on satellite channels, basking in the attentive spotlight. Mahmoud scoffs at how, all of a sudden, political activism and political analysis have become professions in Egypt. Agreement ceased to exist. *The road was filled with hurdles of disagreement, some so high up that they blocked the view of the horizon.* Each individual was thinking, "What are my personal gains?" Activists have forgotten the national interests they so eagerly had chanted for on January 25, 2011.

Ikhwan are well organized, have close ties, and rely on a strong communication network. Mahmoud believes that *Ikhwan* deserved to win, having worked for eighty years. They are also well organized. As for the activists, where are they in reality? Activists need to stop lying to themselves. During the first parliamentary elections, activists miscalculated their position and won minor seats. It was like a slap on the face. This should have been a wakeup call for the opposition, to drive them into creating solid and real coalitions. Mahmoud predicts that if the opposition to the *ancien regime* fails to reach an agreement then gradually there will be no opposition, and Egypt will return to a single party rule dominated by *Ikhwan*, just like the former National Democratic Party (NDP).

In Egypt, there are over sixty political parties. Mahmoud refers to the majority of them as 'cardboard parties', weak, lacking a clear vision, and having a weak base. Egyptians need to review the situation, address their shortcomings, rethink the whole scenario and stand united together. This is the only way for Egypt to take a leap forward. Mahmoud warns that if Egypt faces more unrest, it will collapse, as the economy is very fragile. Maybe Egypt needs to consider following models of other countries like the United States, the model of democracy, with only two political parties: Republicans and Democrats.

Mahmoud wonders what the problem with *Ikhwan* ruling for four years is. He does, however, believe that the secret society is willing to do anything for the sake of power. The media is also defaming the *Ikhwan* society by instilling fear in the public that under *Ikhwan* rule, the state would not allow women to work and would force them to wear the veil, which is unfounded. These circulated rumors are intended to cause Christians and liberals to lose faith in *Ikhwan*.

There are overall fears amongst Muslims and Christians alike. However, there is no religious strife, as Egyptians are kind and emotional people. The old *nizam* tried to create this discord, but failed with each attempt. Mahmoud has friends from both faiths. Media is sly and tries to pass along the image it wants to reflect, and not necessarily the reality. Mahmoud avoids watching state television. He is an avid Facebook user and likes to watch the Al Jazeera channel. Egyptian media is a big failure that desperately needs cleansing.

Unfortunately, the majority of activists are living in the virtual world of Facebook, which is their main communication platform. Facebook users are not a true representation of the Egyptian society in terms of mentality and numbers. On the other hand, *Ikhwan* reach people in person, supporting widows, divorcees, orphans and a bulk of the Egyptian people. No new party can win against a party that is eighty years old and whoever thinks it is possible, is either naïve or in denial.

Mahmoud foresees two parties on the scene: *Ikhwan* and the National Movement, former NDP, *feloul*, since these two parties have the experience, brains and the money to play the political game.

When Mahmoud looks at his friends, he can see the divisions. Some were *feloul*, others were activists; the same applies to his extended family. Anybody who benefited from the old *nizam* was saddened to see it go. Some criticized Mahmoud for participating in the protests as he had a senior position and earned a decent living in a company known to be *feloul*. One of the things he hated was the widespread suspicion and mistrust. He could not understand why this happened; did people really lose all their feelings and sense?

The curfew was in place for around two months after former President Mubarak abdicated. The time of the curfew was shortened from 3 to 5 in the afternoon, and so on, with the passing of time. Mahmoud got used to the sight of army trucks and tanks in the streets of Suez.

More Protests

At the beginning of the incidents at Mohamed Mahmoud Street where violence erupted in November 2011, Mahmoud, in parallel, was protesting at the Suez Canal. Nothing had changed and there was no idea when the Supreme Council of the Armed Forces (SCAF) would hand over the reins of power to civilians. At this time, several foreign spies were arrested and handed over to authorities. Egypt has many so-called allies who are jeopardizing its future, with such a great opportunity to do so with the blurry vision after the revolution. Enemies outside and within the borders, attempt to make Egypt fall. If Egypt takes a leap forward, all of the Middle East will leap forward, as Egypt is the country that has historically always been in the lead. The only way to take that leap forward is through a unified country where all Egyptians act as one, and differences are put aside for the good of the country.

By November 2013, Mahmoud joined protests chanting against military rule as he felt SCAF were compromising the revolution. Many of his friends were arrested around this time, the majority of them in Suez. One of them remained in custody for a week while another remained in prison for ten days and a third for three months. The military arrested and beat them, which was the only time they were mistreated. The police arrested another of his friends on January 25 and released him two days later. The police also wounded a few of his friends. One of his friends lost his eye at the Mohamed Mahmoud incident.

The army and the police are foes, as each institution has its own interests to safeguard. It is the interest of the army to sideline the police so that the power remains with the military. For the people to regain trust in the police, they need a lot of time. Mahmoud believes that the only gain the revolution has so far achieved is the downfall of *Dakhleya* (Ministry of Interior). It will take four or five years for the Police Academy to re-write its program and training. Mahmoud perceives that the police were not hurt or killed in the 2011 uprising. However, if the people are suppressed again, he predicts that the police will be massacred by the people.

Uncertain Civil State

Nearly all Egyptians have in one way or another contributed to the corruption that is commonplace in Egypt, including those who give a tip to police officers so that they don't get a parking or speeding ticket. Depending on each one's income, the participation in corruption varies, with the wealthy affording to give bigger 'tips'. When the excellent opportunity came allowing Egyptians to change, why did change not happen?

Mahmoud likes moderation in everything. He joined a political party called '*Mesawaa we Tanmeya*" which means Equality and Development and he is the party's Secretary in Suez. However, after the presidential elections, Mahmoud withdrew from the political scene, as he felt he needs to give the elected president a chance. Regardless of his political affiliations, he is the representative of Egypt and hence deserves respect. Mahmoud believes that *Ikhwan* have the right to appoint their members in all key positions, as they will work well together as a team and achieve better results than if they had to work with the opposition. If you are a new boss and all your team members are loyal to the previous boss, then you can be certain that the old team will do whatever it takes to jeopardize and make the new boss a laughing stock.

Although the parliament had no time to affect change, they have passed a few good laws, including the election observation law. It places observers inside and outside the polling stations. Mahmoud just hopes that nothing compromises the civility of the state and that the rights of the people are upheld; rights such as the freedom to protest and freedom of expression. However, he doubts that a civil state will ever evolve. He is worried about all the political parties, as he is not sure they will respect these newly declared rights. It has become a power struggle, with the people of Egypt caught in the middle.

In the first round of presidential elections, Mahmoud voted for Hamdeen Sabahi and during the run-off, he voted for Morsi as he felt that he did not have a real choice between Morsi and Shafik, the latter representing Mubarak's junta.

Not Working Together

January 2011 was a revolution and not a coup d'état. Its success or failure will only be evident after ten to fifteen years. Now, one cannot decide. If it succeeds, justice will prevail. But if it fails, then there will not be another revolution, as they happen rarely. At some point, the revolution was moving towards becoming a soft military coup. Mahmoud finds it very strange how things are transpiring, as no political analyst could have predicted the unfolding events after Mubarak stepped down.

For real change to happen, agreements and compromises must take place between all parties. One team cannot work solo. If he had sought to include Dr. Baradei, President Morsi would have won the trust of a large portion of society. Unfortunately, he did not. Morsi met with the liberals before the run-off. *The President has a reputation for listening and even agreeing with the opposition in meetings, but then carries on different policies, which people perceive to be Ikhwan-friendly. By not achieving consensus in the constitution, President Morsi has manifested what Machiavelli wrote, "Having made one mistake, he was forced to make others."*[21]

Mahmoud finds it difficult to predict what the future holds for Egypt, as there is an intense power struggle and most institutions are still running according to the old *nizam*. To untangle the intricate web of the deep state that took over sixty years to develop is not an easy task, and will require a lot of time and effort. *Ikhwan* are trying to control the key institutes so that they can work and effect change. Mahmoud is wary that a good portion of society is afraid of the ambiguous intentions of Islamists and he understands people's fear of the radical *Salafists*, but not *Ikhwan*, as their women work and protest.

As long as there is poverty, democracy will not exist. Why? As the popular saying goes, "He who does not own his bread does not own his choice". Ordinary people cannot find bread to sustain them; will they strive for their political freedom? *If the needs on the bottom of the Maslow's pyramid are difficult for a man to meet, then how could that man jump or even think about demanding the top of the pyramid?* As long as capitalism controls the power there will be no democracy, as they rule according to interests. In democracy, a vote is not a vote if bought with money. *Ikhwan* are buying votes by distributing rice and oil to the impoverished. This is fake democracy. Big portions of the voters are directed by a party and not voting based on individual belief. As long as there are hackers and people are working for them, then there is no democracy. The democracy is pretense. Mahmoud views that capitalism has failed in European countries, and is dwindling. Nevertheless, even socialism has failed in the former USSR. A new system needs to be born that is a combination of capitalism and communism. Socialism is the middle ground that meets the revolution's demands of 'bread, freedom and social equality.'

The revolution is not just what Mahmoud has shared and experienced; it is a continuum of interdependent events. Important events like Mohamed Mahmoud, the Council of Ministers and the Port Said massacre, are among such critical events or confrontations. It is a political game from A to Z and Mahmoud hopes that it succeeds and that his children see a better Egypt than he has. *Inexperienced politicians who are committing grave mistakes are governing Egypt. Egypt is facing an 'irrational militarism' as Martin Luther King calls it.*

New Tyrant

Two years later, the revolution is evolving. Mahmoud sees similarities between the different stages of the embryo and the revolution. The revolution is evolving and growing, just like the embryo in the mother's placenta develops into a fully-grown baby.

In May 2013, Mahmoud is very pessimistic and feels as if the revolution never happened. He is no longer active in the political party, having given up completely on the political scene. The old tyrannical system is still in place and people are even worse off than before, with security mayhem and the economy hitting rock bottom. It is strange to find that two years after the revolution many members of the *ancien regime* are acquitted of charges, whereas activists are convicted of charges. The activists, infatuated with the idealism of the revolution woke up with a reality shock.

Mahmoud is saddened to admit that the revolution has brought out the worst in Egyptians, raising all the negative qualities to the surface. *Unfortunately, it seems what George Orwell wrote in 1984 is true in this situation. O' Brien said to Winston, "We know that no one seizes power with the intention of relinquishing it. Power is not a means; it is an end. One does not establish a dictatorship in order to safeguard a revolution; one makes the revolution in order to establish the dictatorship. The object of persecution is persecution. The object of torture is torture. The object of power is power."*[22]

Personally, Mahmoud has no concerns regarding the name or ideology of the ruling party as long as the country progresses. Unfortunately, with the current *Ikhwan* rule Mahmoud sees the future as black and mysterious. Mahmoud feels that he can no longer see, as though blindfolded. Will his blindfold drop to see the light or will he continue to see the darkness? It will take a very long time for change to materialize, as he believes that the Egyptians like to play dirty and are not ready to play clean. It seems Egyptian people are under a curse of stultifying chatter, and are not reaching their dreams.

Mahmoud can no longer see a bright future for Egypt and is trying to leave the polluted environment that is reeking with hatred and shockingly bloody. He did not sign *Tamarod*, although he was upset with the policies of Morsi, as he believes a democracy must allow its president to finish his four-year term, regardless of how bad his policies are. Mahmoud is disturbed at how the Egyptian media are committing grave mistakes and exaggerating. Where is the justice for everyone?

It seems to him that liberals want justice only for themselves and those like them but not for their opposition, specifically, *Ikhwan*. He sees June 30 as a big masquerade by the intelligence to depose of the President and not a true revolution. Mahmoud has reached rock bottom pessimism and is earnestly seeking to immigrate. He does not find Egypt the right place to raise his children any longer. He could continue to live in Egypt, as he is used to the lack of freedom, but he asks himself, "Why should I let my children live in a stifling, unbalanced and unhealthy environment? They surely deserve better."

Only people can change themselves, not governments, as the Tunisian poet Aboul-Qacem Echebbi said in his poem *The Will to Live*, "If the people one day will to live then destiny must respond and the night must disappear and the chain must break."

CHAPTER 6

Missing Man

After meeting Rania, I drove back home crying, with a heavy heart and a painful lump in my throat. What you are about to read is a real life story of love gone missing that reminds us how precious we are and how we should never take anyone for granted. Even though I had prepared myself for a heart-breaking meeting and despite gathering all my strength, I could not help but tear while Rania recounted her plight. It was the first time I met Rania Shaheen at a café at Dandy Mall on Monday the October 10, 2011. We got in touch through Khaled Sharkawi, a friend of my friend, who knows Dalia, Rania's sister. Months after I met Rania I gathered the courage to call her again this time asking to meet her mother-in-law who agreed. I felt I needed to cover the mother's story. I prepared myself mentally and emotionally for yet another unforgettable meeting, which reconfirmed my commitment to see this book through, as it is a true story worthy of publishing. I was glad that Rania's father-in-law joined us as well, so that I am able to write a more comprehensive account, as it turned out he dominated the conversation. I visited them at their home at Masr El Gedida on Wednesday September 5, 2012, which was my only home visit for this book.

Family Members

Tarek Abdel Latif El Aktash: mechanical engineer

The characters listed below are in terms of their relationship to Tarek:

Abdel Latif: father, *Abu Tarek*, retired army general.

Fatma: mother, *Um Tarek*, homemaker.

Mohamed and Khaled: older brothers.

Rania Shaheen: Tarek's wife, interior designer.

Dalia Shaheen: sister-in-law, engineer.

Mariam: 5-year-old daughter

Father-in-law (Rania's father): doctor at Kasr el Aini hospital

His Roots

Tarek's father, Abdel Latif, was born in 1932 in the countryside, in the Kalioubiya governorate to a father who was a farmer. During his childhood, his family moved to Cairo where he was educated. He wanted to fight in the name of God and hence he joined the army. Abdel Latif is a retired army general, in the division of communications, *selah el esharah (Signal* Corps), who fought in the wars of 1956, 1967, 1973 and between those years, was a career officer. He would report for duty in distant places for three weeks at a time and return home for five days per month, leaving his wife, Fatma in charge of the house and their children.

Fatma, Tarek's mother, was born in Cairo in October of 1948. Her father was a businessman and her mother a homemaker. *When I asked them how they met, they smiled and laughed secretly recalling fond memories.* Abdel Latif met Fatma in 1968 in a traditional arranged meeting, which culminated in marriage the following year, 1969. Mohamed their first son was born in 1970, Khaled in 1971 and Tarek in 1975.

His Childhood

Tarek was born on the January 27, 1975. He went to Saint Fatima School and later to the model public school *Yehia El Refaie* Language School at Masr El Gedida, in East Cairo. When he was fourteen, Tarek participated in a student exchange program with the United States and traveled with his school headmistress for the summer, where he was the youngest in his class. *While proudly recounting his son's selection to participate in this exchange program Abu Tarek suddenly sobbed. He took a moment to compose himself and continued talking.* Tarek studied the French language over a couple of years at the French cultural center CFCC at Masr El Gedida until he became fluent. Tarek was also a well-read, devout Muslim. He studied at the Faculty of Mechanical Engineering at Ein Shams University in the early 90's. During his undergraduate studies, Tarek traveled a couple of times to the United States to visit his brothers and relatives where he worked in order to cover his own expenses. Tarek's father did not want to spoil him, so that he would be able to appreciate the value of money and the effort exerted to obtain it. Upon graduating Tarek served the obligatory military service in Egypt.

Tarek was a quiet but assertive person who displayed wisdom beyond his years. His intelligence and creativity resulted in his nomination as the ideal student within his district. He was a good, obedient son who took time off from his work when his mother underwent gall bladder surgery and required bed rest. He cooked her special diet as ordered by her doctor and attended to her needs until she regained her strength.

Tarek was a gallant man who refused anything wrong and unrighteous. He would not want a receiver that would break the cable code that someone else paid for (which is very common in Egypt), but would rather pay for his own cable. His mother recalls that Tarek would stand up for justice regardless of the cost. He declined an offer to take the position of a colleague as he did not want to be the cause of insecurity for his colleague's family and accepted a position in another department for which he did not have any experience. He was very cooperative and loved to research subjects of interest. Nothing stopped him from speaking the truth, even if it hurt feelings.

Lollipop Girl

Rania's parents are both doctors, her father specialized in anesthesiology and her mother in bacteriology. She was born in Khobar, in Saudi Arabia on August 23, 1977. Rania studied in the all-girl German school at Bab ElLouk and later in Dokki where she obtained her high school diploma. The latter was a mixed gender school. After high school, she attended the Faculty of Fine Arts in Zamalek, part of Helwan University, where she studied interior design for five years. Rania is an average build, veiled woman with a big smile.

During these university years, at one point Dalia, Rania's sister, and her classmates asked their friends and family to come and help them with a class project. On the day Rania was at the university helping her sister, Tarek was also there to help one of his friends. Tarek Abdel Latif noticed a short girl with curly hair and a lollipop working on the project, and the girl was Rania. They instantly liked one another. Rania teased Tarek by saying, "What kind of people pass by without adding their ink to the drawing board?" Tarek smiled and ignored her comment. After working on the projects, they would all go out together in a big group, sometimes to celebrate birthdays or to the sporting club during the weekend, but she mostly kept her distance from Tarek. Rania is reminiscent of the friendly fun-filled gatherings.

Rania knew how Tarek admired the American way of life as he imported the concept of 'Deli and more' to his local business in Cairo. Rania vividly recalls a day when she went to Tarek's office to give him some cards that she had designed for his Deli cafe. Although they initially hit it off, Rania was wary in her interactions as she was afraid of embarrassment by Tarek who was reputed to be difficult to deal with. She even feared saying good morning to him. Upon reaching his office, she was surprised to find Tarek smiling. Rania was talking to his partner Sherif, when Tarek left the office to return with a cake box. She thought it was a birthday cake and she told him she was not going to celebrate her birthday in the year 2000 as her grandmother and uncle had passed away.

Tarek said, "Just open it."

Rania was surprised to find "Will you marry me?" written on the cake. Initially she thought it was a joke and broke into hysterical laughter and answered yes to play along. When Sherif hugged Tarek and congratulated him, it suddenly occurred to her that this was no joke. Tarek had just proposed to Rania in a surprisingly romantic way. Rania was dumbfounded, as she had never sensed any feelings emanating from him. That was the beginning of their relationship and they got married in 2004.

Rania worked in small design offices until she got married. Due to health issues, she left work and waited until her daughter went to nursery school before going back to work at Egypt Air's quality assurance department. Two beautiful daughters blessed their marriage, Mariam who was 6 and Sarah who was 1, at the time we met in 2011. At the time of their marriage, Tarek worked for multinational petroleum company for a while then moved to an American petroleum services company in Maadi.

Decision to Demonstrate

On the evening of January 24, 2011, Rania was online and she noticed a lot of activity on Facebook and Twitter calling for demonstrations on January 25, under the hash tag "#Jan25". When she shared this information with Tarek, he quickly dismissed it as being one of the regular small protests. By noon of Tuesday January 25, they heard that crowds were big and Tarek decided that they would play it safe and stay at home. He had no political affiliations. However, he resented the corrupt Mubarak era. His parents stayed at home watching television and following the news. *Abu Tarek* felt that things were about to change after the protestors took to the streets, whereas *Um Tarek* expected a normal day of protests, like Tarek did, after which life would resume normally.

Tarek and Rania were planning to spend the national holiday running errands at Masr el Gedida, but due to the protests, they decided to play it safe and stuck to Maadi. Rania went to visit a friend at the hospital, leaving Tarek with the girls; the streets were empty like most public holidays and when she returned home, she checked the news. By the evening, photos and videos were being broadcast showing unexpectedly populous demonstrations. Tarek admitted to Rania that he was wrong about that day and he sensed that something would change.

The following morning on the Wednesday January 26, they had a scheduled parent-teacher meeting at Mariam's nursery. Rania dropped her daughter off at eight in the morning and waited for the meeting. Shortly afterwards they were informed that all children needed to be taken home as the school, which was at Bab El Louk in downtown Cairo, was going to close. Due to the unpredictable and disturbing situation at Tahrir, the school administration instructed all buses to return schoolchildren to their homes and frantically telephoned parents to pick up their kids. Rania called Tarek to update him on the canceled meeting en route to their home in Maadi, South of Cairo. Tarek had already excused himself from work to attend the meeting, so he decided to check out the downtown area while taking pictures on his mobile, before checking in on his family at home.

Tarek said, "Cars are traveling normally in the streets but I noticed a significant number of *Amn Elmarkazi* (Central Security forces) and police cars. Now I can confirm my feeling that this time, things are different." After a brief silence he said, "I want to participate in the demonstrations."
Rania looked at him, taken aback.
Tarek said, "Don't worry, one cannot run from his destiny. I am going to work now. Let me know if there is anything new from the internet. Surely, I will let you know before I go."

Tarek said that he was joining to raise his voice amongst his fellow protestors in defiance of the state of affairs. He was not expecting a beating and did not fear for his safety. After checking on his family's safety, he returned to his work while waiting for the big crowds to gather momentum so that he could join. Tarek believed that the big numbers would protect him from possible assaults, as he did not want to take any chances.

Preparations
Rania was not worried but rather concerned with the note that the film director and screenwriter Amr Salama had posted on Facebook on January 27 regarding his terrifying beating by the police prior to his eventual release.
Rania said to Tarek, "I agree that it is important to protest but I am worried, look at what they did to Amr Salama."

Tarek and Rania considered physical detainment and abuse to be the worst-case scenario that awaited the unfortunate protestors. Rania recalls sharing relevant messages on Facebook and Twitter such as a call to maintain several protests in many places to wear out the *Amn Elmarkazi*, after a couple of days on duty. There were calls for protests to continue so that the police stay on alert, which would leave them no chance to rest, especially as Friday January 28 was expected to be confrontational.

On Thursday January 27, Tarek and his small family were staying at his mother-in-law's place (Rania's family home) celebrating his thirty-sixth birthday. Meanwhile, on Facebook and Twitter it was announced that a demonstration by members of the actors' syndicate was going to take place, but contradictory information was provided, and Tarek decided to lay low until the big numbers overflowed in the streets. Rania and Tarek kept his intentions to themselves, hiding it from his parents. Tarek, being very considerate, refrained from worrying his parents and his in-laws and lied to them by saying that he was going to work that Friday.

Tarek pondered lengthily before deciding on important matters. He was very cautious and meticulously planned for the day he left to join the demonstrations. He removed all his credit cards and ATM cards from his wallet and only left his national ID, his business card and engineer's syndicate card. He removed the keys to his parents' home as his ID lists their address, and he feared someone breaking into the house should something happen to him. Rania later noticed the keys hanging on the key holder, unaware that he had removed them. Tarek left a list of important information for Rania, in case of emergency, and the steps that she should take if he disappears. She had his ATM card to withdraw money for the girls' school and a cheque with the full amount in the bank so that she could manage the household. Rania knew the passwords to his computer, e-mail account, Facebook and Twitter. Tarek was very organized and she knew where he kept all-important documents should Rania need to revert to them. Normally she was never concerned about these things as he was always in charge. Tarek clearly instructed her to contact his father, his brother and his colleague at work if police detained him. At that point, Rania was thinking of two scenarios: that either he would be beaten and released like Amr Salama *(His story elaborated in chapter 7)* or that he would be beaten and imprisoned. In her mind, there was no third option.

Tarek wanted his children to have another option in life and so he applied for immigration to Canada, seeking a better life for his children. Even if he managed to make a living in Egypt now, his daughters would not in the future. Tarek believed that Egypt was regressing and that eventually a hunger revolution would take place. He believed that if former President Mubarak died the country would collapse. Rania and Tarek wanted to have another passport where they could have another place to move to without requiring a visa. If the hunger revolution happened, he would take his family to the airport and try to buy tickets to leave without worrying about obtaining a visa. If he could not bring up his daughters as good Muslims abroad, only then would he return to Egypt, bearing another passport and hence being treated properly. They were waiting for the medical checkup for their application to immigrate to Canada. Before joining the demonstrations, Tarek told Rania not to worry about the outcome of the immigration, as the medical checkup was going to take time and if something happened to Tarek, Canadian authorities would automatically cancel their application as it was in his name. Rania told him to stop saying that, and she said worst-case police would beat him and he would later return home. Tarek prepared Rania in case matters got bad, and he feared arrest. He told her to take the girls and the money and leave to the United States (as they had a visa) and to contact his family there, should he be arrested. When he was released, he would go to their home and take his passport and travel to her wherever she may be.

On the evening of Thursday January 27, he made calls to arrange a meeting place with his friends. Rania had read online a recommendation to exchange landline numbers, as rumor had it that authorities would sever mobile phone connections. Tarek and his friends agreed to meet in Mohandseen, in East Cairo, at Mostafa Mahmoud mosque where they were planning to perform the Friday noon prayers. *Muslim men are required to perform the Friday noon prayers at a mosque.* On Thursday, the famous social media sites, Facebook and Twitter, were briefly suspended. Messages circulated on how to work around this shutdown. Few people were able to use the proxies that week, however, and the majority were disconnected.

Friday morning was quiet and solemn like the calm before a storm. Rania and Tarek were talking in their bedroom.
Rania said, "Watch out, it is rumored that mobile phones are going to be cut off today."
Tarek said, "I don't think so, at 7 o'clock this morning I was just talking to my friend in America."
Rania replied, "Just check your signal now." He told her that he had a full signal.
Rania told him, "Switch off your mobile and turn it on again, maybe the signal is false."
Tarek did as she asked and said, "You are right, there is no signal."
He showered and wore his blue jeans, black sweater, and a dark blue jacket. Before the Friday prayers, he hugged, kissed and said goodbye to his wife and daughters as any other Friday and left, heading to the mosque and afterwards the demonstrations.

Rania was attentively watching television that afternoon. Initially there was nothing worrying, until later that afternoon. By the evening, Tarek had neither called nor returned. Rania knew something big was keeping him from returning home that Friday night, as he did not take risks lightly. She is sure that Tarek stayed in Tahrir with a strong conviction, as he raised his voice high amongst his compatriots in peaceful demonstrations. He stayed when danger was imminent, with live bullets being fired at the demonstrators. She heard rumors about the army mobilization and a curfew put into place. The rumors materialized when at 5pm, the army took up stations at key locations and authorities announced on national television that a curfew was effective from 6pm. Rania, increasingly apprehensive, was expecting Tarek's return, since the curfew was in effect. That did not happen. She imagines Tarek witnessed civilians assaulted by tear gas, water cannons, birdshots and live bullets. This unjust violence against peaceful men and women would have evoked in him so much emotion that the rational side of him was outweighed, and he stood proudly side by side with his compatriots. Rania imagines so.

Across town, Tarek's parents watched private and state channels, wary that the latter was not broadcasting the truth. They were clueless about their youngest son's whereabouts.

Gone Missing

Before the curfew was in effect, Rania went to the nearby grocery store and stocked on food essentials like cheese and bread. She had heard nothing from Tarek and her worry was gnawing at her. She tried to gain access to his office to acquire the landlines of his colleagues but unfortunately, to no avail. She called her brother-in-law on the landline around nine in the evening.

Rania said, "Khaled please help, Tarek did not return home until now."

Khaled asked, "Where did Tarek go?"

She replied, "He said he was going to prayers and then to work." Rania feared telling the truth still hoping that he was on his way home. She did not want to create havoc within the family, knowing well the dangers of demonstrating, expecting fearful reactions.

Khaled's wife said, "I heard he wanted to join the demonstrations," and Khaled confirmed this saying, "Yes I heard him say that."

Rania then said, "Yes he most probably joined."

Khaled said, "We have to wait till nightfall, maybe he will return home late."

Later that night, Tarek still had not appeared. Rania called Khaled a couple of times again that night so that he would get through to Hany, a colleague of Tarek's, and try to get the numbers of his other colleagues.

Saturday morning Rania grew more nervous. She knew that Tarek would have stopped at any shop and called her. His silence was unusually out of character. She was thinking something must have happened to him. He might have decided to spend the night in Tahrir with his friends or the police may have arrested him.

She could no longer keep quiet, and that morning, Rania told the truth about Tarek's whereabouts to his family. His brother Khaled and his cousin started searching for him. His brother Mohamed was in the United States at the time, and cut his vacation short to search for his missing brother. They called his friends and colleagues. Rania asked his mother who she calls, *Tante Fifi (Tante is like Auntie and Fifi is the nickname for Fatma)* to stay put at home hoping that he might call her, as he only knows their own home number, his mother-in-law's and his mother's by heart. *Um Tarek* was very worried. Rania moved in with her mother who lived upstairs on the ninth floor of their building, when Tarek disappeared. Anxiously, she flipped through national, regional and international news channels, desperate to understand what was happening and hoping to get a clue about her husband's whereabouts.

Manhunt

A manhunt ensued, starting with the morgues around the Tahrir vicinity. It was an unbearable, stomach-turning situation, which ended with no trace of Tarek. They could eliminate the morgues after thoroughly searching through them on Saturday and Sunday. Next, his family searched hospitals. Those were treating hundreds of wounded civilians, but still there was no trace of him. They deduced that the police must have arrested Tarek, which would explain his disturbing silence.

The whole family tried to contact friends at the police force, *Amn Eldawla* (state security) or the army. While they were relentlessly searching for Tarek, *Abu Tarek* personally delivered letters to the minister of defense and the minister of interior, but received no replies. He also sent a written message to Ahmed Shafik, the former Prime Minister, via his daughter, and another to Sami Annan, member of the Supreme Council of the Armed Forces, SCAF. Rania remembers the final talk show on ONTV when Shafik and the novelist Alaa Al Aswany were guests. The talk show host Reem Maged asked the former Prime Minister Shafik about the whereabouts of the missing people, and he replied that he did not know where they are.

They heard that Tarek was under arrest in Giza, which an *Amn Eldawla* general confirmed. *Um Tarek* believes they were deceived into believing that police arrested Tarek, as some leads said that he was with *mokhabarat* (the intelligence). Every night his mother would go to bed hoping that the following morning she would hear from Tarek, and his conspicuous disappearance would be unraveled. She was a bundle of nerves on the edge of a breakdown.

Meanwhile, prisoners were escaping from local prisons and fear infested neighborhoods like a viral outbreak. Young and old men took up watch posts on the streets, blocking *baltegeya* from entering. Khaled stayed with his parents during these troubling nights. Mohamed and Khaled wanted to join the demonstrations, however, they did not want to hurt their parents. It was enough for them to bear that Tarek was missing. Things became chaotic and there was no control over the people in Tahrir. It was no different in Maadi, where Rania's brother joined the civilian checkpoints. He had heard that there were issues in the neighborhood, but was not an eyewitness to any of them.

As the days and weeks passed, they heard about a new set of unknown bodies at the morgue and with dreadful fear, they ventured there. The list of unidentified bodies was long and so was the list of missing people. Rania's father checked the morgue at Kasr El Aini hospital where he practices and did not find Tarek's body. During their search, they came across a similar missing case, that of Ziad Bakir. Rania decided to contact the family of the missing civilian Ziad Bakir, who shared their plight, and stayed in touch. They agreed to inform each other if anyone reappeared or a body was discovered. They shared any leads or contacts in the hope of finding their loved ones. Rania would talk to Mirette, the sister of Ziad, and give her hope that Tarek and Ziad will likely end up being cellmates sitting in the same prison. Rania hoped that they would reappear and become one big happy family.

In desperation, Rania got in touch with media, informing them that Tarek El Aktash and Ziad Bakir were missing; their names appeared on the written strip during news bulletins. She called ONTV, and several known talk show hosts like Amr Adeeb, Lamees El Hadidy, Khairy Ramadan, Tamer Ameen and she conducted several televised telephone interviews, all in the hope of knowing Tarek's whereabouts. It all seemed to be in vain.

Rania remembers the bloody battle on the February 2, 2011 when she was praying that the protestors would be able to stand their ground. She feared that if they were defeated all Egyptians would pay the price. Rania imagined the old regime would be like an injured lion that eats all his assaulters and bystanders.

Tarek was very protective of Rania and did not like his wife to appear in crowds for fear of harassment, which has become a common phenomenon in Egypt. Apart from this, Rania did not endeavor to participate in the demonstrations, as she knew that Tarek would reprimand her for placing herself in danger and leaving their two precious girls without either of their parents' care. It was enough that one parent was missing, she did not want to take any more risks. Moreover, she was worried that if she participated and Tarek was in prison, it would cause him more torture and trouble as the police would brand his wife a 'revolutionary.' The only time she joined the crowds was on the historic February 11, 2011 when President Hosni Mubarak abdicated his power. She went to celebrate with her father and her two daughters in the car, waving the Egyptian flag up high. She did not risk going further than Cairo Sheraton Hotel at Dokki. For once, she did not feel distant and disconnected from people. She shared with her compatriots the triumph, but with a heavy heart. She was thinking, "Where are you Tarek?" Rania was wishing that he could be beside her in this gigantic celebration, hoping that wherever his whereabouts he would not be in agony.

Shattered Hopes

A few times contacts would inform Rania that Tarek was indeed arrested and under investigation at *Amn Eldawla* at Sheikh Rihan or Gaber Ibn Khayan stations *(Where Mohamed, featured in Chapter one, was imprisoned)*. The contact would claim he was not sure which station, as they are similar. One of the leads told her that Tarek was very nervous, and gave the police a hard time during his investigation. Rania bought this claim, as it seemed a lot like Tarek, who was very proud and did not like anyone to step on his toes. Among the misleading lies, they heard that Tarek was at Wadi El Natroun prison. Another day they would hear that all prisoners under police custody were transferred to the army and thus they would search within their known network of army officials.

Meanwhile, Rania told her elder daughter, Mariam, five years old, that her father participated in the demonstrations and many protestors were staying at a 'hotel'. Protestors were unable to leave without a ticket that would allow them to pass through the civilian checkpoints, which was something that had risen during the revolution. Her younger daughter Sarah was less than a year old. Rania told her daughter that they were looking for Tarek, the father of Mariam and Sarah, and could not find him. Once after a promising lead, Rania mistakenly told Mariam that they almost found her father. The heart-broken girl had so much hope that she would be seeing her beloved father soon. Disappointingly, her hopes were shattered a few days later, when nothing unraveled from that lead. Rania had to disclaim what she had said and could feel and see Mariam's deep, unrelenting pain. From then on Rania never raised her daughter's hopes again for fear of letting her down.

She wanted to personally search at the morgues, but could not gather the courage. Once, through one of her contacts, she heard of a man supposedly confirming that he found Tarek El Aktash. They were using the family name as it is an uncommon one, and there were fewer chances of getting him confused with someone else. They were getting different bits of information from various sources across all the family members, and not just one single lead.

On some days Rania felt hope, and on others she was overwhelmed with despair, crying behind closed doors. She felt suffocated, waiting helplessly at home for Tarek to return. As the days passed at a dreadfully slow rate, she would feel and believe that Tarek was somewhere out there. She just did not know where.

The Lead

Elsewhere, on February 26 all the unidentified corpses were moved to the main morgue in Zenhom. On March 3, a doctor was conducting an autopsy and while removing the man's clothes she found a big wallet containing an ID and money. The ID was Tarek's and the address on the ID was that of his parents' home. A marble worker passed by the morgue in search of his brother, and found a resemblance with the corpse of Tarek El Aktash and talked to the deputy prosecutor. The prosecutor told the marble worker that this man could not be his brother, as his ID identified him as Tarek. The marble worker asked him why the body was still at the morgue, and why they had not informed his parents. The officer replied vaguely that they were unable to locate his house. In reality, nobody had tried, as the area was on high alert. Tarek's parents wonder why the General Prosecutor never sent an investigator to inform them that they have possibly found the body of their dead son. The marble worker asked for the parents' address, and volunteered to inform them in order to expedite the body's identification.

On Tuesday March 8, 2011, the simple marble worker passed by Tarek's apartment, referring to the address on the identity card and met Tarek's cousin.
The marble worker said, "Is there a missing person who used to live here?"
The cousin replied, "Yes, why?"
The marble worker said, "There is a body at the morgue with the ID of Tarek El Aktash, but he looks like my missing brother. The prosecutor insisted he needs someone to verify whether the body is Tarek's or not. May someone come with me and identify the body? If he truly is your son then I would have earned a good deed, and if he is not, then he really is my brother."
The cousin anxiously asked him to wait.
Tarek's cousin called another cousin, and recounted what the marble worker had said. Arrangements were made so that they could head to the morgue together.

With mixed feelings of anticipation and fear, Tarek's two cousins accompanied the marble worker to the morgue. Indeed, they identified the body as that of Tarek El Aktash. However, the General Prosecutor insisted on a DNA test to confirm that it was in fact Tarek's body, and said that they needed a sample of his closest blood relative. The cousins called Tarek's brother and debriefed him. The following day, his brother Mohamed went to the morgue, where he provided the required DNA sample, to confirm Tarek's identity.

Mohamed told his younger brother Khaled, breaking the devastating news to him at the airport upon his return from a business trip. The two surviving brothers hesitated before telling their parents the news. Features change forty days post-mortem, and they wondered if they should wait until the DNA results are ready. They decided to inform them without delay. Mohamed, the oldest son, went to his parent's house and broke the heart-breaking news to his parents the same day. It was a traumatic day filled with tears, sobs and anguished screams as the loss of their beloved youngest son hit home. Until that point, there was hope that Tarek could still walk through the door. Now, their worst fear had been confirmed, something no parent or wife, son or daughter, brother or sister ever wants to hear.

Denial

On that terrible Wednesday afternoon, *Um Tarek* called Rania and informed her that her sons had identified Tarek's body at the main Zenhom morgue in Sayeda Zeinab. Rania was shocked and screamed hysterically on the phone.
Rania said, "Don't believe them *Tante Fifi*, I will go myself to make sure."
Um Tarek said, "Mohamed went and recognized him, my daughter."

Rania replied, "I am the only one who saw him every day and can identify his body." Hysterically, Rania continued, "Mohamed has not seen him in a long time and could have made a mistake."

Rania was restlessly in denial, as her heart told her that her husband was alive. If something had happened to Tarek, she was sure she would have felt it. She downright denied the news, and even implied that her brother-in-law was mistaken.

Rejecting the news she'd heard in the disturbing phone call, she decided that she had to go see for herself that same day, otherwise, she would live every day doubting Mohamed's ability to identify his brother's body correctly. Rania wanted to make sure that if her daughters one day questioned or doubted their father's death, that she could confidently confirm it. They arrived upon the calling of the *Maghreb* (sunset) prayers. It was very difficult and brave for Rania to go to the morgue. She felt her intestines tied up in a huge knot of anxiety and her breathing was strained. The smell of the morgue was stomach-wrenching and nauseating.

They met a man in charge at the morgue and asked to see the body of Tarek El Aktash. The man informed them they were not sure if the body was that of Tarek or Ibrahim, the brother of the marble worker. Once the DNA test was out, they would know for sure. Rania's father reassured him, telling him that she was Tarek's wife, and wanted to see for herself.

Closure

The rancid smell of death emanating from the freezer was suffocating, and the room was very cold and quiet. Rania, like most human beings, is uneasy with death and being around the dead. She had to ignore her feelings and gather the strength to go inside and look at a man's body, hoping and praying it would not be that of her husband.

The room was dark and cold, with big metal square refrigerator drawers stacked on each other, each containing three bodies. When Rania entered the room, her eyes rested on a certain drawer on which the word *maghoul* (unknown) was written. The employee shoved a large squeaky, rusty metal trolley right in front of the drawer, which had caught Rania's eyes. She did not make much of her sixth sense. When the man opened the drawer, she saw the dead man's hands above his head. His fingers were very dark, shrunken. His nails appeared long and dry blood coagulated at the tips of his lifeless fingers.

Hastily, Rania said, "This is not Tarek. Look at how his hand appears dark with long nails; it must be the other man."

Her father said, "Wait until you see the whole body."

Rania was searching for a brown *zebiba* (scar on the forehead or leg from prostration during prayer) on the front of his leg that came about from his frequent prayers. It typically looks like an old dried up bruise. The first thing she looked at was his leg where she instantly saw his *zebiba,* and she admitted to her father that this was Tarek, her late husband, while shaking her head in reflex disbelief. She carefully looked at the rest of his body, recognizing his toes, his stomach, chest and arms. But his face, she looked at squeamishly as it had changed drastically. Yellowish in color, his face was thinner, most likely because the blood had dried up. One of his eyes was shrunken, and his nose seemed thinner. Unshaven hairs surrounded his goatee, his brown hair appeared black, and his face was distorted; familiar yet unrecognizable. This was probably why the marble man had confused him for his own brother. Heartbroken, finally Rania knew that Tarek was dead. She pinched her eyes closed as warm tears rolled down her cheeks.

Tears soaked Rania's cheeks as she stood by her husband's body for the last time. She finally knew where he was, and why he had never called or returned home that life-altering Friday, January 28. He couldn't call, as he had died dramatically. She bid him farewell and left the morgue. She was crying, and feeling an aching emptiness. She had a big lump in her throat making her breathe heavily, but she somehow felt relief. During the previous two weeks, Rania had been tormented by thoughts of Tarek being tortured physically and emotionally by the police, and she could not bear his hurt or pain. She had prayed to God that nobody would touch him or disgrace him. Now she knew that he had not been tortured and did not suffer long, as he had died on the spot. Rania knew that Tarek would have liked to die while standing, and he did.

Rania stopped worrying about Tarek. She knew she would miss him and mourn him every hour of her days to come, but she no longer needed to worry about him. Her father, who was driving them home, recited the verse from Quran "Be sure we shall test you with something of fear and hunger, some loss in goods or lives or the fruits (of your toil), but give glad tidings to those who patiently persevere" *(1:155)*. Their faith was tested by the sudden death. Rania felt that her father was more unsettled than she was, and she kept him calm by citing the verse: "to God we Belong and to him is our return" (1:156).[23] When she returned home, she found the wives of her brothers-in-law waiting for her to comfort and attempt to soothe her for the tragic loss of her husband. She called her mother-in-law and told her she was sorry to confirm that her son is dead. She hung up the phone, both women crying hysterically. At the young age of thirty-three, Rania had become a widow.

After she gathered her senses, she called Ziad's family the following day. She informed them so that they would also check unidentified corpses at the morgue, and apologized that she had previously told them that they would find them alive together, raising their hopes. She also told them that she wished that they would find Ziad in a better place. Ziad's older brother went to Zenhom and recognized his young brother's cold lifeless body lying on the iron plate at the morgue. Mirette called her later and told Rania that she was right to have thought that they were going to find them together at the same cell, but as it turned out it was the same morgue. A DNA test ran on Ziad proved positive. A sniper had killed Ziad Bakir with a shot that entered his head from above and exited from below as per the medical autopsy report. This happened while he was defending the national museum at Tahrir from *baltegeya*. Ziad was taken to the Al Hussein University hospital and did not have a wallet on him. Therefore, classified as unidentified, he eventually was moved to Zenhom. His brother recognized the corpse through a nail scar on his leg.

The majority of the bodies discovered died in prisons. Strangely, the authorities claimed that other bodies that had not died on the spot, had died from an indirect injury. Such was the case of Karim Banouna, a martyr, who was shot and returned home but died three or four days later on his bed.

After Tarek's family visually identified him, they had to wait for a full week rather than the usual 2 to 3 days for the DNA results to appear. *Abu Tarek* cannot believe the faulty state of the DNA equipment and material, which in turn, sheds doubt on any results. The police force has not mastered this delicate operation yet. The results of the first test were inconclusive and a second DNA test requested. Results were still inconclusive but the doctor said since he has his ID card then the result is positive, as recounted by *Abu Tarek,* who suddenly breaks into sobs. After the longest, darkest forty days, on March 15, 2011 it was confirmed that they have lost their youngest son. *Abu Tarek* and *Um Tarek* could not venture to the morgue to identify the body of their son. They knew that they could not bear such a gruesome scene. Finally, Tarek's family buried him on March 15, 2011.

The forty days of not knowing the whereabouts of Tarek were horrid, even worse than when they discovered his body at the morgue. Not knowing and feeling helpless is a horrible state. Different accounts from different places brewed uncertainty. Doubt crept into their home, casting black smog blurring their vision and shocking them. *Abu Tarek* refers to a popular saying, "a catastrophe befalling is better than waiting for it to happen". *Abu Tarek* compares his son's plight to a life sentence and death penalty. For Rania, those forty days were unbearable. She said, "It was like waking up and dying each day." Not knowing his fate was worse than when she finally discovered his lifeless body.

Abu Tarek said, "If bodies were thrown into the Nile they would surface eventually. However, bodies could have been buried in the dessert without ever being discovered."

Um Tarek said, "I never imagined that men in high positions would be evasive about my son's whereabouts. I did not doubt their words."

Despite their ordeal, they are grateful to know that their youngest son was in fact dead, unlike other families whose loved ones have been missing for over two years. Until September 2012, the marble worker was still searching for his brother.

What Happened?

As it turns out, Tarek never met up with his colleagues on the Day of Rage, Friday January 28. The one and only day Tarek ventured to participate in the demonstrations ended up being his last day alive, one day after he turned thirty-six. The unity demonstrated by the Egyptians was moving and a force to reckon with, men and women from different parties and faiths were protesting against the police. Without mobile communications and the overflowing crowds, it was impossible for them to meet, so they each headed off on his or her own trajectory that day, with some walking in the demonstrations, and others returning home.

After finally finding Tarek, his family had answers to many of the perturbing questions, which haunted them for those forty days. Tarek was killed late on Friday 28 at 11 or 11:30 at night in Tahrir square. He died from two 4mm shots wounds, one at the front of his head and the second lethal shot, to his neck. The shot cut the artery carrying blood to his brain, hence instantly killing him.

One of Rania's friends coincidentally saw Tarek at the intersection between Kasr El Aini St and Sheikh Rihan St amidst heavy shooting. He saw him for a few seconds at around ten that evening and then retreated among others to Tahrir, as the police were aggressive at that end, where apparently Tarek met his fate.

Tarek was brought to the morgue of the French section of Kasr El Aini Hospital before midnight, as reported. He remained in the freezer during the whole period. She heard that his case was initially concealed since he was instantly killed from behind, an instant kill caused by a direct injury.

One of the workers at the morgue informed Rania that an unlicensed Lancer car was moving bodies from Midan al Tahrir to the hospital's morgue. Apparently, this same car transferred Tarek's body. At the morgue, they searched his pockets to identify him but did not find anything and recorded him as unknown. However, his ID was in his pocket. Did they search in a hurry and miss it? Did they find it and choose to lie? It took them forty days to find this painful closure, though it was still incomplete. The ever-arching question on Rania's mind was why she was not informed of his death. Why did the authorities hide his body all this time at the morgue? *Abu Tarek* says there is a hidden morgue which even Rania's father (a doctor at the same hospital) was unaware of at the hospital, as the French section of the hospital does not usually accept bodies from outside the hospital.

Tarek's mother believes authorities wanted to reduce the number of martyrs in a feeble attempt to cover the situation and hence his body stayed hidden for so long. Um Tarek said, "A large number of men died in the prisons and were buried without authorities informing their parents." His family did not challenge the prosecutor's report, which stated the time and place of Tarek's death and the shots that killed him.

However, his father has a different point of view. He says, "I do not think my son's body was concealed. The sheer number of bodies made it impossible to identify them. The desperate workers would steal what they could use like shoes, glasses or money. With all the false leads they got, it never occurred to Tarek's family that he was dead. Tarek was not a revolutionary character; he cherished Egypt and sought justice for all."

Losing their son brought them closer to God and did not shake their faith. It was a tragic shock, which caused a feeling of numbness and coldness. His parents lost sense of time and place, as if they had lost their souls, unable to hear their loved ones; at times believing and other times denying the loss of their son. As they are devout people, they knew they must accept destiny no matter how painful it was. *Abu Tarek* quotes the *Quran*, "For every term there is a decree"(38:13)[24]. It was his destiny and they must accept it. *Um Tarek* admits it has been a very difficult loss and test of faith. God brought Tarek into this world and He took him away. It is the circle of life.

Martin Luther King said, "In every battle for freedom there are martyrs whose lives are forfeited and whose sacrifice endorses the promise of liberty...They become symbols of our crusade. They give their lives to insure our liberty."[25] *Tarek is among those symbols for Egypt.*

In hindsight, during the manhunt, her brothers-in-law did not check the bodies, but checked a list of names that were badly hand written. As for the unknown bodies, they viewed pictures. Rania doubts that the morgue actually showed all the pictures of the unidentified bodies when family members came searching for missing loved ones. They probably showed pictures in intervals. More bodies were announced after the renaming of *"Amn Eldawla"* (State Security) to *"Amn El Watani"* (National Security). Tarek's wallet was not in a hidden pocket as was claimed, but in a regular pocket, and Rania finds it hard to believe that someone could have missed it. Among the probabilities, with the overwhelming number of bodies, is that perhaps nobody physically checked Tarek's body in the first place, and another probability is that Tarek was identified but intentionally overlooked. *This is a mystery, which his loved ones will forever ponder.*

Why the Cover Up?

During the funeral, the colleagues of Rania's father, who work at the hospital where Tarek's body lay for a month, told Rania's father that the president of the college had given orders not to reveal all the bodies.

Rania sometimes feels angry and stressed that Tarek is gone and other times she feels her faith has strengthened her capacity to deal with difficult matters. She misses feeling safe; her husband gave her the sense of security just by being alive. Tarek was a loving, kind, principled man who was loved by his family, friends and colleagues. Rania is living in her apartment alone with her two girls and when she hears someone at the door, she becomes shaken by fear, scared that someone would attack her. Tarek was a committed, cooperative husband and father who left a huge void that nobody can ever fill. She has lost her companion and her best friend.

Tarek was a very devout man who believed his faith was a private matter between himself and God, and not an external façade. Like any regular Muslim man, he fulfilled the basic pillars of Islam. He had no position towards *Ikhwan*, as they were a secret society with minor supporters. *Abu Tarek* is not against *Ikhwan* but is against their approach to politics.

According to Rania, Tarek's death certificate states that he died instantly during the incidents at Midan alTahrir via live bullets. Not many victims have such a statement as evidence, since many deaths were attributed to health issues such as heart attacks. During his court case, the deputy prosecutor said that the autopsy report was written well. Prosecution granted a martyr certificate that enabled Tarek's family to get compensation of around one thousand five hundred pounds (around two hundred dollars) monthly, payable to his mother, father, wife and two children. Further to this, a social affairs institute issued a one-time check worth five thousand pounds (around seven hundred dollars) as compensation.

The compensation does not really mean much to Rania, as she wants justice to befall on whoever killed her husband in the form of imprisonment, facing a trail and eventually serving a sentence according to court verdict. She is not simply seeking revenge, but justice; she wants the murderers of her husband to face sentencing, so that an example of how unwelcome injustice is, can be set. Actually, no one knows who fired the lethal bullet that took the life of Tarek, which leaves Rania wondering every time she sees a Central Security uniform, was it him or not? Every time she picks up and drops off her daughters at school, Rania passes by the street where Tarek received the fatal shot, with her heart racing. She is scared to look at the paved road and see a bloodstain, imagining it could belong to Tarek. When she passes by the ministry of interior, she does not want to detest it but in reality, she believes one of the police officers in there killed her husband with no justifiable cause. The police authorities need to bring forward the guilty among them so that not all the officers fall victim to societal hatred. She knows that police officers are just men; cousins or friends or fathers or grandfathers or brothers, they are all Egyptian brothers. How can she convey to her daughters that police are good and protect civilians when one of them killed their father? Good police officers need to be separated from bad police officers.

Breaking the Bad News

After Rania had calmed down and pulled herself together, she took her older daughter Mariam to her bedroom and closed the door to have the talk. Rania reminded her that Tarek was in a hotel and was trying to leave it. She told her that her father Tarek had gotten very sick. The doctor said that Tarek was very sick and that God wants him so that he could heal him as the medicine could not, so Tarek went to God. Mariam was shocked and as Rania explained that they would not see her Pappy again, the young girl burst into tears. Rania calmed her daughter down by telling her that Pappy will always be around them and that they will sense his presence and love. Rania also explained to her child that it is better for her father in heaven than to stay very sick on earth.

Sadness and fear engulfed Mariam, who was trying to make sense of her father's absence. Holding onto her mother, begging her not to leave the house, she was paranoid that she might lose her mother as well.

Shortly after this difficult discussion, Rania took Mariam to a psychiatrist to check on how the girl was coping. The doctor told her that she was alright, but that she needed to hear the word 'death' to grasp it and reach closure. Therefore, Rania had another talk with her daughter, and slowly introduced the subject.

Rania: "Marioma, you know that Pappy died?"

Mariam was shocked and said: "Died! You did not say that Pappy died."

Rania: "Did I not tell you that he went to God?"

Mariam: "Yes."

Rania: "Those who go to God are those who die."

Mariam still shocked: "Did Pappy get hurt?"

Rania: "Do you think that whoever dies gets hurt?"

Mariam: "Yes."

Rania: "No, not necessarily. I can get a big bruise and not die, I can get a big bruise and die, I can get a big bruise and get hurt but not die, I can get a small bruise and not die. Just because you die it does not mean you were hurt, and just because you are alive it does not mean that you are not hurting. Those who get hurt or bruised do not necessarily die and do not always feel pain. Don't you see me feeling hurt from a bruise, and other times I don't?"

Mariam nodded her head.

Continuing, Rania said, "Nothing is constant. Maybe Pappy did get hurt and maybe he did not hurt and maybe he felt pain and maybe he did not feel pain, but what matters is that he is in a better place. He is now in heaven and is now building a house for us when we get there *insha' Allah*."

Calmly, Rania soothed her and told her daughter that death happens anywhere at any time. It could be at their home, or office or the street, and no one can control or prevent death. She explained that God wanted her father to die so and that God would provide for Mariam and Sarah.

Mariam said, "Mammy but don't go to heaven before me."

Unable to control herself anymore Rania cried and said brokenly, "I don't know who will go first; maybe you will go before me. I will tell you what I want in the house (in heaven) and if you go before me, you tell Pappy what I want. If Sarah goes first we will tell her what we want too, a pink room or a red couch or a white curtain. Pappy can hear what we say as God sends him angels with our words. Let us read the Quran for Pappy, so that the angel takes our *hasanat* (good deeds), on a silver platter to him, a gift sent from Mariam and Sarah to Pappy."

One evening they were returning home and once Mariam entered the apartment, she said, "Hi Pappy!" Rania was surprised, but kept quiet. A short while later, while they were showering, Mariam said she felt that her father would open the door now and tell her to finish up quickly as he also wants to take a shower. Rania asked her "Do you feel that Pappy is in the house?" Mariam said yes. Rania told her that is because he is a martyr she and Mariam feel he is still around as if he was just traveling.

I believe when Albert Camus said, "Martyrs, my friend, have to choose between being forgotten, mocked or used, as for being understood: never" he omitted how much martyrs will be missed, Tarek's family will never forget him and will miss him deeply, more than words can ever describe.

In Hindsight

Rania did not recall this conversation at his party but her mother reminded her later; Tarek said, "Whoever is assaulted and dies in the demonstration, would be honored and anyone would pray for such honorable death."

At another occasion, one of the colleagues he was going to join during the Friday protest, with told Rania what he remembered her husband had said: "I am going to join the protest and if something happens to me consider me amongst God's martyrs." When Rania discovered Tarek's underlying wish to die a martyr and that

God almightily granted him his wish, she found some sort of peace with her destiny. *Referring to the idiom, 'Be careful what you wish for lest it come true," attributed to a Chinese proverb, Tarek's wish came true.*

Rania recalls a couple of years previously, when she'd had a discussion with Tarek about *jihad,* and the Palestinian plight. Tarek told her that if *jihad* were declared he would volunteer and fight to free sacred Jerusalem and hence come closer to God and heaven. He said back then that he would love to die a martyr. He hated injustice.

Tarek represents the well-to-do class who did not have any personal demands, but joined the demonstrations for his people, demanding the end to corruption, humiliation and undervaluing of Egyptian life. He wanted the end of second and third degree citizenship in his beloved country.

Rania wonders about the unpromising current situation in Egypt. Should she take her girls and leave, as he had instructed her the last day she saw him alive? Yet, she cannot bring herself to leave his final resting place and to abandon what he sacrificed his life for, a better Egypt. She cannot turn her back on that. Rania was planning to return to work once Sarah was a bit older and now she needs to find suitable work earlier than planned due to the sudden change in circumstances. Her in-laws sense that Rania is still unsettled and cannot believe she lost her husband. Every second, she remembers Tarek who had an active role and a strong presence in his family's daily life.

A little before the second anniversary of his martyrdom, Rania posted a note on Facebook on October 10, 2012. In a drawer, she found a letter Tarek had written to Rania and Dalia, her sister, and his classmate when they were just friends. He had been facing a difficult, uncertain period at his work. Twelve years after he wrote this letter, Rania felt goose bumps reading it. Below is part of the letter.

"P.S: Rania...If I'm not able to see you again, I would like you always to remember me not as anything but as a ....kind hearted, white dressed, flying soul, which came in a dark moment, put a torch of light on the wall, smiled in your face, & went away.... where peaceful waters flow.

Remember me girls..."

A Father's Reflections
In June 2011, Tarek's parents appeared on a recorded You Tube interview, talking about their late son. It was too difficult for Rania to participate in it. The interview is in two parts.[26]

Abu Tarek recalls the announcement made by the late vice president and challenges it because if the president steps down then in what position can he appoint the Supreme Council of the Armed Forces, SCAF to rule the nation? He should have appointed them before stepping down, not the other way around. He cannot understand why the activists did not insist on creating a transitory council to manage the country in alliance with the army. Why did they accept the military? The army design and build is to plan a war, not manage the political theatre. For this reason, when President Mohamed Naguib overthrew the monarchy, he said that the army would manage affairs for the short term and hand over Egypt to civilian rule. However, Abdel Nasser had a different vision than Naguib. Eventually Nasser succeeded in forcing Naguib to resign from presidency, and even placed him under house arrest for eighteen years whilst Nasser instilled military rule for over half a century. *Abu Tarek* blames this on power craving. Mistakes built over mistakes end in a very complicated situation. *Abu Tarek* quoted the Arabic proverb *'ma bonya ala batel fahowa batel'* (what is built on illegitimacy is illegitimate).

"Whatever misfortune happens to you is because of the things your hands have written, and for many (of them) He grants forgiveness" *(42:30)*[27]. After quoting this verse from the Quran *Abu Tarek* sobbed and tears filled his eyes behind his glasses.

Any revolution needs time; it starts up without a leader as the people rise against injustice. *Um Tarek* views the lack of leadership as the main reason why the revolution has not delivered on its promises. After the revolution, political parties claimed to have independently carried out the revolution and hence claimed power. Revolutions take time, Egyptians need to be patient. The president needs to love Egypt, not himself and not the palace. If one leaves a stone in the desert for decades and then removes it, surely you will find all sorts of insects, snakes, scorpions, spiders and much more underneath it. *Abu Tarek* draws this simile to former President Mubarak's three-decade reign. *"We've got to stay together and maintain unity…Pharaoh…kept the slaves fighting among themselves"*[28] *Martin Luther King said this, which dates back to our ancestors, and although it is an ancient war strategy, it is still practiced to date, and commonly referred to as divide and conquer. Former President Mubarak and Ikhwan adopted this strategy. Abu Tarek,* realizing this implores, "And hold fast, all together, by the rope which God 'stretches out for you', and be not divided among yourselves" *(3:103)*[29] This contradicts the announced plan to divide the Middle East map, which the American Congress had discussed as early as 1983. He believes that the foreign plan is to divide Egypt into three countries: Sinai goes to the Palestinians, North Egypt and Delta to the Muslims and Upper Egypt and Nubia to the Christians. *Abu Tarek is wary and wonders whether Egyptians can stand united, or if foreign hands will succeed in their master plan of breaking up the country.*

Unfortunately, Egyptians were nothing but disunited under *Ikhwan* rule. *Abu Tarek* predicts that *Ikhwan* will be committing the same mistakes as Hitler. *Ikhwan* are not acting as a group, since they move according to the Supreme Guide and hence are ruled by an individual. They are radicals who believe that the Supreme Guide is their prophet. Muslims need to address matters simply, without complications. As Prophet Mohamed PBUH said, *"el deenyosr"*, which means that religion simplifies and does not complicate.

Abu Tarek does not like the name *"Ikhwan"* (literally meaning brothers) and he finds it annoying, as all Egyptians are brothers and sisters. He prefers the Freedom and Justice Party, which addresses the revolution that demanded justice. *Abu Tarek* points out that the name of the political party of *Ikhwan*, Freedom and Justice Party is an oxymoron. It delivers neither freedom nor justice, due to their repressive approach. Many countries are yearning to control Egypt. *Abu Tarek* sees the Iranians hoping to spread *Shi'ism* in Egypt, the Saudis wanting to spread *Wahhabism,* and the Turks wanting to reassert their Ottoman influence over the Islamic world, ignoring Ataturk's secular statement in the 1930s. Egypt's geographic location and its history make it desirable.

Abu Tarek views the events of January 2011 as a white non-violent revolution. That is why it appealed to world audiences. He predicts curriculum in schools, and universities will cover it. *His son Tarek has contributed his precious life to writing Egypt's history. His loss is hopefully not in vain. As Indira Gandhi said, "Martyrdom does not end something, it is only a beginning."*

God helped the revolution succeed, not the army. The army has protected the revolution against the old regime. However, the army has mishandled affairs. *Abu Tarek* blames this mishap on several *sharazem* (splinters or scattered groups) who have different agendas and visions. Now is not the time for the protests and strikes, which have flooded the country. The country needs productivity to move forward. In Egypt, each party demands its piece of the cake and in the process, they are dividing the country rather than uniting it. Moreover, Egypt suffers from very high levels of uneducation and even higher poverty rates. Egyptians have watched the mushrooming of slums and the growing number of street children sleeping under bridges, and have done nothing to halt or reverse this alarming phenomenon. Unemployment is rampant and educational systems demolished. Early in the twentieth century, one of the English Prime Ministers had said that the best way to combat Islam as a power is not as a religion, but via its education system. This is reflected in Al Azhar University, whose curriculums *Abu Tarek* feels are spoiled by callous tampering. The West has succeeded in weakening Al Azhar by introducing topics into the curriculum. It used to be independent, but recently came under the ruler's influential wing. In the old days, the theologians would nominate three of their scholars for the position of *Sheikh Al Azhar,* and the ruler, either the King or the President, would select one.

Abu Tarek believes that the revolution will continue until equality is achieved, and only then, will it have attained its goals. The old *Nizam* is still in place and corruption is alive, if not growing. The revolution has succeeded in breaking the fear barrier, which the military rule and imperialism had built. This courage is a double edge sword, as crime is now on the rise with no shame or repercussions, not even feeble attempts to conceal the blatant misdeeds. He sees the president of Egypt as dark and bleak, however, he cannot predict the future. Today, matters are moving from bad to worse. There is no blueprint for the future state of Egypt.

Tarek's father is not concerned with who is in power. What matters to him, is how they rule and how Egyptians are treated. *Ikhwan* have taken key ministerial positions in the Ministry of Interior and reputedly, in defense. In September 2012, *Abu Tarek* predicted that the next blow would be against the judges, especially as the General Prosecutor was the same GP as the one during the Mubarak era and Ahmed Meky, his brother is the Minister of Justice. He was right, as on December 2012, President Morsi illegally fired the GP. How can there be freedom with a party based on listening and obeying? *Abu Tarek* wants Egypt's president to love Egypt and strive for its interests.

Um Tarek is uncertain about the future, however, she still has hope that tomorrow is another day.

Two Years Plus Later
It is very painful for Rania to think about this traumatic memory so she has decided to switch off from the political world. She has reached the point of saturation and cannot handle matters any more. Rania is realist and an optimist. She quotes Diasaku Ikeda, "The deeper the dark, the closer the dawn" For now, it is pitch dark.

Rania did not participate in the referendum vote in December 2012, as she felt the theatrics ignored the essential crisis of corruption and injustice. Much as she tried, Rania could not really completely shut off, as she believed former President Mohamed Morsi was incompetent and should not finish his term. Therefore, she signed the *Tamarod* (rebellion) form, although she did not participate in any demonstrations. She never had enough courage to take to the streets. Rania remains optimistic although baffled by the sweeping second revolution against President Morsi on June 30, 2013.

On the other hand, Rania was uncomfortable and questioned the army's call for the people to delegate them to combat terrorism. Although, she was against the vigils at Rabba and Nahda. The bloodshed saddened her. Then again, she could not visualize a third option, as the Islamist protestors were adamant in their vigil. Egypt needs the rule of an iron fist, like that of General Sisi, however it must be just. Rania sees that matters are grey, neither black nor white, but hazy, and hence prefers to be silent.

There is no doubt that Rania feels disturbed by the fact that Egyptians do not cherish human life. A Church wedding turned into a killing spree in Giza, leaving three dead, including an 8-year-old girl, in October 2013. Where have ethics and morals gone? It appears to her that basic ethics have become a utopian idea, far removed from reality. Rania wishes that any of the parties would stand up and admit that they have made a mistake. *Thoreau defines action as follows, "Every free action is produced by the concurrence of two causes; one moral, i.e. the will which determines the act; the other physical, i.e. the power which executes it."*[30] *Rania feels disturbed, as many actions in Egypt seem to have lost their moral grounds.* Another disturbing phenomenon is how people who once stood together on common grounds are now differing in their positions, a phenomenon that is leading to *fitna* (sedition).

Tarek Abdel-Latif died fighting for the rights of Egyptians. He dreamed of a better country for his girls to grow up in. He is among eight hundred and forty-six men and women who parted with life during those eighteen unforgettable days and we Egyptians will forever be indebted to them. As Martin Luther King said, "In every battle for freedom there are martyrs whose lives are forfeited and whose sacrifice endorses the promise of liberty… They became symbols of our crusade. They gave their lives to insure our liberty."[31] *It is difficult for Rania and her family, as this promise of liberty seems unreachable. When will Egyptians live in liberty? Will Egyptians ever live in liberty?*

"It is the cause, not the death that makes the martyr." Napoleon Bonaparte

121

CHAPTER 7

Freedom Fighters

"Sometimes it falls upon a generation to be great,
You can be that generation." Nelson Mandela

While I was talking on the phone with Randa, one of my best friends from university, my idea to write this book was formulated, and Randa whole heartedly encouraged me to pursue my long standing dream of becoming a writer. Initially she was hesitant to feature in it, but eventually she came around and we met at La Roma café in Zamalek on Saturday June 11, 2011.

Baheya

She worships Egypt more than words can describe. She is a warm, tolerant woman but one should be wary around her, as she is strong and can sting like a bee if anyone steps on her toes. Randa Haggag was born on October 24, 1974 in Cairo, where she grew up. She is a well-educated, young, modern and patriotic Egyptian woman in her thirties. Randa has simple tastes; she likes to wear her hair long and dresses in her own individualistic western style. She recently studied fashion, and has launched a new local designer brand called 'Baheya', reflecting her love of Egypt. Randa is tri-lingual, speaking Arabic, French and English, and studied at College du Sacre-Coeur, following which, she majored in Business Administration at the American University in Cairo. Not content, she continued her higher education at RITI University in Cairo where she obtained a Masters of Business Administration (MBA). Before her Masters, she had embarked on the popular marketing career trend, working in several multinational companies across various industries. Randa is a very independent, modern, non-conformist and open-minded woman, who left her family home to live in the Gulf as a single woman *(which is still not a very common thing to do in Egyptian society)* in order to pursue her career aspirations. Randa was fortunate enough to have moved back to Egypt with her husband before the revolution in 2011. Little did she know what she was signing up for when she joined the activists on the streets of Cairo late January 2011.

Day 1: Watching from Home

Randa thought that the protests were going to be business as usual, with a few hundred, or a maximum of a few thousand, on the streets. Moreover, on the first day, she did not know anyone who was joining the protest. She opted, instead, to stay at home and work on some designs for her *"Baheya"* fashion line. She felt that everyone could convey their patriotism in their own manner and *"Baheya"* was her own personal way of showing her love of Egypt. As the day unfolded, she discovered that she had been mistaken, and that several thousand people had gone out of the safety of their homes and into the streets, demanding basic human rights that Egyptians had been deprived of for decades.

While she was online two days later, she came across a brutal story on the *Rasd* News Facebook page about Amr Salama, a director who was kidnapped by armed police officers on January 25. Randa recalls the story vividly as the officers took Amr to the ground floor of one of the buildings in the downtown area, where four officers kicked him all over from head to toe. He repeatedly told them that he owned a house, a car, and a mobile and had a well-paying job and pleaded with the men beating him, saying he was protesting for their sake.

After the initial beating, an officer gave orders to the officers saying, "I am leaving to get another good for nothing traitor. By the time I return you should have beaten him to death."

The officer left and one officer asked Amr: "Can you walk? You need to run away." Another officer added: "You need to disappear quickly before he returns."

Unfortunately, while he was about to leave, the commanding officer returned with another victim. The kicking started all over again until another officer came in and miraculously released him. Randa actually personally met Amr Salama in May of 2011 and he directly confirmed his ordeal with the police.

Day 3: Preparing

By Thursday January 27, Randa had managed to find some friends who were protesting and decided to join them on Friday, knowing that she was better off going with someone than by herself. That evening she wrote her will, carefully closed her apartment, and did not plan to return home. She even compiled a document stating all the money she owed people, and what people owed her from her freelancing jobs. *Muslims have to settle their finances before their death, as they will be accountable for them on the Day of Judgment.* She was so anxious about joining the protests that she only slept for a couple of hours on the living room couch. She was fully aware that if she left, there was a very high chance that she would never return home.

The *ancien regime* cut off mobile communications and her landline was not functioning. Literally, Randa was cut off from any means of communication. Also, at the time, her husband was away, and she was living on her own. The upside was that she had a flexible schedule and hence could dedicate her time to participating in what turned out to be a historic revolution. Randa believes that this was God's mysterious way of shaping her destiny so that she could participate in the revolution. If her husband had been with her, Randa is sure that he would not have permitted her to leave the house during this insecure period, out of fear, like many other protective men.

Day 4: Volleys of Tear Gas

On Friday January 28, Randa went to her friend Nirvana's house. Finding Nirvana's mother being supportive and comforting gave them much-needed confidence. The mother was joining a march in Zamalek, whereas Randa and her friends Nirvana, Moroog and Nermeen took a taxi to join the larger protest in Giza. Dr. Mohamed El Baradei, former Director General of the International Atomic Energy Agency (IAEA) announced he would be present at Giza, so they assumed it would be a safer place. When they arrived, they could see that the number of *Amn Elmarkazi* (central security) officers on the streets was incredible. When the four women arrived at Istekamah Mosque at the Giza roundabout, they prayed the Friday noon prayers outside on the street, as the mosque was overcrowded.

After the prayers, Randa joined the crowds and started chanting at the top of her voice. The first chant was *"Ya Askary mestani eh, enta betakhoud kam geneh?"* which means "You, policeman, what are you waiting for? How many pounds are you earning anyway?" She felt that was a very intelligent attempt at getting the police's sympathy and merging their forces. Nevertheless, that chant did not do the trick. She saw sympathy in the police officers' eyes, however. The commanding officers were watching police officers closely to ensure that they would stick with the regime and the party rhetoric. Randa also chanted *"Yasqot yasqot Hosny Mubarak"* which means, "Down, down with Hosni Mubarak", *"Taghyeer, horeyaha, karama ensaneya"* which means, "Change, freedom and human dignity" and *"Al Shaab yoreed esqat al nezam"* which means, "The people want the downfall of the regime." The last one, the crowds chanted continuously for around ten minutes, and it was beautiful. Randa felt that they were human beings; they were proud, worthy human beings. While she was marching in residential areas she was chanting *"Ya ahalena endamou lena"* (Our families come join us). People were joining the crowds and others were waving from balconies.

Coincidently, someone in the crowd recorded a video[32] of Randa chanting "Yasqot, yasqot Hosni Mubarak". They later met in political lectures after the revolution, and he sent her the video on Facebook.

Randa was overflowing with pride as the march moved from the mosque to Giza Street. She looked around, and saw the crowd growing exponentially. It was as if the people where coming out from under the ground! *She connected to how Nelson Mandela felt during his initial years of activism when he said, "I found that to march with one's people was exhilarating and inspiring."*[33]

Once the crowds reached Cairo University, *Dakhleya* (Ministry of Interior), blocked the road behind them, a road that did not have side streets, essentially trapping the peaceful protestors. It all started at that moment! It was unbelievable! Randa had heard about tear gas but it was nothing compared to what she witnessed. Once the police started firing off canisters of tear gas into the crowds, she felt she could not breathe. Her skin was burning, and her eyes were tearing profusely. The canister itself was very hot to the touch. Some of the men would kick the canisters to another part of the crowd. They did not have a safe haven to dispose of them, unlike the crowds on the bridges who discarded them into the Nile, far away from bystanders. Protestors advised each other to run to the sides when the police attacked. So the crowds ran to the sides, but upon doing so, they found themselves surrounded by the high walls of the university. Some men climbed the walls and managed to break open the gates for the rest of the crowd to seek shelter from the gas. Gallant men escorted Randa along with other women to safety. During this commotion, Randa felt terrified, and began to cry non-stop. Fear gripped her bones; she was hurting, seeing her beloved country in such havoc, for the first time in her life. She tried to get out of the gates, but seeing ongoing attacks, she retreated inside the faculty of engineering campus. Randa saw more brave men carrying the wounded from outside into the safety of the campus. This battle-like scene lasted for a couple of hours. One young fellow was bleeding intensely from his nose and her friend, Moroog, who has a stronger stomach, helped this man. Unfortunately, it was to no avail, as Moroog learned from the man's sister that he passed away just a week later. Randa was in a state of panic. She saw doctors appearing unexpectedly to attend to the victims with no medical supplies - all they had were simple products like cola, vinegar and cotton. The former was recommended by our Tunisian brothers to reduce the side effect of the tear gas, based on their own experience, and it worked like a magic potion.

The university students, who had finished their exams, managed to gather a few women and helped many escape through a back gate. After Randa escaped, she wanted to return to the safety of her mother's home. Nirvana, who was an exceptionally brave woman, wanted to search for other protests and to observe what was taking place there. Randa therefore walked with Nirvana, Moroog, and Nermeen, intending to go to her own mother's house afterwards. She rested on the ground by a fruit vendor on Tahrir Street, who had his TV tuned to Al Jazeera Channel. They were reporting the protests taking place all over Egypt, and the police firing tear gas at all the crowds. This made sense according to what Randa had just witnessed. After resting, she got up and walked through side roads, avoiding the police. A passerby guessed they were activists and told them that another protest was underway on Galaa Street, so they went in that direction.

By the time they arrived, the police attacks had mysteriously ceased. The protest had returned to being peaceful, with people chanting slogans while the *Dakhleya* secured the sides of the roundabout. Randa could still smell the suffocating gas in the air, an unforgettable odor forever engrained in her memory. She stayed there from 2:30 until 4pm, observing that the number of protestors was quite small. However, after 4pm, the crowds began to grow dramatically. Randa could not believe what she was seeing as she surveyed her surroundings. Tens of thousands of people were flooding the streets from all directions, north, south, east and west, all heading to Tahrir. It was something out of this world! It was a victory! At that moment, Randa felt a sense of hope and euphoria. The Ministry of Interior forces held their fire, standing guard until around 4pm.

Randa noticed the security forces retreating into the Dokki police station, and assumed that they would start shooting at the crowds from the station's rooftop. However, this did not happen. Some people listened to the Al Jazeera news station from the neighboring homes and took upon themselves the responsibility of spreading the news to the crowds on the street. Randa recognized some of those spreading news, as they were former colleagues from university. This system of communicating by word of mouth was one of the means that had kept the crowds up-to-date as telecommunications were down. At Galaa Square, she saw many celebrities, the director Khaled Youssef, the movie stars Khaled Abou ElNaga, Amr Waked, Khaled El Sawy and Gihan Fadel. By 6 pm all the police had mysteriously disappeared. Randa heard a man next to her shout *"Allah Akbar"*, which means 'God is great'. The power of the *shaab* (people) vanquished the bloodstained police. She heard about the army mobilization and newly set curfew.

Around this time, Randa decided to head back home. She walked in the deserted Nile Street, taking the 15 May Bridge, and exiting in Zamalek. She bumped into her longtime friend Tayssir Ibrahim *(featured in chapter 8)*, who she noticed was limping. Tayssir recounted to her that a coward had shot him with a rubber bullet in his calf and it was hurting. But he was ignoring his wound as he was heading with his friend to Tahrir. Randa was beside herself with joy seeing Tayssir at this unexpected time. Although tempted to join Tayssir and his friend, after so much effort and the tumultuous events of the day, Randa, beyond exhausted both physically and emotionally, opted to go home. Arriving home, she knocked on her friendly neighbors' door to ask them to use their telephone. She called her parents to reassure them that she was safe, as she had no landline.

That night was probably the worst that Egypt had ever witnessed. Fear, anxiety, shock, betrayal and unbelievable anger was welling up inside so many Egyptians, like a dormant volcano on the verge of explosion. Many convicts escaped or were released from various state prisons across Egypt and were on a looting spree, wreaking havoc across the cities. These unprecedented prison breaks occurred simultaneously, leaving the country haunted by thousands of criminals, which lead to sleepless nights for many Egyptians. This night seemed like an endless nightmare. Out of fear and anticipation, Randa 'slept' on her couch, wearing her shoes, with a kitchen knife under the couch pillow, on full alert. She was afraid, and had hidden all her valuables, ready to run for her life if need be.

Day 4: Cairo Burning

The following morning, January 29, Randa's eyes were puffy and her cheeks sunken, as she had not had anything proper to eat or drink, and it did not matter. She was feeling tired from the sleepless night, but food, and drink, and sleep all seemed insignificant. She had a mission that day to reach Midan alTahrir. She was adamant to reach the square that day and rather than going alone, she preferred taking her younger brother along. Many young women had difficulty convincing their parents and gaining their approval to participate in the demonstrations. However, Randa was lucky, as her parents understood what she was doing, and were without a doubt very proud and supportive of Randa, their only daughter.

Randa walked to Tahrir and was dismayed at the sight of burning tires and police trucks on the roads. Some fires were freshly ablaze. Others were about to die out. She hated the stench of burning rubber, as it made her queasy. On the 6th of October bridge, she saw a heavily armored truck that had been destroyed by flames. The previous night, angry men had tried tirelessly to push the truck over the side of the bridge and into the Nile, but it had been too heavy. She recalls seeing the visuals of the incident on television vividly. Now she was looking at the aftermath. When she saw the National Democratic Party, NDP, building on fire, Randa knew deep down the activists were not behind it. She has a strong position against the use of violence and destruction. Once she reached her target, Midan alTahrir, she felt elated and on top of the world. She was feeling joy, pride, hope and patriotism, all at a new higher level; something she had never felt or imagined before. Randa saw a few civilians and army officials cleaning the square. The past couple of days had moved and inspired so many Egyptians the world over, to act and build a better nation.

Out of a sense of ownership, of belonging, and the unrelenting urge to contribute, Randa voluntarily helped translate for a few foreigners who were out in the square. One Islamist within the group mistook her for a foreigner and talked to her in a manner that displeased her. She quickly lost her temper and got into a quarrel with him, shouting at him. Tarek, her former colleague, came suddenly and carried her away with her brother, Khaled, who took her home to safety. She admits that she was wrong in her hostile reaction to the Islamist, as she had no grounds for losing her temper. She obviously felt carried away with the strong surge of emotion running through the air.

Once home, Randa turned on the television and watched with dread and disbelief the rest of the looting from the previous night. In the neighboring district of Mohandeseen, banks were robbed, the Duty Free shop torched, and other shops broken into. Across the Nile, a commercial center called Arkadia was set ablaze after all the shops were looted. The fire filled the sky with dense black smoke.

The once peaceful country was violated post the insurgency, as the police force conspicuously vanished, and civilians set up a makeshift security system at the speed of light. As Randa lived in Zamalek, an affluent neighborhood, she went on foot from Tahrir to her home. After the curfew had gone into effect at night, she ritualistically passed by the civilian checkpoints. At one of the control points, she once saw a former telecommunications CEO, Mohamed, sitting at the checkpoint under his home, with a bunch of youth and house porters guarding the street. Sometimes, they would actually drive Randa home, as she was feeling so rundown from the abnormal daily stress and struggle. But it was all worth it. The community's organization and commitment to keeping Zamalek safe impressed Randa. Every day they used a new, and usually funny, code as a security measure for people who moved in and out and throughout the area. The voluntary neighborhood security also changed the color, sometimes white or yellow, of the ribbons they wore tied around their arms as a precautionary measure to avoid any breaches in security from outsiders. The Zamalek community also had a list of phone numbers to contact in case of emergency. Luckily, Randa never had to use the numbers. Randa heard about the honorable cooperation between the army and civilian check points in cracking down on criminals and intruders. Mohamed was one of the leading individuals securing Zamalek (Zamalek Guardians) and he was what you call a Harley Davidson biker dude with average build. Zamalek, being an island, was easier to secure as it has less exits and entrances, unlike a populated neighborhood like Imbaba. Nonetheless, they were very wary, as this is residential area known to be affluent with many diplomats and wealthy families.

Day 5 – 8: Overflowing Love

Randa visited Tahrir every day and in the evening went home to catch a few hours of sleep. There were days when the square was very crowded, those were referred to as the *milyouneya* (million-man march), other days the numbers were much smaller. Yet, regardless of the size, the crowds were always overflowing with solidarity, standing up for their demands and legitimate rights.

The atmosphere in Tahrir showed a respectful, decent, developed and modern nation. Everyone, irrespective of social or economic standing in society, displayed this. Nobody was harassed, not even the women! *These times were extraordinary but ephemeral, as women frequently and sadly are harassed on the streets of Egypt.* The crowds were not judging one another, but rather, accepting each other, as they were all Egyptians. There were mixed crowds, including Muslims and Coptic Christians, men and women, and no polarization. They were all unified Egyptians. The social-economic strata of rich and poor were suddenly insignificant and classism was completely absent. It demonstrated the Egypt that Randa wanted to be a part of, a proud, respectful, dignified and responsible nation. *This apparent unfolding of tolerance echoes Gandhi's words, "Before they dare think of freedom they must be brave enough to love one another, to tolerate one another's religion, even prejudices and superstitions and to trust one another. This requires faith in oneself. And faith in oneself is faith in God. If we have faith we cease to fear one another."*[34]

When Randa surveyed her surroundings in Tahrir, she saw men and women sitting side by side, some with bandages on their heads, arms, legs or chest. She saw proud and unified Egyptians gloriously waving their flag. Many were taking photos using cameras and more commonly their camera phones. Tents completely covered the center of the roundabout. At times Randa found herself overwhelmed with emotion and as a result, she broke down in tears. Consequently, seven or eight people would surround her out of concern, asking if somebody had bothered her and they tried to soothe her. Randa was profoundly touched by how quickly her friends and fellow Egyptians responded to her need for comfort. She did not feel alone. They were all in this together, fighting for their rights, their freedom and their dignity. *They were all freedom fighters. The revolutionary and romantic atmosphere mesmerized Randa. Che Guevara first introduced this notion as Michael Casey described, "Che converted the very idea of revolution into a romantic vision for millions."*[35] *Randa Haggag, an Egyptian newborn-activist is one of those millions.*

This beautiful aura of emotion was displayed in simple acts of kindness. One sunny afternoon, Randa was sitting on the sidewalk when an old veiled woman in her sixties approached her.

The old woman said, "*Salam (a greeting used like Hello meaning peace)* my young girl, please have a date," offering her one from a blue cloth bag filled with dates.

Randa said, "Thank you, but I am fine."

The old woman replied, "You have to take one to keep your energy and continue your fight for freedom. I insist you take one date."

Randa, feeling embarrassed, took one and said, "Thank you. May God protect you." Randa did not feel hungry but she was feeling drained and she sincerely prayed for the old lady who continued distributing dates to the crowds, providing them with much needed energy, something Randa needed as well.

The men and women used to go to the neighboring Mosque to use the rest room. Randa stood in a long queue. All the women respected the queues and politely waited for their turn. She felt high spirits, filled with support and positive energy, among the women. The women reciprocated tolerance, respect and acceptance equally between the modern and conservative women, among the veiled and curly haired.

Day 9: Under Attack

The morning of Wednesday February 2, Randa's father called her and told her not to go to Tahrir, as rumor had it that snipers were going to attack the demonstrators from rooftops. On the other hand, her mother warned her that if she did not go to Tahrir, the police would pick her up from her home, along with all the other activists, one by one, and it would be as if this uprising had never happened. Her mother told Randa: "You started something, you have to finish it." *Her parents' opposing opinions became normal in many Egyptian households during the revolution; it opened the door to acute differences in society.* She was going to go Tahrir regardless of what her parents had said but she was very proud of her mother's stand.

Randa arrived at the square a little before 2 pm, and the *baltegeya* (thugs), had gathered in small trucks, but had not instigated any trouble just yet. She was entering Tahrir with a group of protestors, referred to as 'supporters of Mohamed ElBaradei' by the Tahrir checkpoints. They checked her ID and a woman frisked her to ensure that she has no weapons of any sort. At this time, she was not a supporter of ElBaradei, however after the revolution she became one.

That day Randa noticed that the protestors were few, around a few thousand, possibly due to the prevailing rumor that danger loomed ahead. She found it quite concerning that the *baltegeya* were disembarking from mini trucks. It had been rumored that they had been paid by members of the ruling National Democratic Party (NDP). Protestors were warned not to talk to the hooligans, and not to react. It was clear that criminals were trying to provoke fights with the people who were arriving to demonstrate peacefully in Midan alTahrir. Since they were few in numbers, the protestors either called up friends to join by phone or via the internet, as the *ancien regime* had reconnected the latter. Politicians were also calling for people to go out and protect the square against the *baltegeya*. After that day, Randa condemned the political parties, as none of them showed up in person in the square during this 'medieval' battle. Previously they had made appearances in Tahrir in an attempt to gain access to microphones and preach their ideologies, but on this day, they were noticeably absent.

Around 4pm, one of Randa's Alexandrian friends was suddenly shouting, which was abnormal in the newly formed peaceful Tahrir character and spirit. Nermeen told her that some man was politically provoking her and was raising his voice, and all of a sudden, Nermeen was replicating his behavior and shouting as well. In no more than around 15 to 20 minutes, this incident multiplied among many individuals and rapidly many people were arguing at Tahrir. It was evident that those opposing the sit in had planned this, so that the protestors would break out into fights amongst themselves, or so it seemed. Miraculously, they realized this plan and the uproars were muffled very quickly. They started chanting "*selmeya! selmeya!*" (We are peaceful, we are peaceful!), and the situation was under control.

The ruthless ruffians were determined to create chaos and havoc, hurling stones and ceramic pieces at the protestors, after around half an hour. Randa was amazed to see horses and camels run into the square, with offenders riding them and attacking the protestors. This incident with the horses and the camels striding was very brief, only around a couple of minutes, but the media exaggerated the role of the animals in this battle, possibly due to the medieval imagery it evoked. It was termed the 'Battle of the Camels', which annoys Randa, as it simply was not a battle of the camels. The anger and hatred the thugs displayed towards the protestors was unbelievable, especially as the demonstrators just wanted a better life for everyone in the country, the *baltegeya*, included. The men, those honorable men, those brave fighters, stood by each other and constructed human barriers to stop the thugs from entering the square. They made numerous lines protecting the square. While recounting this Randa cried. She will never forget this heart-warming sight.

Randa viewed several single women, young and old, protecting and fighting for Tahrir and the freedom it embodied. The men asked the women to stay inside the square so that they could be able to protect them. People from all walks of life; some were university professors, some were from villages, men and women, were all willing to die for their beloved Egypt in their fight for freedom. Right before sunset, Randa heard gunshots in the vicinity. She ran towards the gunshots, thinking that this was their end and the shots would kill them. Shortly afterwards she realized it was an army officer, Maged Boulis, who had shot rounds into the air to scare away the assaulting thugs and had moved his army tank into the middle of the street. On his own initiative, he was protecting his fellow Egyptian demonstrators from the aggressors and was later considered a hero, and given the title 'The Lion of Tahrir.'

Randa will never forget what happened that night around 8pm or 9pm. Every couple of minutes the protestors carried the wounded inside the square for treatment by the volunteering doctors. Demonstrators arrested the *baltegeya*, who attempted to enter Midan alTahrir and took them as prisoners of war, with their hands tied behind their backs and confined in the underground station. The demonstrators confiscated the personal identifications of the *baltegeya*, and upon observation of the ID cards they realized that around 80% of those they arrested who were wreaking havoc in Tahrir were members of the National Democratic Party (NDP), the old regime's corrupt political party and Ministry of Interior soldiers and officers. Randa saw a 60-year-old man holding a teenager, one of the captives, hitting him on the head. He was telling him the wealthy had come to Tahrir to say "No" to Mubarak, "and you son of a ... are telling him to stay." The teenager was crying and it was clear that he did not understand the meaning of his actions and his subsequent situation. Randa broke into tears as she felt that the older man was spot on in identifying the truth about why she risked her life.

Members of the *Ikhwan* (Muslim Brotherhood), and Ultras, the fanclub of Al Ahly Soccer Team, did a great job in organizing the activists that day. Randa joined a group of people who were breaking the sidewalk into small pieces and placing them in plastic bags to hand over to the men on the front lines as a form of self-defense. She did this for a couple of hours. While she was preparing the 'weapons' she was crying as she was thinking, 'Sorry Egypt! I came here to build you and not break you, but they are making us do this.' She was defending their freedom and trying to build a better nation for its entire people.

At the time, there was a shortage of water, so she had to improvise. Randa, along with other women, filled bags found in the trash with water, to send to the courageous men fighting the *baltegeya*. They used the water to wash their faces and wounds, and quench their thirst. They were collecting scarves and anything that could aid the wounded and stop them from bleeding to death. A little before midnight, one of her friends got hurt. He was lucky it was not his eyes or his head, which were common areas for injury in that horrendous battlefield. Somebody had run to Randa and her friends, and informed them that one of their friends had fallen victim. Randa has no idea how that person knew they were friends. They ran with him to fetch Ahmed. The magical teamwork in place bewitched Randa that bloody night. She felt that angels were helping them. They carried Ahmed back into the secure area where the doctors were literally running after them to treat and attend to his leg injuries.

The struggle seemed endless. The men were taking shifts to protect the square. Every two hours the women would wake up the men to take their turn in defending Tahrir and their liberation. Many of the men fell injured that night and they were all exhausted but nothing stopped them. They went repeatedly to the front lines, fighting for their freedom and dignity.

In one of the side streets, unrest was unfolding and they were summoning help from the protestors, men or women. Randa searched for some weapon for self-defense and found a metal stick. A teenage boy approached her:
The boy said, "Why are you holding that metal rod?"
Randa replied, "In case the rogues break into the square."
His eyes were piercing and he said, "But that is why we are here, we are here to protect you."
Randa replied, "Thank you, may God protect you, us and all of Egypt."
Randa gave him the metal rod with tears in her eyes. The bravery and the chivalry of the Egyptian men was unprecedented, as displayed by this teenager.

Day 10: Holding Up

Randa was proud of every single moment and every single human being she met. She wants to affiliate with the like of those Egyptians. The night of the thugs' attack, she wanted to spend the night in Tahrir, but when it was 2 am, she could not stay any longer and headed home. That night had been bloody and it was unbearably chilly; Randa was very scared and very cold. Rumor had it that *baltegeya* were waiting for the live talk shows to end so that when the stations switched off their live camera feeds, they could massacre the demonstrators without recorded evidence. She wanted to be there, but until 2 am, they did not show up, so she shamefully left. Randa had seen too much bloodshed for one day. She was rebuking herself, thinking, 'I am a coward.' On her way home, she met a man from the civilian checkpoint, who had left earlier, at 6 pm on the previous Wednesday evening, overwhelmed with fear. He could not grasp how she had been brave enough and stayed fighting until the first hours of Thursday, February 3.

When Randa returned home a little after 3 am that early morning, she watched the news channels until 9 am, in anticipation of the alleged planned attacks on Tahrir. Sources say that there had been an order to attack the square but the army had refused to follow orders that would kill civilians. She watched in agitation, waiting for the rumored massacre to start. As it turns out, it was just invalidated hearsay. ONTV maintained live transmission of Midan alTahrir, without stopping, that entire night.

Back at home, Randa realized that she'd lost more than a couple of kilos, and looked run down and exhausted. She mostly forgot to eat during those eighteen days. Sometimes Randa ate dates or a cheese sandwich, which strangers generously offered. With unusually high numbers of people at Tahrir and the ongoing clashes, restaurants opted to close for security reasons. She had terrifyingly lost eight kilos overall, and looked like skin on bones. Randa felt she had aged at least five years in the preceding couple of weeks, noticing that the white hairs on her head had increased with the trauma she had witnessed.

Day 14: Overcoming Fear

Although the dominant mood was positive and filled with optimism, the recounts of arrests tainted it. Months before the revolution, in June 2010, police brutally beat Khaled Said, a young Alexandrian man, to death, pulverizing his face to the point it was unrecognizable. His family had fought hard in an attempt to bring the police officers to justice, but the system was protecting their own. A young man, Wael Ghonim, took it upon himself to create a Facebook page anonymously, trying to bring attention to this hideous, unpunished crime. He named it *"Kulluna Khaled Said."* (We are all Khaled Said). On this page, Wael spoke the naked, agonizing truth, posting appalling videos of police abuse, initiating silent stands and, most successfully, calling for mass demonstrations on January 25, 2011. The number of followers on Facebook was phenomenal.

Randa heard of people arrested during the demonstrations and held for interrogation for two days, unusually, without torture. Apparently, it was the state security's strategy to select individuals who were highly active on Twitter and Facebook, who would ultimately declare online that the police did not physically abuse them. One such person was the administrator of the *"Kulluna Khaled Said"* page, Wael Ghonim, whose identity police discovered, and swiftly arrested him in Tahrir on January 27. Authorities released him after eleven days, on the evening of February 7, and he directly went to a talk show with Mona El-Shazly on Dream TV. He spoke genuinely, simply telling the truth and it struck a chord with millions of Egyptians that night. When Mona brought up the subject of the martyrs, he emotionally broke down in tears. His sorrow was overwhelming, and spilled through the television screens into the homes of millions of viewers. Wael cried on air saying, "It should not have been like this. People shouldn't have died." Randa is sure that the *ancien regime* did not expect that this interview would backfire as it had. The state security probably expected that the fear he went through would scare the masses. Little did they know that his fear and his ordeal would create such momentum, which ultimately solidified their resolve. After Wael's live appearance on TV, the masses in Tahrir grew in numbers on the following day.

Randa heard of other arrests. If a detainee was loud and dared to chant slogans, the police would beat him with the wooden bed planks, muffling his voice to ensure that he would remain silent. Before January 25, Egyptians were looking straight ahead, minding their own business, fearing the unscrupulous security monster. They felt crippled by fear of arrest and imprisonment. *After January 25, there was a paradigm shift for Egyptians, who finally broke free of this paralyzing and debilitating fear. Mandela correctly said, "For fear of imprisonment is a tremendous hindrance to a liberation struggle."*[36]

One of the distinguishing factors of this revolution is the reality that it was leaderless. Randa recalls that certain parties who had gotten a hold of the microphone, advocating their ideologies, were quickly stopped by protestors who withdrew the microphone, chanting, *"shaabiya, shaabiya"* meaning "from the people, from the people." Neither a political party nor an ideology controlled the will of the people. *Shadi Hamid told <u>AUC Cairo Review</u>: "Like Tunisia, Egypt's was a leaderless movement consisting of angry, ordinary Egyptians who came, not with ideologies or partisanship, but the simple overarching demand that President Mubarak step down...That these were leaderless revolutions meant that the regimes had no one to demonize, except their own people."*[37] The Egyptian revolution was not only in Tahrir but also in Suez and Ismailia, whose people Randa perceives as braver than Cairenes and other governorates. She met a few activists who told her they had handled the situation with the police and the army in Alexandria, so they had left for Cairo to help there too. Alexandrians are more assertive than Cairenes. It was never about Tahrir square alone. The revolution was nationwide and Tahrir was just a symbol, which the media honed in on.

Day 17: Swelling Anger
On Thursday February 10, Randa finished her work in Garden City at 2 pm, after which she walked to Tahrir to re-join her friends. One of the soldiers climbed on a platform and announced via microphone that within half an hour, they would meet all the people's demands. He requested two things; that the crowds refrain from aggression, and that they do not riot. He advised against overreaction and violence. She recalls vividly her friend Tayssir's green eyes widening with excitement. Tayssir asked, "Is he gone?"
Randa replied, "No, not yet."

From 5:30 pm to 10:30 pm, they waited for former President Mubarak to deliver his statement, announcing his resignation. The mood was tense. People were literally afraid to cheer. The masses grew in numbers during those few hours. Randa estimates that the numbers had tripled, as they could not find a place to stand because of the overwhelming crowds. As announced, the president delivered his speech; a disappointing one, clearly stating he was not leaving office. Furious is an understatement as to how the crowds and people at home felt. The atmosphere was unsettling, like the aftermath of a bomb explosion. Randa was red with anger; she could feel her blood rushing to her face. She was sure that the crowds would lose control and revert to violence as an outlet for their anger and frustration. She is sure that the *ancien regime* had been relying on such a reaction from the masses. However, the people rose to the occasion and maintained their peace. People were fuming. She saw a boy turning around in circles screaming in wrath. Chants commenced, calling for a move to the Parliament. Others wanted to go to Maspero, where the state television has its headquarters. The most effective chant was *"Selmeya! Selmeya!"* "We are peaceful! We are peaceful!"

Day 18: From Despair to Rejoicing

After midnight on February 11, Randa and her friends decided to leave the square and head back to their homes. The disappointment was more than they could bear. As they were making their departure, they saw soldiers for the first time. Around 30 to 50 of them, holding rifles, were forming lines on two sides of the square. This time, she sensed, they were alert and not friendly. She felt the soldiers were anticipating that the crowds would turn violent and that they, in turn, were ready to kill. She believes that God bestowed peace upon the demonstrators so that they could keep their precious lives and understand that a spider web was being weaved to trap its prey. Randa is sure that angels were guiding the people to think correctly and avoid this web. Despite the stress and anger, heavenly forces ensured that the masses maintained their clarity of mind. Egyptians have proven their bravery, day after day, their courage and peacefulness. *As Gandhi said, "non-violence requires much more courage than violence."*[38]

Tired and desolate, she had reached her home a little after sunset when her friend Mohamed called, asking about her whereabouts. He had participated in the morning demonstration in Heliopolis, in front of the presidential palace. He told her what happened, and she was baffled, not understanding what he meant, as she had just walked home. She switched on the news and heard the statement by former Vice President, Omar Suleiman, stating that Hosni Mubarak had stepped down and entrusted the Supreme Council for the Armed Forces (SCAF) with the powers to run the country. In her living room, she started jumping with joy and exhilaration. Tayssir, Mohamed and Mazen, a Lebanese friend of Mohamed, who flew to Egypt to support his fellow Egyptian brothers, passed by her home and together they went into the streets to celebrate history. They were holding the Egyptian flag, running, jumping and leaping in the streets, overwhelmed with ecstasy. They returned to Tahrir to join the crowds in the big celebration. Egyptians from all walks of life stood cheering in perfect unity and harmony. It was a sense of uncomparable achievement. She had never witnessed the like in either work or personal achievements. It was phenomenal!

Day 19: The Clean Up

On Saturday February 12, after the extensive celebrations, Randa returned in the afternoon with brooms, gloves and garbage bags to clean the historic square, and could not find one piece of paper or cigarette bud or any garbage on the streets. Volunteers had cleaned up the streets already. She felt disappointed and angry that she did not have the chance to participate in the clean-up process of Tahrir. Many volunteers showed up as early as eight in the morning, and got busy cleaning the streets. It was the best thing ever. This is the Egypt that she had dreamt of living in.

6 Months Later

Randa is unsatisfied with the government compensation policy towards martyrs, as it is stirring discontent among civilians. The government had announced that they would compensate the families of the victims with one thousand five hundred pounds, a little over two hundred dollars; however, they needed to submit proof of relation to the deceased. In reality, this would require the parents to dig out their sons or daughters to get proof, a DNA sample, which would cost them around half of the compensation to dig, move the body to a morgue and run the test. This is not something Islam as a religion takes lightly by any means. Moreover, the financial burden is usually more than the family can afford as they struggle to make ends meet. Many have not been able to claim their rightful dues, though they only represented a symbolic means of support.

Recalling the horrendous police officers who had maimed people for life, Randa broke into tears. The injured were in hospitals with nobody visiting them. She was questioning humanity. Why did the police shoot to maim the demonstrators rather than shoot to kill and leave them their dignity? She was troubled. What was happening? How did she get here? There are missing activists who have disappeared and for the last three or four months their whereabouts have been unknown. She cannot understand how these activists are a national security threat. The police have summoned some of the activists for a couple of hours of interrogation after which they were released. Randa feels threatened, as she knows it could have been her. She has witnessed less fortunate people, who have no access to Facebook or Twitter and have no political inclination, abducted by the police, without any notice, in front of their homes. Their families are clueless. Randa and her fellow activists have saved a pre-written message on their mobiles in case of detainment so they can inform their friends and family who would ultimately make efforts to release them. The less fortunate are not able to plan and do not have the connections to help them in such incidents.

Randa believes that in any society there are fundamentalists, moderates and liberals. In Egypt, the main faiths are Islam and Coptic Christianity. She believes the terrorist acts against the Coptic population, like the New Year 2011 attack on a Church in Alexandria, are a by-product of the decaying regime. It is normal to have extremists in any society and it is a fact-of-life, so to speak. When corruption co-exists with extremism, brutal inhumane acts of terror take place. However, the way the *ancien regime* express themselves is not normal. The old regime's strategy was to instill terror and fear among the Egyptians with these devilish crimes against humanity, which all worldly religions condemn. Randa, naive and gullible, like many others, fell for their trap as she could not fathom how evil politicians' intentions could be and how far they would go to further their interests. *Nobody imagined how far the old regime was willing to go in order to maintain power. The popular saying by nineteenth-century, English historian and moralist, John Acton rings true; "Power tends to corrupt, absolute power corrupts absolutely."*

Randa believes the future is in her hands today. If all Egyptians unite to do something for Egypt today, the future is certainly positive. If people focus on the future without doing anything today, then nothing will change. Practically speaking Mubarak is not gone, as the ruling military is running the country during the transition in the same manner as before the revolution. Much has not changed, though some are different. Randa was driving to work one day and a police officer was standing on the sidewalk of Kasr El Nil Bridge, so she moved her car to the left to avoid him. He stopped her car.

The police officer said, "May you please stick to the right shoulder of the street once you are about to take a right turn. That way you do not disturb the traffic on the left lane.

Randa said, "Thank you. Yes, I will do that," and drove on.

The officer was informing her about the proper traffic rules and she immediately accepted abiding by the rules after that. This is change on a micro level.

One sunny afternoon Randa was walking home from work and two young men were about to harass her on the street, when a man wearing the badge of the revolution, held them by their necks and scolded them for attempting to harass her. She stopped and told the man that through his action he is able to explain to them that what they are doing is morally wrong. These moments were as if touched by an angel. The future starts from today.

After the revolution, Randa quit her marketing job to join the communication campaign of Dr. Baradei. Randa is an avid supporter of Dr. Baradei. She felt she needed to be part of the solution. In hindsight, she believes if Dr. Baradei had run for the elections he probably would have won against Shafik or Morsi, even though polls were not showing support for him post revolution.

One Year Later

In a hundred years, Egypt has witnessed four revolutions, 1919, 1952, 1971 and 2011. History would agree that these are far too many revolutions in two centuries. This phenomenon is mainly due to the silence of the majority of the masses. A better life will not fall upon a people while they are procrastinating. Randa deserves a decent life where, when she calls a plumber to fix her bathroom, she knows that he would fix the faults and demand his just fee and would return if needed. This is basic and yet it does not happen. The plumber comes when he wants to, demands an absurdly inflated fee and, worst of all, he fails to fix the faulty plumbing. She believes this takes place, as the plumber is overlooked. For the past thirty years, the dominating topic was food, and nothing about dignity. But what makes a nation, is people with dignity.

Randa is embittered at the pace of change in Egypt and has witnessed days were she has given up. She believes there is always hope. However, if people do not want to change, then she cannot do anything. She feels as if she is inside the depths of a proverbial tunnel and keeps trying to see the light that is meant to be at the end, but it is in vain. She has lost her zeal, like many others, the dispassion apparent in the voter numbers for the second wave of elections for the *Shura* Council (the upper house of parliament). Randa is one of many who did not vote. In fact, less than ten percent of the population actually participated in the poll. Disappointed at the newly elected parliament members, people have quickly fallen back into complacency and despair.

Randa dreams of a better Egypt and will continue to hope for it. Days pass when she feels defeated, and other days pass when she feels there is still hope. In her view, the revolution has failed in fulfilling bread, freedom, social justice and human dignity, as she had passionately demanded. Matters are worse than before and the power of the people has transformed into a monster. The activists have proven to be incapable of listening to one another, immersed in their own inflated egos and failing to unite forces. Randa has realized that to effect change she needs to work for a party within a true democracy and not via demonstrations. At this political stage in Egypt's life demonstrations will not achieve the revolutionary change demanded. Therefore, she has decided to be part of the change and is one of the founding members of Dostour (Constitution) Party, which Dr. Baradei pioneered.

The nation will not progress when citizens stay immersed in themselves. Randa is an example of a brave woman who has left her comfort zone for the sake of her nation. For things to improve, a miracle is needed, as now she has lost trust in Supreme Council of Armed Forces (SCAF), the Muslim Brotherhood, parliament and even the activists. Since January 2012, Randa has chanted against Mubarak, *Dakhleyah*, SCAF, and *Ikhwan*. She will not rest until her promise to the martyrs, which she made by joining the demonstrations, is fulfilled. She will not rest until her promise of bread, freedom, social justice and human dignity for all Egyptians becomes a reality and not a mere dream. This quest keeps her motivated. *Although on some days Randa has fallen victim to despair, she is still hopeful, with her quest arbitrating her hope. Martin Luther King, Jr. had forewarned, "But revolution, though born in despair, cannot long be sustained by despair…one thing that keeps the fire of revolution burning: the ever-present flame of hope."*[39]

Two Years Plus Later

Randa is still politically active in the Dostour Party. On June 30, 2013, she joined protests again, demanding the end of President Morsi's rule and early presidential elections. On July 3, 2013, Randa was celebrating the ousting of President Morsi. However, when General Sisi requested that Egyptians demonstrate on July 26, 2013 to give the security the green light to deal with terrorisms, she backed down. Why does the army need the go ahead in securing the country when it is their job anyway? She was uncomfortable as it was like giving a blank cheque to the suspicious security state. Egypt is certainly not back to square one, as the Egyptian people have changed. The people elected President Morsi and when he failed to deliver, toppled him within a year in office. This is phenomenal. Randa is optimistic in the long term, as she knows change takes time and she is confident that Egypt will get there. 'We will get there.'

CHAPTER 8

Bold Bravery

"We were men and we stood up like men."
Kona regala we wekefna wakfat regala
Actor Mahmoud El Melegy in movie Al Ard, the Land in 1969.

Tayssir is a friend of my former colleague Zeyad El Tahawy who suggested that I meet Tayssir knowing he had a lot to share. We met for the first time at Cilantro Café on Monday March 28, 2011 right across the street from the old main campus of the American University in Cairo (AUC). It was the closest I had ever gotten to Tahrir after the revolution. It was sunny and he was sitting on the tiny balcony smoking a cigarette and drinking his cappuccino. I was unfashionably late due to the unbelievable traffic, given the traffic police had withdrawn from duty with the wave of hate targeting them.

Tayssir Ibrahim is a handsome young man who prefers having a shaved head, smokes heavily, and usually wears big sunglasses, ones that hide his amazing, big green eyes. He was born in Kuwait on October 14, 1979. Like many members of the modern Egyptian bourgeoisie, he spent most of his childhood as an expatriate while his parents worked abroad for a living. He returned to Egypt when he was nine, and completed his primary and secondary education at the French School Le College de la Sainte Famille. Hoping to diversify his schooling, he pursued his higher education in English at the American University of Cairo, (AUC), majoring in political economy. Hungry for more knowledge, and following the popular trend, he pursued an MBA at Heriot-Watt University from Cairo. Like many of the urban elite, he has worked in hybrid multi-national companies and ventured into banking. His work has led him to live in the Middle East for a while, and he returned to Egypt a few years ago. Recently, he ventured to create his own business, renewing kiosks. He is a well-educated, cosmopolitan, tri-lingual man who is conscious of all the issues his country is mired in and was willing and brave enough to do something about it.

Day 1: Defying the Police Day

January 25 is a public holiday celebrating police in Egypt, a practise starting three years prior to the 2011 revolution. Over the years, the police lost their standing and became extremely unpopular among civilians, including Tayssir. This has happened mainly due to certain policies and practices, such as torture and wrongful incrimination. Activist Aida Seif El Dawla justified why people took to the streets on this particular day: "People went down on the 25th on the Day of Police to defy the police and to reject police policies."[40] Tayssir, like thousands of others, received the invitation on Facebook to join protestors on January 25 at Tahrir. Initially he thought it was a prank. Several bloggers sent out invitations on the internet calling for demonstrations either in the form of videos on You Tube or as invitations to an event on Facebook. The youth managed to initiate the impetus that snowballed from there. Tayssir was just one person within this overpowering energy. It is true that this Egyptian revolution lacked and still lacks a leader; however, the youth beautifully orchestrated it with a vision. *This is close to what Gandhi meant when he said, "Civil disobedience, once properly launched needs no leaders,"[41] and the Egyptian protests may possibly be an example of such 'civil disobedience' though others may disagree.* The night before the revolution, there were calls warning people against joining the demonstrations. Heedless, Tayssir went to Midan alTahrir (Tahrir Square) early on the morning of Tuesday, January 25 and found it empty. He next went to Mohandeseen, which he also found deserted. He waited for a little while, smoking cigarettes in the warm sunny winter morning. Tayssir was feeling slightly agitated, not knowing what to expect. Would it end up like the past as he had seen on television, just meek and small numbers? Would this time be different?

As the hours passed, the numbers increased to a couple of hundreds, then five hundred, then thousands of protestors. Tayssir was overwhelmed with a sense of pride and awe witnessing all these brave men and women boldly defying the police on their day. An unprecedented, mega statement was actually happening. Tayssir realized that hordes of more people were heading downtown and decided to join them. He walked past the *Amn Eldawla* (State Security) building at Batal Ahmed Abdel-Aziz Street, making his way through Dokki Square, all the way to Tahrir Street. He joined others in chanting: "*Eish, horeya, we karama ensaneya*" (Bread, freedom and human dignity). Tayssir was very gratified that the demonstration was peaceful, without clashes with the police, just as Gandhi had preached.

The police stopped Tayssir and others at Dokki Square. They were standing side by side, a black-clad human barrier, wearing helmets and carrying rods and shields, a force to reckon with. They were daunting but humane. After a short while, they allowed Tayssir to move on towards the heart of Cairo, towards Tahrir. Tayssir was glad to notice that the police were showing respect towards the demonstrators at the onset of the revolution. Within a couple of hours, he arrived at the city center. He underestimated the masses to be around 10,000 when he arrived at Tahrir square. As per the media, they were five times that number, estimated at around 50,000. Initially, before the violence erupted, Tayssir thought that people were just joining to say 'No' and at nightfall they would all return to their homes. But at some point, he realized that this demonstration was very serious. A realization that the police also came to, and to which they reacted by using force. This was no joke! A fire engine started to spray water on the demonstrators in an attempt to disperse the thickening crowds. The police strengthened their offensive by surrounding the square and firing tear gas bombs at the masses in all the streets leading to the square, Midan alTahrir.

Subsequently demonstrators, among them Tayssir, decided to stay in Midan alTahrir, objecting to the harsh police crackdown on the peaceful protest. The first evening at Tahrir was probably the best; people sang, or recited poetry or the *Quran* and charitable people brought food and water to the square. By nightfall, the chants merged into one rallying cry: *"Elshaab yoreed eskat el nezam!"* (The people want the downfall of the regime!). They were relentless and the persistent cries were like those of a deprived wolf howling and crying watching an older, experienced wolf enjoying his prey whilst he, uninvited and unwanted, watches on with frustration, envy and hunger. His life is cursed with discomfort, as nobody ever taught him how to catch his own prey, and struggles with his bad luck.

The bitter cold blanketed the night, but Tayssir and the crowds were not driven away, despite being unprepared for the finger- and foot-freezing weather. After midnight, reinforcements came from the State Security. They were moving into the roundabout from the peripheral streets, closing in on the protestors like hunters pursuing their prey. They persisted in their aggressive strategy, firing tear gas bombs into the masses. In response, those on the receiving end defiantly approached the police while trying to avoid the gas. The police began firing rubber bullets at the protestors for the first time. People tried to evade the bullets and were forced to retreat to the center of the square, bombarded by tear gas. It was all overwhelming! Tayssir was suffocating from the cloud of smoke, struggling to breathe while coughing persistently. His eyes were burning, and he couldn't see properly. The 20,000 or so people around him were experiencing the same symptoms, keeping their eyes shut from the stinging gas. Some people fainted, others broke down in tears. Some were trampled on, and others were bravely ready and willing to die. A few unfortunately did. The most vulnerable were those who had respiratory or heart conditions. During those moments, Tayssir was thinking that this day was indeed different. "This was no demonstration; it was a revolution."

Tayssir never imagined that one day anyone would fire a weapon at him, or that he would stand up against it, tall and brave. Fear, confusion, shock, panic, anxiety, hurt, betrayal and sadness were among the numerous feelings that filled the air enveloping Tahrir, along with the burning sensation caused by the chemical compounds in the tear gas. Amidst all this emotion and turmoil, Tayssir fell down, hurting his leg and limped towards the Egyptian museum. If he had stayed on the ground, he would have probably died. When he fell, he saw something that he will never forget: an old man wearing a white *galabeya* (traditional robe), sitting in a wheel chair. The old man could not see anything because of the stifling smoke from the gas, nor could he move with all the commotion engulfing him. Tayssir heard him say the *shahada* (there is no God but God and Mohamed is his prophet) and then he covered his face with a towel in surrender to *Allah*, as he was about to die.

Tayssir did not flinch in the face of death, but anger was building up inside him. He walked within the vicinity of the museum, where he saw suspicious-looking empty buses. One man with a stick was beckoning him to get on the bus, calling him "My son…my son." Instinctively, he decided to pretend to be vomiting behind a wall, suspecting a set up by regime-paid *baltegeya* (thugs). Luckily, he did not fall into their trap, and got away. Shortly afterwards he hailed a taxi and left for home. Skirmishes took place in many of the side streets leading to Midan alTahrir. He heard about another group that police pursued from Talat Harb Street all the way to the Azhar tunnel.

When he got home, he checked the RNN news channel; much to his relief, it stated that people were gathering at Ramsis to return to Tahrir. The police had not been able to suppress the movement. After this pivotal first day, protestors took to marching in groups of around two dozen to stay protected and avoid arrest. Tayssir tossed and turned throughout this first night, recalling the danger he faced, the pandemonium, the rollercoaster of emotions and the death he saw. Guilt kept him awake - he had not been able to save the old man, for he had barely been able to save himself.

Day 4: Tide of Rage

Friday January 28 was declared the 'Friday of Anger'. Tayssir, like everyone else in Tahrir, was infuriated by the police offensive during the preceding days, and was unwilling to be silenced by anyone. This time he went prepared for the tear gas. He had masks, Pepsi, vinegar, onions, and water on him to limit the side effects. Tayssir, a diabetic, also brought his medicine and food to sustain him through this long and arduous day. At noon, he prayed in Mostafa Mahmoud Mosque in Mohandseen – by then there were around 5,000 demonstrators. The mood was uncertain, tense and unknowing, as the government, in the early morning hours, had switched off all modern forms of communication. There was no mobile communication and no internet connection. Egypt switched back into the dark ages just by disconnecting a few wires. The *ancien regime* was attempting to cripple the movement by severing their communication lines. A simple tactic led to an unequivocal, resonating backlash. Tayssir and millions of Egyptians became more determined than ever to get their rights and dignity back.

Tayssir then made his way to Dokki Square, where he and others were targets of volleys of tear gas canisters for nearly two hours. Nonetheless, Tayssir along with the other activists, managed to move on and reach Kasr El Nil Bridge, traversing it after a struggle with the police. At the last section of the bridge, the protestors halted for the afternoon prayer, and shockingly, the police drenched them with water hoses mid-prayer. It felt as if it had rained heavily on them. This heathen act was a disgrace that provoked the people into persevering and advancing onwards. Absolutely nothing was going to stop them. After the prayers, the skirmishes escalated into brutal assaults. The bridge was packed, and once the police started firing, people started retreating. Panic ensued and it was disastrous. The sheer numbers of people running on the narrow bridge, pushed some over the sides and into the Nile River. Others hung on to the bridge rails for dear life, and many more were trampled upon.

The police were despicable and inhumane as they aimed their guns at people's faces, especially the eyes. They could have aimed for the legs or the arms but they did not, they aimed to kill or maim. They might have assumed that their brutality would scare people back to the safety of their homes, but they were very much mistaken in their assumption. Witnessing such brutal atrocities and injustices did not arouse fear; on the contrary, it overcame fear and transformed into a greater resolve. This horror did not lead to retreat; rather, it led to a strong will to advance. In fact, after these cruel events, the protesters succeeded in pushing through until they joined the main demonstration at Midan alTahrir. *This watershed victory by the protestors reflected Gandhi's idea when he said, "I can boldly declare and with certainty that so long as there is even a handful of men true to their pledge, there can be only one end to the struggle – and that is victory."*[42]

He Was Targeted

Tayssir, for the first time in his life, saw an immense amount of bloodshed. There was a man standing beside him, one second, whole and well, and the next second a fountain of blood spurting from his eye. He had been shot. Tayssir tried to stop the bleeding with whatever he had at hand, getting his hands and clothes stained with this stranger's blood in the process. He will never forget the rusty, stinging smell of blood. He looked around him and saw blood, shock, anger, fear but also a contagious resolve, enforced by the sheer number of people there. The injured were not walking away. The crowds were carrying them. Eventually the crowds separated him from the wounded man. After around half an hour of battle, the masses retreated to the square facing the Opera House. Some people returned to Dokki and some made their way through Zamalek. This is where Tayssir, as he was walking away, took a bullet in his left calf. Only a coward shoots a man who is walking away from behind, especially one who is unarmed. The rubber bullet caused minor bleeding, and paralyzed his leg temporarily, making him unable to walk on it. Fortunately, he came across Zeyad El Tahawy (*our mutual friend*) whom he was able to lean on.

The quiet, empty streets of Zamalek, made it seem like a ghost city. Upon reaching 15 May Bridge Tayssir discovered another battle, smaller in scale. Across the Nile, he could see yet another clash on the riverbank, the Corniche next to the building that houses Al Ahly Bank. When he heard the minarets calling for the sunset prayers, he and Zeyad prayed, below the bridge in Zamalek. After prayer, Tayssir looked for a pharmacy as his leg was swelling up, but in vain, as most pharmacies and in general, all shops were closed. This is when he parted from Zeyad and crossed paths with Ahmed, his cousin's fiancé, whom Tayssir leaned on for the remainder of the day and until late at night.

While he was walking along the Nile bank in front of the *Nadi El Ahly* (Al Ahly Sporting Club) he met an old colleague from a company he worked for in Dubai, Randa Haggag *(featured in chapter 7)*. Tayssir had not seen her in over a year and was in awe with the coincidence. *I was surprised to realize he knows my friend Randa who inspired and encouraged me to write this book, it truly is a small world.*
Randa said, "Hi Tayssir, what happened to your leg?"
Tayssir replied, "While I was in front of the new Opera house, I got shot from behind."
Concerned, Randa asked, "Does it hurt?"
Tayssir replied, "Not really, it feels numb. I cannot really walk on it. Earlier I bumped into another friend who I have leaned on for many hours."
Randa said, "What is happening is crazy. I have seen enough for the day and am beyond exhausted. I will go home, rest and recharge."
Tayssir replied, "Ok, stay safe Randa. It is great seeing you."
Randa smiled her radiant smile. "You too. Stay safe Tayssir."

Tayssir returned to the bridge and could not find anyone there. He heard they had left to Mohandseen, so he decided to head there as well. Tayssir was baffled. It seemed to be another city a few hours ago, with intense clashes, and suddenly there was almost nobody.
Tayssir asked, "What happened? Where is everybody?" And a pedestrian replied, "It seems the police have withdrawn and so have the protestors."

Little did he know that the police had actually withdrawn not just from the streets of Cairo, but most of Egypt.

He walked past the Opera House, making his way to Galaa Bridge. Men and women were coming down from their homes with their children. They were saying that the police had withdrawn and Tahrir Square was now the people's square. When Tayssir returned to Tahrir, he discovered that the National Democratic Party's, NDP, building was unexpectedly an inferno. Under the Kasr El Nil Bridge, thieves were carrying the safe of Ahmed Ezz, former leading member of the NDP and business tycoon. One man was stamping the hands of passersby's with Ezz's stamp. The looting men took out knives and fought over who would take the safe. It was surreal, like watching a medieval sword battle over a treasure. No doubt, people had been injured, if not killed in the process. It appeared that the people who had broken into the party's headquarters were not the same as the revolutionaries. They were calling people to join them in burning the building. They called Tayssir and, after giving him a thorough once-over, let him go, recruiting other people, who appeared like thugs instead.

Chaos Ensued

It suddenly dawned on Tayssir that there was a serious breach of security in the city, and perhaps throughout the country. He heard that the army had mobilized but nobody understood what was really happening. People were saying, "Suez is burning." Some even started a rumor that "Suez has declared its independence." It was complete chaos. Tayssir went into the square to look for his friends but found a battle underway instead. People were hiding in the side streets. His leg hurt and he felt powerless and vulnerable. *Shabab* (youngsters) were driving police cars and had confiscated tear gas canisters and guns. The mob wanted to storm the ministry of interior building, demanding the removal of Habib El Adly, its minister at the time. Tayssir decided to stay outside the building, as he was unable to walk with the excruciating pain in his leg, let alone run. He sat for a while next to the mosque, where they were bringing in all the bodies and using it as a makeshift morgue. He swallowed his pain and while keeping an eye out for his friends, seemingly in vain, he somehow mustered the energy to help the wounded. Tayssir saw people set two police vans on fire. The first floor of the huge bureaucratic building called *Mogamaa* was on fire from the tear gas the police fired in an attempt to frame the demonstrators as outlaws. Machine gun fire and gunshots were heard through the windows. A mosque on a nearby side street was transformed into a hospital treating the injured victims of the revolution. He saw four bodies at the hospital. Tayssir was disconcerted. He wanted a better Egypt but did there have to be bloodshed? *Machiavelli once said, "Nobody should start a revolution in a city in the belief that later he can stop it at will or regulate it as he likes."*[43] *The revolution in Egypt was unstoppable and nobody knew what would unfold.*

In the evening, the streets were alive and full of angry men. Some of the men swarming the streets had either revenge or hooliganism on their minds. It was not justified by any means. There were also revolutionaries who were outraged by the bloodshed, violence and death. They wanted to punish the minister of interior whose hands were stained with the blood of all the innocent martyrs, shot dead in the streets during the previous three horrendous days. That night civilian checkpoints were set up on most streets to fill in the void left by the abrupt withdrawal of corrupt police. At Tahrir the people welcomed an army vehicle at 9 pm, only to realize that it was loaded with ammunition: tear gas canisters and rubber bullets. This meant that the army was dispatched to reinforce or replace the police, who had mysteriously disappeared. Tayssir saw people confiscating the vehicle and its ammunition and setting it on fire. By this time, he could no longer feel his wounded, numb leg. Fortunately, he met his friend Omar, he bid goodnight to Ahmed, another friend, and they each headed home. Tayssir and Omar took a taxi and along the way, they saw several army tanks heading into Tahrir. When the people felt assured that the army was not going to fire on its own civilians, they resumed their protest in Tahrir square.

Day 5: Out of Touch

On Saturday January 29, Tayssir attentively watched and listened to the television from the safety of his home. The then President Hosni Mubarak made his first speech addressing the revolution. He announced that the government had resigned and, for the first time in thirty years, he appointed a vice president, Omar Suleiman, previously the Head of Intelligence. He also appointed Ahmed Shafik, former minister of Civil Aviation, as Prime Minister. These were his mediocre attempts to placate the people. As had been characteristic of the unpopular regime, Tayssir believed it was too little, too late. He was angry at Mubarak's complete dissociation from his people, as if he was living in another country, another world for that matter. It was typical of the phenomenon known as 'dictator's solitude'.

Machiavelli had a perfect explanation for Mubarak's disconnection with the people: "Being on the spot, one can detect trouble at the start and deal with it immediately, if one is absent, it is discerned only when it has grown serious and it is then too late."[44] His detachment had started years before the revolution. Political activist Amr Hamazawy said, "After 2005, Mubarak started to lose track of what was going on in Egypt. He distanced himself from the population."[45] Mubarak had left his people behind.

Day 6: Hyde Park

On Sunday January 30, Coptic Egyptians held mass in commemoration of the fallen martyrs. Tayssir and all the activists were mourning and felt solemn at the loss of human life. Despite the solemnness, Tayssir was overjoyed at the spectacular sight of all the people cleaning the square before the mass. They organized themselves into checkpoints at the entrances of the square in order to check the personal IDs of those wanting to come in, as a safety measure. The *Ikhwan* (Muslim Brotherhood) officially appeared then and helped in organizing Tahrir. They organized a station for the blankets (as nights were getting colder), another station for medical supplies and yet another for the food. Doctors, who had only come to drop off medication, wounded up volunteering and stayed for the remainder of the eighteen days, attending to the victims. They could not leave after seeing the extent of the wounds. These doctors proved to be brave, patriotic men and women.

The overall feeling in Tahrir was that of euphoria, the kind that only freedom can inspire, and you could sense the power of a united people in the air. Tayssir compared it to being in Hyde Park; it felt like a forum or an open political debate. People stood up on the stage erected in the *Midan* and expressed their views without criticism or shouting. They were ready to die for their country and for their freedom. It had started as a dream and had turned into a destiny...the *rayees* (president) will go. The second speech by President Mubarak worried Tayssir, but he was willing to give the *rayees* the benefit of the doubt and a one-month grace period to address the legitimate demands of the people.

At Tivoli, a restaurant and café complex at Heliopolis, Tayssir met some of his friends to discuss the issue and decide upon which course of action to take. The majority did not want to accept the former president's concessions and were determined that he must leave. What surprised Tayssir the most was that average Egyptians, the uneducated and poor, were more shrewdly skeptical of the political rhetoric than the more educated urban elite, who argued that Mubarak had earned some measure of tolerance.

After this day, Tayssir's leg had developed an infection from the rubber bullet. His doctor asked him to rest completely for two days and while he rested at home, his friends witnessed a real war.

Day 9: The Attack
On Wednesday February 2, after the former President's conciliatory speech, rumor had it that the ruling party sent their men on camels and horses to beat and kill the protestors in Tahrir. It was a scene of war from the nineteenth century. Tayssir could not reach his friends and he was very restless those two days while he recovered at home. He watched the news channels throughout the night, unable and unwilling to sleep. He heard the *Ikhwan* had saved protestors' lives. They displayed strong faith and willingness to die for a cause, *Jihad*. Their resolve was unshaken. They organized the square by placing fences and barriers. Their strategy was to throw stones and then retreat, and they generally gave very good advice to withstand the attacks. He was

told about a brave woman that day wearing a black *abaya* (loose robes) and *hijab* who passed by all the entrances of the square with a bottle of water and a glass, quenching the thirst of those on the front lines.

The woman said, "Drink some water," offering Tayssir's friend, Mohamed, a glass of water.
Mohamed said, "*Ya Haga (Haga is the term used to address a woman who went on a pligirmage to Mecca)* thank you but you should return to the safety of your home," and he drank the water.
The woman explained, "How can I go back home after I lost my son! At least here I feel closer to him, may he rest in peace. I might be fortunate and God will remember me too so that I may join my son in heaven" Tears welled in her eyes.
Mohamed said, "May God grant you patience and justice will be rendered, you will see." She moved on to the next man serving him water. Losing her son, she felt there was nothing left for her. She was not scared; her bravery gave the men and women strength to keep going. *Fischer once said about Guevara: "Che was utterly fearless of death."*[46] *In Egypt, women and men of all ages had demonstrated this bold fearlessness.*

Mohamed saw girls hit on their faces by rocks retreat to place a bandage and return to the battlefield, unshaken by their injuries. These acts of courage by heroines certainly empowered them all into continuing the battle and eventually prevailing. The attackers were not willing to die. Once one of them got hurt he would run away like a coward. They were not fighting for a cause and therefore lacked the solid resolve and will of those who were. The day of the camel and horse attack, his friend Mohamed and Randa Haggag told Tayssir, an F16 fighter jet flew over the square. People were wary of the army as the minister of defense, Field Marshal Tantawi, was an old friend of President Mubarak. The army officers were all talking at that time, as they had allegedly gotten orders to attack Midan alTahrir. However, they had decided to disobey.

Maged Boulos, a Coptic army official, was watching the battle and suddenly broke into tears and started firing his gun at the supporters of President Mubarak, killing them, and yet saving many lives. It was at that moment that the demonstrators understood that the army was with the people. They chanted *"Al Geish wel elshaab eed wahda"* meaning, "The army and the people are one hand." One of the tanks was facing the people, so they asked the soldier to turn it around, and he complied. *The former Ambassador to the United States, Nabil Fahmy said, "The minute the army went down in the streets, the government lost control. Let me re-phrase that, the minute the army hit the street, it was clear that the demonstrators had won, because the Egyptian army does not shoot at Egyptian civilians. It has never done that and it's code of honor is that it will not"*[47] However, post those eighteen days, there were incidents when the army

150

did shoot at civilians, as was the case at Maspero in October 2011, whether provoked or following orders, time will tell.

Day 10: Invincible

Tayssir re-joined his friends on Thursday February 3 after the appalling so-called Camel Attack. He felt ashamed that he had not been there, side-by-side with his compatriots. Tayssir was overwhelmed and humbled when he saw the people welcoming any newcomers that were coming to help. Their gratitude was genuine and deeply moving. They were saying "Here are the men" and "Here are the Egyptians." at the entrance. Spirits were high. Tayssir saw local musicians playing guitars and singing patriotic songs. It was definitely contagious. Their soul was ecstatic, a feeling that actually gave him goose bumps and made him cry. He kissed all of their heads, thanking them for their bold courage and perseverance. They are brave heroes that history will remember. At the exit, they chanted, "We are waiting for you tomorrow".

Tayssir realized that the numbers increased in Tahrir, not just during the weekend but also on weekdays. People brought changes of clothes, placed them in their tents, and were willing to spend months in protest until President Mubarak left. Some were lucky to have friends allowing them to use their apartments in the vicinity. They expected to stay for months until the *rayees* resigned, as they were comparing the situation to that of Tunisia's former President Zine El-Abidine Ben Ali who had withstood for one whole month before fleeing. To their thinking, this meant Mubarak would take longer.

The week of endurance commenced and nothing happened. On the contrary, the newly appointed prime minister, Ahmed Shafik, was talking about the youth in a condescending tone, denying that this was a revolution and saying it was merely a demonstration. Shafik's tone and statements infuriated Tayssir. He underestimated the power of the 'movement'. The revolutionaries felt the need to escalate the pressure on the regime by calling for a million-man-march to the government ministries and institutions. However, many did not welcome this suggestion and so they continued with the sit-in at Tahrir square and reportedly on some days, the number of demonstrators reached the millions. When the banks reopened, Tayssir would go to work until 2pm, after which he rejoined his friends in Tahrir for the remainder of the day.

Tayssir once mingled for a couple of hours with a man who turned out to be a pickpocket. He had stopped stealing during the revolution, believing that the people were writing history with this great revolution, which would bring providence. Because of that, he was not tempted to pick up any of the handbags lying all over the square. He had promised not to pick pocket until President Mubarak left!

Another time he talked to a long bearded man from the *Salafists*, a radical hard line Islamic group. Tayssir offered him a cigarette.

The *Salafist said*, "If you had offered me a cigarette two months earlier, I would have gotten up and left. But today things are different." He waved his hand politely declining.

Tayssir said, "We are all brothers and sisters and we respect and tolerate our differences."

Agreeing, the *Salafist* said, "I am very keen on seeing changes in our beloved Egypt. We need a good leader and president."

Tayssir replied, "Me too. Who do you think would be a good president?"

The *Salafist* said, "I would like to see Bin Laden as the president of Egypt!"

Tayssir taken aback, said, "I would tend to disagree with you. I would like to see Dr. Mohamed El Baradei come as president."

The *Salafist* replied, "I will disagree with you, he is an American agent. But let us focus now on getting Mubarak out and worry about who will come later when the time comes."

This conversation prophesied what actually took place after Mubarak abdicated. There was much discord among the different parties.

Day 17: Anticipation

Anticipation peaked on Thursday February 10 as the army announced that their first statement would be aired shortly, proclaiming that the demands of the people would be met. Tayssir, surveying the activists, sensed and saw high, excited, winning spirits all around him. Meanwhile, international news channels announced that former President Hosni Mubarak was going to resign. Tayssir saw a man in a group behind him who had brought a cake and candles expecting to celebrate the great victory. After the build-up, President Mubarak's speech was a big letdown to say the least. The president's speech did not have the tone of a resignation, but rather filled with self-righteous expressions such as, "we will do" and "Hosni Mubarak did this... and that..." Not surprisingly, when the speech was over, the man with the cake threw it in the garbage. Tayssir cried, as did several men and women. The weight of disappointment was unbearable, to the extent that some people's breathing became strained and heavy. It was as if a thick black cloud had settled above the city, hiding the moon and all the stars. It was a very dark moment.

Prospects were gloomy and the mood was thick with with a feeling of suffocation. Some people had fainted after the speech and some were admitted to hospitals. Many were hysterically running and crying in an attempt to deal with the ugly dire reality. Despair was widespread until Tayssir heard people calling for a march to the presidential palace. Tayssir was chain smoking, inhaling the smoke deeply into his lungs and strongly breathing it out, in a small futile attempt at relaxation. He predicted the presidential guards were surely not going to be peaceful if the activists stormed the palace.

Tayssir joined protestors heading to Maspero, where the national state TV building was located and, surprisingly, the army did not hinder them, allowing them to enter and walk in the corridors. It seemed that the soldiers understood their frustration and their need to vent, so they permitted them access to the building in this exceptional situation. The soldiers were distributing their water and biscuits to the people in a gesture of solace, like a mother soothing her child with candy after getting hurt. The masses had come to a verdict: on that Friday President Mubarak would resign, so they chanted this rhyme *"bokra el aasr hankharogo men el asr"* which means "Tomorrow in the afternoon we will evict him from the palace."

Day 18: They Won
On the celebrated Friday February 11, 2011, Tayssir, headed to the presidential palace after noon prayers. Astonishingly, the Presidential Guards treated them with respect, stopping cars in the street for them to cross and handing them water. He had been mistaken in thinking that they would kill the protestors. He saw three helicopters land at the Palace and instantly assumed that the former President was running away. Tayssir's mother had gone to Tahrir with her friends and needed him to return her home. So he headed to Tahrir where he met his mother. After dropping her off, he saw the historic announcement by the Vice President Omar Suleiman who solemnly declared that President Hosni Mubarak had decided to step down and pass all presidential powers to the Supreme Council of the Armed Forces, SCAF. That was a climax!

Tayssir could not believe his ears, so he went to Tahrir to see the interpretations of and reactions to the announcement. The mood was joyous, everyone was smiling and crying. It was a huge celebration with men, women and children going into the streets, proudly waving the Egyptian flag. Overtaken with joy, Tayssir turned around and hugged several strangers, fellow compatriots. He met his friends from the revolution, friends with whom he still feels very close after sharing such unforgettable, testing moments. They were ecstatic having successfully passed through a crisis together and were forever bound to each other.

Friday February 11, 2011 was marked as a day of celebration and the activists agreed that they would not return to Tahrir, as they needed to give the new government a chance. A month later he realized it was the biggest mistake the protestors made, leaving Tahrir too early after the military forcibly emptied the sit in.

Two Months Later

Tayssir's driver, Arafa, turned into a friend; Arafa attends lectures and seminars with him and sometimes attends on Tayssir's behalf if two overlap in time. Arafa diligently debriefs Tayssir later. Arafa was a *Salafist* with a good understanding of politics, better than Tayssir himself. *Amn Eldawla* detained Arafa due to his beard and participation in meetings, after which he decided to shave his beard and stay away from any activity, to avoid any more trouble. Tayssir learned that education is unrelated to political understanding, and he can now talk with Arafa about current affairs more than he could with his regular friends. Under normal circumstances, he would not have politically heated debates, but the revolution paved that road. Tayssir truly respects Arafa's thinking. They both agreed that the whole regime must go, not just President Mubarak, for he was just the tip of the iceberg. Now they had to focus on melting the entire iceberg. Tayssir did not feel safe with the regime still in power, despite the fact that the *rayees* had stepped down, as he had heard that some revolutionaries were arrested at that time and others had simply disappeared.

The police actually believed their own lies that the activists were spies. Tayssir did not notice anyone suspicious at Tahrir. At the same time, he cannot say whether these claims were sound or not. The police who were convinced of their spy accusation beat up one man, Ramy, among others. Tayssir had met Ramy, a singer, on the first day of the revolution and noticed that he liked to take a slogan and write lyrics to match it. Ramy became very popular in Midan alTahrir. Police detained and brutally beat Ramy, the peaceful revolution's singer. After Mubarak had stepped down the activists were interrogated by the police with the latter slowly starting to believe that they were acting as brave patriots and not alleged spies. They would blindfold activists, question them for a few hours and then release them. When Hilary Clinton, U.S. Secretary of State, wanted to meet the revolutionaries, they refused, as they did not have and did not want to have external relations. Another reason stated for that refusal, was that Clinton had initially undermined the revolution by saying "the Egyptian government is stable".

The focus of the activists was now on Prime Minister Ahmed Shafik, and his government. Tayssir personally vouched for the fact that Shafik was as corrupt and crooked as the suspects in Tora prison were. Rampant corruption tainted the airport institute. Tayssir's friend was the project manager of the bid to rebuild the airport and witnessed bribes paid under the table that ultimately and sadly led his friend to flee the country in despair, seeking a decent, moral and ethical country to live in. Eventually, the Supreme Council of the Armed Forces reputedly asked Shafik to submit his resignation. This was right after a humiliating broadcast talk show with novelist, Alaa Al Aswany, author of *The Yacoubian Building*, in which he bombarded the prime minister with accusations that Shafik failed in responding to, let alone in defending his position. Tayssir recalls it well.

Tayssir, at the time, trusted the army, as he believed that they were trying to play it right, but at the same time, were not on the side of the youth. The senior officials who did not object to the old *nizam* climbed the ladder of seniority, whereas those who opposed it did not. One clear example of the former is Field Marshal Tantawi. The whole regime was corrupt and the army was part of the regime, but Tayssir did not believe that they were all corrupt. Not all the apples are rotten. The army and the people are on the same wave length but the Supreme Council of the Armed Forces, SCAF, expectedly, lacks training to administer and run a country. Such a task is outside its military curriculum. Their role is to defend the nation. The masses chanted *"al gheish wel shaab eid wahda,"* which means "the people and the army are one hand," not out of love but out of political savviness and social shrewdness. The army is playing friends with the people and in turn, the people are playing friends with the army. The revolutionaries would definitely join the soldiers had they initiated a military coup against Generalissimo Tantawi to protect the integrity of the revolution, but that seemed highly unlikely. For the time being, as long as the army was delivering on the demands of the revolution, any sort of reasoning was not necessary. But with the passing months, Tayssir realized that the army's intentions were not as he had initially thought, as the army intended to stay above the law. *The road ahead for Egypt is not straight, as freedom does not come free. As India's former, Prime Minister Nehru said in the title speech after independence in 1953, "There is no easy walk to freedom."*

Tayssir went home, back to his normal life but with one major difference: his initiation into political activism. He arranged meetings and organized activists with different groups; he attended brainstorming sessions, lectures and seminars. Tayssir feels that Egypt will truly change, as there is a newborn spirit of ownership and freedom. He mingled and got involved with his driver, Arafa, and people from low-income area of Sayeda Zeinab in the city center and was glad to discover their level of political awareness. This was more so than his friends, who unfortunately are tainted by classism and an elitist upbringing, making them focused on the details and sometimes losing sight of the big picture. On the other hand, the average people he met on the streets were very aware of the big issues; they realized that the *ancien regime* had fooled them for thirty years. They know exactly what they want and they know how to get it quickly. An example of this was seen in the video clip of a baker who explained why the revolution took place with overwhelming clarity. He portrayed the *ancien regime* as a cancer and not a snake wherein cutting of the head of the snake was not sufficient. The cancer needs complete cleansing from the heavily manned public service; it was not enough to remove the President, dissolve the parliament and change the government, as the cancer is in the complete political body. He explained why former Prime Minister Shafik needed to resign, as succeeding in renovating an airport simply does not qualify him to preside over a nation. People referred to him as the *'alkhabaz al faseeh'* (the articulate baker)[48].

Tayssir believes that if one truly wants to change his country then he needs to go down on the streets and enlighten the people. The March 2011 referendum was a big shock for all the Facebook lobbyists. It was as if a lightning bolt had struck a house, a quick, much needed reality check to get them back on course that made it very apparent that the campaigning needed to be on the ground and in the governorates, not just in Cairo.

Tayssir joined the Justice Party led by Mostafa El Nagar as he felt aligned with its agenda. He was an active campaigner prior to the parliamentary elections and his candidate actually won the elections. Tayssir even allowed the Justice Party temporarily use his vacant apartment, to serve as the party's headquarters. He later left them to join Dr. Baradei's *Hezb ElDostour*. Dr. Baradei was the person who inspired Tayssir to join the world of politics. When Dr. Baradei resigned from the post of vice president in the summer of 2013 Tayssir was disappointed but not surprised, as he knows Dr. Baradei would not accept the violence and repression of civilians.

Post-revolution, Tayssir feels worthy of something great and he feels free. One now has the freedom to talk about politics with anyone. One can search for a suitable political party. Previously these were dreams and not realities. From a religious angle, Muslims and Christians in Egypt have never suffered from divisions, and Tayssir is confident that this will never be a serious issue as it is in other Arab states. Sectarian strife was the stick that the *ancien regime* used to distract and silence people from talking about the real issues.

A year and a half before the revolution, Dr. Mohamed El Baradei, diplomat and former Director General of the International Atomic Energy Agency, IAEA, said in an interview that he would not run for presidency until the constitution changes. Back then people would have considered him a dreamer, but now his dream has become a brief reality. For Tayssir, El Baradei is a man with a vision. Tayssir foresees a bright future for Egypt and feels that the sky is the limit. Tayssir has a dream too; his dream is that in five years' time Egypt will surpass the United Arab Emirates, UAE in terms of development, efficiency and opportunities. He is sure that there is no going back; it is like a new-born-child who can never re-enter its mother's womb. Tayssir believes that after tasting this feeling of worth and freedom no one can deny us again.

The American President Barack Obama's speech after Mubarak stepped down moved Tayssir, when he said, "we saw a new generation emerge." He also quoted an Egyptian: "Most people have discovered in the last few days that they are worth something and this cannot be taken away from them anymore, ever. This is the power of human dignity and it can never be denied…The word Tahrir means liberation.

That is a word that speaks to something in our souls that cries out for freedom and forevermore will remind us of the Egyptian people, of what they did, of the things that they stood for, and how they changed their country and in doing so changed the world."

One Year Later: Square One

Tayssir is sure that the fear barrier has been broken. Like many, he was mistaken in thinking that the revolution would be a straightforward road, as disappointingly, it has turned out to be winding and full of detours. Now, in the current state, things are back to square one, but this year, Tayssir is still active in politics and has hopes that the revolution will eventually succeed. One decisive factor will be the outcome of the presidential elections scheduled for June 2012. He was among many Egyptians who voted for Mohamed Morsi, as he did not want any person from the *ancien regime* to rule again. The election came and went and Tayssir was grateful that Ahmed Shafik lost the run-off, as it would have been a clear victory for the counter-revolution. He was actually dismayed with the polarity of the choices voters faced during the run-off. Ahmed Shafik, the former Prime Minister and Mohamed Morsi, the head of the Muslim Brotherhood. For a while, Tayssir felt that the revolution had died with the run-off in the presidential elections and the whole point of the uprising was lost in the debris. However, shortly afterwards he was adamant that the revolution had not failed but had been stolen by parties for their own self-interests; parties like, *Ikhwan* (Muslim Brotherhood), *Salafist* and Supreme Council of the Armed Forces, SCAF.

Randa Haggag, the old friend that Tayssir bumped into in *Zamalek*, and he have become closer friends because of Tahrir, socializing together and working on the Presidential Campaign of Dr. Baradei. They are currently both members of AlDostour Party, which Dr. Baradei founded working at the grassroots level in order to gain support and win the next elections. Tayssir has realized that the time of demonstrations is over and it is now time for him to work on the streets addressing the country's most pressing issues. He believes that the Muslim Brotherhood, *Ikhwan,* are incapable of leading the country and have proven repeatedly to be incompetent. He was working with them, however, to try and uplift the state of affairs, as he felt Egyptians are all in one boat and need to work together to keep it afloat. President Morsi won the elections fair and square; a democrat respects the winner and works with the winner for the benefit of the nation and not against him or her to the detriment of affairs. Tayssir does not believe that *Ikhwan* are the enemy, as they are not the *ancien regime.* However, he knows that they have struck deals with the *ancien regime.* He does not believe that Egypt will fall back into the dark ages as many Egyptians fear, under the steering of the *Ikhwan.* However, under President Morsi's rule, he feared the looming dark ages.

Over Two Years Later: Square Zero

With the passing of time, Tayssir realized that he had been wrong in trusting *Ikhwan*. He had believed that *Ikhwan* deserved a chance for the people to know their true colors. They have proven to him to be an enemy, and players in the counter-revolution.

After the Itihadiya incident in December 2012, where *Ikhwan* killed protestors in front of the presidential palace, Tayssir became politically passive as the game was no longer political, and possibly never really was in the first place. However, Tayssir wholeheartedly endorsed *Tamarod,* the rebellion movement that called for early presidential elections in 2013, in an attempt to oust newly elected President Mohamed Morsi. Tayssir was among millions who flooded the streets on June 30, 2013 demanding the ousting of President Morsi and stayed put until July 3, 2013 at which time the military announced the ousting of President Mohamed Morsi and the appointment of an interim president.

Tayssir rejected the roadmap that *Tamarod* announced in alignment with the military as he signed up for early presidential elections only as written on the *Tamarod* document. He was against the nationwide protests, which General Sisi called for on July 26, 2013 delegating the army and police to deal with 'terrorism'. In Tayssir's opinion, if security forces were doing the right thing then they would not need the support of the public to do so. Only if actions are shady or a bit grey in nature could the support of the people tip the scales to their side. Tayssir was not in town on the controversial July 26 and even if he had been in town, he would not have joined.

Since June 30, 2013, Egypt has been fighting a war on terrorism with nothing achieved on the ground, leaving a pessimistic, gloomy portrait. Tayssir is not happy with the turn of events, as Egypt is back to point zero, a security and police state, with the deep state apparently intact. It is very likely that General Sisi will run for elections (despite his claims that he will not) and another Pharaoh will be in the palace. One thing Tayssir is certain of is that *Ikhwan* are finished politically, *fait accompli*. The sad part is, there is no other organization to take over their social grassroots work. Tayssir, fed up with the polarization between military and *Ikhwan* and the general polarization throughout the country, boycotted the constitutional referendum in January 2014.

The only thing that gives Tayssir hope and a sense of optimism is the country's bright new generation that will not accept repression. On a happier note, Tayssir is engaged and plans to be married in 2014. He hopes no more turmoil unravels, as he wants to start his matrimonial life in peace and with security.

CHAPTER 9

Strong Solidarity

"All for one and one for all, united we stand divided we fall" Alexander Dumas

I wanted to meet a smart but uneducated woman who uses basic logic in understanding current affairs. Nadia came to my mind. She is the daughter-in-law of my gardener and some days she helps him in the garden. We met in my small garden on Monday May 14, 2012, as it was her preference to meet in my home rather than hers.

Sunshine Smile

Nadia is a young, twenty-two-year old woman who is full of positive energy and has a great, big and contagious sunshine smile. She is a modest Egyptian woman from the countryside who moved to the city with her husband when they married. Nadia usually wears a bright colored *galabeya* (traditional robes) with a small colorful scarf covering part of her hair. She was born on October 22, 1990 in the town of El Beyadeyah, in Mallawi an area in Menya, Upper Egypt. Nadia is a devout Orthodox Christian with a heavy, unmistakably southern Egyptian accent.

As a young girl, Nadia entered a literacy program in Mallawi for two years, but stopped at the age of twelve. This is quite common in Egypt, where many youngsters, especially girls, never finish high school. During her short literary exposure, Nadia learned the Arabic alphabet and can read simple sentences, headlines of newspapers, and can write her name. When she turned twelve, her father began to have severe back problems, rendering him incapable of working for a year. Her older brother, Walid, was in the final year of high school and wanted to finish his studies, as did her younger sister. This left Nadia with the burden of working at their farm and *diwar* (a family house in the countryside), a sacrifice she made for her younger siblings. Nadia had stopped going to the literacy program classes, as her family's financial situation was dire. Her father was incapacitated, and there were seven mouths to feed: two girls, three boys and her parents.

Nadia's mother took over the farm work, *which has become a very common practice in Egypt's rural society as many men travel seeking employment in the cities or resorts to complement the meager farm earnings*. When her brother, Walid, earned a diploma in agriculture, he moved to Cairo where he started working as gardener and would send back money to the family, allowing them to pay for medical care, which their ailing father desperately needed. Nadia recalls that during the time her brother sent money their family's situation improved significantly. Their father began walking, with difficulty, but eventually with medical care, rehabilitation and rest, he was finally able to regain his ability to walk normally again. Eventually her brother, Walid, left the big city and now works on a farm along the Alexandria – Cairo highway *(known as the desert road)*, and both her parents and siblings live with him and his wife. When Nadia married, she moved with her in-laws to Giza, closer to her parents and siblings, allowing them to arrange family reunions every couple of months or so.

Teenage Marriage

In rural Egypt, it is normal to see girls engaged at a young age and Nadia was no different from the rest. At the tender age of sixteen Nadia met a young man by the name of Magdi in her grandmother's house, and a year later they were married. Nadia and her husband Magdi lived and grew up on the same street and actually have common family relations. Nadia moved to Giza with her in-laws when her first-born was a toddler.

One year after their marriage, Nadia and Magdi had their first boy, Mena, whom they named after Saint Mena, one of the more famous Egyptian Saints known as a martyr and miracle worker. After having her first child, Nadia decided to take birth control pills for two and a half years, but eventually stopped as the pills provoked an allergic skin reaction over time. Nadia informed her mother-in-law that she would stop taking the pill due to this allergy and her mother-in-law supported her decision. Within five months, she became pregnant with her second child. Nadia and Magdi named their daughter Marina. At the time of the interview, she was ten months old. Nadia then resumed the birth control pills and did not suffer side effects. Nadia would have loved to have three children, but her husband told her that two is enough. He wants to be able to provide well for them. *This is quite different from many other families throughout Egypt, as the average fertility rate in Egypt is 3.92 children per woman.*[49]

During the time Nadia was living with her in-laws, Reda, her father-in-law, was the man of the house, as her husband was off serving his compulsory military duty.

Reda did not like the idea of Nadia working as a housekeeper while she was under his responsibility. If her husband, Magdi, were around and he agreed, then Reda would not object. However, under his house and his rules, he did not want Nadia cleaning and working in other people's homes, just as it was with his own wife. Nadia did not mind not working, as she had her hands full in any case, with the house and her children. Moreover, it is common that men from Upper Egypt do not allow their women to work.

Magdi is illiterate and a farmer, so he was obliged to serve three years in the military. Had he been educated with even a high school diploma, then he would have only had to serve two years. During his 3 years of military service, his month was split; twenty days in the army camp and ten days with his family.

Nadia, her husband and children, live in the basement of the villa in which Reda works as a porter and gardener. Reda was using two rooms in the basement. When Nadia moved in, the owner of the house readily agreed to let the family use all three rooms in the basement. She occupies one room with her kids, her brother-in-law and his wife stay in another room, and her parents-in-law in the third.

Nadia reads the newspapers and later proudly informs her husband and father-in-law, who cannot read and write, the headlines. The family all watch the news on television after, to supplement the headlines she was able to understand. On the television screen, Nadia is able to read the news ticker on the bottom of the screen.

Old Tradition

Concerning the controversial topic of female circumcision, Nadia is wholeheartedly against it, as she believes it is wrong and the practice should not take place. Circumcision is all right when it comes to boys but not for girls. Nadia believes that God created girls as they are and that society should not harm or mutilate them in any way. She strongly believes it is unjust to intentionally hurt and mistreat a girl; on the contrary, girls and women should be *mastourah* (protected). In the old days, people did not know better and were cursed by ignorance and hence, this horrible practice of female genital mutilation *(which some call female circumcision)* was deemed a tradition that is widely practiced in Egypt. *To place this in context, 96% of women in Egypt are victims of the practice, according to the latest Demographic and Health Survey (DHS).* However, now we know better, and Nadia cannot understand how parents could hurt their own daughters in this way. Nadia's parents did not circumcise her, and she in turn will not circumcise her daughter.

The tradition of female circumcision dates back to ancient Egypt. Since then it has been widely practiced across the country in both Muslim and Christian families.

When we met, Nadia said she thought both her mother and mother-in-law were victims of this old custom but she was not sure. The topic is so embarrassing that Nadia did not even talk about it with her own mother; hence, the vagueness about her mother's condition. As a girl, she felt embarrassed talking about such matters with her mother. However, as a married woman living under the same roof as her mother-in-law, Nadia has spoken with ease about circumcision with her mother-in-law, who underwent this practice. *After talking to me, Nadia asked her mother about her circumcision.* It turns out that Nadia's mother was not a victim of circumcision, unlike her mother-in-law.

Nadia is unable to understand why there are people who are convinced that girls need circumcision. Within her social circle sometimes, she and her family and friends talk about the practice, but Nadia does not know of any circumcised friends or relatives. Surprisingly, as far as she learnt by talking with her friends, none of them within her generation had to go through circumcision. *Then again, this topic is taboo and friends may not disclose this information.* She has never heard of any girl who was in a critical condition or died as a result, of circumcision. Nadia unfalteringly says, "Circumcision is ignorance." Any doctor who performs this mutilation, society should immediately report and reprimand.

Nadia is a simple woman who seeks justice and equality for all and she hopes for peaceful coexistence of both religions in Egypt, especially with the turbulent time after the revolution.

Shocked

Although the slogan of the revolution, "Bread, freedom and social equality" resonates with Nadia, she did not participate in the revolution. She is among the silent majority. Nadia recalls that in Mubarak's first speech to the nation, he said things that sparked anger among the public rather than relief, with her boiling with frustration. She did not like his speech, as she felt it failed to address the demands of the people.

Nadia vented her frustration, saying to her family," I wish I could enter the TV screen and choke him! It is his fault how he has destroyed Egypt like this. He has caused this bloodshed."
Nadia's family laughed at what they felt was a ridiculous notion on her part, but understood where she was coming from as the entire family had the same sentiments. The second speech by the former president where he managed to gain the support of a large portion of Egyptians, stirred some emotions in Nadia. However, she did not buy into his speech, which she viewed as an attempt to gain sympathy. Nadia was adamant that he had to go.

Nadia was perplexed, and filled with questions when Egyptians on camels and horseback rode into Tahrir and beat the peaceful protestors on February 2, 2011. She could not understand the use of unnecessary violence between compatriots. She could not believe her eyes when she saw men holding other men and beating them to death. This was wrong and *haram* (impious), it was a massacre.

Nadia asked Reda, "Why, my father, are they attacking the protestors?"
Reda said, "I don't know. It is heart-breaking."

Gun Shots

During the security vacuum and the widespread paranoia during and after the revolution, Nadia witnessed random acts of hooliganism in her neighborhood, like the stolen electricity cables and other nuisances. Consequently, they would have no electricity from dawn until dusk. Another time, thieves removed manhole covers from the streets, presumably to sell.

Usually Reda, her father-in-law, uses a certain gate to enter and exit the villa. However, one night he used the other gate as he was walking around the house with his grandson, throwing stones to deter stray dogs. He saw a conspicuous looking black car parked outside with a man and a woman inside. It seems the man thought Reda was throwing the stones at the car, because he took out his gun and fired two shots in Reda's direction. Hearing the two gunshots, Nadia ran quickly outside, desperately looking for her son. If Reda had taken the regular gate, the shooter could probably have hit him with his shots, as he would have been unprotected. The car drove off after the shots, before Reda could even take note of its license plate.

Another night, Nadia and her in-laws were sitting in the garden when they heard screams and shouts. They saw young boys running after a car with four men inside. The men in the car were firing shots and the car escaped. Elsewhere, Nadia's brother-in-law saw a car with six armed men inside it, and to his surprise, he was suddenly facing a weapon directed at him. He told Nadia "I could not stop them, as how can I, an unarmed man, stand up to an armed man?" He had no choice but to let them pass.

A little while later they heard that some men who had been arrested turned out to be escaped convicts from a nearby prison. Nadia could not believe that there had been a prison break and that they happened to break free during this time of turmoil throughout the country. She is prone to believe that either the families of the convicts, many who were *Salafists* or *Ikhwan*, or the police, opened up the prisons. The *Ikhwan* or *Salafists* in order to release their loved ones, and the police to create commotion and wreak havoc in the country. This is what many Egyptians believed at the time. The other theory is that the prisons might have simply been over their capacity, forcing the guards to open the gates. In any case, thousands of convicts were roaming around the country free and clear.

Army Duty

During the eighteen days of the revolution, Nadia and her in-laws were on edge and they would be startled any time the wind banged the windows or doors. Any otherwise normal sounds, seemed to cause fear and anxiety. In the evenings, they would have their dinner outside on the streets to keep an eye out for *baltegeya*. Some days they would eat cheese sandwiches or *foul* (fava bean) sandwiches and other more fortunate days, chicken if their budget permitted. With Nadia's husband away on army duty, he left his family to fend for themselves with her father-in-law Reda taking charge.

Whenever Reda went outside on the streets to be on neighborhood watch, Nadia and the other family members followed him.

Reda said, "You should stay inside the house, don't be scared."

Nadia replied, "No we will stand with you."

Reda said, "Have your dinner inside and when you finish I will go inside and eat."

Her mother-in-law said, "No whatever you do we will also do. We can take whatever is destined when we all stand together."

One very cold winter night, Reda lit up a fire to keep his family warm. Nadia recalls starring into the fire and suddenly breaking into tears as she thought about her beloved husband in the army, wondering if he was safe.

Nadia said, "When Magdi comes this time, I will not let him go back to the army. It is too dangerous."

Her mother-in-law replied, "Nadia he must go back, otherwise he would be imprisoned."

Nadia said, "Where is the government? There is no government. Nobody can harm him if he does not return to the army."

Nadia was very scared, given the fact that Magdi was obliged to go back to the army; she was petrified that he would never return to her. When she saw the images of dead bodies on TV, her fears engulfed her even more. Her mother-in-law also cried for her son, and prayed that God would return Magdi home safe and unharmed.

During his holidays, Magdi returned home safely and Nadia felt her soul was alive again; without him, she felt empty. During one of his visits, she spoke to him when they were alone.

Nadia said, "Please stay with me. Do not go back. Just give them an excuse, tell them you are tired."

Magdi said, "Nadia that is impossible. I have one more year left in the army. If I am destined to die, I will die like the others; and if I am not, I will not. I am not better than anybody else. Besides, my location is safer than others."

Nadia recalls how Magdi had refused to go to the army at the very beginning, but she and his parents forced him to fulfill his obligations. After two years, and with the political turmoil in the country, Magdi changed and matured into a responsible man who refused to shy away from danger and insisted on standing by his friends and colleagues.

During his military service on many occasions, Magdi told Nadia how he wanted to get out of the army lines and move to the protestors' side, to defend them but he could not defy his orders.

Finally, in May 2011, Magdi completed his military service and returned home to his family. Magdi was greatly relieved, as the last months had beeen the most dangerous that he had ever witnessed. He was grateful to be going home to his family.

Now that her husband was back, Nadia was waiting for her daughter to grow up a little bit more, at which time she would be open to the work opportunities that come along. However, as it turned out, like father like son; her husband, like his father, did not want Nadia to work. He felt that her place was in the home, take caring of the children and their house.

Changed her mind

In Mubarak's final speech before he stepped down, Nadia felt that he was glad that the protestors died and that they deserved it. His tone was spiteful and defiant, as if he was saying, "You asked for it." After the revolution, when guards carried the overthrown president on a stretcher to court, Nadia was praying and hoping he would die. This was completely uncharacteristic of Nadia, as she usually harbors no malicious thoughts.

Initially after the revolution, Nadia felt that the army was good and would lead her country on the right path. However, despite her disapproval of former President Mubarak, with the worsening of the political scene, Nadia could not help but long for the days that Mubarak ruled during which in the very least, security prevailed.

Nadia said, "Can you see what happened to Egypt when he left it? Now I wish he did not leave." She started feeling that Egypt under Mubarak had been better, despite all the thievery and corruption. Over a year after the revolution, Nadia feels that authorities largely restored security but she is wary of the situation. It can be maintained, if and only if all Egyptians remain united. Nadia feels that equality amongst Egyptians will lead Egypt into a higher rank and a prosperous state. Without equity and unification amongst the people, she foresees that they would mourn the deaths of the country's *shabab* (youth), both Christian and Muslim. If the unity she speaks of is shattered, Nadia predicts that the bloodshed will escalate and both the Muslim and Christian communities will suffer the destructive consequences.

When Nadia watched the television broadcasting of the Maspero massacre in November 2011, where many Christians were protesting and demanding equal rights, she saw the army in conflict with the civilians, and thugs or *baltegeya* roaming the streets causing destruction and havoc. It is true that some soldiers were hurt in the arm or injured on the face, but the tanks trampled protestors, running over some of the bodies. It was a horrible, gruesome sight. The *baltegeya* attacked the army and the army was on the defensive, wounding and killing many innocent protestors. The army came out almost unscathed. Who came out destroyed? Nadia asked, the army or the civilian who was swarming in his own warm pool of blood? So who is at fault? The army or the civilians? For Nadia the answer was clear. She holds the army responsible. Yet, she could not understand how soldiers in uniform could beat civilians as they did. *Many lives were lost in front of the state television building in a massacre referred to as Maspero, in keeping with the buidling's name. State television characteristically broadcast the ancien regime's lies and propaganda. However, to this fact, Nadia is clueless* and refers to national state television as her main source of news and she watches satellite channels for news and the talk shows. All the channels seemed to be broadcasting the same troubling scene.

Under Attack

Nadia is not pleased with the turn of political events in Egypt, as she felt safer under Mubarak, being clueless to the corruption. Prior to the revolution, Nadia did not feel any differences between religions. All Egyptians were one hand. But now, after the revolution, she felt that things had changedin this regard. Nadia does not recall a church ever coming under attack before the revolution. Nadia was brought up where Muslims lived side by side with the Christians in harmony, and enjoyed a common sense of hospitality and fraternity. When in need, Muslims and Christians would assist one another. For instance, when a loved one had died, the Muslims paid their condolences in the church and the Christians did the same in mosques. There were no boundaries or divisions, and religion never hindered their human relations. Her father-in-law, Reda, has been working as a porter of a villa, owned by a Muslim, in the suburbs of Egypt for the past five years and never once did Reda feel any sort of discrimination. The owner jokes with Reda and treats him like a brother almost unconditionally. Nadia recalls that back in her hometown, she would hear the mosque calling for *fajr* (dawn) prayers, and the neighboring Church bells ringing simultaneously for the dawn mass. Egyptians cared and feared for the safety and well-being of one another.

Nadia likes the good people in Egypt who treat neighbors well and employers who are generous with their employees. She is aware that not everybody is alike; Egypt has the good and the bad. Nadia, although from a modest background, has self-dignity and self-worth and does not feel like a second-class citizen. Some people may look down on her as is if she was a slave, but she chooses to ignore them. Nadia does not take a liking to those people who attempt to make her feel inferior; she knows from the facial expressions, from the smile, how the person feels towards her. She knows and concentrates on those other Egyptians, the ones who treat one another with respect, equity and without discrimination or classism. Nadia feels that she can talk and laugh with the well to do, without feeling uneasy. Egypt has good people and has a lot of wealth.

Nevertheless, Nadia questions her belief as she is confused at how her Muslim Egyptian brothers could ever kill Christians and set ablaze the churches, as they did in Alexandria and Atfeeh in 2011. Apparently, the year 2011 was void of any security. Nadia could not understand how a Muslim could hate a Christian so much as to kill him and burn his church. What kind of person can live with his conscience and sleep at night, knowing he killed so many innocent lives? Nadia has heard rumors that a foreign hand committed this crime while others say it was the *Ikhwan*. When Nadia imagines herself in a compromising situation alongside a Muslim woman, she feels certain that the two women would look out for each other and protect one another until the end. Nadia prays that Egyptian unity is rooted in the soil forever.

While we were sitting in the garden, her son Mena was with her. She could not manage both children so she left her daughter with her mother-in-law. At the time, Mena was not feeling well, with a runny nose, and a cough. It was a wonder how she was able to talk to me with her son asking to go home every ten minutes. She told him that if they went home there was a man who would give him an injection and they needed to wait until he goes away. She gave him her mobile to play with at one point, and at another told him to water the garden.

One day Nadia was on an errand with Reda and while in the microbus, they overheard another passenger refer to Christians as 'bastards'. They kept quiet. Reda was too scared to confront the man, as there were a couple of bearded men who he suspected were *Ikhwan* and *Salafis* and he worried that they would attack him if he spoke up in defense of his religion. Nadia was confused by the derogatory insults because until that moment, her interactions and experiences with Muslims had all been positive, and Muslims had always treated her with respect. After the revolution and seemingly all of a sudden, she was seeing a different kind of treatment, which left her baffled.

Nadia recalls a conversation with Reda on this occasion.
Nadia asked, "Are all long-bearded Muslim men bad, and insult Christians?"
Reda replied, "Not all men who grow their beards are bad people. The troubling kind traveled from foreign lands to destroy and spoil Egypt."
Nadia wondered, "Weren't we all standing as one during the revolution?"
Reda said, "Yes, but an external hand has played a destructive role."

When the protests started to happen and casualties reported, Nadia cried at the turn of events, for the lost and the injured souls. She prayed to God to protect Egypt. Nadia will never forget the television screen panning over the bodies of thos who had died during the protests, or the deformed faces. She could not stand the injustice. *As Martin Luther King wisely said, "Injustice anywhere is a threat to justice everywhere. We are caught in an inescapable network of mutuality, tied in a single garment of destiny. Whatever affects one directly, affects all indirectly."*[50]

Nadia feels for the mother who lost her child and the wife who lost her husband and the child who lost his father. She was touched, and cried as she could empathetically picture these tragedies befalling her own family. She feels that she and they are one, regardless of religion, we are all Egyptian. The cost has been heavy for all of Egypt, and what happened during the revolution has left people walking in the streets weary and fearful.

Mixed Feelings

In Nadia's view, the Egyptians who took to the streets on January 25 were defending their rights and the rights of all Egyptians. They were not at fault to protest against the blatant corruption and thievery that was taking place. Violence and death was not what the protestors were seeking. The brave who dared to speak up and stand up for their rights met their end on the streets of Egypt. The spilling of blood has irreversibly broken the fear barrier. Hope, after having been lost in the alleys of Cairo, has been reborn at Tahrir square. Nadia prays that God will send Egypt a good leader like Gamal Abdel Nasser to uplift the spirits of the Egyptians in the aftermath of the loss of life.

Nadia is proud of the young people on the streets and their families, as they genuinely care for their neighbors and their property. With the disappearance of security forces, civilians gathered to stand in vigil in front of their cherished homes. Egypt still has good youth and integrity. When Nadia called her relatives back in her hometown, she was pleased to know that their men also stood guard over their families and properties, armed with sticks and a few guns. Back in her hometown, her family was scared, as there were cases of kidnappings of children. Kidnappings were happening in the capital, but that was far from where Nadia lives.

They were days filled with cooperation and compassion amongst all Egyptians, where neighbors would pass by and ask if Nadia and her family needed anything. Egypt was witnessing a great time in its history, demonstrating strength in unity. *Martin Luther King wrote, "There is amazing power in unity. Where there is true unity, every effort to disunite only serves to strengthen the unity...What happened to one happened to all."*[51] Unity is essential.

Nadia believes that it must have been a foreign hand causing the chaos. She refuses the notion that an Egyptian could ruin his own country, and believes that they are incapable of pulling such an elaborate scheme on their own. Former President Mubarak has his supporters inside and outside the country. Nadia is against violence and the shedding of Egyptian blood by fellow Egyptians. It is a horrendous crime, unnecessary in order to bring about a new regime. She is wary that the *ancien regime* instigates religious strife to divide the people. However, she is a devout Christian who believes what the Bible says, "If one member suffers, all suffer together; if one member is honored, all rejoice together" (1 Corinthians 12:26).

The revolution does not bring pride to Nadia, as it has negatively affected her life as well as that of others. She had never worried when the men left the house for work in the morning, but now Nadia is apprehensive and prays that they return home safely. Worry has now come to cloud her daily life and the smallest things unsettle her.

Nadia will never be able to erase the sight of blood on her television screen from her memory. She hates blood and uncalled for death. She has changed after the revolution. She used to slaughter chickens with ease, but not anymore, as the act now reminds her of the blood of men and women spilled on the asphalt streets of Egypt. Nadia is now faint-hearted; she grasps her father-in-law's hand when she sees a man with his hand maimed or a wounded street dog. Reda was surprised to see this drastic change in Nadia. In the middle of the night, Nadia often wakes up screaming from nightmares, which still happen two and a half years after these events. Now, when one of her kids gets hurt, Nadia is anxious and her heart grows heavy in her chest, having seen people wounded and killed on the news has made her even more wary.

Nadia prefers her old rural life where she lived with a big family and felt safe. When she moved to Giza three years before, things were all right until the revolution happened. Ever since, Nadia is living in fear, always careful that the door is closed. During Mubarak's era, Nadia felt safe, but after his downfall, Nadia realized that he stole from the state, upsetting and draining society. She is worried about what tomorrow will bring.

A Good Just President

It is difficult to judge whether the revolution has succeeded or not. As Nadia contemplates shortly and says, "As long as we stay united, hand in hand, and fear for the safety of one another, it will succeed." Our strength is in our solidarity. Although, many perished and many were injured and much destroyed, the nation will move forward. The revolution is not over yet, and will continue until the time a good and just president who treats the civilians like his own children rules Egypt. We need a ruler who rules with conscience and in a manner wary of God. Having a fair president is not enough though, as the people have a big role. *Gandhi said, "Before they dare think of freedom they must be brave enough to love one another, to tolerate one another's religion, even prejudices and superstitions and to trust one another. This requires faith in oneself. And faith in oneself is faith in God. If we have faith we shall cease to fear one another."* [52] *Nadia believes that a just President and love of all are essential for a brighter future.*

Nadia predicted that if the *Ikhwan* presidential candidate won the elections, the Christians would be in danger. However, if former Prime Minister Ahmed Shafik won he would be protective of all Egyptian citizens. Nadia perceives that the army protected its interests and standing, and not the revolution. The police and the army are pulling at each other.

Around June 2011, a month before he finished his army duty, Magdi and his colleagues were going home for their monthly leave. They had just dropped off another colleague after leaving their platoon and were driving on the ring road, when a car driving in the opposite direction collided with their car. His colleague died from the sudden collision, but Magdi was lucky, although his ribs fractured requiring him to endure gauze wrapping. Magdi took sick leave and returned home to Nadia. The night he returned home, his face was ghostly and his clothes disheveled. Magdi recounted what he saw and Nadia grew more petrified and protective over her husband, pleading with him not to go back to his army service, but it was useless. He was adamant and unwavering. The army pays sixty pounds, less than ten dollars, to each soldier; when they discovered he was married, they raised his salary to one hundred pounds, less than fifteen dollars.

There was one time, Nadia was watching television and could have sworn she saw Magdi on the screen protecting an institute at Ramsis street. At this time, unknown people had attacked the army by throwing stones, wounding a few soldiers and killing one.

When Nadia ponders on her plight as the 'unfortunate poor people', Reda appeases her. Reda says, "God could have created us all the same, but he created the rich and the poor, to judge if each one of us accepts his life or not.

If one day her husband gets a normal civilian job and a decent wage, she would be grateful and thankful to God. They are faithful people who accept whatever destiny brings them, the good and the bad.

Nadia wanted to vote during the presidential elections, but she was unable to afford the transportation costs. One could only vote in his or her own hometown, and transportation to Nadia's hometown was one hundred and twenty pounds, the equivalent of twenty dollars, which she could not afford. Her personal identification states that she comes from and lives in Upper Egypt and hence cannot vote in Giza. *If voters can vote wherever they live and not just in the district on their ID's it will probably increase voter turnout.* In a family of six adults, only her father-in-law traveled to vote. Reda voted for Amr Moussa in the first round and Ahmed Shafik in the second round. The Church beckoned its followers to return to their hometowns to vote. Authorities announced that voters who abstained might be penalized one hundred pounds – around sixteen dollars, but as it turned out, nobody penalized her.

Future
Nadia hopes for Egypt to be a strong nation where its *shabab* (youth), take on their rights and fulfill their dreams. She dreams that life will return to normality and security where everyone enjoys his or her rights.

She lives day-by-day, and does not think about tomorrow as she has faith that God will take care of tomorrow. She reads the Bible and prays to God as she perceives herself to be a weak person and God responds to her prayers. Nadia likes to quote Pope Shenouda who said, "God is here." The future is unknown. Nonetheless, Nadia remains optimistic, as she believes Egypt is sacred and protected. She believes that *Ikhwan*, although they won the election, will not continue their term. Bottom line, Nadia does not understand what *Ikhwan* stand for, nor any of their members for that matter. At the Church, she comfortably signed a form by, *Tamarod*, 'rebellion' that withdraws confidence in President Morsi and asks for early presidential elections.

Alexandria
In August 2012, Nadia moved with her husband and children to Alexandria, where Magdi found work as a villa porter. Nadia prefers the coastal city to the desert city as the latter is a busy, crowded city, unlike the suburban residential area where she stayed with her father-in-law, close to the desert. She is very happy being in Alexandria with her husband after three years of army service and separation.

In Alexandria, Nadia has seen marches and protests, which she had never seen in the suburbs of Giza. Recently, many youth have taken to the streets in protest of the unrepresentative constitution and the constitutional declarations. Nadia is convinced that the people ought to refuse the draft of the constitution, as it does not guarantee rights. She foresees that Christians will not be able to build Churches if this constitution passes.

Nadia is taking care of her children and the house demands, including shopping. One day she was taken aback while buying food at the *souk* (market).
The vender asked her, "Are you Christian or Muslim?"
Nadia replied, "I am Christian."
The vender did not comment and treated her well, playing with her children. However, she does not understand why he asked the question in the first place. She senses that some people do not like her son Mena's name. There is only one man who asked her about her faith. Nadia and her family returned to Cairo after a year in Alexandria, as their landowner gave Magdi low wages and expected him to work exclusively in the house. Magdi is now the villa porter in the suburbs at 6th of October City, close to where his father Reda works. Nadia is happy to be back in town close to their families.

The cutthroat tension in the air is unbearable, with each religion pointing fingers at the other as the party at fault. It breaks Nadia's heart that people attacked churches. President Morsi did not change anything, Muslims and Christians are still fighting in isolated dramatic cases. She is disappointed, as he did not stand up to protect them. *Martin Luther King wrote, "Something tells me that the ultimate test of man is not where he stands in moments of comfort and moments of convenience, but where he stands in moments of challenge and moments of controversy."*[53] In this sense, President Morsi did not pass the test in Nadia's eyes and she felt even more scared two years after the revolution than she did during the first year.

With the eventual ousting of President Mohamed Morsi, Nadia feels even more optimistic. She personally did not join on June 30, 2013, as she could not leave her children. When the army called on people to come to the streets and counter terrorism on July 26, 2013 Nadia supported them, but did not join in the street demonstrations again as she could not leave her precious children. Even after the ousting of President Morsi, Nadia does not feel that security is as it was during the Mubarak era, especially with the spiraling of crimes like murder, previously unheard of.

Nadia insists that the people must stay united in solidarity. *Che Guevara wrote, "La gente undid jam as sera vencida!" (The people, united, will never be defeated!)"*[54] No force can stand against people power, as was demonstrated by the Egyptian people.

CHAPTER 10

Frightful Fear

"Of *Allah*. Verily never will *Allah* change the condition of a people
until they change what is in themselves." *Qur'anic verse (13:11)*

*We graduated from American University in Cairo (AUC) in '97 and our paths crossed
once more at work. Lina was working at an advertising agency and the multinational
I worked at, at the time was her client. While I was searching for someone who opposed
the revolution, Lina crossed my mind as I had noticed from her Facebook posts her clear
rational opposition and I was keen on understanding her viewpoint. We met at Dandy
Mall on Wednesday September 14, 2011. She prefers only her first name to be used.*

Climbing up the Ladder

She is an exceptionally strong, bright, diligent Egyptian woman, who knows how to
get things done. Lina is a pretty petite who keeps her hair long and her skin tanned.
Born in Cairo in February 1974, as a young girl, she attended the then famous Port
Said School in Zamalek, and later Misr Language Schools. She studied Business
Administration, and minored in psychology at the American University in Cairo,
graduating in 1997. In Egypt, youth usually start working after university, but Lina
was a non-conformist choosing to work in the advertising industry when she was
merely a young sophomore in college. Lina's mother was a teacher and her father
worked in the sales domain. He offered to call his contacts to help Lina land a job at
the beginning of her career, but she firmly declined any help. Yet again, she refused
to follow the norm, rejected any *wasta* (using connections), and starting from ground
zero. She ambitiously climbed the career ladder to become General Manager of one
of the international advertising agencies in Egypt. With her eighteen years of work
experience, Lina's work and life has exposed her to various calibers of people within
Egyptian society. She got married in her thirties and has a four-year-old daughter.

Premonition

Like many Egyptians, Lina felt provoked by the unjust actions of the *ancien regime,* especially when it came to their stronghold over the media. In October 2010, the Egyptian government suspended 12 satellite channels, mostly religious and prone to the Salafi inclination. *According to an article in Egypt Independent, some twenty other channels received warnings due to their alleged "incitement of religious hatred, unlicensed medical advice and obscenity".*[55] The following month the government cracked down on around four or five independent media channels, actually shutting them down, including the one hosting Amr Adeeb's talk show *Al Qahera Al Youm* (Cairo Today). Adeeb was a leading, bold Arab presenter who did not shy away from controversy. This shutdown took place during the parliamentary elections that were flagrantly fraudulent.

Freedom of expression had been denied. Concerned by the reactions of the government, Lina felt betrayed by those in power. *As Martin Luther King said, "Law and order exist for the purpose of establishing justice and that when they fail in this purpose they become dangerously structured dams that block the flow of social progress."*[56] Lina was concerned, as the old *nizam* (regime) was no longer upholding justice, but rather representing the tainted hands of injustice, thwarting freedom of expression and causing society to regress. Her instinct told her that something significant was about to happen, a premonition of the revolution. She recalls sending out a Facebook message on January 7, 2011 to her friends abroad. The intention of Lina's note was to share her concern about the state of the nation and Lina was seriously considering buying real estate abroad far away from Egypt. All her friends gave her affirmative advice on places to invest.

> "Subject: Investment
>
> Hello friends
> Strange message, but here goes. I am a bit worried about the future of our beloved country, and decided to put the minimal money that I have outside *3alashan* (so that) I don't get screwed if things go bad....
> I nearly decided to sell the house I bought here and instead, buy something small in USA, to rent, and get income, and *tekoon madmoona in shaaallah!* (Something reliable, if God permits)
> My budget is LE XX *masalan* (for instance), translated to USD. What would be your recommendation? State, area, next steps???
> Please help. If you have a suggestion, I will take whatever route you recommend, and I will come finish the deal. Cash.
> I am lost and too confused :("

Change Not Revolution
From the first day, January 25, Lina wholeheartedly agreed with the initial valid demands of the protestors: *"eish, horeya, karama and adalah"* (bread, freedom, dignity and equality.) Individuals have the right to ask for universal human rights and to call for anti-corruption measures. However, she believes they should not revert to blackmail and full-scale revolt.

The people voiced demands to topple the regime on the night of January 25. Lina remembers watching the live coverage. The protestors' demands escalated to chanting, *"Yaskot yaskot Hosni Mubarak"* (down, down with Hosni Mubarak.) This is when Lina felt they were crossing the line and she turned against the hardline nature of the protest. She believes that if the activists had protested every day after work, asking for their rights, for twenty consecutive days, they would have gotten attention. They could have chosen a mature, well-spoken representative to negotiate, with a clear list of demands, with the regime. She is sure that the government would have met their demands without former President Mubarak abdicating.

Lina respects the law and expects that protestors also abide by the law. The activists were planning to protest and return home in the evening, but they did not. Moreover, since they were blocking movement in the roundabout, they fully violated the protest law.

Paranoia
After the protests commenced, Lina went to a local hypermarket and stocked plenty of food and household necessities. There were long queues, as everyone was thinking along the same lines. At work, she issued salaries earlier than usual, as she expected the worst, and personally withdrew money from the ATM. Lina was ready for the unwelcome street war she had predicted. The first two days, she was attentively watching the news on television and on the internet, both of which reported violent incidents. Nationwide panic was escalating at an alarmingly rapid pace.

Lina was edgy, angry, scared and paranoid. Nervous, she started lashing out at her family and fighting with them, insisting they leave their downtown homes, close to the action, and move into her villa in an up-scale compound in the suburbs of Cairo, thinking it would be safer for all. She then had a houseful of extended family: her sister and her niece, her mother, her mother-in-law, her sister-in-law and her husband and kids. She was missing her aunt and her cousin, who insisted on staying in their homes, which was a nerve-wracking ordeal for Lina, especially given the communication shut down.

Early on Friday January 28, the government cut off all mobile communication and internet in an attempt to curtail the called for demonstrations on this 'Friday of Rage'. Protesters calling for the downfall of the regime threatened national security; therefore, the government felt it had the right to protect the nation by cutting off the internet and mobile communication. Lina viewed this government action pragmatically, however this is not how the majority felt. *Most Egyptians felt the government wrongfully denied their rights by this infringement, which instigated them to swarm the streets.*

Lina was bewildered as to how educated people could not analyze the situation and realize the potential negative consequences of their demonstrations. She was politically unaligned with the escalating demands of the protestors, particularly *"eskat al nezam"* (ousting the regime), and she personally panicked. It was absurd not to expect any harm would befall the protestors when their demands became so radical. She strongly believes that the government has the right to defend the nation and it is its rightful role and duty. It is normal practice worldwide that police use water cannons and tear gas to disperse crowds. As for the identity of those who fired live bullets, she believes it needs investigations; however, she is skeptical of any closure being reached.

What do protestors expect as a reaction to their demand for the downfall of the regime and the president? That the president will pack up his bag and leave obediently and quietly? In any country the world over, if the people ask their queen to abdicate, will she do so willingly? Is such a request reasonable or realistic? They cannot expect to return home unharmed and untouched. Lina cannot fathom their naivety.

Fear Enveloped Them

In the still and quiet of her suburban neighborhood, Lina used to sleep soundly at night. That was until after her husband went to a meeting at the compound following the first 'Friday of Rage', and returned panicking. He ordered them to shut all the window blinds and took out his licensed guns, all in front of the children. It was terrible. She could see the fear in her husband's eyes when he said, "They are coming." The house helpers were crying, the children were crying, and gone were her sound nights of blissful sleep, replaced with shocking fear. Lina will never forget that horrid night when her husband took out his guns to protect his home and family if necessary.

The *baltageyas* (thugs) are criminals who perceive the residents of these luxurious compounds as the ones who took the money from the less fortunate people and in turn, wanted to reclaim what they thought was rightfully theirs. She reached this conclusion from the way people look at her and seem to be talking about her on the street. The hooligans deny that the money is hard-earned cash from the residents' long hours of work at an office. This money is not a privileged right and there are those amongst the downtrodden who want to move into their homes and live their lives instead, the poor robbing from the rich. She heard from her neighboring friends that criminals were about to attack a neighboring compound among others.

Lina was fearful of any outcome; would they come to steal, move in, rape, kill, or what? She was terribly frightened. Her husband joined their neighbors, rotating in shifts in an attempt to safeguard the compound. The children were afraid, especially those old enough to understand what was happening.

Baltageya burned the hypermarket, Hyper One at Shiekh Zayed. Her sister had been there just two hours earlier and her husband was actually there when the fire spread to the second floor. It was disturbing that these acts of vandalism and arson were so proximate, so close to home.

Elsewhere, closer to the city center, within the populated district of Mohandseen, thugs broke into several shops at Shehab Street, where her aunt lives. Her cousin gave her a frantic call on the landline, terrified that the loitering hooligans would break into their house. The tension was shattering and definitely left Lina more discontent with the unfolding, desperate events. Lina's cousin called to tell her about the arrest of four men, who were subsequently beaten to death. Soon her aunt and her cousin went through nervous breakdowns, continuously crying, and refusing to step outside their apartment. The phone calls and crying were troubling and unsettling, building up Lina's uncontrollable fear. The uncertainty and fear was literally eating her alive. They stopped driving their big expensive cars and used their smaller, cheaper cars that would not attract attention, as a safety measure.

Security was absent in Egypt. People could not walk in the street; employers and employees could not go to work; children and teachers could not go to school; men and women could not withdraw money from ATMs. Lina knew that the security was beyond restoration for a very long time ahead. She was aware that Egypt has more than an estimated twenty three million[57] uneducated citizens, most likely unemployed and easily susceptible to becoming *baltegeya* at the promise of some quickly earned money. The police seemed to have withdrawn their iron grip on the country, as she knows of thieves who robbed homes of her friends or stole cars from them. The police did not proceed with any investigations for these crimes. This was no revolution. It was a criminal outbreak.

During the ten days of the revolution when security was absent, Lina and the adults slept in their training suits, ready and alert to run if needed. They abandoned the first floor and camped out in sleeping bags with the children on the second floor. She felt safer on higher ground. Mostly, they could not sleep, catching a few hours of rest here and there.

As if the lack of security was not enough, at her full house, everyone was against the revolution except her mother and her sister who were standing on the borderlines. This created an atmosphere of tension, filled with intense arguments. These were hard times to say the least. Since they had only one main television, they all tuned to the same channel but had different reactions. Some defended and others criticized. It was a time of paranoia and unease.

As panic peaked, Lina's husband decided that his family should leave Egypt, as it was no longer safe. Lina was perplexed, as she had always loved her country. She married late and had many opportunities to work and live abroad, but she always chose not to. She could not understand; leave Egypt? Go where? Lina is a General Manager of an agency, where would she work if she leaves? What would be the fate of her family? What standard of living could she afford in another country? Would it be a high standard of living, as in Egypt? Was this forever or just for a few months? She went through a nervous breakdown. Lina started cursing the revolution. Life was peaceful before the revolution. There were plenty of flaws that needed fixing, but this was the wrong approach to fixing them. She met the idea of leaving with complete rejection, and her husband eventually dropped it.

Unethical Role Models

The way people were talking about former President Mubarak offended Lina. For example, an actor said, "He is a pig that is worthy of spitting on." It was a clear display of the rampant disrespect and lack of ethics in Egyptian society. She never felt any emotions towards Mubarak, but after the revolution she developed a soft spot for him, due to the unnecessary humiliation he was facing. Lina is very concerned about how adults have become bad role models to the children, who have gotten accustomed to hearing younger people disrespect and humiliate the elderly. At one of the popular sporting clubs, Nadi el Gezira, children were told not to use the inflatable jumping castle and she clearly heard them boldly and rudely reject the order, saying: *"Mesh hanemshy entatemshy"* (We are not leaving, you leave), a slogan chanted by the demonstrators.

Lina's sister, who works in the educational field, recounted that even at the elite schools, students protested against the food at the canteen. Students did not like the Arabic teacher and hence did not enter the class. This is the overshadowing, pricy lesson that our children learnt from the revolution. A bad example has not just been set for the children, but also for adults, as nobody answers to the elderly anymore.

Kebeer (meaning elderly and pronounced in reverence) has sadly become extinct, a distant memory.

Lina is not proud of anything that happened during those eighteen days. On the contrary, she is embarrassed of everything as she felt that it has proven to be a very bad example for the children. The outcome of the eighteen days set bad ethical standards and showed how the men and women have been displaying barbaric behavior, given all the destruction, assaults and looting. Unfortunately, the meaning of freedom has been misunderstood for disrespect and disobeying orders, erasing the code of ethics; freedom stood for anarchy.

Joining the Demonstrations

As Lina got furious with this growing resentment and disrespect, she joined the supporters of the *ancien regime*. With the insecurity looming over the country, it was not easy convincing her family to join a demonstration. She had to argue with her husband to get his permission for her to leave and of course, her mother was wholeheartedly against it as she supported the revolution.

Lina said, "I have to be proactive and go to the street to show support to Mubarak."

Her mother replied, "You must be out of your mind. Did you not see the men and women who have been wounded or killed?"

Her husband said, "Lina, it is not a good idea. The situation is dangerous."

Lina replied, "Well I have to go protest and get my point of view heard. Not all of Egypt wants President Mubarak to step down right away. We need to go to show our support that he should finish his term."

Her mother said, "I am not comfortable with this at all," her eyes swelling with tears scared for their safety.

Her husband said, "Well, we need to go in a group."

On Wednesday February 2, Lina eventually got her way and joined the protests at Mostafa Mahmoud Square in Mohandseen with her husband, her sister, her cousin and sister-in-law. Lina was convinced that Mubarak had to leave, but after six months, when he would have completed his presidential term with a stable transition period, not right away.

The supporters of Mubarak were ordinary people like herself, peaceful, polite without an overarching demand. *"Al Shaab Yored el Rahma"* (The people want mercy), *"la leltakhreeb"* (No to destruction), *"Nam leltagheer, la le ehanet al kabeer"* (Yes to change, no to insulting the elder). Lina is certain that all Egyptians want a better country void of corruption, but what happened, had happened. Let former President Mubarak be. *Martin Luther King said, "Let us not seek to satisfy our thirst for freedom by drinking from the cup of bitterness and hatred.*"[58] Egyptians cannot keep crying over spilt milk. The people need to move on and overcome this hatred, but they have not.

Media Bias

Lina contacted several broadcast channels including CNN, BBC, CNBC Arabia and Al Arabia in order to ensure proper media coverage representing their view. Egyptians were claiming that *"el shaab yoreed…"* (The people want…) but she among others disagreed with the end of their chant, 'the downfall of the regime', and felt obliged to make it clear. She felt that the supporters were emanating positive energy and were hopeful that they would outsmart the activists and save the country. The international media, however, did not want to report this demonstration at all. They sent their crew but they never aired it. She had friends waiting in front of the television to see the event covered, but it never went on air. Lina called these stations several times to record viewer comments but none of them aired. This was a shocking, bitter realization for Lina. Why was international media ignoring the supporters of Mubarak?

Moreover, Lina found it strange that the Egyptian media sent a camera man and reporter to cover the demonstration, but did not cover the protests well. Their report failed to reflect the big numbers that actually showed up, estimating them at five to ten thousands, where she saw much more. The crowds packed all of Gameat El Dewal Street in addition to all the side streets. On the other side of town, the media amplified Tahrir numbers, giving the activists in Tahrir preferential coverage, or so it seemed.

It was a media game, and once Lina realized that the media had interests in supporting the revolution, her hope evaporated into thin air. The role of the media in the revolution has been negative and unethical to the worst possible level, both local and international, on television and in newspapers.

Whilst at Mostafa Mahmoud Square, Lina remembers waving at the supporters riding the camels and the horses, who were passing by. She heard that they were people from the area of Nazlet El Seman, next to the pyramids where tourists ride horses. Due to the protests at Tahrir, all the tourists had left Egypt and their departure had had a detrimental effect on their business. Their livelihoods were abruptly cut short. Lina was unaware when the flock of camels and horses attacked Tahrir. She received warning calls that Tahrir protestors were heading towards the president's supporters, so she left quickly with her husband and sister. They returned to their home before the curfew fell.

Lina finds it bewildering that the protestors were asking for their rights and yet did not respect the curfew. Within the walls of her suburban home, she saw the bloodshed on television. A theory she heard was that the pro- Mubarak protestors were the ones who had started assaulting the supporters at Tahrir, which caused the fighting that ensued. She saw evidence in a video online. However, she does not believe that the alleged members of NDP hired those people to go beat the protestors, especially as the day before, most of Egypt was siding with former President Mubarak after his emotional second speech. Another theory is that enemies of Mubarak planned this attack, possibly even the army, as they did let Mubarak's supporters enter Tahrir Square after all, knowing well that this would cause clashes. Lina will never understand how the army let a battle continue for over six hours without interfering. She believes the mystery around this street war will never be truly unraveled. However, over a year later, she suspects *Ikhwan* were behind the attack as it was an excellent opportunity for them to grab power after decades of injustice and oppression.

With her advertising background, Lina does not view the videos on You Tube as the blind truth. Depending on the angle and the timing of a video, a viewer can see a number of different perceptions of the same event. Lina is skeptical, for only if one were actually present in person, can one judge fairly. Back in 1986, the Guardian produced a great advert called 'Points of View'. It starts with the view of a man running, and one would assume he was running away from something. They then move onto the next clip, showing that the man is running towards a man holding a briefcase, presumably to steal it. However, the third clip shows the running man pushing the man with the briefcase, to save him from some falling masonry. The Guardian effectively shows the viewers that a story needs viewing from all angles to see the big picture.[59] Photos and videos from the demonstrations hence, did not move her personally, as she is skeptical, with the portrayal of only one angle.

Too Little Too Late

Everything seemed to go wrong with Mubarak's speeches, and it was apparent that the president had very bad advisors. All the speeches were at the wrong time, in the wrong way, with the wrong tone and the wrong message. Lina does not doubt that the revolution unfolded the way it did due to his advisory team's misreading of, and mediocre response to, the demands of his people. Additionally, the President could have prevented many events if he had responded differently, and more quickly. All the speeches were too little too late. Why did he deliver his speeches on different days? Why did he not say it all at once, the first time? Lina found his second speech good, but too late, as the bar of demands had risen due to his silent ignoring of the people.

His last speech prior to his stepping down, she found hilarious. It was a joke. Lina was worried about the safety of her activist friends, relentlessly advising them to stay at home. She called one of them after the third speech and they both cracked up in hysterical laughter. The speech had the unlikely same reaction from his supporters, by then known as *feloul* (remnants), and the activists.

Friday February 11, was Lina's worst birthday. The Vice President had announced around 6 pm that Mubarak was stepping down, at which point her birthday became the saddest day for her. Many of her friends were saluting her for being born on the best day in the world, when the tyrant finally fell, but she felt otherwise. For Lina it represented a sign of defeat, a giving in to chaos. To Lina it was the start of a horrible day and a horrible life.

Propose Don't Just Criticize

It is almost impossible for one human being to enjoy unanimous support; the same impossibility applies to a manager as it does a president. A subordinate can evaluate a manager as bad or good, strict or lenient, popular or unpopular. Lina, as a manager, is no different. The employees' verdict is the base on which managers are judged. It has to be noted that employees vary in experience and hence, maturity, leaving many unable to see the bigger picture. Senior positions are required to view business on a macro level. Most management take decisions considering the general good rather the individual good. Junior positions, on the other hand, tend to base their judgment through the micro lens rather than the macro lens.

Management is tough; it requires tough decisions, which not all employees will like. There are employees that do not perform up to standards but stay on the payroll to avert unbudgeted ten-year tenure, had the management fired them. As a result, some may consider a manager lenient with these types of senior employees. A manager may hear that there are employees coming to work late despite strict attendance policy, and deduct the missed hours from their salaries. An employee may tell his manager that one of his colleagues is taking an unethical commission, and although the manager may agree that it is a possibility, he turns a blind eye to whatever he might be pocketing, given that this employee is getting him good business, and as a result, the revenue is good. The list of employee concerns or dissatisfactions is endless.

If employees perceive that management is making mistakes, someone like Lina for example, would invite them to a meeting to propose alternatives, and not simply criticize. Lina would consider all valid options. Do not just judge. Present a better plan and she would be willing to implement it. She would challenge them to take her place, daring them to do a better job, and show her that the proposed plan is doable. This is what she expected from the activists when they took to the streets and revolted. However, in her opinion they failed dramatically.

The political scene is similar to the business scene in the sense that she is certain that former President Mubarak faced situations where he opted to be practical, and turned a blind eye in certain instances. Some will ponder the state Egypt has reached today, and where it could have been under a different President. One cannot judge unless placed in the same position. Lina was indifferent to former President Hosni Mubarak, whereas she showed preference for Sadat over Abdel-Nasser. Lina does not believe that President Mubarak is an evil person. On the contrary, she thinks the problem is that he lacked assertiveness and was overly kind and weak, succumbing easily to the influence of his close circle of confidence.

In a different context, it annoys Lina to see fans watching a football match, cursing, as a player loses a good shot at getting a goal; she challenges the fan to take the place of the player in order to realize that the player is doing his best.

Contagious Corruption

It exists in almost every society, democracies and autocracies. Many are corrupted by the system and follow the 'if you can't beat them, then join them' approach. *Moore referred to this notion in Utopia, "Besides, what chance have you got of doing any good, when you're working with colleagues like that? You'll never reform them-they're far more likely to corrupt you, however admirable a character you are!"*[60] *Similarly, in Egypt the corruption has turned into the assented silent conformity, with the non-corrupt the awkward minority.*

Lina witnessed corruption in the old *nizam*, yet shockingly it has doubled in rate after the revolution. Her cousin's husband works in the agriculture industry and deals frequently with customs. Before the revolution, if he needed a permit, a known Mr. X expected a bribe worth fifty thousand Egyptian pounds – eight thousand one hundred dollars- for the necessary permit. After the revolution, the fee doubled! Pre and post revolution, bribes have been normal, if not more so now. As salaries are so low, many public employees perceive demanding a bribe is their moral right. The revolution succeeded in removing the tip of the iceberg, but many of the fundamental problems in the Egyptian society are within the iceberg. Bribery and corruption is the accepted norm and this needs to change. Unfortunately, post Mubarak this has flourished even further.

Reform

In order to melt the whole iceberg, major reforms need implementation. Either that, or the emergence of an assertive, cold blooded, tough and daring leader. Someone the likes of Saddam Hussein. Otherwise, no inherent change will take place. Whoever is in power needs to take immediate action against the endemic lawlessness and deficiencies. He or she needs to take their head out of the dreamy clouds and come down to earth to tackle this gigantic issue of lack of discipline and ethics in all fields.

Real reform will be a lengthy and tiresome process that is likely to take many years, not mere months, until the unwanted iceberg has melted down, joining with the deep waters of the oceans.

It will require difficult but essential decisions. The cleaning up and purifying process needs to be thorough. If an employee is corrupt, he must be fired on the spot. A zero tolerance policy towards corruption must be the new norm, and no more *maalesh (I am sorry in a laid-back way)*. Reform needs to be all-encompassing, laws need reviewing, and changes need to be made to ensure justice upheld. Referring to the labor law, which protects employees who do not work and are unproductive, Lina deems that it desperately needs alteration, allowing employers to fire such inefficient and ineffective employees. If the reformed system is solid, then corruption will become the rare exception. *This echoes what Thomas Moore wrote in* <u>Utopia</u>, *"He should prevent crime by sound administration rather than allow it to develop and then start punishing."*[61]

Egypt is lacking good management; plagued with an utter lack of punctuality and degrading work ethics, and lacking conscience in work. Egyptians need to be educated in matters of work ethics: how to work properly, manage time, and for management to assert a firm fist. Unethical behavior needs swift and merciless dealing. Lina gives a simple example of househelp: compare the Egyptian work ethic to that of a Filipino. The difference is clear, and sadly, Egyptians do not want to work, are frequently late or absent, ready with excuses to avoid work. She gives another example of the lack of punctuality: she called up the air conditioner maintenance hot line for an appointment, and was given a three-hour range wherein she needed to sit and wait for them to show up. Eventually, the maintenance team arrived two hours after the agreed time range, wasting her entire afternoon. If one does something wrong once and it is accepted then he or she can repeat it indefinitely, and it becomes all right. The fault is not just on the doer but also the acceptor. In Egypt, the acceptor is the people, the silent majority.

Law is Above All

Lina saw a video on Amr Adeeb's talk show where the police asked a man to descend from a bus, asking for his papers - which he failed to provide, and hence the police assaulted him. She is not supporting violence and those assaulters need imprisonment, but law and justice must rule. Yet, in her opinion, police brutality needs viewing case by case, where in some cases it is justified and in others, it is not.

Lina is against violence but cannot rule it out completely when it comes to the police force. She cannot expect the police officer to treat a mass killer kindly. Lina personally does not know any innocent people maliciously hurt by the police. There are many question marks around the late Khaled Said. Whether he was framed as a 'drug dealer' or an innocent young man, as is the popular belief, may remain a mystery.

Resolving the mistrust between the police and the public will not take place over night. Lina believes that the police need to use the iron fist approach again as the tender *laissez-faire* approach has failed. What Egypt needs is aggressive, assertive leadership in the coming years to ensure it sails in the right direction.

Those who break the law need to be charged and those who uphold it need recognition; an example needs to be set. There are numerous methods with which to manage people and the government can call upon consultants to assist in selecting the most appropriate method for the country and its people.

Lina cannot fathom the new trend of street brutality, wherein civilians believe they have the right to assault the police. Civilians are complaining at the harsh treatment of the police and yet are demanding a harsh sentence on the former president. In their eyes, it is justice that the court may sentence former President Mubarak to the death penalty, merely based on public opinion and not concrete evidence. Civilians need to practice what they preach. The people on the street want the former president to face death, regardless of whether or not he ordered the killing of the peaceful protestors. And yet there is an outcry when a civilian is sentenced without proof. *The double standards must end.*

It is My Way or the Highway

Lina draws a simple simile between the revolution and the corporate world. In her agency, she has around one hundred and fifty employees on the payroll. If one morning, they strike and demand that the manager leaves or else they will stop working, Lina would not succumb to blackmail and instead would invite them to go ahead and leave. If one allows this overthrow, just once, then one becomes buried in chaos forever, and certainly in Egypt's case, miring it in mud post revolution. She detests immature attitudes such as 'it is my way or the highway.' Mothers face this with their toddlers who throw a tantrum and burst into tears in order to get their way, and if a mother gives in, then the toddler will know, 'this is the way I get what I want' and intelligently will repeat this technique, because it works!

Lina would be willing to listen to her employees if they delegate a speaker, who would represent them to management and state their demands. For instance, if it's a salary raise or increased benefits that they want, she would look at her financials and if there is room to implement such an increase, she will agree. But if not, then she would need to set a plan to include it in the next fiscal year. In a mature, quiet, reasonable manner, the employees will get their rights. Immature, loud and irrational behavior is unacceptable, just like a revolution asking for the downfall of the ruling regime. Lina finds it ironic that the protestors were asking for their human rights, but denied the personal freedom of Gamal Mubarak in running for presidency. People cannot decide who can and who cannot run for elections, law defines the candidate. Eligible voters just vote for whom they want from the choices they are given. She is certain that the protests will continue, as it is impossible that eighty plus million Egyptians will come to an agreement and will be content with the government or cabinet. It will never be unanimous and hence, some will voice their disagreement, demanding change. *As Machiavelli nicely wrote in* The Prince, *"There always exist malcontents and those who want a change."*[62] *It is inevitable.*

Revolutionaries

Lina's view has not changed much over the passing of the months, as all her fears have materialized. The revolutionaries did not have a vision and only focused on the short-term with no long-term plan. She is very disappointed in the educated elite who took to the streets, unaware of the dire repercussions. Their actions have led Egypt to unchartered and unsafe, chaotic deep waters. Lina is aware that the activists had good intentions, but they were too naïve to anticipate the effects of the revolution. She categorizes the revolutionaries into three groups: first, the highly educated with good intentions, second the followers, and thirdly the un-educated and unemployed victims of the society calling for personal justice. Among the third group are a few who figuratively got high on blood after the kill. Some of them were side tracked and others had plenty to gain. Some people were *ghawghaa* (mobs). She knows that the educated did not take to the streets, loot the shops and break into the prisons. This third group continued the momentum of the demonstrations whereas the followers now have become *feloul* against the revolution and the first group admitted that the revolution has led Egypt into a path they were not calling for.

Lina is baffled that the activists did not realize that the Islamists would rise to power with the fall of the *'ancien regime'*, or that the absence of a leader would lead to confrontations and disunity. And further, that by succumbing to one demand, they opened the door to over eighty million demands. Lina is very pessimistic, knowing that it is impossible to get all Egyptians to agree on one course, given the diversity in society.

The activists found themselves mixed up in a complicated political situation, having no clue as to what is needed to unravel the potential of this nation. In Lina's view, the activists have acted very childishly, expecting that after Mubarak steps aside everything would function normally. After the revolution, they should have united to form one political party rather than dozens, to deliver on the dreams of the revolution and to play politics. Activists cannot just fight over who gets a bigger piece of the pie, neglecting the state of the pie that has gone sour in the process.

Counter-Revolution

Lina recognizes that internal and external forces are probably supporting the counter-revolution. The world balance of power and the status quo need maintaining within the region at any cost. One cannot really understand the politics going on but clearly, Egypt is a strategic country with many enemies disguised as 'allies'.

Lina does not doubt that the politics playing out post-revolution are far too complicated for an average person to comprehend. There is an aggressive counter-revolution in place cracking down on the nation. Lina refers to the notorious attack on prisons on Friday January 28, 2011. There are several conspiracy theories behind the lethal hanky panky. Was it the Islamists setting their members free, or the ruling NDP sending hired thugs, attempting to distract the people from the protests in order to gain ground against the revolution? The proof shows that prisons were broken into from outside. If it were an internal plot then they could have just opened the gates. No one seems to have the answer, and perhaps no one ever will. There are plenty of unanswered questions. Why did the army let armed men into Tahrir? Who started the fighting? Why was there no interference when a full fledge battle was underway in downtown for over 6 hours? No one will know the naked truth or the constructed truth, even after the trials.

A black and white portrait is painted, with the counter-revolution labeled as bad and pro-revolution labeled good. This is clearly depicted by the black list, indicating all supporters of Mubarak. It stated that any actor or politician supporting former President Mubarak would be placed on this list and was susceptible to attacks. *George Orwell's Animal Farm predicted the bad and good labels in his fable. After the animal revolution kicked out the men from the farm, the animals came with a simple maxim, "Four legs good, two legs bad," labeling all people associated with the former regime as bad and all revolutionaries, the farm animals as good. Orwell analyzed and predicted generic revolution mechanism brilliantly yet gruesomely. The pigs, the new ruling elite at Animal Farm slowly took over the place of man at the farm and eventually brainwashed the animals into accepting the changed slogan to "Four legs good, two legs better."* [63] *Similarly, in Egypt, many are shocked to see Ikhwan reinstating a new fascist dictatorship far worse than the previous one, where they have brainwashed their members into believing the opposition are traitors and infidels, burying any hope of a democracy. Will Egypt prove to be an exception to the Orwellian revolution? Only time will tell.*

A few days after February 11, Lina went to Mostafa Mahmoud Square again, to find the numbers scarce and celebrities missing due to the ominous black list. People definitely got scared and there was almost no media coverage. It was a sad day, as if the supporters were practicing a religion in secret, fearing discrimination and persecution. One of the discriminating factors amongst the activists and the *feloul* was that the latter were fully aware that havoc and chaos were going to rule; this was the new name of the game. Lina looked around her and saw men and women, herself included, crying at the state of despair Egypt had reached.

After the revolution a group called '*feloul and proud*' was created on Facebook to share their common anti-protest and demonstration sentiments. The page served as a forum for them to express their views freely, with the overarching feeling that activists and pro-revolt folk were attacking them. Unfortunately, many highly educated people have removed friends from Facebook, as their views were conflicting, exercising zero tolerance and respect. However, Lina did not. She respects all her friends and their views, regardless of whether they agree or disagree with her.

Military Rule Will Prevail

In Lina's view, when one faces an unknown situation, one should follow through with the right steps. When one buys a new appliance one should read the manual before operating the appliance. Unfortunately, Egyptians did not refer to the manual, which asserts that after a revolution a new constitution must be the first step towards reform. Hence, Lina voted no to the constitutional referendum, like most activists. Way before the voting day, the Muslim Brotherhood printed posters advocating a yes to represent stability. In mosques, sheikhs openly stated that if you wanted to go to heaven, you should vote 'yes'. Is this not blasphemy?

Islamists were distributing and aggressively hammering to the public, Islamic driven campaign posters and publications, two weeks before voting. Just two days before the ballot box, the army announced the banning of religious messages, strangely after leaving them for over ten days. It was too late, after the message had already been delivered. It was unbelievable, and when the weird results came through, misrepresenting the truth in her view, her skepticism grew even more. To her astonishment, after the referendum the army declared that the constitution was no longer valid and declared a constitutional statement with the accepted clauses during the vote. So why did they call for the referendum and spend millions of Egyptian pounds on a useless exercise?

Although the army's role is fundamental, it has dismally failed to play any positive part. Since the beginning of the revolution, they have sided with the wrongdoers: no action, no reaction; wrong action or slow action; wrong reaction or nothing. There is no doubt in Lina's mind that the army has been unable to live up to the role of managing the country, and due to the complete lack of security, she realizes the possibility that it was their intention to let havoc rule. It can be one of two scenarios; either they are not smart, or they are steering the country in their preferred direction, pretending a naive facade.

It appears that the reigns of the horse are uncontrolled, allowing the Arabian stallion to run wild with no destination. However, over time, it has become apparent that the army wants to maintain its superior power clearly guaranteed in the 2012 constitution. Lina believed there would officially be a military rule and no democracy. She was not convinced that there would be elections by the end of the year. However, she was proved to be wrong, as the parliamentary elections did take place as scheduled in November 2011, in which the *Ikhwan* won the majority of seats.

Future

Lina wears a solidarity bracelet, as she sympathizes with her Christian Coptic brothers and sisters, who suffered heartless attacks. She is a devout Muslim and does not believe she needs to wear the veil to show that. She believes faith is measured by what is within the individual, and not the appearances. Faith is a very personal relationship with God, and differs from one individual to another. Nobody has the right to interfere with a person's relationship with God. She is sad for Islam because of how Islamists are interfering with this sacred, private relationship, tarnishing the true image of Islam. Lina, a Muslim woman, believes the Islamists are a disgrace to Islam, especially Bin Laden, who has tainted the image of Islam worldwide. Whenever she sees a woman wearing a *niqab* (full-face veil) or a man with a long beard, she stereotypes them as being a bad representation of Islam, and curses. She cannot imagine what a foreigner would feel. If within the religion, there is no tolerance then one should not expect tolerance from people of others faiths. In every religion there are extremists and lunatics. The issue with the Islamists is how they view all Egyptians, both Copts and Muslims.

What Egypt is facing is neither freedom nor democracy, but chaos. One cannot expect change while he or she persists with the same old corrupt manners. People are still littering, and cutting each other off on the roads, and women are still being harassed. A popular Arabic proverb goes, "That which is built on a wrong foundation regardless of the construction will also be wrong." Lina does not feel that the Egyptian people will change themselves to become better citizens and hence a better nation, and refers to the verse in the Quran, "Of *Allah*. Verily never will *Allah* change the condition of a people until they change what is in themselves." (13:11)[64] She is pessimistic and does not see the light; the future is glum in her eyes.

180° Change

In 2012, Lina was living in a vicious cycle of recurring negativity that was affecting her mind, and it became difficult to remain sane. She toiled for months after a Plan

B. If things got bad in Egypt, where would they go? Lina and her husband arranged to acquire a residency at the United Arab Emirates, U.A.E. During this period, Lina collapsed into a zombie state. She barely talked with her friends and family. She was on edge, to say the least. Lina was seeing, feeling, and talking blackness. Once she attained her goal and secured a plan, Lina regained herself and her sanity; she became once more positive and optimistic.

Lina would never give up and leave the country that she loved behind because of the radical policies of the ruling *Ikhwan* party. Lina was not giving up on Egypt and its identity. She started becoming happy, content to be living in her beloved country, and became assertive, standing her ground. This was a turning point in her view of current affairs. Suddenly Lina joined forces with the opposition and activists. She entered into an imaginary tug of war. The more she saw bearded men, the more revealing clothes she wore. Lina started to wear sleeveless tops to work for the first time.

At the time President Morsi was announced president, Lina shut off completely from newspapers, Facebook and news broadcasts. She isolated herself in her bubble. However, she remained very optimistic, as she believed the *Ikhwan* rule would not last long; another change was bound to happen sooner rather than later.

Her bubble burst when President Morsi issued a presidential decree on November 22, 2012, furnishing him with sweeping powers, and making himself literally above the law. This declaration caused a lot of unrest on the streets. Protests were called for, and revolutionaries were once more filling the streets of Egypt. One day Lina switched on the television and watched a moving patriotic song that made her want to cry. For the first time, Lina found herself swept by a hurricane of emotions and she finally understood what the activists felt. Lina thought, "I have to be there." Anyone who had died, peacefully protesting, was a martyr.
She said, "I am confident that the activists are strong enough to demand change. We should all stop working and make a statement. It is now or never."

From this day on Lina changed one hundred and eighty degrees. She has been supporting the protestors by collecting funds and will continue in her support despite the fact that a government institute has harassed one of her colleagues, due to her political philanthropy. Lina believes Egyptians cannot back down now because if they fold, their efforts will evaporate into thin air, and their hopes and dreams for a better Egypt will become history.

On Tuesday November 27, 2012, Lina wanted to join the demonstrations for the very first time; she wore black to work in support of the protestors. Unfortunately, swamped with work on a pitch at the agency, she left the office very late, at two in the morning. She needed to return home to be with her daughter who was sick at the time.

The following week, Wednesday December 5, 2012, the protestors opposing the constitutional declaration and the biased constitutional committee were violently attacked by *Ikhwan* at al-Ittihadiya massacre, where around half a dozen people were brutally beaten to death and around several hundred wounded. It was one of the most horrible days for Lina, as she was stuck at the office in a meeting with the CEO and twenty employees. She was torn between watching the television live broadcast of the street war and trying to concentrate on the meeting. Lina was petrified that one of her friends would fall victim and appear on the TV screen. She was crying from inside. Once again, Lina is disappointed in the skewed and scarce international media coverage of the second wave of the revolution in Egypt, which is a *déjà-vu* of the media position during the coverage of Mostafa Mahmoud demonstrations during the last days of Mubarak's reign.

Despite how uncertain and how dark the atmosphere has become, Lina's metamorphosis into an optimistic Egyptian is remarkable. She is confident that Egypt will return to its citizens sooner rather than later. Rightly, so, on June 30, 2013, Lina joined millions of Egyptians flooding the streets of the country demanding the ousting of President Morsi, and the military swiftly obliged.

She did not join the demonstrations on July 26, 2013 when General Sisi called for the delegation of the army to combat terrorism, as she was in her summerhouse. Lina is no longer following the political scene, as she trusts the Egyptian army and is certain that they have a plan for the country. She is optimistic about the future, unconcerned with the return of military state. She wants stability so that the economy can prosper, and to ensure that Egypt is the best place to bring up her children and the children of her friends.

PART III

The Watchdogs

"The gem cannot be polished without friction,
Nor man perfected without trials."
Confucius

CHAPTER 11

Jarring Justice

"Egypt is not a country we live in but a country that lives within us"
"Masr laysat watan naeesh feh bal watan yaeesh feena"
Pope Shenouda III

I believe that fellow artists genuinely want to help each other out, given the usual cold shoulder from society. This is why I think Yehia El Elaily, a professional photographer, eagerly tried to help me in finding authentic perspectives for my book. When we coincidently met at Gezira Club and I shared my book project with him, he was enthusiastic and volunteered to get me in touch with some of his friends. One of them was Ehab Kamel whom I met at Brioche Doree at Hilton Zamalek Residence Hotel on Thursday November 24, 2011.

Supreme Court

He is a handsome eligible bachelor of medium build with big wide brown eyes, a wide smile showing his perfect white teeth and has a distinctive coarse voice. Ehab Kamel Selim had recently turned forty years old. He was born in Cairo on April 27, 1971. He attended Port Said School in Zamalek, where he graduated high school in 1990. Ehab studied general law at Cairo University's Law School, attaining his degree in 1995, after which he pursued his masters. Following university, law graduates need training in law offices for two years in order to attain a certificate of training that gives them a title of a preliminary lawyer.

Ehab was fortunate to have started practicing law right after his training. Being an only male child, he was exempt from military service. Ehab worked as a lawyer in various companies for seven years until he gained enough experience and a good base of clients to set up his own private law office in Garden City, in 2003. As Ehab acquired more law experience, his ranking rose in the hierarchy of lawyers. To reach the level of appeals lawyer, he needs ten years of experience before appearing in front of the court of cassations or the Supreme Court. The most senior level in this hierarchy is the Supreme Court, which Ehab will apply for in January 2013 after completing ten years in appeals.

Although Ehab did not specialize in a certain domain in law school, due to his work, he has been able to focus and hence prosper in the field of criminal law. Ehab further successfully narrowed his scope on felonies. With the help of word of mouth, he gained new clients from old ones who had won lawsuits with him. Ehab has an established reputation. He prefers to stay away from representing people in cases related to drugs and though he once won such a case, he is happy not to have acquired any more since then.

Inefficient Bureaucracy

The major weakness of the Egyptian legal system is its extremely slow motion, arguably, uncharacteristic of other countries. Egyptian key institutions like the ministries of interior and justice are like many intertwined chains. If one chain is cleansed from corruption and inefficiencies, the rest of the chains will follow. On the other hand, the people need to seek self-improvement. For instance, one neighbor should not raise a ludicrous lawsuit because of water dripping from the laundry hung by his upstairs neighbor! One of the reasons behind this slowness is the huge number of cases per judge. Usually, the courts issue decisions towards the end of the month. The pile of cases keeps rising, with many postponed cases in addition to the newly submitted ones. Lawyers know the tricks of the trade, postponing the lawsuits in their favor.

As a lawyer, Ehab deals with people from all walks of life; criminals, police officers, coffee boys, and managers. Ehab needs to deal with people successfully and diplomatically in order to win his cases. Through his dealings, he realizes that the country is running a shamefully corrupt system across all levels. He has seen corruption of the mind where hypocrisy is the lord; it is like graves within graves of corruption. Improper use of resources is the norm in Egypt. The environment is polluted by negative thoughts and energy, making it normal to deal with the surroundings negatively. Before the revolution, Ehab was sure that something was going to happen, but did not know when, where, how or by whom.

Ehab recalls foreigners who wanted to establish a recycling company in Egypt, but faced endless bureaucracy and red tape. Eventually, turned off by the complications, they gave up on the idea of opening the company. Initially, any foreign company wanting to operate in Egypt needs to get security approval for the go-ahead to set-up.

There is no attempt to facilitate and encourage investment in the country. All the ministries are working within the same atmosphere of bureaucracy. Ehab once won a case, proving that he had paid double taxation, against the minister of finance. However, he only got his refund check worth fairly a substantial sum, after a year and a half, due to the corruption. Ehab compares the structure of corruption to that of a pyramid, with the tip of the pyramid being the head of the corrupt state who allows this negative, unjust atmosphere to prevail. On the lower layers of the pyramid, the corruption continues, and ultimately, the base of the people, the majority, are the ones who suffer the negative effects of corruption the most. The norm is to give people such a hard time when trying to get their legal work done that the only way they can achieve it is through *wasta* (contacts or nepotism). The environment today is filled with dissatisfaction, envy, and hatred. *In the past Egyptians were always smiling and courteous, known for their hospitality, which drew tourists to Egypt. Today, many tourists visit the country one time and are not encouraged to re-visit due to the infested environment and spirit.*

A qualified president needs to manage the people, just as any family needs to be run by an efficient husband and father in a traditional patriarchal society. If you take a nuclear family where the parents are not good managers, surely their children will likely end up bad managers. It is the same with the country. If the administration and the executive branches are mismanaging, then all the people will also follow their lead.

Former President Mubarak had many good achievements. However, his failures out-shadow and outweigh the successes when placed on the balance of scales. The security glitz, the Nile basin issue, sectarian strife and football matches, all are part of the plan to keep the population distracted. Observers have noticed the cauldron boiling and some are reacting by withdrawing into depression, while others vent their anxiety with outward aggression, and still others, became ardent change advocates.

Ehab believes since Egyptians are naturally religious, they should pray to God to save the country and deliver justice. Ehab has a strong belief that God orchestrated the revolution via his creation: Egyptian human beings. There were many things at fault in Egypt, and the uprising meant to correct those wrongs, having come after many missed chances. The universe is God's property and He has the right to change things He does not like. Homeowners have the right to change the home décor if they do not like it, what about God with His creations? Ehab was shocked when early in January 2011, when the newly fraudulently elected parliament was in session and protestors were outside the building, former President Mubarak said, "Let them amuse themselves." People despised the president more than words can explain. Ehab's parents brought him up to understand that lying is wrong. He wonders, is rigging elections not a form of lying?

Egyptians took to the streets demanding justice, however almost two years later, it has failed to unfold. As Martin Luther King wrote, "Demonstrations, experience has shown, are part of the process of stimulating legislation and law enforcement."[65] In Egypt this 'process of stimulating legislation and law enforcement' has yet to materialize.

Court Adjourning

Police Day, Tuesday January 25, was a pre-announced day of protesting. Ehab had been enjoying his Caramel Macchiato at Beano's coffee shop in Zamalek, and later met his friend in a suburb called 6th of October, where he watched the unfolding news. He had previously seen protests with people lying on the floor in their underwear, in an attempt to draw the authorities' attention. The authorities, however, blindly ignored them. *Amn Eldawla*, Central Security, expected, and prepared their forces, that there would be bigger than usual crowds, forecasted to be in the thousands. Ehab expected the Ministry of Interior to attack the protestors, just like in other countries when protestors go to the streets illegally. He never expected that an uprising would take place. This was not a mere disturbance, but more like the Palestinian Intifada. Who was their leader? There wass no leader and no symbol, but they had very clear goals. Former President Mubarak, deep down, just could not make peace with his people, as he does not see his dire mistakes. Ehab believes that Mubarak must have approved, on all levels, the aggression towards the protestors. In Ehab's mind, the president must have given his consent. Mubarak never apologized for the deaths of protestors during his three infamous televised speeches. The son of Ehab's neighbor took a live bullet in his leg. In the eyes of the *ancien regime,* that young man committed treason by calling for the end of the regime and hence deserved the shot. Ehab supported the demands of the activists but personally did not participate, representing the silent majority.

Ehab called his friend, a police officer, who explained to him that their forces were scattered, with some officers being re-located - the improvised plan for the huge turnout. Police officers were exhausted, staying alert from January 23 until the 27th without sleep. Officers from *Kasr El Nil* Station were relieved by nearby Abdeen station officers. Moreover, they were not dressed for the very cold weather, wearing T-shirts and jackets, and did not have enough to eat. Police officers were stationed in groups of four and every few hours, one of them would go to buy water and food to sustain them. Ehab thinks that either the intelligence community did not have enough information about the event, or those in charge opted to abstain from making a decision as to a plan of action, hence compromising the security forces. His friend told Ehab that if thugs were to attack the police station, he would defend it using the twelve bullets he had, and shoot at the assaulters, ready to die defending the station. His friend warned him that authorities would order the internet shutdown the following day and true to his word, it was unplugged.

Ehab went to his office on January 26, 2011. It was business as usual for him, but the traffic was gridlocked, as people were protesting at Tahrir.

Caution is one of Ehab's characteristics. However, he strayed from his circumspect nature when he ventured out to see the demonstrations on the Friday of Anger. He needed to see it with his own eyes, to believe the footage on the television screens; the masses of people that had flooded the streets. He walked to Kasr El Aini Bridge, only to find it barricaded. It suddenly dawned on him that the situation was bigger than he had imagined. Ehab retired to the safety of his home, and watched the events on television. He had a morning court session on Saturday the 29th, next to Zenhoum morgue.

On his way to court, Ehab passed by the Kasr El Nil Bridge. The scene had dramatically changed. Police cars and vans littered the street, up in flames. It was surreal, as if a civil war had broken out in the once safe and lively streets of Cairo. Over the serene Nile banks, the loathed headquarters of the former ruling National Democratic Party (NDP) was an inferno, with the mysterious absence of fire engines. Ehab arrived at the courtroom to find astonished and baffled faces, everyone questioning each other about the sudden danger outside. The judge quickly postponed all the cases for the day. Relief swamped Ehab, as he wanted to get away from all the madness on the streets. With the internet down, he realized that no ATMs were functioning, and suddenly Ehab found himself in an awkward situation with little money on him. The mobile network intermittently turned on, and he got a call from a friend informing him about a torched café, and an army tank that was in flames close to his office. Mindlessly, Ehab still wanted to go to his office at Garden City, very close to Kasr El Aini and Tahrir, which was a feat. He managed to get there and took some money, locked up and apprehensively returned to his home.

By Saturday January 29, broadcast reports of casualties haunted the screens. Ehab found it hard to believe. How could the police shoot at thousands and thousands of Egyptians?

Ehab did not participate in the demonstrations, as he believes that everyone has a role to play, and he knew that being an activist was not his role. It is not his nature to shout support or chant a slogan, not even in a football match. He joined the civilian checkpoints near his apartment building, where they would search incoming cars thoroughly to maintain safety in their vicinity, with the absence of the police. Ehab was very glad to see the newborn harmony amongst neighbors who had previously never met. Before the revolution, families were so self-involved with their affairs; work, school, household, parents, children's activities, buying their groceries and paying the bills, that they never had time to meet their neighbors.

Ehab simply classifies the protestors into two main groups. The first group was the decent people who had good intentions; the second group was people who had bad, vengeful intentions. During any conflict, one party needs to let go if no clashes are to take place. Ideally, that would be the offenders, not the defenders, according to Ehab.

One Hand
Army officials from Special Forces 777 team, a lieutenant and a captain, helped Ehab's checkpoint near the Army Club. They asked him to call them whenever he needed. Ehab was amazed at the type and number of weapons, which came out of the Zamalek homes, for instance a rifle slung over the shoulder like in a Sylvester Stallone movie. He even saw Samurai swords! Residents at key locations protected each major street. Ehab mostly took the evening shift from 6 pm until 2 am, as he usually cannot stay awake very late. There was also the late morning shift from 2 am until 10 am. Neighbours managed the shifts together by communicating via their landlines.

During his shift, Ehab arrested two thugs; one, ironically, was a lawyer and the other, a doctor. One was unarmed, but had a plastic bag, which he refused to show them, and declined to answer their questions. After a phone call was made, three armored cars drove by the checkpoint to escort the *baltegeya*. The officers, well built and tall, wearing masks on their faces, thoroughly checked the thugs before leaving. Every day, security code words were changed. One time it was 'God is with us'; another was 'Koraish's Eagle'. The codes were changed in coordination with all the checkpoints at Zamalek, to avoid any confusion. The leaders of the checkpoints wore different color bands around their arms to distinguish them as security marshalls. Zamalek is known as a quiet, affluent residential area where many embassies are located. All of them normally have officers securing them but they were absent during those turbulent times. It would have been suicide, as many targeted or hunted the police.

One of the residents had a red Dodge Ram car that was used to trap suspects and drive them to the army officials. They arrested a criminal who was transferred to *mokhabarat* (intelligence).

Power of Prayer
Ehab viewed the first and third speeches of former President Mubarak as a waste of time. However, the second speech was brilliant, as it struck the emotional cords of Egyptians, resulting in division amongst the people. One camp sympathized with President Mubarak and the other camp did not buy his emotional sweet talk. Ehab was surprised to see some of his friends going to Mostafa Mahmoud Mosque to show support for the former president. During the third and last speech, Ehab noticed that Mubarak was frail and needed to support himself, a possible sign of retributive justice.

Being a devout Christian, Ehab believes in the power of prayer, and this is what he reverted to during those unforgettable, stomach wrenching 18 days. When life becomes suffocating, tight and pitch dark, a worshipper would look up to the sky and ask for God's help. He heard some people explain the ugly situation as punishment from God, for steering away from Him, and Ehab wanted to get closer. Prayer was Ehab's only solace, and after 18 rollercoaster days, God seems to have heard his prayers. When the late Vice President Omar Suleiman announced President Mubarak had actually stepped down, Ehab was in shock and disbelief that it really happened! He was thankful that it did not take longer for this historic day to materialize. It was a joyful day for Ehab and for most of Egypt. Ehab drove his car in the streets of Zamalek, joining the public celebration and jubilation. His mobile was constantly ringing with calls from friends and family, sharing congratulations and confirming the astounding news. It was a miracle. Ehab could not help but ponder on the power of prayers.

Even though President Mubarak did not resign in person, the constitution allows the president to resign for health reasons or due to popular pressure. He cannot come back, as his legitimacy was lost in the streets. With the downfall of the president as head of the executive power, automatically the constitution also fell. The former president was the superior ruling officer of the army, police, and judiciary. With this huge power vacuum, there were two legal alternatives. First, the head of the Supreme Court, Farouk Sultan, could legally be assigned to lead the nation. Second, a representative political committee that would either establish a preliminary temporary constitutional declaration or proceed directly with establishing the new constitution, could be summoned. The ruling party, in this case the Supreme Council of the Armed Forces (SCAF) would nominate or select candidates for a vote. The people withdrew their trust and hence the legitimacy of the former president, and the president handed over this legitimacy to the Supreme Council of the Armed Forces. The representative committee could include key figures such as the head of Supreme Court, the head of the appeals court, constitutional experts, representatives of church and Azhar, representatives of the political parties, and the people's assembly. However, the Supreme Council of the Armed Forces did not opt for this path.

The worst thing that happened, in Ehab's point of view, was the relentless killing of the protestors. An image that he will never forget is the photograph of a young boy sleeping on the caterpillar treads of the army tank, which symbolized the army protecting its people. In his mind, the most remarkable time was the first day of the revolution and the last day, with Mubarak's abdication.

Shaky Transition

On March 19, 2011, the Supreme Council of the Armed Forces (SCAF), held the first constitutional referendum on changes to the old 'overthrown' constitution, after which they strangely issued a constitutional declaration with the rules the country would abide by during the transition. This path baffled many activists and intellectuals. How could the country vote on changes to a constitution, already overthrown with the abdication of former President Mubarak?

Common fears were that *Ikhwan* would take over the reins of this magnificent Arabian horse. The Islamists subtly confirmed this underlying fear when they called for a million-man march on November 2011. Ehab believes that Egyptians do not want Islamists to rule. He resents *Ikhwan's* manipulation of people's fears based on religion. *To this day, this fear is widespread, more so after President Mohamed Morsi has been in office for over forty days. Many people want to separate religion from politics in opposition to the Islamists who want them married.*

The Egyptian Republic is built on the base of separation of powers, similar to the French Republic and actually, many Egyptian laws are based on the revered French laws. For instance, the French Republic has no vice president in its structure and likewise, in Egypt. The legislative, judiciary and executive powers each have independent functions. Laws are issued by the legislative power, the executive implement those laws, and the judiciary supervises both. The problem in Egypt is that the executive power changed its role as it supervised the legislative and judiciary powers, which led to an absolute tyranny. Today, some reformers are advocating a parliamentary system similar to the British system, with the prime minister ruling the country, and a figurehead president. Legislative power has come under the jurisdiction of the executive, which has been catastrophic. Ehab noticed that midway, as the post revolution Parliament was writing up a new law on the parliamentary system, there was a change of heart and the presidential system was upheld.

It is crucial for Egyptians to have the proper mindset so that a smooth transition takes place. The constitution, drafted by the best hundred scholars back in 1954, is a great starting point. Unfortunately, the Supreme Council of the Armed Forces (SCAF) did not opt for this possibility, but rather, went for parliamentary elections. In November 2011, there was street trouble close to Tahrir at Mohamed Mahmoud Street where *Dakhleya* headquarters is located. Many civilians were wounded and died during this street war. Rumor had it that the parliamentary elections would be postponed due to the circumstances but the army clearly stated they would stick to their word, which they did. The elections forced the people out of the street and stopped the skirmishes so that there would be a vote. Ehab was not worried at the prospect of *Ikhwan* winning the majority of the seats in the parliament. However, he could understand how women would be concerned if authorities forced them to wear the *hijab*, stifling their personal freedom. This did not happen. Ehab could not imagine that Egypt overthrew a system of outlaws and non-disciplined abusers, to select other perpetuators of greater abuses under the name of religion.

During the Mohamed Mahmoud Street war, protestors provoked the police. His friend, Mourad, told Ehab police hired *baltegeya* to attack themselves and take photos as proof that *Dakhelya*, was under threat. Mourad was injured when a bullet entered his calf from one side and out the other, luckily causing little damage. More accustomed to the innocent decent protestors at Tahrir, the sudden attack surprised police officers. Each party was playing defense. The police would not allow assaults on public institutions, and refused to stand by watching their demise.

Ehab has heard that *Ikhwan* gather men from the rural governorates of Tanta or Kafr El Sheikh into big buses and pay them a hundred pounds, around fourteen dollars, to travel to Tahrir to stage a sit-in and return to their town by the end of the day. *Ikhwan* mobilize the crowds using money rather than logical, reasoned demands and an overarching vision. The activists sitting openly at Tahrir realized *Ikhwan's* plot of hiring phantom activists. With the passing of months, many people have lost trust in *Ikhwan*.

Distrusting Police
Ehab believes some laws in Egypt need to be changed. For instance, the criminal law is feeble; women and children need laws that provide them justice; and police need the law to be on their side, granting them more power in order to uphold law and order on the streets. Law needs swift implementation but the rooted bureaucracy hinders this. Some helpful laws do exist but lack implementation, like the law against insulting religion. *The police have a critical role to play in upholding justice as they hold the keys to law and order. As Martin Luther King said, "law and order exist for the purpose of establishing justice and that when they fail in this purpose they become the dangerously structured dams that block the flow of social progress"*[66] After the revolution, the police lay low for a long period and were not visible to civilians, thus thwarting progress.

Ehab talked with his police friend, who was disgruntled to say the least, with the country's affairs. The problem is, like the flow of water, the current of the law flows against the waters of the police force. For instance, the law does not protect the police officer who stood up defending his station, as society branded the police officer a criminal, and the assaulting civilian a martyr. The supervising lieutenant who allowed his police officers to shoot at the protestors is now in prison and therefore, the officers are left feeling vulnerable. This explains the absence of the police force in the Egyptian streets in addition to the burning hatred emanating from civilians towards the force.

Ehab believes a written constitution along with an elected parliament, and qualified government, will address the complete lack of trust among the civilians and the police force. Once these essentials state apparatus are in place, the trust will automatically grow back. As long as those in charge during the transition period insist on patching up matters like an old rag sewn onto a worn galabeya, the people will reject the distasteful ugly-looking *galabeya*. What authorities need to do is to buy new clean material of good quality for the tailor to sew a new *galabeya* that is closer to the people's new taste and liking. Once this happens, the wheel of productivity will run smoothly. Gone are the days of patchwork.

Betrayed Friends

Ehab believes the issues between Muslims and Christian have old roots, which could have been resolved during the 70's, in the era of President Anwar Sadat, but have been ignored. When a Church was demolished in the town of Sol in Bani Suef in March 2011 and another at Imbaba in May 2011 the army stepped in, rebuilt them, and shouldered its cost. However, they did not address the root cause or the reason why the assaulters targeted and demolished the churches in the first place, continuing the Sadat and Mubarak strategy. In 2000, terrorists killed thirty Christians at Koshoh, in Assiut. Some were forced outside their homes and burnt alive, and others shot dead as they came out of work. One story Ehab heard which he could never forget is about two close friends, one Muslim and one Christian. They worked together at a warehouse. That day after work, they had dinner together, and bid each other farewell, parting to their respective homes. In the evening, the Muslim friend went up to his Christian friend with a gang of Islamists demanding that he convert to Islam or else the gang would kill him. The Christian man refused and was confused at the betrayal of his friend who watched his merciless execution. The Islamists torched the house in an abhorrent act of unjustifiable hatred.

Martin Luther King wrote about the dangers of hatred, "Hate is just as injurious to the hater as it is to the hated. Like an unchecked cancer, hate corrodes the personality and eats away its vital unity..."Love or perish"[67] A Muslim lawyer, Maged Yakoub defended the Christian victims at court after this horrible crime. When the convicts were sentenced to life imprisonment and death their cases were appealed, and ended with their acquittal. This was a clear, jarring social statement declaring the acceptance of hate crimes against Christians, as they will go un-punished. *How could a defendant be found guilty and sentenced and upon appeal became innocent? This indicates that either the law is flawed or the judge is not upholding the law and in either case, reform is mandatory.*

The nation is heading into darkness with economic recession, and vast lies and deceptions cover hidden agendas. At the neighborhood of Omraneya, in Giza, workers were restoring a church in August 2010 when outlaws fired at them. People blamed Hezbollah for this atrocious act of evil, which they quickly denied. Shortly afterwards on the January 1, 2011, the All Saints Church was attacked with many worshippers suddenly and brutally dying. Despite the sporadic spurts of violence, Ehab does not believe that Egypt is at risk of a civil war breaking out. He is convinced that Egyptians have inherent good seeds of love and tolerance and will not let religious differences divide them.

The building law number 120 issued in 2008 has instigated protests at Maspero in front of the national State TV building. The law requires approval of *Amn Eldawla* (State Security), before proceeding with building a church. The new law issued in 2012 has amended this requirement and therefore it will be simpler for Egyptians to build churches.

Ehab has not personally faced any sort of religious discrimination. He has a conviction that it is a matter of self rather than other, following the old golden rule, "do unto others, as you would want them to do unto you." Ehab lives with a positive attitude, minding God in everything. He respects everyone he deals with and hence demands respect in return. Ehab never rejects anyone and hence nobody rejects him. Ehab abides by this verse from the Bible, "Set a watch, O LORD, before my mouth; keep the door of my lips" (Psalms 141: 3)[68].

Screeching Injustice

Egyptian law has fundamental errors that are not conducive for justice to prevail. An example is how laws affecting women's rights under the family law are upheld. For instance, if a married woman requested divorce as her husband had physically abused her and she presented a medical report supporting her statement, the judge can grant her a divorce based on the official medical report. However, in Egypt, the judge proceeds in demanding two witnesses to back her story, hence prolonging the process and delaying justice, which is unquestionably traumatic for the abused wife. Another example where the courts do not uphold the law is in the case of *nafkah* (alimony), where at times of separation, the law requires the husband to pay his wife a temporary allowance until the case is final and a final settlement is paid. However, often courts do not demand this lawful temporary alimony for the wife, as the court possibly intentionally ignores and overlooks it. Ehab is handling a divorce request by a wife beaten by her husband, but the court will decide after six months. During those months, her life is on hold and she lives in fear. The articles of law protect women on paper. However, the judgment is not swift, and hence, it is unjust. As the saying goes 'justice delayed is justice denied'.

Ehab cites a documented case where a father of his client owns a plot of land, one thousand square meters, and rents it to a company. The father had set up two contracts with the same company, splitting the land; one contract for seven hundred square meters, and the other for three hundred square meters. As per the law, after forty years, the landowner has the right to evict the tenant and reclaim usage of his land. Ehab's client raised a lawsuit to reclaim the land and lost the case. Ehab proceeded to the appeals court. Legally, there were two cases for the two contracts, with a two-week lag between them. The ruling in the first case was that the tenant evacuates the land and hands it back to the owner. Ehab and his client were very glad and were confident that the second case would end with the same ruling. However, they were wrong. The second case was rejected in the appeal, with the court ruling in favor of the tenant to continue his usage of the land. How could the same case have two opposing rulings under the same rent law and the same judge? The plaintiff was the same, the defense was the same, and yet the outcome was very different. This is a clear example of the inconsistency and error in some of the articles in Egyptian law, especially when it comes to its implementation. If the court rejects an appeal, only the Supreme Court can reopen the case. This, however, is a very lengthy and bureaucratic process, possibly lasting up to two decades.

Similarly, inconsistencies arise in inheritance laws. The law does not guarantee rights, and certainly does not uphold equal rights. Ehab predicts from current discussion on the constitution, that the predominating Islamist wave would compromise women and children's rights. For instance, among the discussions is one on allowing children of twelve years old to work, which is in conflict with international laws against child labor. Twelve year olds need the care of family and state. The argument brought forward for reducing the age of the work force is that there is a need to utilize the millions of young and idle children who roam the streets of Egypt begging, or cleaning windscreens or pick pocketing. Ehab was baffled and shocked at this rationale; rather than creating an institution in charge of these children to provide them with support, it will be easier if authorities legally employed the children. At the time of this interview, there is a request to cancel the constitutional committee, based on illegality and misrepresentation but the judge postponed the verdict. *Similarly, one of the laws protecting women is the one banning female 'circumcision'. The law, however, has not stopped the widespread mutilation of young girls and the former dominantly Ikhwan parliament were discussing revoking this law under the pretext of providing safer 'circumcision'.*

Constitutional Vacuum

Ehab believes that the right path to the constitution and ultimately good laws is to reveal the truth to the people. The recent rise to power of the *Ikhwan* has indicated repeatedly, their hunger to grasp power and head the country. For Egypt to get out of the political blunder, the newly elected ruling party needs to face the facts, admit their mistakes, and take corrective action. They need to state that they are incapable of managing and leading the country and appoint qualified politicians from outside their party to move forward. The 'cream of society' needs to set a constitutional draft committee from a selection of the rich, the poor, the intellectuals and the goal achievers all combined.

The rules of the game should be that whatever standing law needs abolishing should go, and that which is new and has majority support should remain upheld. Egypt needs a constitution from within its boundaries and does not need to borrow from other countries. The committee needs to consist of people who have no interests in power, to ensure it is unbiased. Ehab can only deduce that whoever is in the political scene today is corrupt, and whoever has stayed away is principled. In order to affect reform, the whole team needs change, regardless of individuals being qualified. Ehab compares the situation with a child whose hair has been affected with an imaginary disease. The doctor orders all his hair shaved off in order to heal his hair, and for the new healthy hair to grow. If the doctor only treats the affected area, how could he guarantee that the rest of the hair is not infected? The handsome boy will surely not look his best with his bald head, but this is for his own good, and to combat the disease. Eventually, he will look good again when his hair grows in even a better condition, thicker and shinier than before. Similarly, in Egypt, the ruling government needs to resign for a new, healthy regime to take over.

The president should only appoint a constitutional committee, and not its members. Ehab recommends a small committee to select the one hundred representatives to write the constitution, including individuals who are elderly, independent, and non-partisan. This mix of individuals would write a supreme constitution, which ensures the rights of all Egyptians, a true revolutionary charter.

Ehab has no political interests or aspirations, and jokes that for one to live a decent life one needs to stay away from the political arena. He refers to the sacking of the general prosecutor in October 2012 by the president, who defied the rule that clearly states that this action is not within the power of the president, as the judiciary is independent. Ehab explains this awkward, spiteful situation came about because the general prosecutor had issued warrants for the arrest of Mohamed Morsi when he was among the top leadership of *Ikhwan,* along with many of his colleagues, on Friday January 28, 2011. *He escaped one or two days later when many prisoners escaped from several prisons. Police arrested Morsi in 2006 and imprisoned for six months, for protesting against the rule of Mubarak.* Ehab believes that the former general prosecutor was fair and worked according to the law, as he had issued warrants to arrest members of *Ikhwan* as well as former President Mubarak and his sons.

The infamous trial of the Battle of the Camel did not go through via the general prosecutor, but through a juridical investigation. It is legal for the judge of a court to assign a case to juridical investigation, which is known to be under the authority of the president's office. One of the laws in Egypt is, if an accused is proven innocent by court, the case cannot be brought forward again in front of the district attorney, or any other court. This is a fundamental law, which protects the innocent. The trial of the Battle of the Camel is an example of the defects in Egyptian criminal procedures law, where the case was presented to the improper court. Certain articles of the criminal law, specifically articles 64 and 65, need to be anulled. The whole situation was like going to a dentist for treatment and being referred to the Head of Faculty for treatment, which is outside the protocol. Even if this law is revoked, the case of the Battle of the Camel is closed and no court can re-open it. Many view this as a miscarriage of justice, with so many people dying and nobody being held accountable. One will never know if the accused were actually guilty, they may have been innocent. Ehab believes that the men behind the Battle of the Camel were the *Ikhwan* in liaison with *Hamas*. He bases his theory on pure logic, as the day prior to the Battle of the Camel, many of the activists had decided to quit Tahrir and accept former President Mubarak's six-month transition period. The revolution was losing steam and the one party who would clearly win with the downfall of the regime was *Ikhwan,* who had fought long for a chance to rule and were not going to let this opportunity pass them by. Ehab cannot believe all the accusations on the former ruling elite, as it was a very dangerous time for any of them to play dirty, being under the intense spotlight. Time will surface the carefully concealed evidence.

Not all civilians understand how the judge rules. If evidence does not prove a defendant guilty, then the court should set him free. A judge cannot convict a defendant if he has an iota of doubt; it has to be beyond reasonable doubt. The plaintiffs are the ones who requested to change Judge Ahmed Refaat, who was in charge of Mubarak's trail. The prosecution's ground was that the judge had been unfair and hence, did not allow for a proper defense. Instead, he orchestrated a media show at court, in favor of the defense.

In this historic case against former President Mubarak and his entourage, only Mubarak and the former minister of interior, Habib El Adly were convicted due to the lack of evidence incriminating the other men. The normal human's reflex to danger is to protect himself. In this case, it was done by destroying evidence through burning incriminating documents. Criminal judges can only issue sentences based on material evidence and hence, cannot charge the accused with hypothetically destroying evidence. For instance, to convict a killer, the weapon has to be on hand; in the case of fraud, proof of the original cheque is necessary.

Clashes

With the first confrontation, while running the country, Marshal Tantawi lost his credibility as he allowed the police to fire on civilians at Mohamed Mahmoud Street. Just as Mubarak allowed the shooting, the Generalissimo made the same grave mistake. Ehab expects that the Defense Ministry will not stay in power for long. Tantawi was a witness in favor of the former President Mubarak, in the trial of the century. Now, if at any point Tantawi is charged, then it automatically revokes his previous testimony. Ehab predicted General Sami Annan could have turned against Tantawi, as his days were ending. Even if he left, the army establishment would be unchanged as he was only its symbol. Tantawi called for a national referendum when opposition demanding his resignation grew. However, it did not happen. The people give legitimacy, and that is why Mubarak stepped down, as his people withdrew trust in him. *Ehab was right with his prediction. As I write this chapter, Tantawi and Sami Annan have retired abruptly and the president has rewarded them both with the Nile Medallion and Medallion Republic.*

Events have been rapidly unraveling within the course of the past twenty-three months. It has appeared that *Ikhwan's* loyalty is not to Egypt. Even *Salafist* have broken ties with them, although they joined forces during elections. Two main polarized parties are the main characters of the theatre, *Ikhwan* and the army. Ehab compares the relationship with the Ahly and Zamalek national soccer teams, who have been competing for over two decades. National elections are like the national soccer championships, when two rivals join forces against another external competitor.

Currently the country is a big vessel struggling to survive a deadly thunderstorm; many times, it has almost capsized from the incredibly high waves. Ehab is not worried about this storm because he is confident and has faith that God will sail this ship outside the storm and eventually to safe, calm, light blue seas. Ehab quotes the Bible, "The Lord is my helper; I will not be afraid" (Hebrews 13:6)[69].

Many Christians have decided to pack their bags, fearing this deadly storm and seeking new homes in new countries. Ehab is not worried about this exodus, as all his friends and family are sticking out the storm. The overall stories that media covered had some truth to them, but not entirely. For instance, not all the families at the city of Rafah have left their homes as reported. According to Ehab, the real number stands at around five. An inexplicable incident took place at Rafah in October 2012. Initially a verbal conflict between families of different religious beliefs escalated into physical violence and assaults. This conflict led to families leaving their life-long, cherished homes. Circumstances drove some families away from homes and neighborhoods they were accustomed to. Ehab expects adults to act responsibly and maturely, resolving conflicts in a civil and respectable manner, which sadly, in the case of Rafah was far from the reality. Extremists blew the situation out of proportion.

During the clashes at Itihadiya palace, in December 2012, Ehab went with his fiancée and friend to save one of their girlfriends. For a moment his group was susceptible to a beating by the supporters of the president when suddenly one of the assaulters called to him. Just like that, Ehab and his friends ran for their lives and were saved from possible beating and looming death.

Detour

Ehab did not join *Tamarod* as he feels he should maintain his observer position, like a judge who should not participate in politics. He feels he should not be politically active. However, Ehab felt that something was brewing in the pot for *Ikhwan*. Nonetheless, he succumbed to social pressure and joined the protests on June 30, 2013 for the first time. He went with his fiancée to Salah Salem Street and walked amongst the throng of classy people displaying unparalleled happiness. He remembers two old women took their stylish couch and placed it on the street and sat on it, joining the protests.

Scales represent justice, which means that most times the scales tip to one side, clearly favoring the tipped side. During *Ikhwan* rule, it was apparent that the scales were tipping in favor of *Ikhwan*. *Ikhwan* unfairly treated any non-Muslims and even moderate Muslims. Ehab believes with the ousting of President Morsi, matters are moving in the right direction and it is important for Egyptians to accept that change takes a while to be in effect. In early 2014, Ehab noticed that corruption is a tad bit less and commitment is still required to drive the reform.

In Ehab's mind, a few things need addressing in the country along with reforming the existing institutes. Firstly, all intelligence personnel need official disclosure and subsequent expedition, which media must propagate. Secondly, all people need to work and continue to focus on work. Thirdly, any traffic offenses like those committed by street vendors, police must firmly address, and clear the roads of such violations.

Despite the bumpy road, the warning signs and the detour Egypt took before ousting the *Ikhwan* rule, Ehab remains confident and optimistic that the nation's future is bright. He is hopeful, as he has an unfaltering belief that God is surveying, and guiding Egypt to a better place. In the New Testament there is a verse, "All things work together for good to them that love God" (Romans 8:28). Egypt is moving to higher ground but the road is muddy and foggy and the horizons invisible, but hopes are high. Rigorous reform must be visible in all aspects of Egyptian life, and justice is a crucial block that needs addressing. *As Martin Luther King said, "It must be remembered that genuine peace is not the absence of tension, but the presence of justice"*[70] *Egypt desperately and vehemently needs unwavering justice.*

CHAPTER 12

Cheeky Cynicism

"When it is said to them: 'Make not mischief on the earth.' They say; 'We are the only ones that put things right.' Of a surety, they are the ones who make mischief, but they realize (it) not."
(Quran 2:11-12)

One rare evening, my husband, Tarek, and I were out for dinner with old friends and I mentioned that I needed a police viewpoint for my book. Two of my friends, Randa Haggag (featured in chapter 7) and Amr El Tobgy, instantly told me I should meet their friend Shaimaa whose brother is a police officer, and her father a retired police officer. Shaimaa readily agreed and we met at Beano's Café in Zamalek on Sunday September 17, 2011.

Feloul

The term, *Feloul,* was unheard of before the January 25 revolution; people used it after the uprising to refer to the loyal supporters of former President Mubarak. Some say that the Muslim Brotherhood, *Ikhwan,* initiated it. In Arabic it means, the remains of a battlefield, the closest words in English are the remnants or the remains. Shaimaa fits well into this category of *Feloul,* especially given the fact that she is the daughter of a retired police officer. The police have played an integral role in the Mubarak era, implementing the emergency law hence instilling fear among civilians, as they had the power to arrest and imprison anyone for up to six months without proper charges or a lawsuit.

Shaimaa Abdelaziz does not believe in revolutions. She is utterly pessimistic and predicts the revolution would lead to pandemonium. *George Orwell holds a similar belief as he said, "All revolutions are failures, but they are not all the same failure"*[71] She is well read and up to speed with current global and local affairs. She has a fresh perspective in her original theories and thoughts. Shaimaa is a petite, attractive, confident, single, working woman. Her very pale complexion contrasts with her dark long hair. She was born in Beni Suef on April Fool's Day 1980. Curiously, she enjoys monitoring human behavior, finding it complicated yet fascinating. Not many people marry their interests with their studies, seeking instead, a better fortune. She pursued an altogether different subject in computer science at Sadat Academy, a public university. As both her parents were in public service, she quite naturally attended public schooling in Hurghada, located on the Red Sea. Her good judgment and decision-making has taken her across the digital media industry, quickly ascending the ladder of success and reaching the executive level. She has a passion for learning and has set aside time to further her knowledge in pursuing several relevant diplomas and an MBA.

Anti-Revolution Skeptic
Shaimaa's vision of the Egyptian people is not rosy. To her mind, they have fallen into mediocrity, passivity and worst of all, non-productivity. Shaimaa believes demonstrations need to be conducted with more civil manners and organization with a clear list of demands. These would ultimately lead to a meeting with the superiors to discuss the requirements. She cites the Japanese who are superior in manners and work ethics. When workers protest, they simply wear a ribbon on their arm while working until management sits and discusses their issues. The question is, would Egyptian managers heed to such a subtle protest? From her reading of history, she has not come across any insurrection that has led to a better life than prior to the uprising. In her opinion, the famous French Revolution in 1778 was a failure, as it led to a military dictatorship, followed by the Napoleonic Empire established by Napoleon Bonaparte and eventually re-establishing a monarchy. The French Republic came about after three other revolutions within the course of a century.

The Egyptian revolution had no leader, which Shaimaa links to utter chaos. She reverts to the popular proverb, that a ship with two captains will sink - this ship has eighty million captains! Can you imagine what will happen to the ship? Shaimaa was also anti revolution due to the continuous change in the list of demands. She viewed newcomers to Tahrir square adding their own list of requests, which she finds endless, as embarrassing. They were unsatisfied, and even greedy. This made it difficult to find a spokesperson for the revolution. To top it all off, the different political parties were all trying to get the largest piece of the cake.

On Tuesday January 25, Shaimaa was at home, attentively watching the news channels' broadcast of the demonstrations. She admired the approach of the youth. However, she was cynical about the fact that the demonstrators were not representative of the masses of Egyptians living below the poverty line. For Shaimaa, the activists were from high socio-economic classes, representing less than five percent of the population. Their demands were on behalf of fellow compatriots. She is skeptical of their benevolence, challenging them with the fact that they have not all personally witnessed the plight of the masses, except for a meek minority. However, she respected them for taking the initiative to shout out these long forgotten human rights. Dignity, self-respect, equal opportunity and freedom were the demands. Days, nights passed by, and the activists maintained their position at Tahrir square. In hindsight, she believes the protestors got drunk from their own people power and unfortunately, eventually they lost it.

Lawlessness

Friday January 28, commonly referred to as the 'Friday of Anger', was the day when the whole security apparatus collapsed, like an old building crumbled by the strong tremors of an earthquake. Shaimaa was anxious, furious and sleepless. Rumor had it that the police had received orders to withdraw from Midan alTahrir, as the army was mobilizing.

Shaimaa remembers watching the outbreak of vandalism on a television programme one evening.
She shouted, "Mom! Dad! Come quickly look at the news."
The broadcasters were announcing a rise in crime, and the disappearance of police presence from the streets.
Her father said, "Surely this is a high level betrayal by the police, Adly (Minister of Interior) in specific."
Her mother asked, "You really think so? How could he?"
Her father replied, "It must be, as the police force cannot all disappear without orders."
Shaimaa said, "That is possible, but don't forget that there is no mobile communication, so maybe the policemen were outnumbered and decided to withdraw."

When the *baltageya* (hooligans) attacked the police stations, two theories dominated; one was that the police ran away, which Shaimaa believed; and the other was that the police got orders to withdraw, which is what her father believed. As for the prisons, from her viewpoint, relatives of convicts broke into them. Shaimaa disagrees with the popular theory that police officers opened prisons. *Baltegeya* attacked police stations and prisons, killing police officers and setting free thousands of prisoners. She is confident of that, as not only was her father a police officer, but also, her brother is a police investigator in Hurghada, on the Red Sea. Shaimaa knows things that authorities did not communicate to people and she cannot fathom why the secrecy was necessary. She truly believes that the police force and the army have severe communication issues. Prior to the revolution she had sensed this conflict, and the insurgency confirmed her instincts afterwards as it had become all too evident that the two security entities did not collaborate or communicate effectively.

During the period of the revolution, more than 425 police officers were killed. Shaimaa knows that police officers were shot dead defending the prisons but this fact has conspicuously been kept from the media, incommunicado. It is clear that a high level of treason took place. The truth will never really be clear, but what she is certain of is that *Hamas* benefited from these prison breaks. One of the convicts who had escaped, crossing the border into Palestine within seven hours of breaking out, was among their ranks. According to Shaimaa, the masterminds behind the prison breaks most likely carefully planned them, as the escape took a record time. She considers several parties who could have masterminded these events. Internally, it could have been former Minister of Interior Habib El Adly, or the dominant National Democratic Party (NDP) and externally, Hezbollah or Iran. With the passing of time, Shaimaa added Hamas and *Ikhwan* to the list. It is very likely that Egyptians will never reach closure regarding this mutiny, similar to the lack of closure surrounding the assassination of former U.S. President John F. Kennedy.

There were videos on Facebook showing police officers opening cells, telling convicts to hurry and go home, which Shaimaa believes do not reflect the truth. These were not convicted criminals, but detainees. The police officers knew that families of convicts were in the neighboring vicinity, and were approaching the station to burn it to ashes and thus, let the detainees run for their lives. Should they have left them to burn in their cells? Police authorities gave orders to police officers not to shoot at the assailants, so many officers fled for their lives, while others stood their ground and consequently met their end. The raiders stole vehicles and artillery from the stations. The majority of the police force remained in their homes when there was unrest, as the demonstrators literally wore them out during the first four days. Shaimaa was boiling with rage, how could the regime no matter how degenerate, fail so drastically in having an emergency plan to facing such aggression? No backup plan unfolded. She compared the Egyptian situation to the more developed British system during the London Riots of August 2011, which led to unimaginable anarchy. However, within a few days' time the UK authorities had everything under control. London and the UK did not collapse, but Egypt has collapsed like an old bridge tumbling into the Nile after years of ignoring regulations, and overlooking the dire need for maintenance.

This plight reminded her about the movie *'Ayam ElSadat' (The Days of Sadat)* about the 1967 defeat, when former President Anwar Sadat asked El Mosheer, the Minister of Defense, what his backup plan was in case of defeat. The latter replied that his forces would withdraw into the desert. Sadat was dissatisfied with this contingency, as it would lead to many casualties, prisoners of war and utter chaos. Shaimaa believes that this is exactly what happened on the cold bleak bloody Friday January 28, 2011.

Shaimaa finds the scariest part was when the police officers attempted to contact their superior officers for updated orders, and were unable to. Mobile communication had been severd on that day, in an attempt to thwart off the protests. With this strange reality, each police officer had to improvise and take independent decisions. Some officers defended their lives and the stations, getting injured or killed. Plenty fled. Many had to take off their uniforms and run off in their underwear, to save their lives. People had suffered as the underdogs for far too long under the unwaveringly hardhearted police, the watch guards of the old regime. When the underdogs saw the excellent opportunity to strike back, they did just that.

As the days unfolded, the police force continued to be conspicuously missing. This continues for months on end, and was largely attributed to the negatively charged vibe towards all the police officers after the deaths and injuries at the protests. Civilians felt betrayed by their own police force.

After this huge tide of lawlessness swept the country, Dr. Mohamed El Baradei, a key political figure that embodies change, appeared on a satellite channel beckoning the Muslim Brotherhood to join forces and protect the square, Midan alTahrir. The Muslim Brotherhood has a reputation of being good in organization and the protestors needed their assistance. On February 2, 2011, the Muslim Brotherhood was one of the key contributors in organizing efforts, giving clear instructions, which aided the protestors in withstanding the attacks they suffered. The police took off their shirts to show their uniforms once the assault commenced. The protestors quickly organized themselves into *saraya*, (platoons) each one with an appointed leader, medical supplies, medical treatment, food, communication, and the like. The training of *Ikhwan* on how to safeguard people and how to beat aggressors in crowded areas played an instrumental role.

'Revolutionary Dictatorship'
Her sentiments aside, Shaimaa agrees with the demands of the activists. She wants the country cleansed from the prevailing corruption, which requires the nation to go on a long period of fasting to absolve itself. Shaimaa's brother was supporting the revolution, as he truly wanted an end to the flagrant corruption and perceived it as God's mysterious hand. However, after the police force were under attack and chaos ensued, his perspective changed.

Prosecuting the corrupt figures and improving the standard of living were among the list of demands; however, she disagrees with how the activists pursued their goals.

If the activists had stopped after the abdication of former President Mubarak, then she would have supported the revolution wholeheartedly. It was time to settle down after February 12, 2011. They should have stepped back to let the transition take place, with proper elections and the Supreme Council for the Armed Forces, SCAF, transferring power to the elected officials. She opposes how the activists threaten the SCAF, frequently by calling for and instigating further demonstrations. The activists were demanding a presidential council to govern the country but she finds this autocratic, as this is not what the Egyptian people want, since it has no backing in the form of a referendum.

Mona, her friend, came up with a catchy creative term referring to the revolutionaries, calling their attitude "Revolutionary Dictatorship". Democracy advocates listening to other parties and yet the young free spirits advocating democracy were labeling their opposition in a treacherous "black list", erasing their freedom of expression. How were they different from the former regime? It seems that the activists believed that the means justified the end, wherein the means was the chaos they imposed with the demonstrations, which paved the road for the infringements on public and private properties by criminals. *How you attain the goal is as important as attaining the goal. As Martin Luther King Jr, said, "I have consistently preached that nonviolence demands that the means we use must be as pure as the ends we seek…But now I must affirm that it is wrong, or perhaps even more so, to use moral means to preserve immoral ends"[72] The ultimate goal is to achieve a liberated civil society where all its citizens have equality and good living.*

Shaimaa cannot trust the activists, as they have not considered other people's opinions as she is skeptical what the new police force would do to her if they actually held power. What are the guarantees that they would not steal and abuse just like the *ancien regime*?

History Repeats Itself

Shaimaa draws a parallel to the July 23 Revolution of 1952 when the security forces surged against corruption, feudalism, monarchy and the King after which they became more abominable than the overthrown monarchy. *This phenomenon is clear in George Orwell's celebrated political satire, Animal Farm. The Animals on 'Manor Farm' revolt against the humans, hoping to get a better life with their own kind, the animals, ruling. Major, the mastermind of the revolution said: "And remember also in fighting against Man, we must not come to resemble him. Even when you have conquered him, do not adopt his vices"[73] He clearly forewarned them but satirically they ended up worse off than before under the tight reins of their new pig dictator Napoleon[74].* Similarly, many in Egypt believe that as a monarchy the nation and its people were better off than after the revolution when the republic, a security state, was born. If Egypt had stayed a monarchy, she believes the state of the nation would have been better. However, now it is quite impossible, as Egyptians will no longer accept a reinstated monarch. In her mind, Egypt needs a fair dictator. Democracy is overrated and Shaimaa does not believe in it.

The political torture came after the 1952 revolution with Salah Nasr as the head of intelligence. They confiscated all property. Shaimaa believes that the endemic decay in the governing apparatus dates back six decades, not just during Mubarak's era. This is why Shaimaa is so concerned with the 2011 revolution, expecting the same exploitation all over again where a deteriorating situation moves from bad to worse. Egyptians were living before January 25; she questions what gains the revolution has brought. To the contrary, there are many unfortunate costs associated with the revolution; the economy is in ruins, there are vacuums of safety and security, and there is no light of hope at the end of the tunnel. Protestors are turning against the transitional government led by the army, chanting: *"Yoskot yoskot hokm el askar"* (Down Down with military rule.) This is a transformation; any transition to civilian rule lasts a few months at least. The army is neither good nor evil. Shaimaa cannot understand the protestors. They demanded the downfall of Mubarak, and their demand was duly fulfilled. As former President Mubarak handed his power over to the army, their chant changed to demanding an end to the military power. She is glad that the activists' demand of a presidential council handling the transition as a nominated body and not an elected one, fell on deaf ears as she believes it could have led to further conflicts.

Speaking about the violence which confronted the protestors on the streets, Shaimaa justifies the use of force against civil disobedience. The means which the security forces used are normal in even developed countries like the USA, England, Greece, Brazil and many other countries. She cited the use of tear gas and rubber bullets. Shaimaa's brother explained to her the mechanism of rubber bullets, which consist of capsules containing tens of pellets. Once shot they disperse randomly, wounding people, as it happened, many in the eye. If the police intended to shoot directly in the eye, they would have needed live bullets and the targets would have died on the spot. She emphasizes that the use of rubber bullets against protestors is a common global police practice.

Economic Downturn

Shaimaa believes what turned this revolution into victory was when eight million workers joined their voices. They were demanding a better living conditions and higher pay. The economy is a wreck and the poor are now poorer, inflation is on the rise, there is more unemployment, the stock market has lost millions, over one thousand factories have shut down, productivity has taken a big dip, liquidity is scarce and the reserve has dropped substantially. Cynically, Shaimaa notices that after the revolution everyone wanted a salary increase without any productivity, a lose-lose scenario. Once the central bank issues bank notes, the Egyptian pound will be significantly devalued and inflation will skyrocket. She cites increased costs to the economy due to the volatile political situation. For instance, China is now demanding upfront payment prior to dispatching orders. The insurance cost of imported freight has taken a leap for Egypt, now considered a high-risk country, almost double the cost of imports into Iraq. All foreign embassies warn businesses, advising advance payments or guarantees. All this is costing Egypt and she blames the activists for not seeing the bigger picture and continuing in their detrimental efforts to end military rule. Shaimaa gives a wonderful example of solidarity that Japan displayed after the horrific and deadly tsunami that hit them in March 2011. She recalls reading in an article how the Japanese, befallen with devastating losses, increased working hours by three hours over the course of one and a half months, to help make up for the losses. Cynically she asks what the Egyptians did. They continued to protest and hurt the economy further.

Blazing Fury

The first speech on Saturday January 29, clearly displayed a huge disconnect between the former president and his people. Even Shaimaa was mad, as he did not address the masses, which to say the least was not very smart of him. He seemed to ignore the events of the previous four or five days before he uttered his first address and to add salt to the wound, he spoke of things that were irrelevant to the matters at hand. The activists were dying for him to listen to them but he overlooked them. Shaimaa's parents and brother also criticized Mubarak's extended silence before his first unpopular speech.

What kind of a leader was he? At critical times like this, his position should have obliged him to act genuinely, even if he felt otherwise. He missed an opportunity to get his house in order several times. Human nature does not respond well to being ignored. Each individual human wants acknowledgement and appreciation, which is common sense psychology that any leader must understand. By giving the masses a cold shoulder, he permitted the rage to rise to this dangerous level, like a dormant volcano erupting with hot, burning lava. Shaimaa admits that her feelings towards Mubarak are contradictory. Before the revolution, she totally despised him, as she believed that he has been the worst leader in the history of Egypt. She preferred former President Abdel Nasser who, although imperfect, was passionate, charismatic and had the ability to be a great leader. Where Nasser failed, in her view, was to direct his followers in the right direction. He took haphazard decisions, was very emotional, and tended to have a bad temperament. Nasser had corrupt friends in his close circle but he could not stand up to them. In Shaimaa's opinion, President Anwar Sadat, who came after President Nasser, was a genius. At the very least, during Sadat's era the

Egyptian citizen was valued in his or her own country and worldwide, whereas Hosni Mubarak lacked leadership, genius and was not *bona fide*. Shaimaa believes he was an unsuccessful leader in all regard, and holds him accountable for all the corruption that has taken place throughout Egypt over the course of the last three decades.

Change of Hearts

For the last ten years of his presidency, Mubarak was mostly residing in the town of Sharm El Sheikh, a resort on the Red Sea in Sinai. At the time Shaimaa and I spoke, he was eighty-four years old, way past retirement age. During his second speech on February 1, he managed to gain the sympathy of many Egyptians. The population was divided. One camp inclined to allow him the remaining six months, which Shaimaa agreed with, and the other side refused to buy into his emotional blackmail and wanted him out immediately. After this second speech, Shaimaa and her parents agreed that Mubarak was no criminal, and would stick to his word. However, her brother did not buy Mubarak's promise. Her family, like many Egyptian families, had varying points of view.

Unquestionably, Shaimaa detested Mubarak until the day he abdicated his power. For her, it depicted the president's love of Egypt. If he had not stepped down, the alternative would have been for him to order the armed forces to fire against civilians and a civil war would have transpired, like in the neighboring countries of Libya, Syria, Yemen and Bahrain. Shaimaa disagrees with many who say that the army refused to follow orders to fire against people, as she believes the order never happened. Army officials are trained to follow orders without questioning or blinking, let alone refusing. Her belief is that the army would have suffered internal divisions between those who wanted to fire, and those who did not. Mubarak had decided to resign to spare his army and country from any hardship that might have ensued.

Mubarak refused to leave his beloved country and touched Egyptian hearts by declaring that he wanted his final resting place to be in his beloved land. He also declared that he was not going to nominate himself for another term, and handed powers to the newly appointed vice president, Omar Suleiman. In addition, President Mubarak agreed to amend the constitution, just as the masses demanded, and promised to transfer power over September 2011, which would have marked the end of his fifth and final term. Meanwhile, on February 7, former Minister of Interior Habib El Adly, and Ahmed Ezz, former leading member of the ruling NDP, and others were notified not to travel outside the country. Shaimaa was very content with this speech and was happy he had not ceded his powers as had been rumored, as she believes the popular saying, "moderation is the best policy". In her view, he wanted to end his political career in a dignified way. Her parents also agreed with his terms and wanted the chaos to be resolved and business as usual to resume.

Shaimaa draws a simile, noting that when an employee resigns from work in a company, he or she gives a one-month notice and continues to work and prepare a handover in the interim. What about the President of a nation? Mubarak could have declared a military coup wherein the military laws would have ruled, rather than opting to abdicate his power to the Supreme Council of the Armed Forces, SCAF.

On Whose Orders?

In Shaimaa's mind, former President Mubarak did not give the order to attack protestors on Wednesday February 2. Instead, his enemies did, blowing his last chance to exit with honor. The members of the ruling National Democratic Party (NDP) panicked, as they were no longer the untouchables given that the people power was escalating. Hence, the NDP members felt susceptible to arrests on corruption charges. Shaimaa believes that the NDP members paid off *baltegeya* to assault the revolutionaries at Tahrir square. She questions the credibility of any reply from the *baltegeya* if asked who paid them to assault the protestors. Shaimaa cannot picture President Mubarak giving the orders to attack the activists, especially as he had succeeded in gaining support through his second speech. It just does not add up. She raises the possibility that it could have been one of his sons who did it, trying to scare the protestors. Over time, she no longer believes any of the president's sons were behind it. When it comes to politics, you can never tell what actually happened. Who would have benefited? Who would have been hurt? Who were the scapegoats?

That attack on the protestors by the thugs turned out to be very bloody, with thousands of activists hurt and several killed. People were lying in their own blood on the pavement until brave men carried them to the medical platoon. The army soldiers did not prevent this attack, as the army were dispatched only to protect national institutes. Shaimaa believes army soldiers are like programs, and they were not set up to fire, and hence did nothing during this attack. She recounted how at the military academy, all soldiers are brainwashed during their first year and trained not to think before they follow orders. Shaimaa justifies this approach as during a war, if a soldier hesitates for a second to fire once ordered, he is more prone to being shot and killed along with the other soldiers near him. In other words, he compromises the situation simply by thinking, putting himself and his battalion at risk. It is as if the soldiers are programs controlled by the mainframe computer system. Similarly, the police academy trains officers to do absurd tasks without flinching or thinking. Shaimaa cites an example that her father told her, of an officer who was ordered to fill a teaspoon with water and empty it into the dormitory where seventy soldiers slept, until the water reached a hand's height. Another absurd order was to measure the dormitory with a needle. Imagine how much time that would take! They are not trained to question orders from superiors or allowed to ponder on the repercussions, let alone reflect on whether or not those in power are morally correct or not.

Egyptians have no idea about politically sensitive documentation that exists about places like Ethiopia, the Nile River or Israel and how the chaos which followed the revolution, affected the steady balance of power. The country would have been in a better position if the masses had accepted his speech, allowing the army and the people to create an observatory council ensuring that the former president transferred the power as promised. If something were to go astray, she states that Tahrir square is not going to disappear and protestors could gather and demonstrate once again if they deemed necessary.

Revolutionaries fell in love with the spirit of Tahrir and the carnival-like gathering and did not want to let it go. Protestors got addicted to the high of the revolution. Their insatiable hunger to express themselves left them in a position where they just could not get enough and they totally ignored the curfew. The curfew set on the main cities of Egypt was superficial, as the army should have shot at people who moved after the set time, but this did not happen, clearly avoiding bloodshed. Shaimaa thinks that was an unsound decision and led to the continued chaos in the country and disrespect of authority.

Shaimaa is very humble and modest as she is aware that her theory might be wrong, but one can never know. She had hoped her instincts were wrong, but is sad to admit that all her fears have manifested themselves since the revolution.

The Outsider
On February 11, 2011, millions and millions of Egyptians took to the streets celebrating former President Mubarak's yielding of power to the Supreme Council of the Armed Forces, SCAF. It was an unprecedented national celebration. Egyptians partied throughout the night as if dancing up in the clouds with angels. No one could deny them their euphoria. Shaimaa felt like a complete outsider, as she did not share the overarching sentiment, but nonetheless it was an unforgettable day in Egypt's history, for everyone.

Shaimaa recalls it clearly, as if it were yesterday. She was at a friend's party in Rehab compound, one of the suburbs of Cairo, when she heard that the President has stepped down. She cried while everyone around her was jumping and dancing with jubilation; sorrow amidst celebrations. Her friends, mostly single men and women, well-educated elite dressed in tasteful clothes, who like to party and enjoy nightlife and are frequent voyagers abroad, were celebrating as they never have done before. The joy transcended their high school prom party, graduation party, managerial or director promotion and even their wedding celebrations. The loud music muffled her ears; in stark contrast with her friends, she felt as if locked in a pitch-black dungeon with no windows. Shaimaa felt a heavy weight burdening her heart and sadly foresaw the looming anarchy, which the nation has indeed been witnessing since the revolution.

She is expecting more bloodshed in the coming years because of President Mubarak's abdication, more blood than if he had maintained his symbolic power and the vice-president had ruled. Shaimaa is pessimistic and fears Egypt is on the brink of an imminent civil war between the varying sects and parties, similar to that which happened in Lebanon and Algeria. Her only hope is the Supreme Council of the Armed Forces; SCAF embarks on an iron fist policy and fully supports the incoming government, which she senses is going to be the case.

Future Blueprint

The Supreme Council of the Armed Forces, SCAF, organized a nationwide referendum on the constitution on March 19, 2011. They were heedless to the activists' stand against the constitutional referendum, as the revolution overthrew the *ancien regime*, and hence, their ruling constitution. Shaimaa voted yes for the constitutional amendments, along with the majority of Egyptians accepting the proposed changes. Calling an appointed council to write the constitution without elections was nonsense in her opinion. The elected parliament is the rightful body to elect the committee to write the new constitution, not the Egyptian people. In principle she is fine with an Islamist constitution, however as the parliament was ruled illegitimate, the constitutional committee could not be legitimate. Shaimaa calls on the activists to respect the democracy that they loudly and eagerly demanded. Unfortunately, the Islamists played on the ignorance of the masses by promoting the notion that a 'No' vote means that you are an atheist and that a 'Yes' vote means that you are a devout believer.

Shaimaa is convinced that writing a new constitution is not a task that the people can entrust the protestors with. Rather, there needs to be an elected body, like the parliament to do so. *Egypt is witnessing its worst days. As Machiavelli clearly stated in The Prince, "there is nothing more difficult to handle, more doubtful of success and more dangerous to carry through than initiating changes in a state's constitution."*[75] *This is exactly where Egypt stands. All political parties are playing to get the bigger share of the pie.*

The protestors are at a disadvantage as their newly formed political parties are not strongly rooted to win the parliamentary elections and the Muslim Brotherhood, *Ikhwan*, will definitely win the majority of the seats. The protestors dread and fear that the Muslim Brotherhood will dominate politics and hence, do not want this democratic process. Yet, they want an end of the military rule. Activists want a tailor-made democracy that suits their profile, which cannot be democracy. Shaimaa is convinced that the SCAF do not want to rule the nation indefinitely, as to them it is a fireball in their hands, one that they are willing to let go of in due time.

Sparks

One of the catalysts of the revolution was a Facebook site in memory of the late Khaled Said, a reputedly innocent young man brutally beaten to death in public in Alexandria by the police. However, Shaimaa has heard another angle to this controversial popular story. She has heard that the reputed fight took place between Khaled and a couple of police officers over a drug deal and that the police beat him to death. It was a fight between drug dealers and this was not an innocent young man; however, she is not certain as to whether or not any of it is true. Her brother, an officer stationed in Hurghada, denies that they as police would always torture prisoners. She does not deny that there are sick and sadistic police officers who derive pleasure from others' pain, but feels that these officers are not the norm. Just like in any institution, there are good and bad apples. Shaimaa does not support police beatings, but she knows that they are not equipped with proper tools to reach the truth and convict criminals, like in other countries. Tools such as DNA testing. Only people registered as dangerous or who have a criminal record have their fingerprints on file with the police. Moreover, imagine that in all of Egypt, a nation of eighty million, there are only twenty doctors qualified to run autopsies!

Her brother, a police officer, once told her of a case involving a rapist. The rape victim, who was a child, identified the rapist and the rapist himself even admitted to the rape. However, he was acquitted as he had been illegally arrested, and thus he was freed. This is a clear example of laws and a legal system in dire need of reform.

Frustrated by the silent majority in the fight against racism and segregation in the United States, Martin Luther King said, "Shallow understanding from people of good will is more frustrating than absolute misunderstanding from people of ill will. Lukewarm acceptance is much more bewildering than outright rejection"[76] *In Egypt, the worst nightmare the police are facing is the silence of victims and witnesses, the silent majority.*

In addition to unsound laws, fear often paralyzes people from seeking justice. Shaimaa's brother once told her that he is unable to enter the slums of Egypt, which are mainly located outside the capital, because, ironically they are better armed with guns and weaponry than the police themselves. This was before the revolution; imagine the situation now with the surge in unlicensed guns scattered all over the country. The wicked rogue of the shanty slums exercises the self-imposed right: to sleep with a bride on her wedding night, or rape a young boy and ironically ask his parents to pay protection ransom every month. These hooligans are voracious for power and money. They will stop nowhere in their insatiable quest of greed. With the endemic silence and fear, there is no proof behind these stories and if investigations were to start, people would vehemently deny any wrongdoing.

Cynic

Among the chants which activists repeated was, *"Erfaa rasak fouk enta masry,"* (Raise your head, for you are Egyptian). Shaimaa does not relate to it and is cynical, questioning what the activists have personally done to improve the state of the country. The economy has taken a swift ride downhill with rundown breaks and it is not stopping.

Shaimaa is embittered, as it will take several years for the people and the police to re-establish trust and good rapport. Reform needs to be holistic and genuine, and the police need to feel appreciated and needed, like any human. When they earn a salary of L.E.90 plus allowances of L.E.150, totaling less than $40 a month, how could you expect them not to take bribes? If a policeman is not violating the law is it charity? Police officers by nature use more physical effort than verbal and therefore are not good speakers and communicators. This is definitely not assisting them in their plight. Their past training under the Mubarak era discredited them without any substitution.

Human nature tends to mold to its surroundings. Shaimaa remembers that when she was training at a public bank as an undergraduate, she was taken aback at how rude the employees were with clients. After her training, this rudeness rubbed off on her and she was talking in a similar manner. The clientele were simple people, often uneducated, even illiterate and had difficulty grasping financials. For instance, one man came to her demanding that the bank accept a check. But the check was not in his name and thus, Shaimaa could not cash it for him. He was not able to understand why, likely due to his lack of exposure and education. Similarly, the police deal with criminals day in and day out and eventually, their language and behavior are affected by their work. *This needs addressing via proper training to buffer police officers from the influence of their surroundings.*

Shaimaa is hopeful, as more people are standing against the chaos and demonstrations. The army played a meek bystander's role that led to huge losses to the nation, possibly intended to gain public support. She cites the example of the attack on the Israeli embassy. It is ironic that the public considers a trespasser who invades Israeli property and replaces the Israeli flag with that of Egypt as a hero. The governor of Giza endows him with an apartment as a reward, when this man is actually a thief with a criminal record and pending court cases. Cynically, a criminal turns into a hero!

Shaimaa believes that the army should be taking a stronger stand in the situation. Although they have already started to do so, they still need to hold the reins of this magnificent Arabian horse more strongly and steer it to safety and prosperity. The country may return to stability after a while. However, she predicts that religious strife among Egyptian Copts and Egyptian Muslims will grow, as it is inherent to the culture. She fears that the future of Egypt will be similar to Iran.

Shaimaa said she would most likely vote for the Muslim Brotherhood, *Ikhwan*, in the parliamentary elections, as they had the most reasonable moderate viewpoint and were the most organized. She believed that they would win and hoped that they adopt the moderate policy they have been advocating. Eventually though, she did not vote for *Ikhwan* during the parliamentary elections, as she knew one of the liberals running in the Hurghada circle and voted for him. Shaimaa has since discovered that *Ikhwan* had an agenda to rule Egypt. She saw them gain majority parliamentary seats and abuse rather than use the power for the sake of the country.

Initiative

After the revolution, Shaimaa met our common friend Randa Haggag *(featured in Chapter 7)* at a café in Zamalek next to the Um Kalthoum Hotel. They met just after civilians brutally attacked a police officer in Maadi, an increasing occurence with the growing absence of security forces on the streets. Randa and Shaimaa wanted to help *Dakhleya* by proposing a communication strategy.
Randa said, "We cannot continue without police on the streets."
Shaimaa said, "I don't know why it's taking them so long."
Randa proposed, "We need to work on the police image among the people, to fix this sorry plight. They need a good PR campaign."
Shaimaa replied, "Yes, that, and they also need to get a social skills course. Randa they really do not know how to deal with people, zero people skills. I know that, from my father and brother."
Randa agreed, "That is very important, can you get us in touch with the right people?"
Shaimaa said, "Yes, I will try to get in touch with the minister of interior."
With the security situation in Egypt ever changing in the ministry and new incidents almost every month, Shaimaa was never able to get in touch with someone from *Dakhleya*.

The hurdles police face are not only related to communication, but also tools with which to do their work. The police need to be better equipped with the most recent technology and good weapons. Literally, their guns are rusty. Many police officers work long hours, sometimes eighteen hour-days, mostly standing in the heat of the sun. As a child, Shaimaa could not really talk to her father, as he seemed to come from a different world, dealing with abnormal human behavior and crimes. They are having it tough with very low salaries. It is a tough life. Their work requires them to confront danger continuously.

Cemented View

Nineteen months later, Shaimaa has not changed her opinion. She has come to accept Egypt's fate as, abiding by the Hadith by Prophet Mohamed (PBUH) "Allah has decreed (it) and what He willed, He has done". However, she is still skeptical as she feels that the worst has yet to appear.

When it came to the first democratic presidential elections, Shaimaa voted for Ahmed Shafik, as she believed he was the most capable during this transition. Moreover, if he had gone astray, the system would certainly check and remove him. However, she did comprehend the stubbornness of the activists who supported the Muslim Brotherhood, *Ikhwan*, presidential candidate Mohamed Morsi simply because they did not trust Ahmed Shafik and the old *nizam*. She accepted the results of the democratic process. However, in Shaimaa's view, it will be impossible to control, let alone overthrow the *Ikhwan*, should they go astray, and she senses that Egypt has now crashed into the wall with the *Ikhwan* at the steering wheel. In her mind, the *Ikhwan* burnt themselves, and not the people who overthrew them. Their blinded arrogance and disconnect with the demands of the people, as their voters, turned against them since they failed to deliver on any promises. Nonetheless, *Ikhwan* are a power that neither should be taken for granted, nor can be erased. In 2013, Egypt is at a stage of a civil war with all the frequent bombs and killings.

The *Ikhwan* have proven repeatedly that they do not keep their promises and are striving for their party's benefits and not those of the country. Shaimaa was dumbfounded when President Morsi decided to revoke the latest constitutional declaration by the Supreme Council of the Armed Forces, SCAF and recalled the parliament, both of which the Supreme Court legally overruled. During his campaign, President Morsi promised many changes within one hundred days, *almost half that time has elapsed as I write this chapter and the government has only temporarily solved the issue of garbage collection, for example.* During the prior weeks, Egyptian streets were congested with heaps of garbage as the collectors were on strike. Eventually this one issue out of many was resolved, but for a short while, only to leave the streets shamefully littered again. Shaimaa finds it suspicious that President Morsi wants to remove the legal supervision over elections. *Ikhwan* have announced that they will be targeting all the parliamentary seats in the upcoming elections, much more ambitious than their declared thirty percent in the last elections.

Referring to the incident in Sinai in August 2012, when seventeen border guards were shot dead while breaking their fast during the holy month of Ramadan, Shaimaa does not believe that it was *Hamas* behind the attack. However, she cannot completely ignore the theory. As she knows that Gabal Al Halal at Sinai is a military base for *Hamas* from which they can attack Israel, moreover she believes *Hamas* is the military army for *Ikhwan*. She believes President Morsi was not in control, as he promised to catch the assaulters and never did. She still doubts that *Hamas* was behind the attack and heard that the assaulters were in *Ikhwan*'s custody but they could not hand them over to authorities due to a standing agreement amongst Islamist groups. Shaimaa is not convinced of the theory that President Morsi was behind this killing to remove the top army generals.

Shortly after the Sinai attacks, President Morsi sacked two of the most senior army officials, Field Marshal Tantawi and Sami Annan, while rewarding them with medals. Shaimaa is sure that an arbitrated deal amongst them or a soft coup in the military took place, overthrowing its old leaders. She read in an article that post the Sinai attacks, during the meeting between Anan, Tantawi, the head of Intelligence, President Morsi and his campaign head, Annan left the meeting. A friend informed Shaimaa that Annan had left when the campaign manager overstepped his jurisdiction by questioning military plans, and that the military advised President Morsi that he must close the bordering tunnel with Rafah to contain the situation; advice that the president adamantly refused. Given this fact, President Morsi's advisors recommended that he make a public statement to civilians supporting his decision to keep the borders open. After the announcement, President Morsi agreed to close the tunnel, clearly demonstrating that perhaps he did not have legitimate reasons for keeping the border open, and possibly fearing that the public would object and retaliate. Only shortly afterwards, those senior officials were the scapegoats of this attack, and were suddenly made to retire.

Meandering Road
In 2013, four soldiers were kidnapped in Sinai and an officer called Abu Shakra was send undercover to investigate the kidnapping. Only four people knew where he was, three security officials and the president. It was clear that his location and his cover were blown when he was kidnapped and killed. After this, the police no longer took orders from the president as they felt he compromised one of them. Abu Shakra had a *tar* (vendetta) with the high-ranking *Ikhwan* official, Khairat el Shater, whom he had previously arrested.

Shaimaa viewed the constitutional declaration that President Morsi issued as a breach of his oath, and hence an immediate loss of legitimacy. In her mind, after the constitutional declaration in November 2012, President Morsi was no longer the president. What happened in between then and June 30 was a high-level intelligence game to package the ousting in the best way possible, with the army in the background.

When the *Tamarod* (rebellion) movement started surfacing, Shaimaa rejected it, as it was not a legitimate body. It was not a governmental entity and did not have proper supervision and observation (similar to the initial revolution against former President Mubarak). It started as a popular youth movement that succeeded in gaining support and then, the security endorsed it. *Tamarod* became a brand that united the Egyptian people against *Ikhwan*. However, it was a good marketing tool used by the youth to oust President Morsi and gained unpredictable support, which paved the way for the army to stand with the people and declare the President's removal from power. For the first time, in June, Shaimaa took to the streets and protested in Tahrir. She found herself surrounded by anti-police attitudes, and feeling uncomfortable with all the anti-military sentiments, she did not join the Tahrir protest again. She joined the Itihadiyah Presidential Palace protest instead. From June 30 through July 3, 2013, Shaimaa joined millions of Egyptians who flocked to the streets of Egypt demanding the ousting of President Morsi and early Presidential elections.

'Coup-Volution'

After the army announcement, Shaimaa went with her parents to celebrate the great feat of overthrowing the *Ikhwan* rule after only one year in power. She finds events such as the January 25, 2011 protests to be ironic as they are commonly termed a 'revolution', backed up by the *Ikhwan*, but the June 30, 2013 protests are referred to as a 'coup' by *Ikhwan* themselves and western media, since the *Ikhwan* had opposed it. This is despite indicators that the numbers on the latter day were by far more than the former day. What happened in June is something new; she can call it neither a revolution nor a military coup. It needs a new word. Recently she has started to refer to it as 'coup-volution,' meaning a revolution that the people started and the military finished. That describes what happened in Egypt. Based on Shaimaa's readings in history, no revolution succeeded without military backing, and the military is the backbone of Egypt.

A couple of weeks later when General Sisi called for the people's delegation to counter the terrorism on the 26 of July, Shaimaa and her parents willingly obliged and joined millions at Itihadiyah Presidential Palace. Terrorism is the war going on at Sinai, and not the dismantlement of protests in Cairo and Giza that police, and not the army, carried out. On the clearing of the pro-Morsi vigils at Rabaa and El Nahda, Shaimaa believes that those who were bearing arms should have been arrested by the police and that the peaceful and unarmed demonstrators should have been allowed to voice their opinions. However, it was complicated, as residents had made complaints that the sit-in was infringing on their freedom of movement. In the end, police warned the pro-Morsi supporters and asked them to leave within forty days, but the protestors ignored the warnings. The police had no other option but to physically clear the square, forcibly removing the demonstrators.

However, the future is not very bright with the Islamists seemingly attempting to exhaust the institutes and the people, in revenge for President Morsi's ousting.

Shaimaa does not believe that General Sisi would nominate himself for President, and that it is intelligence propaganda. If he does run, she would be against it, but she admits that there are no good presidential candidates on the theatre.

Shaimaa is happy to perceive an improvement in relations between the police and the people, better than she had expected. This is an encouraging first good step towards change. The leadership needs to change and the police officers are trying to change themselves, however pressurized with the violence of the Islamists. Shaimaa senses the spirit is changing for the better and is hopeful. However, Egypt will be traveling through a long and dark tunnel before reaching the light at the end.

CHAPTER 13

Condemned Captain

"Darkness cannot drive out darkness; only light can do that.
Hate cannot drive out hate; only love can do that." Martin Luther King, Jr.

A police officer, a military man and an Ikhwan member were among the difficult perspectives to find for this book. This chapter recounts the point of view of a police officer and given that his profession does not allow him to disclose matters that relate to his professional role, he prefers to remain anonymous. Consequently, I will not share the identity of my lead and Captain Mo is the pseudonym of the police officer. We met the morning of Monday March 5, 2012 at a café in Zamalek.

Eyes on the Sky

His appearance commands attention. Mo is a handsome, tall, well-built man in his thirties with dark black hair and contrasting white skin. He is a heavy smoker and very conscience of his physical appearances; during our meeting, he refrained from eating due to his diet. He was born in Cairo in the late seventies. Mo went to Islamic language schools at the primary and secondary levels in Mohandseen, and studied English and French in secondary school. Mo's father is a retired army official and his mother works in the administration of a private company. Captain Mo has one older brother who tragically died in a car accident a few months earlier; Mo did not want to elaborate on his tragic loss.

As a child, Mo did not dream of becoming a police officer. However, as a teenager, Mo's father encouraged him to apply to the Police Academy. His father told him that if he succeeded there, then he would have a desirable, guaranteed job, considering the fact that at the time, not all graduates were able to find jobs. Mo's father considered the police force to be the better and safer option in comparison to the army, as his father had witnessed wars, which he did not want his son to bear witness to or be a part of. Nevertheless, Mo had his eyes on the sky, dreaming of becoming a pilot and so, he took the screening exam for military aviation. However, he was unable to withstand the ear pressure inside the cabin and hence, the screening committee excused him. Apparently, he was not destined to be a pilot.

Heeding his father's words of advice, Mo went to the Police Academy. By default, the military excuses the police officers from the obligatory military conscription as they undergo the equivalent three years at the Police Academy. Similarly, anyone who attended Military College would automatically be exempt from the conscription. Naïve and gullible, Mo was clueless as to what the police were really made of and to the fact that they are underpaid. Captain Mo has been in the police force for eleven years.

Meager Pay

Captain Mo says, "Honestly, there is nothing to like about my job." His initial net salary was four hundred and fifty pounds, around seventy dollars, including his transportation. As a government employee, Captain Mo paid a discounted train ticket at thirty-five pounds one way for the first class carriage, far from luxurious but the best available option, as the entire train system is in dire need of scrapping. The salary was not sufficient to cover Captain Mo's needs as a single man and he ended up having his father help cover his financial needs; something he is still doing until this day, a common practice in Egypt. Shortly thereafter, an insufficient salary adjustment of over sixty percent took place. By his fourth year, Captain Mo was earning double his initial salary but still falling short of his needs, considering inflation and the extremely low starting point. To date his salary covers only thirty percent of his expenses as a single man. If Captain Mo's family were not well off, he would have long ago been begging or stealing on the streets trying to make ends meet.

Captain Mo resents the low remuneration of the police officer. If he had worked a basic security job in a company over a span of ten years, his salary could have been around ten times more than what he currently earns. Captain Mo stands in the street during the hot summer days of August, or the cold winter nights of January, many days stuck in the middle of a protest, earning a pitiful compensation.

First Assignment

Captain Mo started his police career in 2001 in the south of Egypt, often referred to as Upper Egypt. He vividly recalls his train journey to Upper Egypt. While the train was approaching the station, he surveyed his new hometown in anticipation and anxiety. Captain Mo realized the houses were made of mud. The overnight train trip is quite long, lasting about twenty hours. Mo arrived around noon on a scorching hot August day. Once Captain Mo stepped outside the carriage, by reflex he put his foot back inside the train, shocked at the suffocating heat. For a split second, he considered staying in the train and returning to Cairo. Captain Mo was apprehensive. He felt queasy realizing that he would be living in a mud-house in the suffocating summer heat for the next three or four years of his life.

First impressions are difficult to change, and as it turned out, Captain Mo did not enjoy the four years he lived in Upper Egypt, which he describes as one of those places that are nice to visit as a tourist but not to live in. Captain Mo worked for twenty consecutive days, sometimes even longer, and would then take ten days off which he spent in Cairo. Although legally, Captain Mo was entitled to weekly holidays, the distance between the location of his work and his hometown forced him to forsake the weekends. After four long dreary years in Upper Egypt, Captain Mo was ecstatic when he transferred back to Cairo.

Captain Mo has noticed a difference between urban and rural thinking, the rural being more conservative. However, working in Cairo is more difficult than working in Upper Egypt. Mo is still living with his parents today. *In Egypt it is normal to find single men and women in their twenties or thirties or forties still living with their parents. Moving out is not the norm in Egyptian culture, although it is socially acceptable for a man to move out but not a woman.*

When we met, Mo was a captain in the police force. The first level in the Egyptian police hierarchy is *moulazem* (lieutenant) followed by *moulazem awal* (first lieutenant), followed by *nakeeb* (Captain), then *raed* (Major), followed by *moukadem* (Colonel), *akeed* (Lieutenant Colonel), then *ameed* (Brigadier) and finally by the highest level being *lewa* (General). Promotion of police officers depends on their graduating year, and usually guaranteed, with the exception of those who are black-listed due to violations with a pending legal case on hand that require firing the officer in question. For example, Mo recalls a lieutenant who was fired for selling cheese on the side of the street. The lieutenant was off duty and out of uniform, wearing a *galabeya* at Ramsis square, selling cheese out of a large platter in an attempt to complement his meager income. As police officers are working for the government, it prohibits them to work in any other domain.

On a normal schedule, Captain Mo could be in police service for a consecutive twelve-hour period, from seven in the morning until seven at night. Sometimes work overburdens him and he has to extend his duty, forcing him to work for thirty days without a day's rest.

Resentment Brewing
Before January 25, many of the police officers resented the circulating rumor that Mubarak's younger son, Gamal, would inherit the presidency. Almost the whole force

saw the injustice and opposed this idea in the first place, they remained silenced, too scared to speak up. Captain Mo saw the dire fate of those who dared talk; as per a popular Arabic saying, they were 'thrown behind the sun'. No matter what position in the force, those who spoke up unexpectedly faced trouble and cooked up lawsuits ensued. Captain Mo opted to stay away from trouble and kept silent, ignoring what he saw, as he did not want to compromise his fate.

The popular Facebook page *'Kullena Khaled Saiid'* (We Are All Khaled Said), created as a forum for discussions related to the tragic death of Khaled Said, transformed into a January 25 online communication platform. Captain Mo has a simple mathematical assumption that only ten percent viewership of any media are actively involved. He assumed that ten percent of those who liked the We are all Khaled Said Facebook page will be involved accordingly. That page had around nine hundred and fifty thousand likes during January 2011. Assuming only ten percent were actually going to demonstrate, that would lead to ninety-five thousand people on the streets. After the *Amn Elmarkazi* (Central Security) attacked, Captain Mo assumed that ten percent maintained their ground, leaving nine thousand five hundred protestors, which was the estimated number of people in Tahrir square on January 25, according to his hypothetical calculations.

Captain Mo expected something to happen on January 25 and if nothing had happened, he believed the situation would have considerably deteriorated. Captain Mo deals with all sorts of people, the good, the bad and the ugly; the innocent and the guilty; the smart and the simple-minded. Among the worst kind, he recalls a man married to five women in addition to his first wife; a man who raped a nine-year old; and a child who, unbelievably, beat his own mother. Captain Mo has seen and felt how tough life is for Egyptians. Unfortunately, this is still the status quo. When standing on duty in the street, he encounters people who stop to talk to him, or ask for directions; others have complaints, and Captain Mo always lends his ear to their queries and worries. Protests were inevitably surfacing. Previously they had barely ever happened, and it was as if a giant had awakened from hibernation. People gathered to protest in front of the syndicate buildings of journalists and lawyers.

Bread was difficult to find, with long queues in front of bakeries. Bread is an integral staple food in Egypt. With local wheat supplies far from meeting the demands of the population, Egypt imports the balance it needs, mainly from the United States. Captain Mo has seen families buy dozens of loaves of bread, eating only a couple and feeding their livestock and poultry the rest. The people do this out of ignorance, clueless that ducks should not eat bread; they should not eat food for human consumption. Captain Mo thinks that this is causing a food shortage for humans, where one family is feeding its bread to animals and another family is not able to find bread to eat. A family of five claims that it needs twenty loafs of *baladi* (local thin bread in a shape of a circle) bread a day; each family member eating four a day, certainly significantly exceeds the basic nutritional needs. Captain Mo wonders why the government did not enforce rationing of food when supplies were limited, and people were clearly overeating; something that has happened in other countries during and after wars. Rationing in difficult times is common practice in many countries including the United Kingdom, where, during World War II, food was rationed and bread was reduced in quality and was sold a day after baking in order to be harder, hence discouraged its consumption, according to Wikipedia.

Despite the growing resentment portrayed in the protests, Captain Mo observed no reaction from the men in charge of the country, despite the people's frustration growing exponentially. He saw the ensuing explosion of the bubble. However, Captain Mo expected the explosion to happen later, after the presidential elections in which Gamal Mubarak, as was the common belief, would have run and likely won. This would have driven people to the streets, as Egypt is a republic and not a monarchy. Another scenario Captain Mo had conceived was that of former President Mubarak passing away while in office, after which a military coup might have ensued. Speculation was and still is rampant, with several floating theories tossed around.

Prior to the pre-announced day of demonstration, Captain Mo was with colleagues in an annual training camp session, which police cut short, as *Dakhleyah* needed its forces on full alert for January 25.

January 25: D-Day
Expecting a normal day, Captain Mo was on duty at seven in the morning on January 25, 2011, and stationed at Abdeen square. Their orders were to stop demonstrators from reaching Tahrir square, symbolic, as Tahrir means Liberation. Police officers made a human barrier blocking the people within the square without any physical contact, as the demonstrators were not causing harm. Some protests moved from Tahrir square all the way to Captain Mo's station at Abdeen, chanting *"Ya Ahaleena endamo lina"* (Our families come join us).

After the *zohr* (noon) prayers, around two o'clock the police hosed the demonstrators with water in order to disperse the growing crowds. Police protocol stipulates that no officer is to secure demonstrations with his handgun, as they are not *Amn Elmarkazi*, (Central Security). The police were armed with rods and shotguns (*khartosh*), not hand guns (*bondekya*), to fire the tear gas known as CS. The shotgun has various bullet sizes. The CS gas causes excessive tearing, burning in the eyes, irritation and itching; Captain Mo assures that it does not cause death, contrary to hearsay. When police fire a canister of tear gas, demonstrators would usually run away to avoid inhaling the gas. However, some stayed, in Captain Mo's opinion, to get high. Many protestors were sticking by, not running away, and continuously inhaling the gas. 'Tramadol', is a painkiller, which if taken in excess causes a high. There are protestors who administered this popular drug for their mood whilst inhaling the CS gas, which possibly caused medical complications. On this day in question, the bullets contained small stingy pellets called birdshot. The police were ordered to target the ground, causing the bullets to reflect off the pavement and hit the protestors in their legs, a tactic used by the police to avoid serious injuries.

The police who were under attack were able to contain the assailants and maintained their position. Rocks were hurled at the police, leaving people wounded from both sides. One soldier died from all the pushing and heaving close to Talaat Harb Street. While he was on full alert in Abdeen square, Captain Mo managed to watch the Al Jazeera channel, at a hairdresser shop. Some officers used sound shots that would echo and scare. Microbuses evacuated the square at three on the morning of January 26.

During the course of the day, Captain Mo called his fellow police officers situated close to the parliament building, near Midan alTahrir.
Captain Mo said, "How are things at your side?"
A police officer replied, "Some people came and threw acid on an officer's face, burning it."
Alarmed, Captain Mo knew that the protest was no longer peaceful.

By nightfall, the weather was very cold, having reached eight degrees Celsius. The hairdresser at whose shop he watched the news, felt sympathy towards Captain Mo and gave him his car keys to sit inside for warmth. Captain Mo left his station on January 26 at four in the morning, feeling completely worn out, after working twenty-one hours! By day break matters had deteriorated.

The numbers in Tahrir were considerably lower than the previous day, with many people going to work as usual on Wednesday January 26. Elsewhere, in Imbaba prison, rumor had it that relatives of the prisoners had sent incredibly big men to break into the prison so that their loved ones could escape. Captain Mo believes that some protestors rode the wave of violence and participated in the attacks and henceforth, shifted from activist gear into criminal gear.

Although originally the police approved the protest, since people were intending to leave at night, the following day, the police orders subsequently changed to prevent large groups from protesting. Those who did not heed, faced arrest. Protestors did not want to leave Tahrir late at night, and shifted the protests into a sit-in, which the security forces had not approved, and were starting to hinder the movement throughout the square. Given that the number of protestors was limited on that first night, the police's job was an easy one and they were able to disperse the crowd and clear the square. A stampede or birdshot caused the death of a couple of the protestors; Captain Mo is not sure about the numbers. Chants were targeting the removal of the loathed minister of interior, Habib El Adly, and demanding a decent living, freedom and social equality. There were no demands for the downfall of the regime yet.

January 28: Hell Broke Loose
The scenario changed dramatically on January 28. Captain Mo believes that the unplugging of mobile and internet communications was a grave mistake made by the old *nizam* for it provoked the people and gave them additional justification to demonstrate on this Friday.

On social media, the bloggers were calling it 'Friday of Anger' to avenge the death of peaceful protestors. The protest was scheduled right after the *zohr* (noon) prayers. People were appearing from all sides of Abdeen square, north, south, east and west and in significantly large numbers, in the tens of thousands, a sight that Captain Mo had never witnessed before. Until around three in the afternoon, *Amn Elmarkazi*, (Central Security) was standing solemnly as human barriers, but their facade trickled down rapidly in about five minutes. Captain Mo does not recall any chants on Friday, as he was busy trying to evade the hurled stones from protestors. Captain Mo was standing within the police frontier, safeguarding *Dakhleyah* (ministry of interior). All side roads were barricaded. At a distance, Captain Mo managed to catch sight of the sea of crowds at Tahrir square. He was feeling anxious.

Captain Mo followed the instructions to refrain from talking on the walkie-talkie, in order to avoid drawing attention to himself. When Captain Mo was listening to the radio channels at around three in the afternoon, he tuned in to the Al Azbakiyah police station channel to hear an officer screaming into the microphone. The station is below a fly over on Ramsis Street.
The officer said, "Help! They are throwing Molotov cocktails at the station and the station is on fire! I have detainees in the prison that can die inside, what should I do?" Another officer replied, "Ok I will send you an *Amn Elmarkazi* truck right away." The officer dispatched a truck from Tahrir square.

Almost all the police stations were under attack; it was like a domino effect, one fell after the other within an hour. The first station attacked was Masr El Adeema. These stations are normally loaded with weapons in addition to detainees imprisoned for a short period awaiting prosecution. At the time, Captain Mo believed an organized group must have orchestrated the attacks but he was not certain. However, today he knows that *Ikhwan* were the mastermind behind this attack. He has heard that trained mercenaries from abroad lent them a hand. Demonstrating is a form of activism; but attacking a public institute like the police station is not activism. It is nothing but unlawful aggression. To attack the police stations was an act of treason. Some of the assailants were armed and charged with hatred.

Shortly, the *Amn Elmarkazi* truck, referred to in Arabic as *box* or *Sandook*, arrived at the Al Azbakiyah station to rescue the detainees, but sadly the *box* was set on fire. The help they asked for went up in flames. Despair loomed.
An officer said, "They set the *box* on fire!"
The station manager replied, "Go upstairs and fire your gun."
The officer protested, "Are you crazy? Do you want me to provoke the people?"
The station manager said, "Shoot in to the air."

The smoke from the fire in the station and the truck was thick and heavy, and breathing was increasingly impossible. It was pandemonium. Some police officers ran for their lives, others stayed and fired at the assailants. The officers released detainees to save them from the ferocious flames.

At another police station, the jail had around twenty detainees, who tried to break the gates with metal bars they had broken from their beds and succeeded to enter the corridor. *It is worth noting that reputedly the jails at police stations do not have beds.* The prisoners were trying to escape, but the police officers fired tear gas, forcing them to go in another direction, where the police were able to contain them.

By evening, the officers were exhausted; Captain Mo had his shotgun with him, but was not going to fire it at people around him. He was aware that many good people had joined the protests, like his late brother. The assailants were not everywhere; they were at the police stations. Captain Mo said, "I will never shoot at a person just like that." He did not get orders to withdraw that night, and all police officers acted independently. If the police force had used real weapons on January 28, Captain Mo is sure that Egypt could have transformed into a sea of blood. If the police had used their machine guns, all it would have taken is one shot that could pass through fifteen protestors, just to give a sense of the magnitude of the bloodshed had the police used their weapons on the crowds. Now imagine what one hundred shots in one machine gun can do. One officer could literally kill one thousand five hundred persons with just one weapon! Let alone the whole force fully armed.

Tahrir square drew demonstrators as if it were a powerful magnet attracting and mesmerizing them into a state of hypnosis. Captain Mo anticipated a larger turnout than there was on the first day, but did not expect the targeting of police stations. Whether the police officer was good or bad was beside the point, the assailants wanted them dead. Captain Mo recalls a man who was defending an officer, pleading that the assaulters spare him, as "He is a good man." The man hugged the officer and led him outside the station. *On the perception of the police who the public despise, I would like to refer to Nelson Mandela who said, "Honest men are to be found on both sides of the color line, and the Afrikaner is no exception."*[77] In Egypt, there are good *police officers and bad police officers and the public should never forget that.* It is clear for Captain Mo that *Dakhleya (Ministry of Interior)* were the targeted bogeyman. As a popular Arabic saying, 'when a calf falls down, the knives on him increase'. He compares the police to the calf.

Bomb at Tahrir

Guns aside, the media never announced that twelve kilos of bomb ammunition were located at Tahrir square on the 'Friday of Anger'. Fortunately, the police managed to dismantle them. One of his colleagues who saw the bombs informed Captain Mo, but no one knew who planted them. If the bombs had detonated, a very large area would have gone up in flames. It seems it was part of the plan, to ignite Tahrir once the army got there, positioning the army as the aggressors and subsequently causing a fall out between civilians and the army. Why did the police and army keep this a secret? Captain Mo believes that the army protected the revolution; if the army protected the *ancien regime,* Egypt's fate would have been similar to neighboring Libya or Syria where the army opened fire on protestors, leading to civil war.

Whoever was behind those bombs clearly is an enemy of the state and wants Egypt to tremble and collapse into civil war. Who could be behind this? Captain Mo suspects foreign powers, for instance the USA, Israel, or Iran. According to Mo, an American NGO which advocates democracy and human rights sponsored the opposition movement, April 6 Movement, and has aligned its resources to back it in Egypt. Captain Mo's theory of what is behind this apparent change in American policy towards Egypt, is that they were unhappy about former President Mubarak's refusal to enter the Iraq war and his turning down of their request to locate an American missile base on Egyptian soil sometime before revolution. *Did spies instigate the revolution as payback time? This farfetched theory may have an iota of truth. Nonetheless; the cries of the revolution were genuine and legitimate.*

Commotion

Another incident Captain Mo recounts, is of an officer at Sheikh Rihan Street. On January 28, soldiers next to *Amn Elmarkazi,* the Central Security barracks were attacked. One of them was hit by a shot from a passing bus. Seconds later another soldier was hit and fell to the ground, and just after that a protestor was also gunned down. Who was shooting at both the army and the protestors?

The army and the police have different roles; once the army mobilized, they understood the difficulties the police had been facing, as civilians were boldly disrespectful. Take the simple example of parking in a no-parking zone or even in the middle of the street, blocking traffic. The civilian will justify stopping his car by saying that it will only be five minutes, overlooking the law and unconcerned if the police officer is penalized for not upholding the law.

Captain Mo recounts a scene which his army colleague had witnessed. An army car located on Sixth of October Bridge was set ablaze on the 'Friday of Anger'. One man said in a loud voice, "The army came to help the police!" and then sparked the flames in the car. Subsequently, a man threw pebbles at the driver, hurting him and stopping the car while setting it on fire. Another officer jumped out of the burning car, ran along the bridge with his rifle and jumped into the cold Nile River. Shortly afterwards, the car exploded with a large deafening sound that scared everyone around, causing frantic running away from the blaze. The army soldiers talked to the people and restored calm, assuring them that they came to protect the country. As the police were unable to ensure order, the army mobilized to stand by the police. Captain Mo states that it is unfathomed that the army and the police should not be present at the same time.

Captain Mo recalls that on January 28, he saw a police officer firing his shotgun in Ataba square, causing protestors to disperse. One man froze in shock, and looked at his chest searching for a wound. When he realized he was not shot he looked up at the office, smiling with relief. The police officer ended up laughing and a few bystanders too. It was a touch of much needed comic relief in tumultuous times. *Even in the possibility of death, Egyptians can be humorous.*

On Friday January 28, Captain Mo decided to withdraw when he heard gunshots from all around him, feeling that if he had stayed it would have been suicide. Moreover, staying at Abdeen square any longer had become pointless as the protestors were camping at Tahrir square already, clearly not going home. Captain Mo decided to change into civilian clothing to avoid any clashes and evade looming attacks. Evidently, after officers changed their uniforms into regular clothes, calm returned on the streets of Cairo. At five in the afternoon Captain Mo headed to his police station within the vicinity of downtown. He found its doors closed and its lights turned off. Regularly clothed police officers were leading protestors, telling them, "They ran this way," averting the protestors from the police station. Captain Mo's superior officer asked him to go protect his home and return to duty the following morning.

Elsewhere, one of his colleagues was on his way to Maadi, East of Cairo, when he saw men coming out of police station armed with machine guns shooting in the air. Mohamed's colleagues stayed on the ground, hiding behind a plastic chair for an hour, watching this ghastly security breach and unable to do anything.

Many officers died in service and others thrown into the banks of the Nile, but the police never reported.

Change of Heart

While somberly walking home on Kasr El Aini Street, Captain Mo saw cars in flames and a petrol station in shambles. Civilians were setting cars on fire and destroying whatever they came across. He saw a man with a wooden cart stealing anything he could on the street, even a water hose! At the onset of the revolution, Captain Mo was happy with the demonstrations, until the Friday of Anger on January 28. After he saw people at Kasr El Aini Street filled with hatred and vengeance, Captain Mo reconsidered and became deeply saddened to see his beloved country burning in flames. The police force was withdrawing, collapsing, and Captain Mo stood by watching helplessly. He saw people boiling with envy only interested in wrecking the neighborhood. When he arrived home, Captain Mo washed his face and went downstairs on full alert to join the civilian checkpoints.

Captain Mo gets mad at the lack of appreciation, when people say they can live without the police. The police, him included, had secured the streets for the civilians in numerous checkpoints. In his area, there were police dressed in civilian clothes to safeguard the neighborhood. Captain Mo was standing with another three of his police colleagues at the front row, with the civilians behind them. Captain Mo recalls a man trembling when he heard that *baltegeya* were coming their way. There were men who were too scared to stand in the streets. One time a man brought a street dog to smell the car, assuming he would be able to smell any weapons, clueless to the fact that police dogs are highly trained. Captain Mo could not help but smile, as he did not want to offend the simple man.

Late January 28: The Great Escape

Prisoners escaped from several prisons late on Friday January 28. Captain Mo knows one of the prison guards at Tora, who recounted to him that the prisoners had heard about the revolts on the streets of Egypt and contagiously revolted inside their cells. Mobile phones are smuggled into prison cells, keeping prisoners in touch with the outside world. Hardcore criminals are worse than people could ever imagine. A criminal could go to unthinkable measures, like hurting his own face, to blame it on the police. Nonetheless, at Tora prison nobody managed to escape, unlike at other prisons.

Captain Mo did not see the document that was circulating, which alleged that Minister of Interior Habib El Adly had ordered prisons open. Given the news of prison breakouts all over the country, Captain Mo called his friends on their landlines and alerted them to be on vigil at their apartment blocks and to create civilian checkpoints in order to keep their communities safe. Around three prisons, which largely held *Ikhwan* prisoners, were broken into. Hundreds of prisoners escaped from Fayoum, South of Cairo and killed a senior police officer (*no one has been formally charged with his murder and evidence shows that he was killed by his sniper as he refused to open the prison gates).*[78] Thousands escaped from Wadi El Natrun prisons located at Beheira governorate North of Cairo. *This great escape has happened in other countries during times of political unrest; it happened in Burma, of which Suu Kyi said, "the mass release of prisoners added a new element of peril and anarchy to the dangerously combustible elements...around the country...10,000 footloose criminals."*[79]

Many police cars were stolen during those 18 days, and even after the revolution. An officer who was a colleague of Captain Mo's, informed him that he spotted stolen white American Embassy cars, which had been used to run over soldiers. The following morning, Captain Mo went to his station and his senior officer told him to stay put in his neighborhood, until matters settled. Captain Mo and his neighbors stayed alert at the civilian checkpoints, catching thieves. Every now and then, they would hear that criminals were coming from the direction of the prison, but nobody appeared. Only gunshots resonated. It seemed as though endless rumors were stalking the cities with no way of verifying what was true and what was not.

Around the vicinity of *Dakhleya*, gunshots echoed. Police and the army are obliged to defend public institutions and according to law, can gun down any assailant. Captain Mo was upset when a woman came on TV and said, "Why are they defending *Dakhleya* as if it was *el Kaaba* (The Muslim holy place of pilgrimage, in Mecca)?" Captain Mo cannot understand the complacency Egyptians have in not grasping the right to defend public institutions and the importance of securing the property of all Egyptians. Why does she not comprehend the dangers of a fire? What is the objective of burning down the ministry of interior? It will cost a fortune to build another one; in any case, Mo believes there are more pressing matters to use Egypt's money for.

During the period of civilian checkpoints, civilians arrested seven or eight criminals within his neighborhood and the military police contacted Captain Mo to move them to prison. When he collected the detainees, Mo wore his civilian clothes.

An Outsider Job

Captain Mo can think of many groups who gained from opening the prison gates; for instance, *Hamas*. One of the escaped prisoners was from *Hamas* and he escaped from Wadi El Natroun prison, located in the desert of the Northwestern Nile Delta, in a stolen car; some say it was a police vehicle, others say it was an ambulance. He crossed the border overnight into Gaza. A rented bulldozer drove into the prison walls to release this prisoner, a well-planned escape during the turmoil on Egyptian streets. Captain Mo questions how the police could, while facing unprecedented demonstrations in the streets, conceive and implement the simultaneous prison breaks. In addition to the prison breaks, Captain Mo is confident that a third party was behind the use of live bullets in Tahrir and refers to it as an enemy of the state. The enemy wants Egypt to enter very dark times. Who were the snipers over the American embassy and over the ministry of interior? Despite the commotion, according to Captain Mo, not many people died at Tahrir - around seven or eight, most of them on Friday of Anger. The majority of casualties were in front of the police stations, which law justifies, as they were assailants attacking public property.

Mo rejects the theory that police let out the prisoners. The prison warden cannot open up the gates even if he received orders to do so, as his senior officer will question him about the whereabouts of the prisoners. A smart police officer needs to stick to what is right to avoid getting into trouble.

Additionally, it is very difficult to fire birdshots and aim at the eye, as pellets spread on impact. Police snipers from *Dakhleya* have a specific mission, which does not entail shooting at civilians from rooftops, and they were not at Tahrir on the Friday of Anger. On February 2, 2011, many people died on the bridge, targeted by red laser beams from unknown snipers and then instantly gunned down. The men on the bridge were supporters of Mubarak and were unsuspectingly targeted and attacked. Captain Mo posed a very valid question; if the snipers were really *Dakhleya* or police, would they fire at the supporters of Mubarak whom they protect? Mo does not think so. Why would a sniper use a laser? Snipers' work is always covert. Snipers have very sophisticated lenses that do not need a laser beam to mark their target. Captain Mo is sure that laser beams were used to draw the attention of the media so that they would write a story about snipers shooting at protestors, and leading the public to lose even more confidence in the police. Captain Mo vouches that the police have been set up as the 'bad guys' wearing black with blood stained hands.

14 Days: Clashes Led to Downfall

The day the medieval battle took place in Tahrir square on February 2, 2011 Captain Mo was at Kasr El Nil station. Around one in the afternoon, he saw a group of men and women passing by proudly holding pictures of former President Mubarak, some riding motor bikes. One of the signs said, 'If they are a million, we are eighty million.' He overhead them saying they were going to enter Tahrir and clear it from all the protestors. Captain Mo could hear women ululating, a sound of joy that emanates from the throat commonly heard at celebrations like weddings. Captain Mo went to his home, to watch the events on television, as he expected a clash to take place between the supporters of Mubarak and those who opposed him. He was contemplating who would end up victorious.

One of the theories, which many people were buying into, is that members of the former ruling National Democratic Party, NDP, party hired *baltegeya* to attack the protestors. Captain Mo could agree with this theory, but there were other parties involved as well. Certainly, some of those involved were the men who worked at the Pyramids and were losing their livelihood, gravely affected by the abrupt lack of tourists and halted economy due to the political instability. Nevertheless, with the passing of time, Captain Mo believed the emerging theory that *Ikhwan* were behind the last straw that broke the camel's back, and not the former NDP, as was widely believed.

Captain Mo knows from his friends that on the bloody February 2, 2011 there were shots fired from within the crowds, targeting at the men in balconies and on rooftops. *Ikhwan* were definitely present and armed, indeed they used their guns. The media never highlighted this.

Captain Mo had lost his wallet with his personal ID at the onset of the demonstrations, which he refrained from elaborating on, and hence did not have any proof of his identity, making it impossible to enter Tahrir, as the check points looked at identity cards and frisked everyone before entering the square.

Captain Mo was hoping and praying that former President Mubarak would abdicate during those eighteen days, and was very happy when he did just that. President Mubarak's second speech, after which many Egyptians felt sympathy towards the president, did not affect Captain Mo; he sensed that those were Mubarak's final days and that his service was more than over. By the third speech, nobody believed President Mubarak's words and intentions, including Captain Mo. But over a year later, Captain Mo realizes that former President Mubarak was genuinely scared for the country and wanted to avoid the current situation.

Post 18 Days: Widening Gap

A little over a month after the eighteen days of the revolution, a constitutional referendum took place on March 19, 2011, in which many people agreed to the proposed changes, in order for the wheel of production to recommence and resume business as usual. As a police officer, Captain Mo does not have the right to vote in elections. If he had the right to vote, he would have voted 'No', against the proposed changes, as the constitution needed to be re-written from scratch. As the saying goes, 'out with the old and in with the new'. For his own safety, Captain Mo refrained from wearing his uniform, as he expected the targeting of police during the referendum.

Concern is creeping over Captain Mo that gangs could arise, covering various districts as happened in France after the French revolution, where he recalls hearing that war broke out between different districts that lasted for decades. Captain Mo worries that the poor districts would attack the rich districts and steal from them, convinced that the rich stole from the poor and hence such actions were justified, as with Robin Hood. In Cairo, almost every affluent district has a neighboring squalor of a slum like Zamalek and Kit Kat, Garden City and Sayeda Zeinab. Envy is growing within people; when a poor man sees a rich man driving an expensive Mercedes S 500 in Egypt that is worth over two million pounds, around three hundred and twenty thousand dollars, he is not happy for the rich man. Rather, he thinks that the rich man is insensitive, unconcerned with the unfortunate who sleep without dinners and cannot afford medical treatment, among other necessities. The constant comparison is endless. The less fortunate do not have natural gas pipes connected in their homes and need to queue for long hours to buy the subsidized gas cylinders, whereas almost all affluent districts have gas connections. Captain Mo senses that a real hunger revolution is imminent if the economic situation continues in its downward spiral.

Hazy Definition
People have different perspectives of what happened on January 25. Some view it as a revolution, others as a military *coup d'etat,* and others as an Intifada (uprising). Al Arabiya channel referred to the events as an Intifada and not a revolution. Captain Mo believes that this Intifada succeeded ephemerally but in the past months, its shortcomings have surfaced and it has transformed into a coup.

After the abdication of President Mubarak, some obnoxious people ventured to Tahrir square, demanding trials, and believing that they had the right to rule the country, deciding who should die and who should live. Captain Mo has a theory that the men and women who were at Tahrir after the Friday of Anger had issues, either personal, family related, or mental. There are protestors who joined on January 25 and 28 but never ventured back again. Protesting became somewhat fashionable. Like a nice new Barbie doll in the hands of an excited young girl who does not want to stop playing with it, the protestors did not want to stop protesting. Just the week before, some high school students had been protesting and chanting *'yoskot, yoskot hokum elaskar'* ('down down with military rule').

The people have succeeded in overthrowing the ruler by cutting the head of the snake, with the tail still moving fiercely; but usually it can only move for a brief amount of time before it will die too. However, this particular tail seems eternal, or the snake seems to have grown a new head. Many ministers from the old *nizam* are facing charges and imprisonment. Captain Mo was sad to see Alaa Mubarak imprisoned, as he believes he was genuinely good, unlike his brother Gamal.

Some *baltegeya* acted as if they were revolutionaries and some died, reputedly as martyrs. When men die fighting, which of them will God consider a martyr? The man assaulting the station, or the man defending the station? Captain Mo views the crisis in Egypt as that which stems primarily from bad people thinking that they are good and doing well. This confusion is very dangerous. A political activist proudly confessed on live television that he threw a Molotov cocktail, setting fire to the Science Center, a library that holds two hundred thousand books. Unbelievably, people came out of their homes to defend the man and his crime. Captain Mo was thinking. "How twisted can it get?" People are justifying the demolition of an institute but not blood, *both of which are unjustifiable. Among the destroyed documents is the 20-volume "Description D'Egypte" from the Napoleonic era. As one student activist, Ahmed, told CNN, "Since when are buildings and manuscripts more important than human lives?" Besides Ahmed did not know that the building was a library and blames the police who were hurling rocks from its rooftop.* Captain Mo cannot understand how basic people's thinking can be. When a man sets fire to a building, the people inside may burn to death, and the fire itself can spread to neighboring buildings.

Today, Captain Mo is scared to kill a criminal, as he fears the public may view the criminal as a hero and him as the villain! This warped perspective is something he really cannot understand, and this 'so what' attitude is leading to further disaster.

Many people want the police to return to their posts by any means to reassert security in the streets of Egypt. The police are doing their jobs and almost each day, a mission is out arresting criminals, posting news on the Police's official Facebook page. Traffic police can not dare wear their uniforms and police the streets with a hostile public, fearing assaults.

Deeply immersed in our discussions, we are interrupted by a phone call from Essam, a friend and colleague, asking about Captain Mo's whereabouts. Mo explained briefly that he was in Zamalek and was about to head out to the Council of Ministers to report to duty.

After the revolution, *Dakhleya (Ministry of Interior)* has found itself in a worse position concerning the upholding of security. A police officer cannot go about his job without any law protecting him. Before the revolution, there was not so much violence and lack of security. It was rare to find a man armed with a knife walking in the street, but today this is becoming the norm. Weapons are abundant in the country. They originate from Sudan and Libya. Arms are not smuggled via trucks as is depicted in films, but are loaded on a camel, which walks into the desert, arriving on its own to the desired destination. The deals are paid up front before the goods are shipped.

One evening, Captain Mo was listening to a socialist on a TV talk show who was advocating for the complete downfall of the state before rebuilding a new state, entailing civil war between the people and the army; in other words, anarchy. There was another man called Alaa who said, "We have two options: we either resort to violence which is the faster track, but people will not bless bloodshed, or we take the slower track, diplomacy, that will take around fifty years."

Falling Out with Police

After the revolution, there was a disturbing incident in one of the roundabouts in Maadi. A police officer called El Segeny was driving his big Dodge-ram wearing civilian clothes, when he saw a minibus driver driving recklessly through the street.

El Segeny said, "How could you cut me off like that? Do you own this street?" These words provoked the minibus driver who got out of his vehicle. Seeing the police beret on the dashboard of El Segeny's car sparked the minibus driver's bitter sentiments towards the police. The driver attacked El Segeny with a knife but El Segeny surely would not have retaliated with his handgun, as the weapon according to Egyptian law, is classified as a superior weapon, which is not the case abroad[80]. Captain Mo knows that the police officer was a very decent man. He did not witness this incident, but the driver and other men beat El Segeny, who ended up in a hospital bed with several injuries. El Segeny has since recovered and is back on duty. *This is a disputed and controversial incident as to what happened that day. The people of the neighborhood said the police officer had killed the driver, as he had provoked the officer by ridiculing him, saying that the people had driven officers to stay in their homes. At this, the officer shot the driver. The Ministry of Interior stated that the officer was on leave, as he had psychological issues.*[81]

The right to self-defense is no longer as it was before the revolution. The law does not protect the police officer or any other individual who defends himself. The type of weapon used to defend oneself is fundamental; in fair play, a gun is inequivalent to a knife, even in self-defense. Captain Mo feels as if the laws are hiding in the dark, waiting for any mistake made by the police.

It is worth noting that one cannot expect a police officer to accept unfounded assaults with fear, as police and cowardice do not match. As Fischer notes, "The Prophet of non-violence,

Gandhi, nevertheless declared that 'where there is a choice between cowardice and violence, I would choose violence,' for cowardice reduces a man's self-respect and hence his stature." [82]

Defects in the Law

The Egyptian law needs to be reformed, protecting the police officer in his essential role of upholding law and order in Egypt, as per the example of El Segeny who could not use his gun against a knife. Moreover, the tools used by the police force to gather clues are very primitive compared to those found in developed countries. Like many countries, lawyers in Egypt do their utmost to prove the defendant innocent even when he/she is not. This is probably why very few lawyers accept to defend heroin cases. If a judge has half a percent doubt, he cannot and will not sentence the defendant with the death penalty. Similarly, in the case of former President Mubarak, there cannot be a popular trail. The law requires evidence presented by the prosecution in the court in order to sentence former President Mubarak. Sentences can never be according to hearsay and public opinion.

Throughout Egypt, crime has been evolving. For instance, an imported machine facilitates ATM theft, giving illegal access to the money in an ATM. The police arrested three young men who stole from an ATM in Masr El Gedida, East of Cairo. Certainly, this is considered a crime of theft by the courts, but the arching question is, what type of theft? Current law does not cover ATM theft so what sentence is appropriate? Likewise, with political corruption, what is the law governing and defining political corruption? If an official stole, his defense would need to present proof before he is charged with theft. Armed robbery however, which is popularly termed as *baltaga*, has a very serious sentencing reaching life imprisonment.

Egyptian law allows an individual to protect himself, his property and his land or his neighbors if attacked. For instance, if a man sees another man assaulted and he interferes to protect the target's life, the law protects the man who is interfering in self-defense. However, since the revolution, people now say, "The man had no right to defend or interfere". For instance, the officers who were defending the police stations are now facing charges, although the men who attacked the stations did so with the intention of breaking into the weapons room to steal the machine guns and all sorts of firearms. Those who attacked the police stations cleaned them clear of any weapons, which partially accounts for the insurgence of weapons on the streets. An officer who was defending Sayeda Zeinab Station, in downtown Cairo, killed assailants and hence was temporarily detained. Captain Mo found his detainment strange and difficult to accept. He has not come to terms with the unjustified post revolution changes in the implementation of the law.

The armed man rules the Machiavellian state. Egypt will depend on its arms and security state as Machiavelli wrote, "It is unreasonable to expect that an armed man should obey one who is unarmed, or that an unarmed man should remain safe and secure when his servants are armed."[83] *Some countries clearly practice this philosophy and in other countries it is concealed.*

Tahrir Safe Haven

At the onset of the summer of 2011, an unprecedented wave of armed theft took place near Tahrir square. A state of paralysis daunted police officers, despite daily reports of thefts. At other times, police officers could go into Tahrir and arrest a thief, but after the revolution, it has become a green zone free of the police, a perfect haven for criminals. One such thief known as '*Farkha*' stopped a man walking in the square, threatened him with a knife and stole all his money. It is noteworthy that this thief has a light sense of humor as '*farkha*' means 'chicken'. Just the day before, Captain Mo got word of five similar cases of theft within Tahrir. If Captain Mo were to pursue '*farkha*', at least half a dozen of *farkha's* friends would come to his aid and a gang fight would ensue, which the media would jump on. The media would portray it as an attack by the police, against the 'peaceful protestors' at Tahrir. In a very short time, more people will come to help the criminals, believing they are protestors. The thief who calls himself '*farkha*' tells victims to relay the following message to the police, "The *farkha* just stole from me." In the meantime, '*Farkha*' does not leave the square and camps in his safe depot, accumulating a fortune. Mo is uncertain if the police have arrested '*Farkha*' or not. *I find it amusing that criminals are using animal names as their code names, as in the suburb of Six of October City a famous carjacker referred to himself as 'Asfoura,' which means bird.*

Since the revolution, protestors have been demanding pay raises, apartments, and jobs. But one must ask, what have they done to deserve such rewards? What have they given to take in return? Captain Mo talks about the unemployed, and challenges them: do they really want to work and earn a living? Or are they just seeking a job that is convenient, and is to their liking? Beggars cannot be choosers. Egyptians are seeking a job that pays well and ends at two in the afternoon, a job that furnishes him with an apartment and a car. Wake up from this dream! Are Egyptians willing to relocate to have a job? No, they want a job close to their homes and are not willing to sacrifice.

Condemned Police

Among the reasons why the police were out of favour with the people, was the widespread torture in prisons. Nevertheless, Captain Mo claims that for the last six or seven years, torture is no longer the common practice, since *Dakhleya* has an office for complaints against police officers. As long as there is paper and pen, the police do not need torture. Every day there were complaints filed. Police justifiably beating up heartless criminals, like a man who had killed a seven-year-old girl, or a man who raped a young boy, were being reported.

Regarding the famous case of the late Khaled Said, and the distorted picture of his face, Captain Mo says the picture was not taken immediately after his beating, but after his autopsy. As the police charged him with drug dealing and of swallowing the packet of drugs, they needed to deform his face during the autopsy in order to retrieve the packet. Among the theories put forward was that the police officers who killed Khaled were drug dealers. Captain Mo does not believe this theory. The police officers tried to arrest Khaled, who probably resisted, and hence the beating ensued. However, Captain Mo can never really know what happened, as he does not even work in Alexandria; it is an unsolved mystery, which certainly created an outcry in Egypt.

Public opinion does not believe that the court delivered justice in the case of Khaled Said. Captain Mo wants people to realize that no judge can declare a sentence unless he is certain without a reasonable doubt that the defense is guilty. In the case of Habib El Adly, the court sentenced him to unlawful financial gains and acquitted him on issuing orders to kill protestors. Captain Mo has realized from independent online videos that regular civilians are attempting to act as investigators, presenting evidence that the police shot live ammunition. Mo heard that during the closed hearing, Marshal Tantawy never said that he did not get orders to shoot civilians, nor refuse to follow any. He just said, "We would never fire on civilians."

Civilians do not realize how difficult a life Captain Mo lives as a police officer and in spite of this, he will not quit his job. If he left his job now, who would take care of his responsibilities? When the going gets tough, one just does not pack up his bags and leave. Before the revolution, Captain Mo considered submitting his resignation. Now, after the dramatic changes in the country, it is simply not the right time. If he quits the police force now, he will feel like a backstabbing coward. If all the good men left the force, who would remain?

In March 2012, a case attracted the attention and coverage of news channels. Several Americans who were working for NGOs in Egypt were arrested and imprisoned on the charge of working without permits and illegally raising funds from the United States and funneling them to Egypt. Midway during their trail, inexplicably, the Judge excused himself from the case, literally abandoning it. Within a couple of days, the Americans seemed to have negotiated a deal with the Egyptian government, deporting their nationals and the case was closed. The case created an outcry, as it did not render justice. Hearsay is that the Americans paid 'hush hush' money to Egypt to release their nationals, money needed to get the economy rolling after the huge exodus of foreign investment.

Among the problems facing Egypt in these testing times, is individual or group self-interest over the nation's general interests. Abou Hamed, former member of parliament, tried to address the issues of protestors and ended up protesting himself while the parliament was in session, on a live television feed. Captain Mo used to watch this and break out into laughter. It seemed to him that the new name of the game in parliament was, whichever MP who was talking from the podium would appear on air, mainly talking, but with no action. Each session, the MP earns five thousand pounds, around seven hundred and fifty dollars. *Mo seems to be have confused the numbers, as their salary is 5000 on a monthly basis, and they earn 150 per parliamentary session.* One MP had recommended increasing the number of sessions the parliament held in each parliamentary term, possibly to make more money, as there is no guarantee as to how long the parliament will be in session. *In June 2012, right before the presidential run-off between Morsi and Ahmed Shafik, the court dissolved the parliament. At the time, Captain Mo recalled that Baradei had forewarned this, as he said to the Guardian, "The election of a president in the absence of a constitution and a parliament is the election of a president with powers that not even the most entrenched dictatorships have known." While I am writing this chapter, Egypt has witnessed violence between supporters of President Morsi and opposition who oppose the presidential decree granting him super powers. Will the conflict be resolved civilly or through bloodshed?*

Opportunity Cost

Former Minister of Interior, Habib El Adly, was a powerful man who left the people fearing the ministry. From what Mo perceived, police could get things done with mere talk, rather than physical coercion; for instance if a police officer beckoned a criminal to approach him the criminal would simply obey, but those days are gone. Although El Adly gave *Dakhleya* a powerful stature, he simultaneously ruined the ministry. The reputation of a police officer is now equivalent to a corrupt thief, unsuitable as a marriage suitor. More than once parents of prospective brides rejected Captain Mo as a suitor simply because he is a police officer.

Gone are the glorious days where police officers were proud and respected individuals. Families cannot accept a man who they believe will curse and beat their daughter and will be unable to provide for her in addition to working long hours. Due to this horrendous reputation, many police officers submitted their resignations so that they could live a respectable life in the eyes of society, and marry the women they love. By remaining in the police force, Captain Mo is sacrificing his personal life and societal acceptance. If Captain Mo wanted to leave the police force after less than ten years of service, he would have to compensate the ministry, by paying one hundred thousand pounds, around fourteen thousand dollars, for his freedom. After ten years of service, the penalty no longer applies. So once in the police force, you are rather stuck unless you are willing to pay the penalty, which recently the Minister of Interior, El Eisawy evoked. Moreover, the Police Academy is not free; Captain Mo's parents paid around thirty-seven thousand pounds, around six thousand dollars for Mo's police academy education.

Captain Mo cannot say that the former Minister, Al Adly, deserves his sentence, but he can assure that he did not give the orders to use live ammunition on civilians on January 28, as each policeman decided on his own what he would do. The question of stealing by the former minister is an altogether different matter. If he stole, then it was from police officers, not the people. Salaries need reviewing to reflect a fair and proper compensation for all the police officers, with a clear minimum and maximum wage.

The police are exerting more effort in their work post revolution, though it is not apparent, as the public is simply rejecting the police, viewing them as incapable of performing their jobs. Captain Mo recalls watching a TV broadcast of a man who was on a motorbike, riding in the opposite direction.
The reporter asked him, "Do you realize you are driving in the wrong direction on the bridge?"
The bike rider replied, "I am aware, but as long as the country is going in the wrong direction, so will I."
Captain Mo finds this to be absolute chaos.

Emergency Law is essential only when the nation is in a state of emergency. The expedited cases are of criminals with severe sentences. Now the nation is drowned with illegal weapons, and without this law, the country will slip into the valleys of insecurity and crime. Mo's concerns heightened when the minister of interior was ridiculed in front of the parliament. How will this affect the police morale, with their big boss disrespected? Nowadays the emergency law is in dire need of firm enforcement, due to the security vacuum. Actually, it is more necessary today than ever before. This law facilitates the inspection process, wherein the police are not required to have a warrant prior to inspection. To check out a car, the police need permission from the prosecution. In his view, it was a mistake to revoke the emergency law, which allowed him to stop a car he suspected and search it. Today he cannot stop a car even though he knows it is loaded with illegal weapons or drugs as he needs a permit. Many cases are dropped due to illegal searches without permits.

Twenty minutes after his first call, Essam calls Captain Mo again, asking him when he will arrive. Captain Mo promises to call him shortly. He is late taking over the shift from Essam, due to this lengthy interview.

Naturally Different
There clearly is a different line of thought between Muslims and Christians, as they have different religious beliefs. When a person highlights these differences, he

provokes sensitivities and fallout. Captain Mo quotes an Arabic saying that "religious strife is stronger than killing." Captain Mo never labeled the other according to their faith. He and his Christian friends cared for one another equally and exchanged greetings at religious festivities. Captain Mo believes that the *ancien regime* tried to water down the strife. *Amn Eldawla* (State Security) requests a Christian man, who converts to Islam, after thorough questioning not to announce his conversion, as it could cause havoc in society. Any believer is wary of matters touching his religion. Captain Mo is not comfortable with religion driven protests like those at Maspero in October 2011. Why use religion as a showcase attracting many followers, and creating a story for the media?

Captain Mo is satisfied with the outcome of the revolution, but believes that now is the time for the scene to halt and plans to be set for the future. It is as if going up the stairs, one did not notice the hole in the broken stair, and got a foot trapped in it. Enough looking behind us, it is time to start looking ahead of us. From one demonstration, another sectarian demonstration picks up and in the process, the country is at a standstill, not producing. The demonstrations are endless and many take place at the Council of Ministries. Mo believes that if every man and woman who was in a position of authority during the Mubarak era is discredited then almost everyone faces firing, regardless of his or her field.

Uncertain Future
Captain Mo's outlook is uncertain as be believes the Egyptian people are inherently good, but they need to wake up and realize the reality. If they continue dreaming, then the future transforms into dark pessimism. The downtrodden men of society are forced to steal to survive, and no one can blame them. Society has allowed their plight to continue worsening. *This confirms Moore who wrote, "You create thieves and then punish them for stealing."*[84] *This is the dramatic irony of states.*

Captain Mo predicted that *Ikhwan* would gain power and would spoil the country, just as the Americans planned. Unlike most civilians, the police know the *Ikhwan* inside out, and they have had a blood feud against them for years on end. In Mo's view, the April 6 movement in opposition to the Mubarak regime was and still is a tool and agent of the United States. The Americans do not want Egypt to settle down and prosper. Captain Mo sees Egypt rotating within a vicious cycle of chaos and uncertainty for many years to come. In his view, *Ikhwan* and the April 6 movement are different branches of the same tree, one civilian and the other Islamist, aiming to topple the *ancien regime.*

Captain Mo is sure that the Supreme Council of Armed Forces, SCAF, do not want to rule the country, as they are facing several booby traps. He predicted that

SCAF will shy away from ruling the country and *Ikhwan* would win the upcoming elections. He recalls clearly, when *Ikhwan* protested against the SCAF constitutional declaration, which limited the powers of the president prior to the presidential run-off. Captain Mo is sure that if Ahmed Shafik had won the elections, *Ikhwan* would have created havoc, setting the country up in flames and a blood feud would have ensued.

Police lack the proper tools to aid them in arresting criminals. Among the suggestions officers are discussing is the placement of cameras, like the traffic cameras for the police to better survey and uphold the law. The cameras are costly and may be implemented district by district.

In the United States, if a car does not respond to the siren of a police car, the police officer can hit the car and make it stop. Once the car stops, the officer places his hand on his gun while asking the driver to place his hands on the steering wheel where he can see them. If he does not comply, he asks the driver to step outside and lie face front on the street with his hands behind his head, for the officer to frisk him. If at any point in time the civilian does not respond to the demands of the officer the officer elevates his gun, this is protocol. The officer may fire bullets if at any point in time he feels endangered by the civilian. Unfortunately, this is not the case in Egypt.

Crossroads

Egypt is passing through testing crossroads, almost two years after the revolution. Somehow a second revolution seems to be unraveling, with the country split into two camps; the Islamists supporting President Morsi's constitutional declaration and draft Islamic constitution granting him sweeping powers, and the other camp of moderates and the liberals in outrage at the bold declaration of dictatorship. Captain Mo is pessimistic about the future and wants to wait and see which of these two polarized camps will win. He personally is reading the draft constitution, and has some reservations as to the proposal that Azhar would have a legislative role. As a police officer, he cannot frisk a suspected drug dealer, and yet he can detain someone for up to twelve hours without informing him of the reasons for his detainment, as long as the police release him before the twelve hours are up. If detained for more than twelve hours, then legally the detainee is entitled to an explanation. Where are the rights of the detainee?

Captain Mo can clearly see that *Ikhwan* are *Ikhwanising* all government institutions to wipe out any potential opposition. First came the ministries of defense and interior. Weeks before the controversial constitutional referendum, President Morsi fired the general prosecutor and unceremoniously appointed his replacement. This move created resentment amongst the prosecutors, who protested on December 17,

2012. Strangely enough, after the second round of presidential elections, he actually revoked his resignation as he simply changed his mind. In Captain Mo's view, the ministry of interior should follow law and orders, regardless of who is in office.

At the time of our meeting, Captain Mo was feeling extremely pessimistic. Lying had become the normal policy, and it was reputed that *Ikhwan* have a covert militia arm. In December 2012, *Ikhwan* announced that they were worried that their headquarters may be attacked in several governorates, and were considering arming their members to defend their offices.

Captain Mo has not changed his view over the past months. On the contrary, his viewpoint has been confirmed by the dire trail of events that Egypt has walked since the overthrow of former President Mubarak. *Ikhwan* have committed a grave mistake by trying to rush the constitution, a clear sign of their political immaturity and arrogance. *Ikhwan* have lost the trust and respect of many Egyptians, with the blood spilled at the presidential palace in December 2012.

The constitutional referendum witnessed a low turnout rate of 32% of the increasing voter base. This adds up to less than 11 million of almost fifty-two million voters. The results were a 63% yes vote for the *Ikhwan* constitution. The referendum turnout is a significant drop from the first referendum in March 2011, which had a turnout of 41% of the eligible forty-five million eligible voters, and fourteen million voting "Yes" at 77%. (Figures based on Wikipedia.)

Attack on Terrorism

With the launching of *Tamarod* early in 2013, Captain Mo was uncomfortable, as he knew many members were also April 6 movement members. However, as it gained popular momentum, he morally supported, but did not sign.

Captain Mo justifies the so-called war on 'terrorism' and readily agrees with Machiavelli who once said, *"When it is absolutely a question of the safety of one's country…there must be no consideration of just or unjust, of merciful or cruel, of praiseworthy or disgraceful." Even Prime Minister Tony Blair quoted Machiavelli, signifying that the leader of the ancient British democracy agrees that state comes first in the twenty first century.*

Captain Mo is optimistic about the future. Arrests will take place for those who carry weapons. He defends all freedom as far as it does not overstep the freedom of others. In his view, people should not protest and block the entrance of people's homes as was done at Rabaa El Adawiya, where many Islamists protested. *As Thoreau cited Marquis d'Argenson, a French statesman in the eighteenth century, "'In the republic 'each man is perfectly free in what does not harm others.'"*[85] *Captain Mo's definition comes very close to this one.*

In his view, the media has been playing and working on people's opinions in an unethical way. Police reform is underway, as he senses the ministry is treating its personnel more humanely and showing public appreciation for the number of men who died in service. Captain Mo has seen the younger police officers given more space in their work. Authorities are showing concern for the police officers. Captain Mo believes the slow process of reform has started. Recently, Mo was promoted to (*Raed*) Major. His luck has turned as he finally is engaged to a young woman.

CHAPTER 14

Blinding Bullet

"But it is possible that ye dislike a thing which is good for you, and that you love a thing which is bad for you." (Quran Verse 2:216)[86]

I cried profusely when I saw on television or heard of fallen souls and victims of those eighteen days, feeling a painful lump in my throat. I ardently felt that I must search for a victim of the revolution to record his or her story. One of my university friends, a philanthropist, Yasmina Abou Youssef, collected money during those days to hand over to the victims and to help their families. She got me in touch with Mai Asfour who introduced me to Sayed. When I called him, he welcomed the idea of featuring in the book. Frankly, I felt uncomfortable meeting two complete strangers, as another tall sturdy man, Shawki, joined us in the middle of the interview. We met at Trianon Café at Mohandseen on Monday February 20, 2012.

School Drop Out

He is a tall slim black-eyed man with salt-and-pepper hair. Sayed Attia El Sayed was born in Cairo on November 2, 1967. His father is a simple uneducated man. In the 1940's, after his father married he moved with his wife from Tanta in the countryside to Cairo and specifically to the neighborhood of Shoubra Masr, and started working at the municipality. Sayed's father then took up another job to provide for his big family of six children, as the financial situation was dire. Sayed recalls his private lessons cost a fortune back then, amounting to twenty percent of his father's meager income back in the 1960's. Feeling burdensome and wanting to earn money, Sayed decided to drop out of school, not such a hardship for him, especially as he did not like school much anyway. He stopped going to Omar Makram Public Primary School, barely knowing how to read and write. However, his older sister managed to obtain a diploma.

Sayed still lives at Shoubra Masr, a district known for its brave men, women and children. He started to sculpt back in 1979. He was a professional metal welder, specialized in all forms of metal used for medical equipment. He used a small welding machine, around seventy-five centimeters in length, that produced an effect similar to needlework.

When Sayed wanted to get married, he searched his neighborhood for a decent 'circumcised' woman; his family introduced him to Ibtisam in a traditionally arranged setting. Ten days after they met, he proposed and they announced their engagement, which lasted two years before they eventually got married. Sayed is 45 years old now and has three daughters. He circumcised his two elder daughters in the presence of his mother and mother-in-law. He respects the elderly and believes whatever the elders have done must be also done to the younger generation. Sayed believes it is a proper Muslim ritual. *Women in Egypt and some other African countries undergo female genital mutilation so that sexual desires are curbed and to avoid any dishonor to their men. However, there are some theologians who have challenged this interpretation and it remains a controversial subject with some Muslims who state it is not required religiously, while others deem it as only a preference.*

Sayed is toiling so that his daughters attend schools in order to learn how to read and write, hoping they will not suffer like him. Nonetheless, living in a patriarchal society where men (*and to an extent even women*) do not treat women well, Sayed does not wish to see his daughters or his wife working where they can be maltreated and harassed in the workplace or in public transportation. Sayed has seen how the scum of society treat other women in his surroundings and can never accept placing his women in such a position. Some may say that Sayed is overly protective, as despite his difficult circumstances, he completely refuses the notion that his women could work.

Below Zero
Sayed has lived a difficult life and has faced humiliation under the rule of former President Mubarak. He was unable to cover the basic needs of his family, such as providing food, healthcare and keeping a roof over his one-bedroom apartment that totals around 60 square meters. Egyptian society consists of several socio-economic classes and Sayed believes that the creme de la creme, the men and women in high-end posts, are out of touch with the less fortunate. Each class is out of touch with the class below them. The struggling class faces hard times, where they work and sweat for long hours. Sayed works long days, starting from ten in the morning and ending at eight at night, yet earns a mere twenty-five pounds - a little more than four dollars per day. Moreover, if he works overtime till midnight he merely earns an additional five pounds. On his way home Sayed would buy milk, sandwiches and pampers for his baby and spend at least fifteen pounds. Rent costs him one hundred and fifty

pounds a month, around twenty-five dollars - twenty-five percent of his income. He calculates his daily rate and sadly realizes that his weekly income will not cover basic food costs for the week. He cannot make ends meet with just six hundred pounds, a little less than one hundred dollars for 5 mouths to feed in a month. Sayed says that no economic minister would be able to answer as to how such a salary can suffice a family covering necessities: food, schooling, healthcare and clothes. Moreover, when his mother was alive, he also helped her financially as his father's pension was not sufficient.

Sayed's situation resonates with what Marx described, "The modern labourer, on the contrary, instead of rising with the progress of industry, sinks deeper and deeper below the conditions of existence of his own class. He becomes a pauper, and pauperism develops more rapidly than population and wealth."[87] Sayed may be considered a 'fortunate' pauper in Egypt, as many are even worse off.

Sayed describes his life as a triangle revolving around his home, work and soccer. The only event that actually united all Egyptians, not just the hardline fans, was soccer. Football is an outlet for venting anger and stress. It was one of the few occasions were a feeling of national pride would emerge and the Egyptian flag would proudly float in the air. Otherwise, people felt embarrassed to say they were Egyptian. Sayed compares soccer to alcohol, where soccer quickly becomes a drinker's glass of wine, which temporarily washes away his worries. Soccer was the booze of the average Egyptian, leading him to forget his desperate, worrisome and burdensome life temporarily.

All the shop owner cared for was the work, and the profit he made off Sayed's work. He did not care if Sayed was sick or not, if he had pressing personal circumstances or not. When work was sparse, Sayed believed his boss created work for him keeping him late at night, so that he would never have free time for any distractions. He never had enough free time to search for another job to increase his feeble income. Sayed draws a comparison between his boss and the *ancien regime* who kept its people occupied with pursuing the basic needs of life. This kept them, as the Egyptian saying goes, 'walking beside the wall, out of harm's way and other people's business.' People were too exhausted to think about politics and had reached a point beyond despair. They abandoned any notion of a better life somewhere, somehow, sometime...

The Egyptian people have suffered a lot under the Mubarak regime, and the animals even had it worse. There came a time when stray dogs were plenty in Sayed's neighborhood. He could not believe it, when he saw the dogs mercilessly shot at. He does not believe this treatment of helpless stray dogs occurs in other countries. Sayed could not think of a justification for the way people treat animals. He does not understand how they could be a threat to humanity. Why do Egyptians disrespect life in general?

Sayed came to believe that the former *rayees*, Mubarak, was no longer a human being, as he allowed Egyptians to live in such morbid circumstances; he could not possibly be human. Back in May 2009, Mubarak's twelve-year-old grandson died. Sayed thought that this tragedy would awaken his humanity and a new dawn would shine over Egypt. It was a lesson that no matter how much money or power he had obtained he was unable to save his dear grandson. This was a wakeup call from God, striking the bell, but unfortunately, Mubarak's awareness continued being dormant and he did not change paths at this crossroad. Sayed was hoping that Mubarak would start really seeing his people and listening to their needs and complaints. On Dooms Day, there will be no titles, just men and women with their deeds judged by God Almighty.

One night, Sayed's four-year-old daughter Habiba got an asthma attack and he did not have the needed five pounds for her oxygen session at the hospital. So he carried her on his shoulder at three in the morning, for her to breathe in oxygen. When he can afford the oxygen session at the hospital, he is obliged to give a tip to the nurse. Why should he tip anyone when he can barely afford the treatment itself? Moreover, why should he tip someone who is doing his or her job?

Sayed felt worthless, and in desperate hours, would wish he died and was reborn as a dog living in Europe. He had reached an abyss, feeling utterly unimportant. *As Martin Luther King described it, "when you are forever fighting a degenerating sense of 'nobodiness'-then you will understand why we find it difficult to wait. There comes a time when the cup of endurance runs over, and men are no longer willing to be plunged into the abyss of despair."*[88]

In his mind, the rich people go to clean hospitals for treatment of their ailments and get presumably superior medical treatment, which the poor people can never receive in their wildest dreams. *More than twenty-five percent of Egyptians are living below the poverty line, based on CAPMAS 2010-2011 statistics.* This is why Sayed joined the demonstrations, wishing and hoping that change may happen. On January 25, the rich people took to the streets, objecting to the dire conditions. On January 28, all Egyptians joined them. Ironically, the percentage of people living below the poverty line has increased after the revolution.

Tahrir Calling
On January 25, 2011, while Sayed was working at his workstation listening to a news bulletin on the radio, he heard that demonstrations were underway by activists whom

he referred to as the 'hippies'. *I must say I was surprised to hear Sayed use this term.* Sayed did not heed the news, as change was beyond his dreams and hopes. He heard on the radio that security officers were hosing protestors with water, beating them with batons and shooting tear gas canisters to disperse the crowds at Tahrir square.

The following day, January 26, instead of heading off to work as usual, something drew him to see what the demonstrations were about. He went to Tahrir, where he parked his motorbike in AlBostan Street. He joined the demonstrations, observing that the 'hippies' actually came from all social classes and were all ages, men and women alike, maybe forty or fifty thousand people. He saw both simple and sophisticated people. Sayed anticipated that something was about to happen but did not know what and when.

Confrontations were mild, with gunshots fired in the air escalating on January 27. During his obligatory conscription, Sayed became familiar with the sound of live ammunition. When he heard the bullets echoing in the streets of Cairo he was dismayed, and afraid for the nearby men and women. He did not fear so much for himself, but seeing fear in the eyes of men and women near him made him worry. Sayed will never forget the alert eyes of those ready and willing to die, young and old alike. Suddenly it occurred to Sayed that he must continue his stand with his compatriots. He surveyed the situation and decided to move to the side, away from the confrontation and bullets. Fright and flight were common on this bloody day. The situation was fluid, with people coming and going back and forth. Sayed moved around: Tahrir square, Abdel Meniem Riyad St., Mohamed Mahmoud St., AlBostan St., and Kasr El Eini St., where the fighting was heavier.

Ignoring the Ultimatum
Sayed called his wife from a nearby kiosk to check on her and the girls and assure her he was all right.

Sayed said, "*Um* Basma I am at Tahrir."

Um Basma asked, "Why? I thought you are going to work?"

Sayed said, "While I was heading to work, I was drawn to Tahrir. I feel this is the right place for me to be."

Later in the day he called back home to check again.

Um Basma said, "Your boss called you this morning asking why you did not go to work. I told him that you are at Tahrir and he was very upset and said that you can stay at Tahrir and start looking for another job to feed your family."

Sayed replied, "He never understood me or cared for me. Don't worry *Um Basma*, this is God's will and I will find another job *inshallah*."

Sayed did not go home from January 26 until the 29th as he felt he was in the right place fighting for what was his right. This is probably one of the reasons he ignored the threat of his sacking. *Alaa Aswany wrote in June 2010, "The important reason for these vehement protests is that Egyptians have realized that silence about justice will not protect them from injustice."*[89] *Sayed realized this when he was at Tahrir.*

In Sayed's view, the Friday of Anger was the real revolution. At Tahrir, people offered all sorts of food like sweet potato, *koshari* (a traditional lentil and rice meal), and *smeet*, (a pretzel-type savory snack). As for the rumor that activists were eating KFC, Sayed logically questions how that is possible with the store closed. Many of the shops were shut down during the skirmishes, for fear of damage and looting of property. However, that did not save shops from looting during the revolution by opportunistic *baltegeya*. Many people suffered injuries at Tahrir, or populated districts, or in front of police stations. During those four days, Sayed cannot begin to recount the number of victims or fallen men and women he saw. Sayed will never forget the amount of blood he saw staining the uneven asphalt streets of Tahrir in front of the *Mogamaa*, a government building, and at Kasr El Aini Street. Police were beating protestors with their rod sticks like animals. Others were beaten by hand or were victims of rubber or live bullets. Violence was dominant in all forms. It was truly an ugly sight, Egyptians fighting against Egyptians, hurting one another and even killing one another.

Sayed recalls the famous chant *"eskat al nezam"* (Down with the regime) on Friday of Anger, January 28 and not before. People used to walk incredibly long distances for a couple of hours, from Midan El Remaya at Giza to Tahrir, from Ramsis to Tahrir, and from Maadi to Tahrir. They walked in tides, which brought about awe and inspiration to its participants and even onlookers. *This phenomenal tide echoes similar sight decades ago across the Atlantic, that Martin Luther King described, "The enthusiasm of these thousands of people swept everything along like an onrushing tidal wave."*[90] *These long marches were very unusual, as Egyptians are not naturally walkers, and depend largely on private cars for those who can afford them or the weak public transport network for the majority.*

Sayed was standing next to Sheikh Hassan, possibly a *Salafist* or *Ikhwan* (Muslim Brotherhood) member, beside the colossal government building known as *Mogamaa*, one afternoon, conversing.
Sheikh Hassan said, "Don't be afraid my brother, God is with us."
Sayed did not have the time to reply as gunshots were fired instantly and suddenly Sheikh Hassan fell on the street with a loud thud, at Sayed's feet. Sayed was sickened by the unlawful bloodshed. He managed to carry Sheikh Hassan on his shoulders, moving as fast as he could muster, trying to duck the flying bullets. Deafening sirens surrounded him. Sayed reached the make-shift hospital at *Omar Makram Mosque*

but it was too late, as a doctor told him, "Sorry your friend is dead." Sheikh Hassan drew his last breath in Sayed's company, a stranger.

Around the mosque, he saw familiar men and women carrying or supporting fallen friends or strangers needing urgent medical attention. He saw wounds in various places around their bodies, shoulders, legs, and chest. Ambulances took the injured and reputedly delivered them to police for arresting, rather than admitting them to hospitals for treatment. One victim was his new friend Mohamed, who received a shot to his chest. Sayed was sure that he was dead with the severity of his wound and the horrendous outflow of blood. It was a miracle that Mohamed survived his wounds.

When night descended on Tahrir and cold chills dug into the bones, the men screened off a safe and warm area for women to sleep. There were many looted shops and many people slept inside them. Fires were lit up to keep them warm and the men slept in shifts, with some staying awake, guarding the camp. When the red laser dot appeared in a camp, the men and women ran in unbelievable speed for their lives. If someone tripped and fell down, he surely died from trampling, as with a stampeding herd of wild buffalos during the migrations season at Masai Mara. Nothing survives in their path. There were more snipers on several rooftops and especially, on top of *Mogamaa* in Tahrir. Out of the seventy-two-hours Sayed spent at Tahrir, he slept less than twelve. He would roam around the square, checking on his new friends. Sayed is clueless as to the source of the blankets that were provided to keep them warm on those cold, numbing nights. Certainly there were many good people out there, who volunteered to buy blankets and distribute them among the activists.

Mishap
On Saturday January 29, 2011 at around 2pm, Sayed decided to head back home, certain that his family needed food. He knew his reliable, strong wife was handling their home just as if he were present. He decided to buy some vegetables from Tawfiqia market *en route* to his home; he intended to return later to the square. Nobody was selling anything at the market so he detoured to Shoubra El Kheima, where he passed many civilian checkpoints that had been set up to secure the neighborhood in the absence of the police. Vegetable sellers were trading at incredibly high prices, following the basic laws of supply and demand during those uncertain times. Sayed had no choice but to pay the premium price. He noticed a large gathering on the 15 May Street, around 50 meters before the police station. Unknowing of the situation, Sayed decided to park his bike and light up a cheap Cleopatra cigarette; he is a heavy smoker, smoking at least a pack a day, if not a pack and a half. *Despite the lack of money, Egyptians always allocate money aside for their nicotine intake, with many Egyptians being heavy smokers.*

A short while later, he realized that cars were passing by normally. He threw his cigarette bud in the street and started his motorbike, to head home. He assumed the gathering people were checking on an arrested loved one. A microbus parked forty meters ahead of the police station blocked his view. He had not moved far, when out of nowhere, a pellet bullet hit Sayed. It was around 5 p.m. *Sayed will never know if it was a stray bullet or targeted.* He was at the wrong place at the wrong time.

Suddenly Sayed was swaying, with his eyes shut, as if he had hit a hard, burning wall. The pellet hit and entered his eye and it felt as if his eye had caught fire. On reflex, Sayed placed his hand over his wounded eye and fell from his motorbike onto the street. Quickly people ran to help him. They were reassuring him not to be afraid and rebuking him for passing by this dangerous street, when he could have used side roads, *not very constructive considering the circumstances.* It appeared that the bullet had hit Sayed on his forehead, oozing blood onto his face and jacket. His purchased vegetables were scattered on the dirty asphalt, and his bike dented. He was bleeding and he sensed the blood was coming from his forehead right above his eye.

A Passerby gave him a wet cloth to wipe away the blood.
Sayed said, "I can't see with my eye."
The passerby said, "Don't worry the pellet from your forehead probably caused a temporary loss of sight. You have to go to the hospital for a checkup."

Egyptians enjoy a charlatan habit of giving opinions on matters they really do not understand. We have a word for that, 'yeftou' that describes this compulsion. The passerby did just that when he reassured Sayed that his loss of sight was temporary. However, he was right in advising Sayed to go to the hospital.

Another passerby asked Sayed, "Can you drive?"
Sayed said, "Yes I can, thank you."
Sayed managed to get up on his feet; the passerby turned on the ignition and started the motorbike for him. He rode home, unaware of what exactly had happened to his body. Sayed heeded the stranger's advice and passed by Nasser Hospital right away, where a general practitioner saw him and simply advised that he place ice and a cloth over his eye.

Shortly after that, Sayed arrived home and slowly climbed up the stairway to his apartment on the fifth floor. His wife was shocked to see her husband come in, with dirty and bloody clothes and with blood on his forehead.
Scared, *Um* Basma asked, "What happened?"
Sayed lied and said, "Nothing, I got hit by a rock."

He lied, as he did not want his family to worry. Sayed showered, skipped his dinner and lay down on his bed, unable to sleep from the blinding pain. He was really exhausted after three active nights at Tahrir and tried to rest. His wife and daughters were silenced by shock at the sight of his blood. That first night, Sayed was pondering how he would get money for the household with his wound and inability to work. He imagined that he would return to work after a fortnight or less.

The following morning, Sayed moved with great difficulty. His whole body was dealing with the trauma and he kept his eye covered with cotton, as he could not move his eyelid. He called his older brother, who lives close by, updated him with his story, and asked him to take him to the hospital. His brother borrowed his friend's car to pick him up and along with his nephew, they made their way from his simple home at around nine in the morning on Sunday January 30. To get out of Shoubra El Kheima they passed numerous civilian checkpoints that checked the cars and frisked its passengers to ensure no one was armed. It was not an inconvenience in Sayed's opinion, but a sign of how great the Egyptian people truly are. It took Sayed three hours to reach Ramad Hospital at Rhod El Farag.

Where is the Doctor?
The hospital turned out to be a whole other ordeal. To his dismay, only two doctors were on duty, with many staff members being absent because of security concerns. Sayed remembers meeting a man called Taher there, a microbus driver who had been hit in both his eyes; but his spirits were not broken, and he was taking matters better than Sayed. Staff summoned the doctor while Sayed and his brother sat in the waiting room. When the doctor arrived, Sayed recounted his accident in detail. The doctor said in a serious tone, "You need to be operated on now."
Sayed said, "Doctor, what is the matter?"
The doctor replied, "You have a pellet inside your eye which has caused the blood vessels in your eye to burst."
Sayed, in shock and denial, said, "How do you know?"
The doctor replied, "Look at your eye; it is bloody red."
Fear gripped Sayed. The pain was indescribable. If your eyelash falls inside your eye, it bothers you until you remove it, now imagine how Sayed felt with his retina damaged!

Sayed underwent his first eye surgery the day after his injury, as soon as he was admitted to the hospital. The surgeon sewed back his cornea to protect it from microbes and further complications. It was not a corrective procedure, as cases like his needed operating by a surgeon specializing in ophthalmology, who was not on duty at the time.

A few days later Sayed met with Dr. Mikhail, the ophthalmologist.

Dr. Mikhail said, "We will operate on your eye to remove the pellet but cannot stop the internal bleeding."

Sayed said, "I see shadows, will you be able to save my eyesight?" He had heard that cases operated upon early enough had a greater chance of eyesight restoration.

Dr. Mikhail replied, "No, I cannot stop the bleeding you have."

"Not even with your prescribed treatment?" Sayed asked. He was spending close to his previous monthly salary on the prescription; one antibiotic pill cost ten pounds, which he took three times per day. Sayed moved back and forth between his home and the hospital until his second surgery.

Operating Theatre

His second operation was on February 10, during which they removed the pellet and installed a lens. Sayed had his operation at the Ameeri Hospital in Rhod El Farag, Shoubra. Before entering the operating room, Sayed bent over and kissed the hands of Dr. Mikhail.

He pleaded, "I beg you save my eye; it is my source of income for my children and my wife, please save my eyesight."

Dr. Mikhail said, "Don't worry Sayed, *inshallah* (God willing), you will be alright."

Sayed received local anesthesia in his right eye; the needle caused him excruciating pain in this very sensitive organ. Dr. Mikhail and his assistant Dr. Ahmed sliced open his eye under the strong blinding operating spotlights. They protected Sayed's left eye by covering it with a sterile cloth.

Sayed will never forget the conversations between the two doctors. He felt them remove his eyeball from its socket. The pellet had struck the optic nerve. With a very delicate pincer, the doctor tried to remove the pellet, but it fell. He tried another time, and it fell again. Sayed was very anxious, uncomfortably aware of the pellet falling each time. While holding his breath, he prayed, "Ya Rab (God)", pleading for God to save his eye.

Dr. Mikhail said, "What now, the man's eyesight will be gone, what do we do?"

The doctor noticed tears trickle from Sayed's left eye. He was crying, afraid to lose his eyesight.

Dr. Mikhail said, "Sayed don't be scared I will not leave you. Ahmed, what did you do with yesterday's patient?"

Dr. Ahmed recounted the procedure. Suddenly, the doctor seemed to have an idea.

Dr. Mikhail said, "The eyelid needs to be covered with dressing."

He removed the eyelid, using a sterile dressing, and was finally able to remove the slippery pellet.

While they removed the pellet, Sayed felt an unbelievable weight uplifted from him, as if he was carrying the weight of a Mount Uhud (a mountain located north of

Medina) on his back. Sayed said the *shehada,* thanking God. The doctor continued his work, injecting his eye with silicone and changing his eye lens. They replaced the eyeball into the socket and stitched him up. He waited in the hospital for four hours that seemed like four years. Sayed was in incredible pain and none of the painkillers he was given worked. He was in so much agony that he imagined he would remove his eye if it would stop the pain and the terrible headache.

After his check up and operations, Sayed learnt that the *khartoush* (cartridge) has several small pellets that can cause multiple wounds in the target. One pellet hit his right eye and another was lodged in his forehead. The latter he has kept as a souvenir of his attack.

Recovery

For two months he recovered at his home, sitting upright with his head bent forward, his chin touching his chest. This position safeguarded the silicone. He was not allowed to change his head's position, regardless of whether he was sleeping, eating, talking, or in the toilet. To sleep, Sayed used the ironing table as a pillow and slept sitting on the coach, while his devoted wife slept on the carpet beside him.

When he covers his good eye, Sayed can see light and shadows. It had been better before the cataract came upon him. Sayed was torn apart as he was incapable of joining the celebrations when Hosni Mubarak abdicated, a day after his second operation. Sayed pleaded with his wife to join the festivities. *Um Basma* wisely locked the apartment door and hid the keys inside her cooking pots! Sayed was delirious, threatening to jump from the fifth floor, and she reverted to reverse psychology, coolly saying, "Go ahead and jump". He was beyond sad.

Sayed started thinking about how he could watch television in his unusual position. He wanted to see the plant reap its fruits, especially as he had helped sow the seeds of the revolution. He placed a medium-sized mirror on the floor, below him at a forty-five-degree angle so that he could see the reflection of the television screen. During those awkward two months, this unnatural position exhausted Sayed. Continuous thinking further exhausted him, with his lack of income and piling medical expenses, household bills and daunting debt.

He felt imprisoned, incapable of providing for his family, who did nothing to deserve this predicament. With all that time to think and re-think his destiny he started turning against himself. At those moments of weakness regret swept over him; "What made you join the protests? Your brother and your nephews stayed home, why didn't you stay home safe?" Sayed pondered the reason his young nephews had not participated, given that the protestors were demanding a better future for them.

Here he was, a middle aged man who may live another ten years only, as his family has a short life span, protesting for the rights of all Egyptian people. To reach peace with himself, he recited a verse of *Quran* that says, *"But it is possible that ye dislike a thing which is good for you, and that you love a thing which is bad for you."* (2:216)

Helping Hand

In February 2011, he heard that Yasmina Abou Youssef had helped some of their neighbors in Shobra by collecting money to aid the victims. His friend, Mohamed, suggested that they ask for her help. Sayed is very shy by nature and is embarrassed to ask his sister-in-law for a glass of water, let alone enter the bathroom in his brother's home. How could he ask for help from a complete stranger? Mohamed ended up calling Yasmina, who responded positively and readily, asking him to meet her at a hospital's gardens March 5, 2011 where she gave him an envelope. That morning he had one pound in his pocket and was clueless as to how he would pay the return microbus fee. After she left, Sayed opened the envelope to find two thousand pounds, around two hundred and ninety dollars, which was more money than he had ever held, a real fortune in his world. It was as if he was walking in a hot desert, thirsty and with a dry throat, and suddenly finding an oasis of water. Sayed was supposed to visit the hospital to get his eye checked, but he was so ecstatic with his unexpected fortune that he rushed home to share the great news. He was able to afford the expensive treatment required for his eye. He was also able to pay some of his debts and his children's school fees. Yasmina then helped Sayed out with half of the initial amount a few months later.

The Fallen

With the passing of time, his pain receded, and with his regret forgotten, acceptance of his fate brought him peace. Sayed was greatly offended when compatriots perceived activists as betraying their country and labeled as foreign agents. It really bothered him. Another ludicrous claim was that financial incentives were showered on the protestors to stay at Tahrir. Sayed is bewildered. If this had been true, would not all the needy people have joined? The revolution did not include all eighty-five million Egyptian citizens; maybe around thirty million nationwide took to the streets. The other fifty-five million were the silent majority. *The silence or inaction of the majority, Martin Luther King blames for inhumanity, "Man's inhumanity to man is not only perpetuated by the vitriolic actions of those who are bad. It is also perpetrated by the vitiating inaction of those who are good"* [91]

Sayed was not a silent victim. When he was able to, in March 2011, he went to the police station to file a report concerning the assault on him. Sayed honestly said he could have lied to the police, or myself for that matter, to gain more attention by saying his wounds were inflicted at Tahrir. But he is an honest man who believes that truth will prevail. Without a doubt, Tahrir is the father of squares, heart of the great city of Cairo. Historically called Midan El Ismaliyah (Ismailiya Square). Sayed has heard that during the 1952 revolution, a woman wearing a *niqab* removed it at the square and henceforth the square became called Tahrir. *I cannot confirm this. Actually, authorities unofficially named it Tahrir after the 1919 revolution and the name changed officially, after the 1952 revolution.* Tahrir was the legitimate land for the revolution; however, matters ignited first at Suez before Cairo in January 2011.

Sayed, among many Egyptians, believes the brutal killing of Khaled Said was the explosive power behind the revolution, along with April 6, 2008 demonstrations in Mahalla, a large agricultural and industrial city located in the middle of the Delta. The revolution brought upon a new dawn on Egypt where hope and dreams were once more possible. Hope is that justice will prevail eventually. One year after the revolution, Sayed is a realist, as he knows the revolution has not succeeded yet.

The revolution is not just about changing the regime but more importantly, it requires internal changes within the individual to make for a better life and a better country. For instance, liars, thieves or bribe-takers need to review their behavior and become better people, influencing their society positively. As mentioned in the *Quran*, "Verily never will Allah change the condition of a people until they change what is in themselves (with their own souls)" *(13:11)*[92]. Hence, Sayed does not want to overburden the revolution, as it cannot change everything. The revolution will bring about new laws and a new constitution, new government and parliament and newly elected president, but it cannot change the people. The people must change themselves. Although Egyptians are kind people, they have reached a stage of apathy and non-performance that they must break away from. Egyptians can be so kind that they end up appearing foolish. For instance, when two people quarrel, you can easily influence one of them to reconciliation with the other if you practice a little influence, even if the latter is at fault. Being too kind-hearted, an Egyptian would accept unfair treatment at work and in life and forgive it, forsaking his rights. "Leave your matters with God" is a popular saying among pious Egyptians, resonating the general attitude of *sans façon*.

Unfortunately, Egyptians are trapped in a vicious triangle of poverty, illiteracy and rampant sickness, due to ailing economic, educational and health systems. Sayed has a strong conviction that if Egypt addressed these three major pitfalls, the country would certainly rise quickly to the position of a superpower.

Street War
Even after his eye injury Sayed was not afraid, and ventured many times to protests. He went to Tahrir on May 25, 2011. He also joined *mosabin al thawra* (the wounded of the revolution) in their protest on July 8 where he introduced himself to many

other victims. Among them is Ahmed Harara, a dentist, who lost his eye on January 28, 2011. *Ahmed has become an iconic victim of the revolution with an inspiring spirit, as he lost his second eye in the street war in November 2011.* Another was Mohamed, who underwent an operation, where two valves in his heart were changed. Months after his recovery, Sayed met Mohamed among the many wounded of the revolution. Another victim he met was Ahmed, who suffered serious wounds that caused him partial paralysis.

Sadly, with his eye injury, Sayed had to leave his trade. He is a very religious man who views the loss of one of his eyes as a medal and a key to heaven for him. He is willing to sacrifice once again for his beloved country, as he demonstrated during the Mohamed Mahmoud Street clashes in November 2011, where he went to help teenagers and the youth. This time he rarely found middle aged or elderly people. Sayed went with a bottle of vinegar, sprinkling protestors hit by the suffocating teargas. Many protestors joined the demonstration upon hearing that the wounded revolutionaries were being beaten and disgraced. Sayed started mingling with the protestors, who enlightened him in the world of politics. His eye injury has led Sayed to compare himself with a fish trapped in a tiny tank, who amuses people who just watch it swim.

On November 11, 2011, less than a dozen victims were demonstrating. They were demanding compensation from the state. Sayed and his friend Shawki were camping with them. Islamists declared November 19 as the Friday for Islamists. The morning of November 20, Special Forces 777, violently attacked the protestors and tore down their tents. This day at Mohamed Mahmoud Street may be described as a street war.

Shawki, who accompanied Sayed to our meeting, is another victim of the revolution who lost his eye on January 28, 2011, in front of the State Television building, known as Maspero, overlooking the Nile River. Shawki was hit around four in the afternoon and has been unable to continue his job as a weaver, with only one eye. Sayed and Shawki protect each other and do not meet strangers unless they are together, fearing arrest for their activism. *This information explained to me why Shawki accompanied Sayed to this interview. It was into the middle of the interview when Sayed introduced me to Shawki.* Shawki's previous employer gave him a financial severance package and he takes odd jobs as a handyman, with no steady income.

During this street war, there were many more victims. One victim, called Mohamed, was badly injured, to the extent that he needed forty-eight stitches to close his head wound. Another man lost his leg at this infamous street war. Sayed ran away from the attacks, and being unable to see with his right eye, ran into a concrete wall on his right side. Sheikh Emad Efaat died in close range with a silenced gun, among other casualties. Sayed believes that assailants who used silenced guns were surely not police and army officers. Who sent the assassins with silencers? The ruling regime needs to investigate and question until they reveal and disclose the truth to the public.

Sayed has a name for the so-called external hand that meddled in Egyptian affairs; he calls it Mr. 'X' and believes they instigated or provoked the protests. The government does not take much of the heat for its actions, as conveniently, the unknown hand takes much of the blame. Many of the external factors have been termed as *baltegeya*, foreign agents, or external hand. A little over two years later, he believes *Ikhwan* were behind much of the sabotage. If it was not them, they probably hired *baltegeya*. However, Sayed is confident not all *Ikhwan* had information about such violence.

He is keen to identify 'Mr. X'. On the first anniversary of the revolution, the army had warned that matters could get out of hand; however, they never mentioned who could be behind that. Sayed rebukes the state for not arresting the threats to national security. It was able to arrest activists, who faced charges in the military court where no appeals are allowed, which he vehemently opposes.

When the wounded of the revolution declared to a Brigadier during their protest that they were victims of the revolution, they were baffled by his attack as he barked at them, cursing them and their revolution. From Sayed's army duty, he was able to tell that the higher-ranking officers that were in the clashes that month were not *Amn Elmarkazy* or Special Forces, but more likely army officers trained for the hardships of war. The officers were wearing police uniform, but he presumes they were not police. If an officer does not follow orders in the army, he faces punishment more serious than that imposed on a police officer for the same offence. Sayed says citizens have the right to demand to know whose external hand is meddling with Egyptian affairs. The Ministry of Interior had issued an official statement that the fallen were killed by live ammunition, but were not killed by its forces. However, Sayed was eyewitness to *Amn Elmarkazi*, Central Security, firing at protestors, before losing his eye. Sayed has heard that the police fired tear gas at Mohamed Mahmoud Street worth fifteen million pounds, a little less than two and a half million dollars. Regardless of the unconfirmed cost, Sayed is frustrated. He is a victim of the revolution, who demonstrated to demand that the government help with his treatment. An Egyptian citizen has the right to receive medical treatment when he is sick, let alone if wounded. Sayed cannot understand the sadistic irony that the government prefers to pay money attacking protestors rather than healing the wounded. Where is humanity?

Magamaa El Elmy (Science Center), a library next to Mohamed Mahmoud Street, was set ablaze during the street war in November 2011. A wealth of books was lost. Some people in its neighborhood were clueless of the building and its treasured books. Sayed argues that blood is more valuable than cultural heritage preserved in ink. God Almighty has set the human life as His preference above all living organisms, even angels. Unfortunately, human beings do not realize their true value, especially in Egypt.

The spirit of generosity was overflowing that November, with the Omar Makram Mosque well furnished with medical supplies and Kasr El Doubara Church filled with food and medical supplies. Many doctors volunteered to treat the wounded men, women and children. Sayed asks, if civilians sense the burden of the victims, then where is the government in this equation? What role have they played to elevate suffering of victims? Sayed judges that civil society treated over ninety percent of all the victims on the generosity and love of Egyptian brothers and sisters. Among these philanthropists is a millionaire, Heba, who Sayed calls 'Egypt's Mona Lisa.' Another woman might have spent that money in creating her own NGO or political party. She treated victims at a cost of millions. Sayed was not among them, however, he appreciates her generosity. One time Sayed met Heba and asked her why she was helping all these people. She humbly replied, "I am trading with God."

We are All Egyptians
Egyptians of all creeds have always lived in harmony. For years, Sayed had heard about religious discrimination, but for that to effectively change, each individual needs to change personally. After the revolution, laws that allow injustice and tyranny desperately needed revoking and any person suspected of being corrupt needs to be removed from the equation, by simply relieving them from their position of responsibility. To effect change, Sayed will reform his household and if each citizen follows suit, eventually the whole country will reform.

Sayed had heard about the intense, inhuman torture of youth at prisons. The youth stand tall like a proud palm tree that has not yet produced any dates, still too young to reap its fruit. The irreversible effects of torture on the inmates are like the effect of fungus on a palm tree. *Rather than getting the best date produce, the palm tree is destroyed by the fungus, which turning its fronds yellow, wilted, and eventually killing it. This fungus lives in the soil and is likely to infect new palm trees. Unchecked torture could negatively influence a generation, just like the fungus infiltrating the soil and the palm trees.*

The Muslims and Christians of this country are all Egyptians. A verse in the Quran says, "To you be your way and to me mine" (109:6),[93] 'you' being a reference to any non-Muslim. When asked his name at Tahrir, Sayed replies, 'Sayed El Masry', Sayed the Egyptian, in solidarity with both religions.

Government Help

The Minister's Council created a national council for the people wounded in the revolution. This council sent Sayed to a camp in Alexandria for one week in early 2012, where he enjoyed free meals and a psychiatrist observed victims of the revolution, and questioned them on their views before and after the revolution. The psychiatrist asked about their aspirations and hopes, and how each would re-build his life after his injuries. The victims presented suggestions and requests and openly expressed their ideas. Sayed feels that 'the wounded of the revolution' society established by this council acts according to the policies of the *ancien regime* and accordingly, the attendants were grouped as per their political views. He blames the government for this treatment, as the revolution has not succeeded yet in overthrowing the *regime*. Sayed was among the 'Class of Death' who were hardline supporters of the martyrs and wounded of the revolution. The other group were supporters of the *ancien regime*, which were termed as *feloul*. It was impossible for those two groups to agree on anything.

After the one week of free food and sharing suggestions, the government sent Sayed a letter. They helped provide him with a job in supporting services, a job as a messenger and cleaner. Sayed found it ironic that the revolution was trying to clean the institutes, but was unwilling to clean up the mess in the running of of the institutions themselves. It hurt his dignity to stoop that low. Egyptian society does not view cleaning jobs as being dignified. Sayed refused to dump his twenty-nine years of metalwork profession and pick up a cleaning job. His former patron gave him only one month's salary, so by March 2011, he had no income. To date, Sayed has debts that will take him a full salary of three years to pay - based on his old salary.

Sayed is worried that if he rejects the cleaning job, the government will place a label on him and other victims who refuse to work for the public sector. Initially Sayed did not reply to the offer, feeling it was an insult to his dignity. However, eventually he ceded, as he had no other choice.

Sayed wishes he had died a martyr during the revolution, as his family would have been compensated with thirty-seven thousand pounds, around six thousand dollars. Seven thousand pounds from the ministry of social solidarity, and thirty thousand from a ministry fund worth one hundred million pounds – fourteen and a half million dollars - created for the families of martyrs in addition to a monthly salary of one thousand seven hundred pounds, less than three hundred dollars. Unfortunately, the wounded, today, are lost outsiders.

Former Prime Minister Dr. Kamal El Ghanzoury announced the eligibility of victims to financial compensation and medical treatment at any of the 52 public hospitals. Sayed cynically comments that public hospitals are not suitable for animals, let alone human beings. Social Solidarity compensated victims with five thousand pounds, a little less than eight hundred dollars, and the fund handed out an additional fifteen thousand pounds, around two thousand one hundred dollars. Sayed personally met Dr. Sharaf and shared the plight of victims with him. Subsequently the prime minister raised the compensation fivefold to the five thousand pounds, the equivalent of seven hundred and twenty dollars. Sayed personally met with many key personalities in the government and the army, in order to secure proper support for the victims of the revolution. Dr. El Ghanzoury had proposed a pension of one hundred and eighty pounds for the victims - less than thirty dollars - but Sayed rejected the notion, as he wants to be a productive worker contributing to the economy.

Risk-Taking

Sayed imagined playing a final soccer game that he will either win or lose. He decided to take his destiny into his own hands, as the government proposal fell short of his aspirations. He took a loan from *Bank Masr Al Egtemaie,* Egypt Social Bank, with the help of several people, amounting to twenty-five thousand pounds, around three thousand six hundred dollars. He used the loan for a downpayment on a Suzuki van worth eighty-two thousand pounds, a little over thirteen thousand dollars. He will have to pay monthly installments of one thousand five hundred pounds. Sayed is planning to use the van as a taxi or delivery van, hoping to make a decent living. He licensed the van and is currently facing a hurdle, since he has no school degree as he failed primary school. In order for him to be issued a driving license, he should provide a primary school certificate. Since he has not achieved such a certificate, he has had to present an illiteracy certificate instead, that would cost him a fee of one thousand five hundred pounds, a bribe in his mind. He bought the car in January 2012 and at the time, was unable to drive without the license. Sayed was saddened that he needed connections, since he could not pass his driving test. Weeks later, he received his exceptional license.

With his license, he tried his luck working as a driver on the ring road. Sayed woke up at dawn, preformed his *fajr* (dawn) prayers, and then headed to the streets until noon. He would rest for a couple of hours and return to driving until midnight. He would go on driving, until he collected at least two hundred or two hundred twenty pounds each day, which would cover his petrol, loan, and maintenance of the car as well as his household expenses. After those long hours of driving and cleaning the minivan, in addition to dealing with disgruntled Egyptians, it was exhausting to Sayed, both physically and mentally. He was able to keep it up for five or six months and in early September 2012, accepted a government job as an office boy, searching for files in the archives and moving files among employees at the National Insurance Institute. Although he was initially against having two jobs, he has revisited and changed his stand. Sayed derives satisfaction from helping retired Egyptians obtain their lost documents. When he finds their lost files in the archives and he sees, for example, an eighty-year-old woman smile at him from cheek to cheek, Sayed is content to hear her prayers for him. It is a tiresome job, as he moves and distributes files across four floors, and each floor has two sections each containing around eighteen employees. Sayed has taken to smoking two packs a day since he started working.

Hokouma (Authority)

In retrospect, most of the martyrs died in their own neighborhoods. If a home were under attack, would the homeowner not defend himself and his family? Sayed remembers that during his teenage years, whenever *hokouma* (a term popularly used by the working classes to refer to all forms of authority) appeared, any small group of youngsters who were harassing a woman or just hanging out, would quickly disappear. *The police and police stations are associated with 'Hokouma'.* Police stations have come to represent a house of torture and injustice, as many innocent men and women are popularly believed to be framed by police. Sayed blames the people who attacked the police stations, as even though the stations represented injustice, at the end of the day, they belong to the people. One should remove the corrupt branches but not set the whole tree on fire. It is very clear for him the *baltageya* attacked the police stations, and not activists.

There was no leader for the revolution; internet and mobile communication were cut off, therefore all the violence had to have been planned. The Egyptian people are like an active volcano that has exploded. The unjust never sense injustice until they face it. The police officer who fired at civilians had no choice but to follow orders. Sayed thinks that the *Dakhleya* brainwashed soldiers to believe that the protestors at Tahrir were disbelievers who want to roll the country into regression.

The ministry of interior is not all rotten. Every person and every society has the good and the bad simultaneously. Like a lemon tree that has nice green lemons and a few shriveled, rotten lemons too. He hopes that any citizen entering a police station in a shantytown is treated with respect and dignity, his requests being properly addressed. Police officers need to have a personal barometer, clearly measuring the difference between the good and the bad. The public prosecutor interrogated Sayed with respect and decency, always calling him *'Am Sayed'*, which means uncle. On the other hand, another officer accused Sayed of jeopardizing his eyesight intentionally in order to get monetary compensation. If he could give up all his worldly possessions in return for his lost eye, he would not flinch. So how could anyone even think that he would intend to lose his eyesight?

Police officers need to treat men and women with respect regardless of their social background. No one can blame people for being born into poor families. Rich and poor alike deserve equal treatment by the police force. Sanitary workers are one of the most essential forces however are not treated with respect. Imagine, without their work and maintenance, what would life be? Grotesque is an understatement. The street sweepers, if they stopped working - imagine how much dirtier the state of the streets would be. The cleanliness of the streets is a long way from reaching the proper standards. A Quranic verse says, "How many a small company has overcome a large company by permission of Allah". Sayed knows that change takes time and is not sure, but had heard that the French revolution took decades until it succeeded. There is always hope.

Good police officers need to unite and inform their superiors about the bad behavior so that it quickly changes. If they go unchecked, what will change them? Sayed compares this to an apartment building with a bad neighbor, where all the other neighbors file a complaint with the property owner, who in turn checks the bad behavior, requesting and ensuring corrective action. Only through work will they regain the trust of the people. If one does a job for the first time and fails, surely one will put more effort in until succeeding the second time around. Sayed calls upon all managers and workers to excel in their work, so that the cycle of production rolls again, and the economy becomes productive. All institutions need to master their domains and work in a way that will please God. In Islam, work and behavior are viewed as a form of worship as per the Hadith of Mohamed PBUH, "On those who believe and work deeds of righteousness will Allah most Gracious bestow love." (19: 96).

Sayed does not doubt that circumstances have deteriorated in Egypt, as the people, though pious, have drifted away from God and ignored the importance of ethics. If one works a decent job with a suitable income, would he or she steal? Anger, dishonor, injustice, tyranny, suppression, envy are all the negative factors that have led Egypt into this dark hole.

Rebel in Heart

On the first day of Ramadan in 2011, the army invited activists to an *iftar* (the sunset meal to break the fast). Traditionally the first day of Ramadan is spent at home with families. Sayed broke his fast with his family and returned to Tahrir to discover that the *iftar* had turned into a violent dispersal of the activists and a burning of their tents.

The army hosted a party in September 2011 for those wounded in the revolution, a few days before *Eid El Adha*. Sayed wondered why the authorities honored the victims while providing them with neither medical treatment nor employment. Sayed was fully aware that his name would not be among the victims honored, as the head of the function was a former National Democratic Party (NDP) member. It made no sense that members of the former ruling party were honoring the victims injured during demonstrations against them. How provocative could they be? When he arrived at the event and did not find his name among the victims, he got angry and started shouting at the woman welcoming the guests.

Sayed angrily said, "Where is my name?"

The woman said, "I am sorry sir but your name is not on the list."

Sayed was getting angrier and louder, "How could I not be among the victims, look at my eye."

As the scene got loud, an army officer came to check and confirmed that his name was not among the guests.

The officer said, "Sorry Sir but your name is not on the list."

Sayed asked, "How many medals do you have?"

The officer replied, "We will be distributing one hundred medals, thirty for martyrs and seventy for the wounded."

The hall filled with people all expecting medals or certificates of honor and an envelope with token money. Many of these people could not afford to buy meat for the upcoming *Eid* festivities, whereas Sayed perceives, rich people only eat freshly cooked food each day, never eating leftovers. Sayed, looking around, estimated that there were maybe one hundred relatives of martyrs and around six hundred wounded, indicating an imminent problem.

Sayed warned the army officer saying, "Excuse me sir, but many people are not going to be honored, as the numbers surely exceed one hundred."

The officer abruptly and dismissingly said, "Sir this is none of your business."

This honoring ceremony was taking place in many governorates at the same time. The meager list of people was called upon, and they were presented with a medal of honor. They started with the martyrs, and a mother, Um Ahmed, went on stage with a large picture of her young deceased son, a wild rose untimely plucked. The announced time for the ceremony was nine in the morning, but they started very late, at one in the afternoon.

Sayed asked Um Ahmed, "May I see the medal?"

Um Ahmed said, "Sure, Sayed."

It appeared like the shape of the Star of David.

Sayed asked, "Is this worth your son's blood?"

Um Ahmed was dumbfounded. He repeated his question, louder this time, with tears filling his eyes.

Sayed believes his words moved the people to see the lack of appreciation for the victims, with token medals. Suddenly all those who had received medals started throwing them at a board in the room. Sayed prayed: "For us Allah sufficeth! And He is the best Guardian." *Quran* (3:173)[94] Muslims usually refer to this verse when the going gets tough to seek divine help. The party ended sourly. Sayed believes authorities should either commemorate and honor the people properly, or better, not host such an event in the first place. Mediocrity is the worst option. Sayed did not intend to ruin the party, but his instincts told him that it was an orchestrated play.

Still Struggling

Sayed is still struggling to make a living after he lost his eye. He has hope that Egyptians and Egypt will reform to become a society that respects human beings indiscriminately. Sayed never had and never will have any political affiliations, and only understood a bit more about the topic from his fellow protestors.

During the first round of the presidential elections, Sayed voted for Hamdeen Sabahy, like many activists. However, he boycotted the controversial second round in which there were only two polar choices: The *Ikhwan* candidate and former prime minister, Ahmed Shafik. Sayed did not vote for *Ikhwan,* as one of its MP promised Sayed financial help to assist with Habiba's asthma and did not follow through on his promise. However, he was genuinely happy when President Morsi won the Presidential elections, as he represented new blood, new hope and a new dawn for Egypt. He was optimistic with the campaign announcing the *el nahda* (renaissance) project.

All he wants is a decent living for all Egyptians, and the complete erosion of the disturbing visual memory of people searching the garbage for discarded food to eat. Sayed believes President Mohamed Morsi is a respectable man who is working hard to improve the country, who needs all the Egyptians to support his efforts via a personal revolution. Egyptians need to change how they are living for real change to be in effect. No matter how sophisticated a garbage collection system the government places, the streets of Egypt will never be clean if people still litter. Unfortunately, Sayed senses that there are people who are out to see President Morsi fail, just out of vengeance, with no regard for the country.

With the passing of months, it became apparent to him that *Ikhwan* had no political experience and the party was not qualified to run Egypt, having bitten off more than they could chew. They are good businessmen, but not politicians. Sayed was in opposition to the *Ikhwan* rule however did not support *Tamarod,* as his two jobs did not leave him time to vote. Moreover, he never expected any results.

Sayed once again went to Tahrir on June 30, amongst millions of Egyptians, and stayed there until July 3, 2013 when the army announced the ousting of President Morsi. Sayed believes 2013 was a much bigger revolution than 2011. It started with an idea that exploded on January 25, 2011, which built the momentum that led to the 2013 revolution. In 2013, the revolt was on a gigantic scale, a clear demonstration of unity amongst diversity. Egyptians young and old, men and women, rich and poor,

Christians and Muslims, took to the streets demanding early Presidential elections and the end of *Ikhwan* rule. Sayed took to the streets again on July 26, 2013, a protest to insist that the army deals with terrorism. The police accomplished the necessary clearing of the sit-ins at *Rabaa* and *Nahda* with minimal losses in lives.

Future
What remains from the revolution? The revolution has neither failed nor succeeded as it is still underway and has a long bumpy dark road ahead. Sayed believes that fifty percent of the change brought about by the revolution should be to the state of affairs. The other fifty percent of the change should come from the people themselves. Change needs to take effect in all spheres, from the army to *Dakhleya* (Ministry of Interior), to courts of law, media and journalism. Courts need to ensure the implementation of all laws on the poor and on the rich alike. However, until today, the system treats the poor man as if he is an insect, unlike the rich man who it treats like a king.

What Egypt has taken away from the Egyptians, the revolution has brought back, where precious souls paid with their lives. Youth died, went missing or were buried in groups, and others were maimed for life. All men, women and children are suffering the side effects of the events. Sayed, like most Egyptians, is seeking equality in life, health and education

No Regrets
Sayed believes in destiny and has strong faith. He quotes the *Quran,* "Say, Nothing will happen to us except what Allah has decreed for us: He is our Protector. And on Allah let the believers put their trust' (9:51)[95] He does not consider himself a victim, but a man who carries a distinction and despite his experience, is willing to lose his other eye or his life for that matter, in the hope his children will live a better life in Egypt. He believes Egypt is a special land, as mentioned in the *Quran*. He continues to struggle to make a living and pay his bills.

During the days of Caliph Omar, a messenger asked about the caliph, and searched the village until he found a man lying under the shade of a tree, his old *abaya* full of patches. When he questioned him and realized that he was the Caliph Omar Ibn El Khatab, he said, "You have ruled, upheld justice, and hence can sleep". Sayed is skeptical that Egyptians have learnt the wise lesson and understood its teachings, as Egypt is yet to see a just ruler.

Around six thousand Egyptian men, women and children were inflicted with wounds during the January 2011 revolution and Sayed is one of them, shot in his eye in Shobra El Kheima. He is a fighter who works hard for his money. Sayed is an inspiration to human beings for his perseverance and faith, and undying optimism.

CHAPTER 15

Conceited Conscript

*"It is unreasonable to expect that an armed man should obey one
who is unarmed, or that an unarmed man should remain safe
and secure when his servants are armed." Machiavelli.*

*Since the revolution, the army has been on high alert and it was with great difficulty
that I reached an army conscript to interview. Eventually my cousin Aya was able to get
me in touch with her friend's friend, known under an alias as Karim, due to his former
sensitive position as a conscript. We met at Pasqua Café in Mohandseen on Saturday
January 19, 2013.*

American Sweetheart

He is a handsome, tall, well-built man with brown hair, and brown eyes that emanate
energy. Karim was born in 1989. He studied at Port Said Language School and earned
a Bachelor of Arts in Commerce in English. His late father worked in the foreign
ministry. His mother is a social affairs and insurance manager in the government,
close to retirement. Karim was six years old when his father returned from his post
for a holiday and seemed sickly and thin. While prostrate in prayer, he passed away.
His family discovered post-mortem that he was suffering from heart problems. Their
mother did not inform Karim and his brothers, who were staying down the road
at a neighbor's house at the time of their father's death. She informed them several
months later. Karim has two brothers, one of whom is a police officer.

During his undergraduate years, Karim was involved with an American Jewish
woman, a semester abroad student at the American University in Cairo. He was
eighteen when they started dating and over time, their relationship evolved into

a serious one. Usually, an extramarital affair in Egypt is taboo and shunned as religiously sinful, which put pressure on Karim to marry his girlfriend.

In the Army

In Egypt, all men are obliged to serve military conscription with the exception of those who have no brothers. After graduating, Karim presented his documents for conscription and in November of 2010, he entered the *ergha* (some form of lottery, during which potential conscripts find out if they will serve their conscription or may be exempted). Another decisive factor determining whether a potential conscript is to enter the army is whether he has a needed profession or skill, people such as medical doctors, engineers or people with knowledge of Hebrew. Conscription lasts one year for soldiers and three years for conscripts designated as officers. Usually career army officers retire early, at the age of forty-five. If the officer furthers his studies with a masters degree, he is given the title of *arkan harb* (staff officer), then he retires at age of sixty.

The army admitted all conscripts born in the range of twelve specific days in 1989 to the army. Karim's birthday was within these 12 days. All his plans were shattered, as he had not expected the army to enlist him. Karim had two options in the army: to be *askari sika,* which is a soldier assigned to the service of a particular officer, or a regular soldier. *Sika* is a form of military servitude where the soldier personally cleans, washes and cooks for the officer he is assigned to, and serves him in any manner demanded of him. He even eats his superior's leftover food. This option is not physically demanding, however, it is psychologically damaging and demeaning. Karim could not imagine growing old and telling his children that he was a *sika* in the army, it was simply beneath him. That is why he opted for the full fledge experience of a regular soldier, with all its physical hardships.

Karim's first day in the army was on November 17, 2010. He managed to get a recommendation from his brother, the police officer, and ended up assigned in Maadi, a good training center that was referred to as 'Nancy' due to its favorable conditions. Cold and hot water were available in addition to decent food. Visitors were allowed throughout the week while in other centers, it was restricted to Fridays only. The army ascribed Karim to leadership offices, which meant that after his service ended he would not be listed in the reserve forces and would not be recalled to the army. Out of a dozen college friends, he was the only one selected for conscription. They tried to hide their personal joy, so as not to upset Karim. Nevertheless, he was glad to know of the enlisting of two of his childhood friends.

The initial forty-five days of the army are intense and spent in a training center where they go through essential military training and an assessment phase. After this period, the body is cleansed, strengthened, detoxified and purified from any drugs, ready for military combat. Karim was lucky to have spent less than forty-five days in this training as the revolution started on January 25, 2011.

In front of the training center, Karim could see the checkpoint set up by civilians, similar to those in the majority of Egyptian neighborhoods after the prisons breaks on January 28, 2011. He could not leave his barracks. They stopped a big unlicensed car and a bus, which thieves had filled with stolen items including laptops, only the right shoe from several pairs of running shoes (stolen from displays), mobiles, and scales. They also found a few new stolen cars. It was beyond his understanding what the thieves were thinking when they stole all those single shoes. How were they going to be used?

During those first days of the revolution, Karim caught thieves who had stolen from other thieves. He saw two *Toktok* (Rickshaw) drivers dividing loot between them. Each took an LCD screen and a laptop. There was an extra LCD, so they broke it into two pieces and each one took half! Karim's jaw dropped, as he was unable to believe their ignorance.

Karim took up the task of sorting the considerably large number of stolen items. *Egyptian are known to be humorous even inside the serious army,* as they called part of the barracks where all the stolen commodities were kept, *'ard el ma'ared"* (exhibition center). Normally the barracks had a small prison for recruits and troublemakers, which the army emptied out to leave room for the criminals and thieves who had surfaced in abundance with the nationwide prison breaks. Close to the barracks is the infamous Tora prison from which inmates had escaped, Karim recalls. He is not sure if they actually escaped from Tora or another nearby prison and were on the run nearby. Some prisoners had not escaped for long, before the police caught them. Others gave themselves up, as they had a few weeks left in their sentence and did not want to commit themselves to more time.

Change of Plans
With the changing political scene, on January 27, 2011, Karim moved to Ismailia, in the northeast of Egypt. He was the only one selected from his training camp in Maadi and there was a busload of conscripts from other camps with him on the trip. With this move, the army re-categorized him to the Infantry, where the soldiers are functioning in the field. This was certainly a more dangerous mission, due to the brewing uprising, than his original post in Headquarters. Karim tried to call his contact in the army to help reclassify him. However, his contact never answered, evidently swamped with the current wave of events hitting the country.

Before entering Ismailia the bus stopped, and the conscripts were allowed to buy food, which was against the rules. Karim had loads of cash on him from his parents and from his army stipend. He boldly decided to buy a mobile, which was also against the rules. He already had a SIM card with him. Karim wanted to call his girlfriend to check on her. With the turbulence in Egypt, many embassies requested non-essential staff to evacuate the country. Many expats gathered at Marriot Hotel in Zamalek and rode in secured bus convoys to the airport. His girlfriend cried, as she did not want to leave Karim, and insisted on staying in Cairo. His brother watched over their mother and sister and checked on Karim's girlfriend, buying her groceries, especially when the security level was low. Karim was scared that something could happen to his sweetheart and did not want to shoulder the responsibility. Eventually she succumbed to her mother's and Karim's pressure and left Cairo. As a conscript, he signed a statement that he was not a criminal and not carrying another nationality, nor in a relationship with a foreigner; this was to ensure there was no conflict of interest. If he had been honest, he would have subjected himself to intense questioning. The army designed the statement to identify possible spies.

Before the revolution, very few Egyptians had any sort of political awareness. People were intimidated by politics and opted to steer away from political discussions. Karim even sensed that authorities tapped landlines and was never comfortable saying what was on his mind, for fear that Big Brother was watching. A few brave people did not let the fear paralyze them and spoke their minds. However, they risked arrest and police framing them for crimes they did not commit. This political naiveté possibly worsened matters at this tumultuous time, as many people just followed the current blindly without any critical thinking. Karim felt frustrated by the first speech of former President Mubarak, as the speech belittled the people. Why did President Mubarak wait for the protests to pledge all the valid changes? Karim and many Egyptians wondered.

No Water

Before his time in the army, Karim was very independent, as he knew how to cook and wash, untypical of Egyptian men. Karim washed his clothes by hand in the army, on his days off. He was not a smoker, however, he took to smoking while in the army, for the occaisonal relief and relaxation.

With the growing unrest in Sinai, the army wanted to strengthen the Second and Third armies located in the Sinai Peninsula. Karim was among the reinforcements and after three days in Ismailia, assigned to Brigade 3, under Team 16. The nights were very cold and Karim slept on the ground. Suddenly he found himself with strange men from a different upbringing and mentality. In Maadi, Karim was in the company of engineers and computer scientists but at Ismailia, it was an altogether different scene as his company consisted of farmers and workers along with the educated. One of the best coincidences in his life was meeting his childhood friend, Osman, (also an alias) at the barracks in the middle of the desert. Karim could not believe his eyes.

Karim shouted, "Osman!"

Osman replied, "Karim! This is incredible!"

Overwhelmed by excitement, Osman hugged Karim while still carrying his riffle and although the rifle hurt Karim's chest he ignored the pain. Karim was beside himself with happiness. He had finally found someone he could talk to and keep company with on those long, strenuous, cold days and nights.

Karim asked, "What barracks are you in?"

Osman replied, "I am in battalion 9."

Karim asked, "Which ward?"

Osman replied, "2."

Karim said, "This is unbelievable, that is where I am too!"

They were smiling from cheek to cheek.

The two friends spent the whole year together, which made the experience tolerable. Their barracks were referred to as the barracks of the atheists as it had no water and no electricity. The nights were very cold and they walked four or five kilometers to fill two-gallon jerry cans with water for bathing and drinking. By the time they returned, they would have spilled a good amount of the water on the way. They got the water from the brigade leadership, which is located on the road to Ismailia, 3 or 4 kilometers before the entrance of the city. In the morning, they woke up early and walked a few kilometers with their battalion for the morning drills. It was a demanding physical effort to say the least; here Karim trained to use machine guns.

Transferred to Operations

One day, the operations general approached Karim asking him if his handwriting was good.

Karim replied, "Yes Sir."

The operations general said, "Karim, you will join me in the operations."

Karim replied, "I will only join if Osman my cousin joins me." Karim referred to his childhood friend as his cousin.

The general flashed a big grin and said, "There is nothing called my cousin in the army. You will see dire days ahead. When I give an order, I only say it once. If you do not follow orders you will see the worst days of your life."

Karim learnt from that day that he must always agree to the orders given to him even if he will not obey them, as it leads to an agreeable atmosphere void of tension. In the army, there is no room for arrogance.

One of his mates told him to present Osman as a good asset who can retrace maps, has a good command of English and computer skills. Luckily, it worked. Karim had asked around and was told that operations was much better than the battalion. Karim and Osman ended up both joining the operations, which was fortunately the location that had the water source. Finally, their long daily walk and the lack of water and electricity ended. Karim and Osman learned how to trace maps for war, and how to create government records. One of the affluent officers, who owned a mini-cooper and a BMW, really took to Karim and Osman and allowed them to use their Blackberrys while in the barracks, which was against the rules. The officer even entrusted Karim with a fortune of one hundred thousand pounds – around fourteen thousand dollars- to deliver to his Cairo home address.

Karim and Osman had a few other great connections during this time. One time, a Colonel offered Karim and Osman a one-year peacekeeping mission with the UN in either the Congo or Sudan as translators, or the chance to remain in their positions and translate his personal letters. The commander had a foreign mistress who wrote him love letters in English, which he could not read. With the United Nations, the salary would have been four hundred dollars whereas in Egypt a conscript earns a token 157 pounds – around twenty dollars- per month. Once they agreed to translate the letters, they felt well treated and special. Unfortunately for Karim, the commander who held the rank of *Akeed* (colonel) left to the US for a one-year special forces training. Karim and Osman also had the chance to exercise once a week with the captain inside a hall.

A little less than an hour into our interview, a pretty, young woman, whom I did not know, joined us. I found it strange but remained silent. Towards the end of the interview I learned that she was his Egyptian girlfriend and soon to be fiancée, Sarah (alias).

Unwelcome Kiss
In the army, there are three things that Karim carefully watched: his mission, his money and his honor. Among the rules in the army, is the ban on the conscription and service of gay men. In the physical examination before admitting them into the army all men are stripped nude and examined and if the anus is bigger than usual that man is automatically rejected by the army with an embarrassing red certificate. If inside the army a soldier caught in a homosexual act, the army would kick him out with a red certificate, dishonoring him. Moreover, either his mother or sister would receive the certificate to further humilate the man.

In the army, he met a variety of people, the abnormal, the stupid, the fool, the preposterous and the gay. At one point in time, there were temporarily no vacant rooms, and the battalion assigned Karim and Osman to sleep on medical beds used for checkups. The first day they used this room, Karim and Osman found a man holding a pocket mirror and tweezers, plucking his eyebrows. Since this to them was abnormal, they ignored him and stayed away from this man with very thin eyebrows. They assumed the man, whose name was Mohamed, was gay, especially when he approached them with light talk and touched Osman and Karim's arms in a strange manner. On reflex, they pushed him away.

Mohamed said, "You are very cute and sweet looking."

Karim warned, "Stay away from me. I don't like this sort of kidding."

Mohamed backtracked and let them be.

One of the experiences that Karim will never forget took place inside this bunker while Osman was on holiday. The checkup room had beds positioned below the windows and the cupboards were in the shade. In the summer, the room felt like a sauna. With all the physical exhaustion of the military camp, Karim found it very difficult to sleep in this room, due to the excruciating heat and the persistent, annoying flies with their furious buzzing noise. As if the disturbance from the flies was not enough, Mohamed, his roommate was singing. Karim was inclined to emotional outbursts, especially when he felt very tired and was unable to sleep due to all the noise. He would cover his face with a bed sheet to stop the irritating flies and a bit later, he would remove it again, sweltering in the heat. The flies would then come back and he would cover his face restlessly again, and so it would continue throughout the night. He was sleep deprived and exhausted. Finally, on this particular night, after about an hour he drifted into sleep, only to wake up as he felt a kiss on his mouth. He got up and saw Mohamed leaning over him. Karim, full of rage at this violation, punched Mohamed's nose so hard that he broke it. Karim pushed him on the floor and gave him a beating, while soldiers gathered to watch the fight. Karim was defending his honor.

Eventually the officer arrived at the scene and asked, "What happened here?"

Karim said, "I was sleeping when my roommate kissed me on my mouth."

Mohamed replied, "It is not true, Sir."

All the soldiers sided with Karim's story.

The officer replied, "I know Karim, he is disciplined, he prays with me daily in the mosque. I never saw you, Mohamed, praying. Look at your face in the mirror! I believe Karim. You know what, you stay lying on the floor."

The soldiers managed to stop the bleeding and washed Mohamed's face and left him lying on the floor as an initial punishment. Mohamed was lying on his stomach with his hands behind his back, his face on the dirty ground.

Meanwhile, the officer wrote a report about Mohamed, who ended up in prison for two years. After completing his term, the army handed him the embarrassing red certificate. Karim started feeling guilty that he was the reason Mohamed's future was tarnished, and approached the officer, saying that he forgave Mohamed, as he felt the punishment was exaggerated. Karim's plea was disregarded as it had become the army's right, and not Karim's right, that Mohamed had violated.

In military courts, decisions are irrevocable. If a soldier is caught smoking pot, the official confiscates his mobile and imprisons him in solitude as well as fining him ten thousand pounds - one thousand four hundred dollars. During this confinement, the food is hard to swallow and the treatment is dire. With all this traumatic experience, it is almost impossible for the conscript to remain normal post-release and post-service. Karim was cautious and did not compromise his position.

Arrogant Demand

Karim was getting greedy, asking to have prolonged vacations to join his American sweetheart, as she was planning to visit Egypt in October 2011. He wanted to work for five days and take a leave of ten days. Karim was pushing his luck in asking for this from the new *Akeed* (Colonel). He was informed that it is best to approach him if a contact put in a good word for him. Karim blindly listened to this advice and asked his brother, the police officer, to call the *Akeed* and put in a good word for Karim.

Karim's brother had a pleasant telephone conversation with the Colonel, *Akeed* who requested that Karim present himself to the former's office. Soon after, Karim eagerly went to the *Akeed*"s office but the office manager coldly informed him that he could not meet the *Akeed*. Impatiently, Karim called his brother, asking him to call the *Akeed* once more and inform him that he was waiting outside. Whilst on the phone, the *Akeed* rang the bell, summoning Karim inside. When he entered, he saw the *Akeed* smiling while on the phone with his brother. Misreading the scene, Karim forgot to salute him.

The *Akeed* was beyond furious and said, "Your brother does not know anything about the military. He entered without even saluting me. He is playing with his fingers and he obviously has not learned anything here. He is a spoilt soldier. Don't worry I will take good care of him."
The *Akeed* hung up the phone and the first thing he did was slam his hand hard on his desk. Karim felt so scared he wanted the floor to open up and swallow him whole. *Akeed* said, "Have you lost your mind? How could you not salute your senior officer? You want to leave the operations for follow-up. You think I will cede to your request, forget it. What is your battalion?"
Karim said, "Sir nine."
The *Akeed* replied, "I will reassign you under projects where you will dig in the ground just like a dog. You will see the worst days of your life."

The Colonel complained about Karim to his superior the Major. As a result, Karim was transferred back to his former battalion that had no water and electricity.

Karim felt his temperature rise, profusely sweating despite the cool weather, as he heard those angry words that were certain to be his fate. He felt shocked and strangled with the dismal turn of his state. His luck had run out. In retrospect, Karim learned the hard way, that the *Akeed* detests spoiled men and any special attention. He could not meet his sweetheart that October and consequently his two-year relationship ended in February 2012.

Karim had called his mother to ask his uncle to put in a good word for him with the *Akeed*; Karim was lucky, as his uncle was asleep that night, and never did contact him on the matter. His family was very concerned about his welfare, and Karim used to call them as often as he could. He hid the truth about his conditions and always sounded upbeat. However, his brother knew the truth.

Among his hardships was his assigned service, where he stood guarding an ammunition store. He was forbidden to smoke a cigarette, or even keep his mobile on him. He stood for five to six hours straight in the cold winter. It was freezing, standing with no shelter in the cold desert. What made the time pass, was eating pumpkin seeds! By the end of his shift, he could not feel his fingers. In their bunks, each soldier was allocated three thin blankets. Karim slept on one and used the other two to cover himself, however, the blankets were never warm enough.

The Army and the People
During the first six months, Karim and Osman used to secure the streets in Ismailia. Karim found the coastal people to be very difficult to deal with, as they were hostile to anyone from outside their district. Any outsider was treated like an infidel. On one occasion, Karim and Osman were securing a football match between Ismailia and Zamalek clubs, and Karim was told that fans took a certain drug, *'apetryl,'* that made them aggressive and hostile, so that after the match they would beat their Zamalek rivals. People from Ismailia and Suez are revolutionaries; after all, Suez ignited the revolution in Egypt in January 2011 *(As recounted in chapter 5)*.

The Egyptian army and the people have a special relationship, unfathomable to outsiders. In stark contrast with other countries under military rule like Burma where the "army had killed 3,000 civilians in cold blood-...the nightmare of murder and mutilation that the country was living through right now, day after day."[96] Ahdaf Soueif pointed out to the military doctrine, "Egyptian army...in both 1977 and 1985 it refused direct orders to fire on Egyptian demonstrations. An oath taken by every soldier is that he will never raise his weapon in an Egyptian face"[97]*To date events after 2011, some believe, have undermined this doctrine, however, overall the army honor the oath.*

At the onset, when the army mobilized in the streets, people offered them food and young men and women posed to take photos with the soldiers. However, with the passing of time, people grew impatient with the Generalissimo Tantawi, which reflected on the streets, with people attacking the soldiers. General Mohamed Farid Hegazy of the Second Army gave his platoon orders to use blanks, or pellets and not real ammunition. It was clear that the army was not going to shoot and kill civilians. The army tried as best as they could to win back the people. Seven police stations were set ablaze in Ismailia. People were shooting at the security forces, and on one occasion, Karim's colleague took a bullet in his stomach and died. Another colleague took a bullet in his leg. Karim managed to hide below the tank, knowing his ammunition would not protect him. A rock struck the *Akeed,* bruising his head and causing it to bleed heavily. The people knew the army was vulnerable as they ridiculed their pellets. Unfortunately, the media twisted the facts and positioned the army as the bad people killing civilians.

The people's confidence in the army was solid at the beginning, but after the failed transition the people's trust waned. The only thing that would return this trust is a good and just president. Karim believes this may never happen or at best will take time.

At these times of tension, the conscripts would plead with civilians, stating that they were not part of the security state and were under compulsory conscription, which if they ignored or ran away from, would leave their future forever tainted. Any conscript who runs away from conscription would face a sentence of two years' imprisonment, after which, if he has no degree, he also serves the state for three years and ends up with a 'poor' grade in his end of service certificate. Karim wanted a good certificate upon finishing his service and hence, he endured as much as he could this ineradicable year. It was not an easy plight, as there were soldiers or conscripts who wanted to ruin the lives of the more fortunate due to their inferiority complex and endless envy.

Ahdaf Soueif pointed out, "a case in court proposing that using conscripts for Security is unconstitutional; conscription may be necessary to protect us against invasion or aggression. But to use conscripts to protect the government of the day against the people cannot be right."[98]*Egypt is still far away from such an ideal situation. Many conscripts have sacrificed their lives defending the government and not the country.*

However, Ismailia was mostly secure due to the large military presence. In the barracks, Karim read newspapers and watched the news. He was sad to see the state of affairs in Egypt and felt that it would never regain its status, and saw its future heading on a rapid downhill road.

Soldiers Dying

From this brief one-year exposure, Karim understood that in the army, the weapon is more valuable than the soldier's life, which morally affected Karim. The soldiers in charge are reputed to be overbearing; one of them gave Karim a hard time. Karim was surprised when one night this high-handed security soldier invited him to dinner as a gesture to make up for his unpleasant treatment. The following day this soldier rode in an army vehicle, along with other men. The driver was ordered to make a sudden sharp left turn, as he was about to miss the turn. While making the sharp turn, the armored vehicle overturned on top of the soldiers. The high-handed soldier died instantly, as he was standing and not sitting, and the spear at the head of his weapon went through his throat and came out from his mouth. Karim found this tragedy shocking, as it reminded him how sudden death visits.

Upon hearing of the accident, Karim ran outside the barracks and was disturbed after seeing this bloody sight. The first thing the general did was quickly check the serial number of the guns, without heeding to the gruesome sudden death of the soldier, a human being. In order to check the number, the general had to slip the weapon from the lifeless body. How could the weapon be more valuable than human life? Was this normal military principle? Is there humanity in the military, or are the two mutually exclusive? Officers fought over who would return the body to the family of the deceased, afraid of the family's reaction and possible revenge. In this accident, five soldiers died, and a mere three thousand pounds - around four hundred and thirty dollars - were paid in compensation to their families. Traditional media did not cover this tragic event, with only the internet mentioning it. After the accident, the vehicle was loaded with other soldiers and proceeded on its mission. Karim felt horrible seeing human life being treated worse than animals. *However, is there another way? If the military becomes soft to human life, can they really safeguard the interests of the nation?*

In November 2011, the army dispatched soldiers to secure parliamentary elections held in public schools. Karim and his fellow conscripts traveled by train to their assigned school. Between the parliamentary and the *shoura* (consultative council) elections, Karim, among others, was stationed to secure the intelligence building in Ismailia. There was a group of young men walking normally besides the army when suddenly a man drew a gun, shot and killed a soldier and then fled. Karim hated this, as he could not do anything with his blanks. In the army, soldiers must obey orders. Otherwise, they face marshal law. Karim could understand the hatred towards the police with their heinous torture records, but could not understand why some people targeted and shot dead soldiers. What caused this inexplicable hatred to escalate so much that it led to murders such as this assassination? Fathers, brothers and sons are what make up the Egyptian army, how can an Egyptian kill another Egyptian? The army never disclosed the number of casualties on their side. During Karim's one-year military service, around thirty men were killed, just from his battalion. He believes the army feared that the parents of the dead conscripts could protest against the army due to the death of their sons.

Before his conscription, Karim despised the army, as he believed it represented disguised atheism. His impression was that few soldiers declare that they are Muslims but do not practice Islam. However, after his year in the army he realized that his impression was not correct. As in any organization, there are some people who are devout and pious, and others who are not. He had never been aware of politics before, but also grew to understand matters whilst in the army. He grew to know that the Egyptian army is very strong, though its façade as seen by the external world, be it Egyptians or foreigners, appears otherwise. The army has good arms and in good quantities. The army trained soldiers to respond quickly in a state of emergency, as if war has erupted.

With the passing of time, Karim came to realize that the army as an organization, does not accommodate religion. This means the army gives both Muslims and Christians the same responsibilities and treats both in the same way. The military world is a strict environment where there is no mercy. Orders are made to be followed, otherwise you risk being killed. There are no problems between Muslims and Christians in Egypt, or in the army. However, in some regions like Upper Egypt, conflicts and problems between the two religions are set up and fabricated, while in reality there is no genuine crisis.

Insecure Sinai
As per the Camp David Treaty, the army cannot place large military stations in Sinai. The police force secures the desert. The Bedouins of Sinai acquire many products from Israel. Palestine and Israel provide the Bedouins with products and in return, the Bedouins give them information on locations, which can help smuggle people, arms, drugs and other items into Egypt. The Bedouins are reputed to be concerned with their self-interest more than the national interest. Drugs, such as hashish sourced from Marsa Matrouh, are smuggled into Sinai for mixing, manufacturing, and then smuggling onto Arish, North Sinai, across the border and into Israel. An illegal drug exchange would take place and hard drugs would enter Egypt. The side effects of hashish are a lot less serious than hard drugs like cocaine and heroin. The hard drugs mixed in Egypt give higher output and hence more cash. Besides drugs,

arms are also exchanged. Karim believes that the Bedouins have weapons which are not available in Egypt, but sourced from Israel.

Karim believes that Israel was behind the killing of the seventeen soldiers during Ramadan, in August 2012. He doubts that Hamas was behind this incident. Based on his hypothesis, Israel wants to engage in war with Egypt to occupy Sinai, as they believe that Sinai and Syria should be part of the Jewish State. Karim's American girlfriend accepted an invitation to visit Israel, as she is Jewish, and recounted to him this vision of a much-coveted Greater Israel.

Good to Go

When former President Mubarak stepped down, Karim was happy. However, he became mad when he realized soon after, that stability seemed far-fetched with the results of the controversial constitutional referendum. He cannot recall exactly which outcome he supported, as he did not ponder the matter in the first place, since he could not vote while in the army. No matter how many flaws and faults the army might have, when push comes to shove, it still stood by and saved Egypt during the revolution. The army realizes what Machiavelli wrote, *"In our times it is necessary for all rulers to conciliate the people rather than soldiers, because the people are more powerful"* [99]

Among the reasons behind Karim's despair was the simple fact that he was about to start his life in a shattered scene, which minimized his chances of success. Immigrating was never an attractive option for Karim, as he thought it was some sort of betrayal. When the going got tough, he wanted to stick around and not run away in pursuit of another life.

Based on his experience, he would like his future son to serve his obligatory conscription when there is peace, not during a revolution. Karim believes that conscription is a priceless experience that teaches a man to be fearless, independent and resourceful. Simple pleasures of home life such as a hot shower, television, comfortable couch, family, good food, hot tea, and a comfortable bed are all blessings that Karim never really appreciated before the army.

Hard Bread

During the revolution, the army was distributing extra cash to its forces, compensating them for the extra work of securing the streets, which strictly speaking is not the army's job. Even after the revolution, the army increased salaries to reduce any discontent. Karim spent most of the money on juice or baked items to supplement the army food. The army did not allow conscripts to order food from outside, as a precaution measure averting any possible food poisoning.

For breakfast, soldiers were served bread called *gereya*, which Karim describes as very hard, such that if you threw it on the wall it would bounce back! Breakfasts contained hardly boiled fava beans, which needed slow chewing to avoid breaking one's teeth, as it contained small pebbles. The jam was a mixture of sugar and something else; it did not taste like jam. *Halawa* (halva) was so hard that it had to be broken down so it could be edible. Military factories produced all these food items. Karim avoided the served food as best as he could. He bought milk at the canteen in the barracks for nutrition and a lot of sugar cane.

The kitchen served meat or chicken once a week. A chicken wing would constitute the weekly portion of meat along with rice and watery vegetables. Dinner was a small piece of salty cheese and the aforementioned *gereya* bread and sometimes, tuna of the worst kind. They could buy sausage, egg or liver sandwiches that would be substantially tastier. From time-to-time on exception, Karim's contacts allowed them to order food deliveries such as fish, shrimps, and mangos for dessert.

Initially Karim felt that the army position was very good; it was protecting its people. He was fortunate to enjoy good treatment in the early days of his military service.

Wealthy Army
The army revered former President Mubarak, as he was one of them and it was beyond their imagination that a civilian would rule Egypt; the President must be a military man. They were confident that the President would never issue a decision that would harm the army. The largest budget after the national budget is the military budget. Karim believes that Field Marshal Tantawi is among the richest men in Egypt. Karim recounts one military parade of eight thousand soldiers, that the generalissimo attended. Because he was pleased with the performance, he ordered a three hundred pounds bonus per head, which amounted to two million four hundred thousand pounds – around three hundred and forty two thousand dollars. The army has extensive funds. There certainly is room for corruption, as no external body audits or controls the military budget. *Among the demands of the revolution was that the parliament approve the military budget.* As it stands, it is unheard of that the military budget would become part of the state budget.

When former President Mubarak stepped down, the older officers were emotionally distraught to the point that they broke down in tears. Disbelief and uncertainty crept within the armed forces. The viewpoint of the military is different from that of the people, and likewise, the perspective between the police officers and the army officers also differs.

Army men do not live normal married lives. They only have a sense of normality with their families for a brief amount of time throughout the year, due to the conditions of their service. With the army men stationed away, some wives would betray their husbands. One of his commanders' wives was bold and desperate. The commander sent a soldier to his wife to deliver some important paperwork to her. The wife, who was in her forties and lonely, made a pass at the soldier at her house, and the soldier downright refused.

The wife said, "You are going to be imprisoned."

To which the soldier replied, "Why what have I done?"

The wife said, "I will tell my husband that you raped me. I assure you that you will see the worst days of your life."

In the army, it is impossible for a soldier suffering from unjust treatment to ask for help, as a soldier means nothing at the end of the day. The soldier had to comply with her demands and have sex with her, so that she did not report him as a rapist. This soldier used to cry in front of Karim as the wife blackmailed him, making him victim to sexual abuse. Karim could not advise his colleague what to do, as they both knew if he stopped, she would lie to her husband who in turn was capable of planting drugs in his cell, and his future would be bleak and dreary.

Despite their bias towards the former president, the army protected the revolution, and secured all vital institutions. When they received distress calls the army responded quickly, unlike the police who were mysteriously absent. The army had a weapon called *motaaded*, which had long bullets some twelve centimeters in length, which make a loud noise. *Motaaded* is a sort of machine gun sometimes used in hindering escapes from prison. The army gave clear orders not to shoot live bullets at a civilian unless the civilian was shooting at the army. The army was very careful, treating their soldiers with tact, as they feared a rebellion from within. Conscription lasts for two to three years for those who are illiterate or have a primary education. This means that not many of them are aware of current affairs, and therefore can be easily maneuvered and manipulated.

Machiavelli wrote, "The foundations of every state, are good laws and good arms"[100] *I gather from Karim that the army has good arms. What the army and in fact all of Egypt lack is giving proper value to human life; this was the main underlying instigator of the Egyptian revolution.* The army protected the *ancien regime* and yet it did not. The Supreme Council of Armed Forces (SCAF) ordered the protection of the revolution and its revolutionaries, and the army followed orders. The army secured the majority of locations, although this type of security did not fall within its normal jurisdiction. Karim says that, while appearing to protect the revolution, the army really protected the *ancien regime* and its own interests. This was evident to him due to the simple fact that Field Marshal Tantawi remained in charge, and he represented the *ancien regime*.

Mixed Feelings

From Karim's point of view, the eighteen days were all negative, filled with uncertainty. What would happen the next day? Every morning, broadcast news was more distressing. Police stations were set on fire, soldiers killed, buildings set ablaze and drug dealers caught. It was very fluid. All the news was bad and negative and hence Karim could not visualize anything positive within this context.

Karim is both happy and sad that the revolution took place. He is happy, as he is now able to speak his mind openly without fear, and glad for his newly bestowed freedom. He is sad, however, that the transition is not proper and lacks a good leader. He is proud of only one thing; that the Egyptian people rose up and carried out a revolution. But, he was very upset that the Egyptian people continued on the wrong path by making more mistakes daily. To make matters worse, most Egyptians are not politically aware and are new recruits to the political realm, and yet they claim that they understand, and are intolerably adamant that their view is correct. During the presidential elections in 2012, there were many candidates running. Egyptian public opinion was divided and scattered as to who the best candidate was. For Karim, this in and of itself is proof of their naiveté and lack of political awareness.

Karim has tirelessly recounted his military adventures several times to his friends, as they are months he will never forget. The whole conscription lasted fourteen months. Karim finished his unforgettable conscription on March 1, 2012. After the army, Karim feels he is ready to deal with any sort of boss, and and any situation, as the army has prepared him for the worst. He stayed in Hurghada for a month to cleanse his mind and body from the hardships he faced. He started working in May, and got involved with Sarah, his fiancée, in June 2012.

Rivals

Police officers trained to deal with any harm to society and the absence of democracy is *ipso facto* a reality. Karim will never justify the police shooting protestors, as his loyalty is to the Egyptian people.

Karim discovered the main reasons why police usually hate the army. Police officers are better educated than the army officers, as they study law and can practice it as lawyers if they wish. A police officer is free to quit his job after around six years of service, whereas in the army, he cannot. Police, however, earn less than military as police officers only spend two years away from their hometown whereas those in the military spend most of their career away from their hometown and family.

The relationship between the police and the army has been tainted with rivalry and competition, hence the unspoken tension. Karim does not believe the relationship between the army and the police will improve. When the army took over in 2011, they were gloating, saying that the police could stay at home, as the army had matters under control.

The worst two enemies are the *Ikhwan* and the army. The army does not permit its soldiers to grow their beards, which is a common practice among *Ikhwan*. Rumor has it that in February 2011, *Ikhwan* made a deal with the army in return for withdrawing from Tahrir. Contrary to what many people believe, Karim does not think that any deal took place between the two powerful entities during the revolution.

Media Profiting

When it comes to media, Karim believes they have made big monetary gains since the revolution. He didn't like Jazeera, as he felt it abused the situation to its profit. The media was looking after its own interests, unconcerned with the nation's interests and he came to despise all media. His journalist friends told him that their bosses expected big stories daily and that they had to improvise or risk their jobs to more resourceful journalists. In his opinion, the media ruined the image of Egypt internationally.

The media exaggerated or 'fabricated' news, a fundamental yet immoral role, as they were obliged to report a new story daily and many times used twisted facts, or even their own made up stories. The media were essentially looking at stories to implicate the army but Karim feels this was not fair, as without the Egyptian army, Egypt would have lost its sovereignty, and been susceptible to enemy attacks while at its most vulnerable.

Karim noticed that the army did not encourage its recruits to watch the media, to avoid sympathizing with the people and risking an internal rebellion from within the military. He stayed in touch with his friends on Blackberry Messenger, through which he received broadcasts. In his mind, he grew to hate the recently introduced realm of politics.

Conscripts may not vote in elections but when Karim finished his service, he was able to vote in the presidential elections. In the first round, Karim voted for Amr Moussa as he thought he was the best of the candidates. In the second round he chose Ahmed Shafik. In the constitutional referendum in December 2012, he voted No.

On the Maspero incident, when army soldiers killed Christians in front of state TV, Karim is convinced that the army would not shoot at civilians unless they were seriously provoked. In the army, a soldier cannot act on his own as he simply follows orders, unlike the police officer who has the right to fire back if fired upon. Revolutionary women intentionally provoked soldiers with the purpose of crippling or softening their reaction. It is a lot easier for a man to respond to a man than to a woman. Building on this, Karim recounts that a drug dealer in Ismailia had fourteen women bodyguards armed with knives. If an officer tried to arrest the dealer, a woman would throw herself on him, crippling his movement. If the army had fought a woman, the media would have had a field day with headlines circulating about how the army abuses women. One of Karim's colleagues, Ramy, saved an officer from a woman armed with broken glass, who wanted to hit him on the head. Ramy quickly moved and pushed the big woman to the floor. The army was very sensitive, as it did not want to offend any group in society. However, in some cases the army had to respond; for example, when a woman slaps an officer on his face, should he remain quiet after such abuse? How can a soldier confined with strict rules, living in harsh conditions protecting his country, passively accept a slap? It really hurt the soldiers' morale. You need to think about how he feels as a human being with a beating heart not a heart of stone. Soldiers are human beings that have rights and freedoms that deserve respect and protection.

What happened in 2011 started as a revolution. Karim cannot answer as to whether the revolution is finished or continuing, has succeeded or failed, at least not for another year or more. On January 16, 2013, an announcement beckoned protestors to take to the streets. They had a list of demands, so apparently the revolution was not over yet. *As the months of the Ikhwan rule passed, resentment and opposition grew with no achievements and no improvements. Actually many felt the situation of the country was deteriorating fast.* The revolutionary demands did not see the light of day under President Morsi. *Moreover, the moderate and liberal Egyptians sensed the Egyptian identity was at stake, with the hardline Islamist agenda even including discussions on banning ballet.* Karim believed it was the same regime but with different names and a new, bearded appearance. Actually, matters are deteriorating, with a poor constitution and even placating the Israelis of Egyptian origin, asking them to return to Egypt.

Ikhwan men witnessed dark days under the *ancien regime*, decades of repression imprisonment and torture, ultimately forcing the brothers into an underground, secluded secret society. Regardless of how strong their faith was, they had weak hearts and lived in fear due to their repression. Karim perceives their performance after gaining the parliamentary and presidential elections as pure revenge and payback time.

Future
Karim sees a dark and gloomy future, as *Ikhwan* will not just pick up their bags and leave. A revolution will take place to overthrow them, but he predicts it will

fail. At the time of this interview (January 2013), Karim felt that after the four-year presidential term, new *Ikhwan* characters would take over. He predicted their strength would increase over time and they would stay in power as they would have secured the *Ikhwan* reign. Karim predicted the state of Egypt would continue to deteriorate during their reign. He doubts that *Ikhwan* will change anything in the regime. If they were planning to change anything, it would have been evident by now.

Karim believes that *Ikhwan* are the teacher's pet of the United States, although they may say otherwise. They knew that they were going to win the elections before the results were out. It is in America's interests that the *Ikhwan* take over and for Egypt to fall deeper into an abyss. A weak Egypt is easier to manipulate. The revolution kicked off strong; however, it ended dismally.

No government can expedite transition, as Machiavelli said, "governments set up overnight, like everything in nature whose growth is forced, lack strong roots and ramifications."[101] Under *Ikhwan* rule, Karim believes that Egypt has a fake democracy. Post-*Ikhwan* Karim sees things are getting better day after day. Traffic is better, there are better laws, less theft, and the country is on the way to democracy. The constitutional declaration was an ironclad decision by the ousted President Morsi to secure his status and his rule. Karim perceives rigging took place in the presidential election, as well as the constitutional referendum. Egypt will forever be lost as it is a coveted land of fortune by both Egyptians and foreigners alike, everyone skirmishing to take a larger piece of this invaluable land. In Karim's mind, this unquenched desire will never cease. However, he does still wish that the state of Egypt would improve overtime despite his pessimistic outlook on its future.

Karim never joined any protest in Tahrir, as he does not like politics and did not participate on June 30, 2013 when millions of Egyptians took to the streets demanding the end of *Ikhwan* rule.

In July 2013, after the ousting of President Morsi, Karim remains skeptical, though optimistic; he cannot predict what will happen next, the future is uncertain. Egyptians need to learn how to differ from one another in a civil manner. As Martin Luther King said, *"Certainly we will continue to disagree, but we must disagree without becoming violently disagreeable"*[102]

CHAPTER 16

Tainted Truth

"There are no facts, only interpretations." Friedrich Nietzsche.

It felt as though with every step I was taking forward, that I was taking two steps back with a couple of characters withdrawing. Moving forward I contacted a relative of my husband who works in media who recommended that I meet Samah, as we shall call her in this chapter, as she seemed unwilling to sign the proxy allowing me to publish her story under her real name. We met at Cilantro café in Messaha square on Sunday January 13, 2013.

The Myth of Freedom of Expression

Samah is a twenty-five-year old veiled Egyptian woman with bright shiny eyes. She is a smoker and likes cafe latte. Samah was born in Cairo in 1987. Her mother recounted that as a child, Samah used to use a cucumber as a pretend microphone, welcoming guests who came to her home. From the time, she was seventeen years old, she dreamt of becoming a reporter, infatuated by the media world. She has two younger brothers. Her father is a retired colonel in *Amn Eldawla* (State Security) and her mother is a retired art teacher. Samah went to Nozha School and then studied at an Arts College, as her high school grade point average was one percent shy of getting her accepted into Journalism. As an undergraduate, Samah took up internships in journalism during her summer holidays and graduated in 2008. Within the same year, she embarked on her career in journalism. She has been a reporter for seven years. She kick-started her career at Al Ahram newspaper and for the last five years, has been working as a reporter at a private satellite channel. Samah was entangled in an office romance with her colleague Saber *(also his alias)*, which led to marriage a year later, in 2012.

In Samah's view, all media complement one another; television delivers live and direct feeds, and newspapers deliver analytical stories. Talk shows compensate the news feeds by hosting analysis and discussions. Upon pondering, Samah does not see any difference between state and private media, apart from the social backgrounds or status and the salaries of workers, as both state and private mediums deliver directed media. The private media attempts to portray all the points of views. However, the bottom line is, reports are directed by the interests of the owner and channel manager, the same way state media are skewed to the state interests. Censorship existed before the revolution, and after the revolution during the military rule, as it was taboo to talk about the head of state and head of the Supreme Council of the Armed Forces (SCAF). However, as the state lost its awe and glamor in the eyes of the people, the president of the state commands no respect, as not only is he referred to by his first name, but also shamefully insulted. Samah is not proud that there are no barriers to speech in media; there is no code after the revolution. She compares the country to a household where the kids fear and respect their father. When he travels they fear and respect their mother, but when the mother travels too and the younger kids are left in the responsibility of the eldest, imagine how the household will be…a big mess. *Similar to Willaim Golding's* Lord of the Flies *when the innocent children ended up beasts and murderers on the adultless island.*

Machiavelli wrote, "when it is absolutely a question of the safety of one's country… there must be no consideration of just or unjust, of merciful or cruel, of praiseworthy or disgraceful."[103] *Samah seems to agree with this Machiavellian thought.* She believes censorship is unavoidable; a necessary, acceptable evil when it concerns the public interest or discourse, rather than being linked to self-interest or terrorism. In her opinion, freedom of speech cannot exist in the absolute sense when you have rampant ignorance.

After the self-immolation of Bouazizi in Tunisia, the Kefaya (Enough) movement arranged a demonstration in Egypt denouncing the circumstances, in front of *Dar el Kadah el Aly* (the main court complex). Samah was astonished to hear the protestors asking former President Mubarak to step down. Samah remembers a woman journalist passionately chanting, "Down with Mubarak! Your silence is bringing us down." The woman was waving to the silent majority watching from the balconies. It was fear that muffled people before, but their unwavering belief that President Mubarak would step down was dauntingly indomitable. Samah was awestruck as to how the protestors believed in themselves. Something major had happened and the people were no longer afraid. *Nelson Mandela once said, "I learned that courage was not the absence of fear, but the triumph over it. The brave man is not he who does not feel afraid, but he who conquers that fear."*[104] *The activists chanting had suddenly overcome their paralyzing fear.*

Overcoming Fear

On January 25, Samah informed her satellite channel of the pre-planned protests. She ventured out, filled with excitement, assigned to report from *Dar El Kada El Aly* (High Supreme Court). It was a quiet protest until around two in the afternoon, when the perseverance of the protests broke through the human chain of *Amn Elmarkazi* (central security forces), phalanxes clad in black. Samah was amazed when she saw a fellow journalist chanting "*ya ahaleena endamou lena*")" Our families come join us"). That journalist even rebuked the silent men around her and said 'Why aren't you chanting?' Something different was happening as people were positively responding to the protesters they normally would have shunned. She saw drivers park their cars and join the protest. *Amn Eldawla* (state security) fired tear gas canisters to disperse the crowds. The gas was suffocating. Samah conducted her interviews and went back to Media City, at the western suburbs of Cairo, to edit her report. Another colleague was stuck at Tahrir and was unable to communicate, given that mobiles lines were down. While editing, Samah noticed that the manager of the channel had entered the editing room, for the first time ever. He reviewed her script and she sensed that he wanted to broadcast the report, but fear stifled him. His decision finally, was to air it. *It was the third incident in a week where Samah noticed people overcoming fear.* The night of January 25, she discovered that her colleague Ahmed was beaten and his shoulder dislocated. The night of January 28 another colleague, Kamal, was arrested by the police and released after a couple of days.

Samah took the following day off from work and on January 27 she covered a report about a collapsed building in a slum area, which contractors had built without a license. *Sadly, with the rampant disrespect of law, there are many cases whereby contractors construct buildings without proper foundations, materials and without a license or inspection, often leading to catastrophic structural collapses.* Samah expected another day of protests, under the name of 'Friday of Anger'. She fell in love with the revolutionary Guevara atmosphere. Her infatuation was apparent, as a TV anchor warned Samah to be careful; that she must never forget she is a reporter, neither a protestor nor a member of any party. The army mobilized and a curfew ensued. No photographers were allowed to take pictures at the main mosques. Some were harassed, others had their equipment confiscated, and Samah's team was incapable of reporting live. People expected the announcement of martial measures in the country, but none came.

At around three in the afternoon, Samah went with her crew to observe the demonstration, risking camera confiscation at Tahrir Street in Dokki. The *Amn Elmarkazi* (Central Security) truck was apprehending anyone with cameras, and arresting them. A little after she arrived, Samah was in the midst of tear gas canisters being fired at protestors and pellet shots flying around, with men and women running away. She managed to do a couple of stand uppers, standing interviews, but in the midst of the skirmishes, she was worried about her cameraman. Soon, they were exhausted; it became futile trying to take photos with all the gunshots and canisters flying in the air, so her cameraman withdrew. It was chaos.

Police vs. People

The sun was blazing on January 28, 2011. Samah remembers feeling as if her skin was melting, when a tear gas canister landed beside her while the bright rays of sunlight tanned her skin. She ran away trying to avoid the suffocating chemical gas. The spirit of cooperation amongst strangers bewildered her. She saw that when someone fell down and collapsed from the effects of the tear gas, a stranger would hand them a cloth soaked with vinegar or a splash of coke to limit the effects of the gas so that he or she could move on.

Observing the people in the protests, Samah realized they were either the A class or the downtrodden strata of society, both of which were fearless. The former had contacts to assist if needed, and the latter simply had nothing to lose. Protestors were dressed in their branded clothes, scarves and bags. Some even wore heals, in stark contrast to the march from Shoubra. The appearance of so many obviously wealthy people intimidated her, giving her shivers. Samah did not notice any of the middle class. In the midst of the clouds of tear gas, Samah noticed a young teenage boy wearing jeans and a red t-shirt sitting on the sidewalk crying, overwhelmed with the violence.

On the horizon, she could see the battle between the police and protestors on the Kasr El Nile Bridge, while she stood beside the Opera House. After sunset the police backed away, and Samah reached the bridge and traversed it to reach Midan alTahrir.

At around five in the afternoon, the officers moved back to the sides as if retreating, which led to a wave of cheers from the protestors, 'Here are Egypt's men!' An old woman was very happy when the security cordon retreated, but also fearful to the point of breaking out into tears. The atmosphere was electrifying. Samah, despite the tension, was happy with the protests. She never saw Egypt in such a beautiful spirit. People were happy, conversing civilly. She heard a bearded man wearing a *galabeya* saying, "I was never able to walk at ease with my beard before."

Joy surrounded Samah and the victorious protestors. People were jumping up and down on the bridge, and from the tremendous weight, Samah feared that it could possibly collapse! Rumors were circulating that the police were going to block the entrance and exit of the bridge, and that it would be detached from the middle and raised vertically, such that the protestors would fall into the Nile.

Black Plague

Samah ventured towards the auspicious former National Democratic Party (NDP) headquarters on the banks of the great Nile River. She found men carrying televisions, computers, laptops, and keyboards, stolen from the despised former ruling political party. Some men filled with such fury that they smashed the stolen items onto the sidewalks. Samah observed that once destruction and looting had commenced, some people took a stand, rejecting it. She stayed with her friends a little after nightfall, watching protestors in Tahrir. She was happy to witness the generosity in Tahrir, with plenty of food distributed and shared amongst strangers.

When Samah returned home, she discovered that her fiancée, Saber, had been looking for her in the streets after seeing her video report about Tahrir, which she had recorded at the onset of the violence. Saber did not know where she was, and was unable to reach her due to the communication shutdown, leaving him a nervous wreck. While Saber was driving, another car intentionally bumped into his car on the ring road. The windscreen was shattered and men set a tire on fire. Saber was scared and quickly sped away in his car, far from this commotion. He felt that chaos was invading the streets of Cairo like a black plague. After hours of searching, Saber went to Samah's home, hoping to find her. He was relieved and grateful to see her safe.

One of Samah's friends was going through a nervous breakdown, as both her brothers are police officers. The friend's desperate brothers were forced to take off their police uniform, and ran in their underwear in the cold Cairo streets, evading hatred and assaults. Back at home, Samah turned on the state television and recalls seeing a movie playing, with absolutely no coverage of the protests. Jazeera channel had changed its broadcast frequency, which she had not yet updated. It felt like she was living in two parallel worlds; the one she had seen at Tahrir, and the one on television, that was pretending that everything was exactly as per usual.

On Friday January 28, Samah went to the state security offices in the suburban district of Six of October City, where her father had worked before his retirement. While at *Amn Eldawla*, National Security, she overheard that something was unraveling. She remembers watching the first speech by former President Mubarak, which she found disappointingly out of touch with the people. Samah returned home in her father's chauffeured car, sadly noticing the Giza police station was in flames. While passing by her parent's home within the vicinity of Carrefour supermarket in Maadi, she saw thieves looting the stores at around nine in the morning.

Eventually, Samah slept that night only to be awakened by the sound of her mother screaming. She was terrified, as Samah's brother wanted to join the civilian checkpoint in their street. She was hearing frequent sounds of gunshots being fired, which had previously been unheard of. Samah's mother was arguing with her son, pleading with him not to leave the house. He was adamant that he could not stay, as he felt compelled to participate in the protection of their neighborhood.

During the following three days, Samah was attentive to the television broadcasts. Initially there was no live coverage as there was no main signal issued by state television and no 3G equipment on the ground. The main broadcasting method in Tahrir was SNG, which is a pre-planned broadcast via satellite, which transmits an image. Even state television only had a camera overlooking Six of October Bridge.

After the first presidential speech, Samah felt that many people were changing sides turning against the revolution, seeking the comfort of security and cursing change.

The Rift

Samah fondly remembers her father, a retired Brigadier, walking in their house chanting the popular chant *"alshaab yoreed eskat al nizam"* (The people want the downfall of the regime). Her mother was highly involved with the events and after the emotional second speech, she broke out in tears, as she was fine with the compromise that former President Mubarak offered. Samah recalls watching Amr Adeeb's famous talk show after the speech and noticing a woman from *Kefaya* rejecting the presidential concessions, which the talk show host and members of April 6 movement had accepted.

Among Samah's friends, there were controversial views with vehement support for the activists versus loyalists supporting the former president. In the middle were the indifferent, silent bunch. Her fiancée and her parents were among the silent lot as they sympathized with the protestors, but were not for the revolution. As for Samah, she supported the revolution, and mostly covered it as a reporter; however, she participated on one day only namely Friday January 28.

The second presidential speech created a rift amongst the Egyptian people. Samah was asking people's opinions on February 2, within the vicinity of the Maspero state television building. Unexpectedly she noticed civilian checkpoints created at the entrance to Midan alTahrir. Shortly afterwards Samah managed to enter Tahrir through the side roads and she noticed that many bearded men were among the protestors. She recalled that during the initial days of the revolution in January, she did not notice so many bearded men. She saw Safwat Hegazy, a preacher associated with the *Ikhwan*, however he claims otherwise - carried on men's shoulders like a hero. They were chanting for a war to free Jerusalem from Israel saying, "To Jerusalem we are heading martyrs by the millions."

During the quiet before the storm, Samah heard a desperate man say, "Isn't it enough. I am a doctor and I earn seventy-two pounds (around ten dollars)."

Samah felt that people were fed-up with the old *nizam*. She felt as if there was no choice, with death the certain outcome, whether you live within the power of the regime or you fight it.

Green Iron Fence

Events were unfolding quickly on Wednesday February 2, and Samah noticed bleeding protestors running. Samah was walking within the vicinity of Omar Makram Mosque when her station asked her to record the conflict. While she was recording, out of nowhere she was suddenly in the middle of a storm of stones flying in her direction. On reflex Samah raised her hands to protect her head. Amidst the chaos, Samah noticed an old white-haired man in his fifties or sixties wearing trousers, a t-shirt and a jacket sitting on the sidewalk crying, "What is happening to the country? Why are people killing one another?" Given this man's emotional condition, it was impossible for her to approach him for an interview.

Within minutes of the attack, Samah was suddenly facing a camel while she was standing on the sidewalk. The camels were running very fast and passed in front of her. A green iron fence protected Samah. Men were dismantling the metal barriers to hit the assailants. It was a horrendous scene to say the least. Samah felt heartbroken to watch Egyptians hitting one another violently on February 2, causing bloody wounds and killing many.

Samah managed to record footage in this turmoil, but around five in the afternoon, she left. For some unknown reason, her station mentioned on air that their correspondent Samah suffered wounds in *Tahrir*, which was simply not true. Samah's father remained on edge even after seeing that she was all right. Samah's mother was a nervous wreck and decided that Samah was not to leave the house with all this commotion. Subsequently, Samah laid low for a day and on Friday, she convinced her parents that she had to do her work.

On Friday, she reported from El Nour mosque at Abbas El Akkad Street. While she was conducting interviews, the people on the street chastised Samah, telling her that enough is enough and that the media was wrecking the country with their stories and coverage.

Ironic Tahrir

What bothered Samah about *Tahrir* was the manner in which certain civilians were checking other civilians before allowing them to enter Tahrir, as if they owned the square. If someone with a different point of view, for instance pro Mubarak, tried to enter Tahrir, the protestors would become raucous, making it clear that this person was unwelcome in the *midan*, which signified that they tolerated only like-minded people. Where is the freedom to express? Ironically, Samah believes that Tahrir was the most undemocratic place. According to Samah, Tahrir was a place at which people were calling for freedom, social equality and justice and yet, they did not exhibit these very same qualities when it came to people with opinions that differed from their own.

Samah observed that after what was deemed "the battle" on February 2, protestors were asking one another which ideology they believed in. Ideology was creeping up as an issue within the square, whereas initially it was not the case. People were starting to take strong positions against the opposition (Mubarak supporters), even kicking them out of Tahrir. When the people staffing the entrance into Tahrir asked Samah about her ideological beliefs, she showed her student ID card. She even fabricated a story that she was researching a project for Ain Shams University. She opted to 'white lie' as she wanted to avoid any possible justification that protestors could use to force her to turn away, as had been the case on the previous day, when she and others were refused entry. Protestors wanted to break Samah's camera but did not. The crowds pushed Samah and her camera operator with sheer force, but she was not beaten.

Samah will never forget the historic Day of Anger, January 28, 2011, which she believes to be the true revolution. She believes that those who took to the streets on the day of anger truly risked their lives and took the chance of not returning home that night. Samah considers these brave souls the real revolutionaries. Those who went out that day risked imprisonment, suffocation from the tear gas and even death.

During the final presidential speech, Samah was indifferent as to whether the former President Mubarak would stay in power or step down. At the time rumor had it that Mubarak has already stepped down. People were delirious with happiness shouting, *"Allah akbar"* or "God is great" and prostrating themselves on the ground, as a gesture of being thankful to God. Once the people realized it was just a rumor, they broke into tears of frustration and despair. Mubarak was still the President.

On Friday February 11, Samah went to Midan alTahrir during the afternoon prayers. She will never forget the sight of all Muslims kneeling on the asphalt praying. She noticed that many people were joking about the speech in a desperate attempt to lighten up the atmosphere. Many protestors decided to escalate the protest and headed to the Itihadiyah Presidential Palace. Consequently, Samah's assignment was to report from Itihadiyah.

Samah arrived in Itihadiyah ten minutes before the vice president's announcement that former President Mubarak has abdicated his position. Samah noticed heartfelt cheering by protestors, young and old women and men. Among the chants were "Here Here... Here are the Egyptians". Samah interviewed many protestors and remembers how they were all in a celebratory mood as if it were a religious holiday. Samah could not believe that Mubarak would actually abdicate. In and amongst the disbelief, she could not decide whether she was happy or sad regarding Mubarak's abdication. Certainly, the spirit was contagious, as Samah was happy to see Egyptians so festive. The *ancien regime* never harmed Samah directly, however, she was happy for its victims, hoping that justice would rule. She stayed for a few hours, and headed to her brother who was at Tahrir. After navigating the swarms of Egyptians in the streets, together they returned home a little before midnight.

Harassment Resumed

This euphoria abruptly came to an end the night after the former President stepped down. Samah admired how the men treated women in Tahrir, which was a huge change from the widespread harassment of women by strange men. There was no sexual harassment during the eighteen days, with the exception of the embarrassing assault on the American journalist, Lara Logan. While Samah was walking in Tahrir, in the midst of cheers and tears of disbelief, she felt something brush her bottom. As she moved her hand to find the violator, she caught a man's hand on her bottom. Samah was shocked and aggravated at this harassment. She held onto his hand briefly, and met her assailant's ashen face. She let go of his hand and left without uttering a word, out of fear of more violation. As Samah was alone in the crowds at the time, she did not want to take any chances. She was afraid that if she rebuked the man, she would attract the attention of more men and probably be the victim of group harassment.

Egypt has witnessed a flagrant and blatant rise in verbal and physical harassment of pedestrian Egyptian and foreign women, women wearing niqab, veiled, unveiled, in the streets or public buses or metro, which has escalated after the revolution. Many women are shocked at this abuse and unfortunately stay quiet to avoid tarnishing their reputations. In November 2013, Egypt ranked as the worst Arab state in the treatment of women, according to a Comoros, Thomson Reuters Foundation survey. Unfortunately, women who protested for freedom, justice and social equality have found themselves in a worse situation than during the Mubarak era.

Unclear Relations

Samah believes that Egypt is plagued with religious strife, which varies according to upbringing. She senses sensitivities with Christians who are not her friends, but not so much with her own friends. At work, she heard a producer joking in a deranged manner with a Christian woman, cursing her. Not all Muslims like Christians. One of her dear friends is a Christian who cherishes his friendship with Samah. However, he has an extremely condescending view of Muslims, to the extent to that he wrote something to the effect of, "until when will those Muslims stay this way?" on his Facebook wall.

Many died in the Maspero incident in October 2011, where people protested the maltreatment of Christians. After this tragic incident, Samah wanted to interview the victims at the Coptic hospital with her school friend Mena, who knew a victim she could interview. While waiting for Mena at the morgue, she found herself in a very awkward situation. She heard people chanting.
One man chanted, "Muslims and Christians are one hand."
Another man retorted, "Muslims and Christians are not one hand."
A woman vocally and passionately said, "The Muslims are the reason behind what is happening to us."
Samah was not afraid, however, out of respect she slipped quietly to the sides, when unexpectedly she found a strange woman patting her on the shoulder with tears in her eyes. The woman said, "Sorry they don't mean it. They are upset."
Samah gratefully said, "I am not upset. Thank you."

Accidental Mishap

For Samah the relationship between Muslims and Christians is vague and unfathomable. There never was a grass root solution to the sensitivities. She draws a comparison to a host who keeps his guest on edge by repeatedly saying 'this is like your home,' ultimately making the guest uneasy. In the same way, Muslim Egyptians always refer to 'our Coptic brothers,' consequently making the Copts uncomfortable. In her view, the solution is to drop the word 'brothers' and just simply address Egyptian Muslims and Egyptian Christians. Relations need normalizing; for instance, building a Church requires a special permit, unlike building a Mosque, where no permit is required. Such procedures need revoking.

The rationale behind this discrimination is the unfounded Muslim fear that Christians would build Churches everywhere. *Fear is the human's enemy, as it can consume and blind us, and stifle society.* Repression yields the opposite effect, as once this lid of repression is lifted, the suppressed will virally spread. Just like what happened with *Ikhwan* under the Mubarak rule, once they gained power, they scattered all their men in all fields to the extent that a coined term, *Ikhwanisation*, surfaced. Samah considers this to be uncalculated mismanagement, which created a problem that was nonexistent. A common imagined perception among Muslims is that a Christian rather than a Muslim enjoys preference in filling a job opening. Samah blames movies and soap operas for mishandling people along with public policy. However, Samah does not believe that the mishap was intentional. Rather, it was unwisely overlooked by authorities. The *ancien regime* played on this mishap to implement the long established war strategy of divide and conquer. In short, the *ancien regime* was not smart in this.

When the atrocious bomb killed churchgoers on New Year's Eve at Saint Cathedral at Alexandria in 2011, Samah called all her Christian friends wishing them a happy new year and checking that all is good.

Her friend Mena is a happily married man who was super protective of his fellow Christian friend to the extent that when she was emotionally involved with a Muslim man, Mena acted in an unorthodox way. Mena sinned in an extramarital affair with his friend, just to ensure his Christian friend avoided such temptation and subsequent scandal with a Muslim. Committing a sin so that another sin is not committed, how twisted can you get?

Samah does not view matters as having absolute stands. Referring to another minority group, Samah believes that the Egyptian women enjoy their rights with limited exceptions. In Upper Egypt, women manage many households. Samah believes women's freedom depends on the woman herself. If she wants to claim her rights and freedom, she will, and if she is afraid, her fear will cripple her. As per the labor law, a woman has the right to maternity leave, while there is no equivalent vacation for men. Samah believes the report that Egypt is the worst Arab state for women in 2013 is exaggerated. She believes that female genital mutilation is not as widely spread as before as more people understand that it is an ignorant and wrong tradition. Nonetheless, the report depicts the bad situation for Egyptian women, which has deteriorated after the revolution.

Envious Rivals
The army mobilized at six in the afternoon on Friday January 28, 2011. Police stations were set ablaze nationwide at around eight in the evening; there were two tanks at Juhayna roundabout at the Six of October City but none at the police stations. Samah's reasoning is that if the army wanted to secure the stations, they would have.

In Samah's opinion, the army protected its own institution in dealing with the revolution. They protected neither the *old nizam* nor the revolution. National Security, while lighting a fire to destroy their documents, let out lots of smoke that attracted *Ikhwan* to the building, followed by the army. The army did not stop *Ikhwan* from entering to see what was burning. Samah believes that the army was behind opening up the police stations for *baltegeya* and opening *Amn Eldawla* so that *Ikhwan* would break in. Samah cannot say if there is a deal or not between the army and *Ikhwan*. At Madinet Nasr police stations, the army relieved the police force, informing them that people were on the way. *Amn Eldawla* locations are highly secured sites that cannot be penetrated from the outside. Police and army officials were standing inside the building and civilians were outside. Samah questions how the civilians got inside the well-barricaded building. She is not sure who was behind the prison out-breaks.

The army and the police are not partners in security. At Imbaba, criminals attacked Christians in their homes. An army official was hitting the people while police officers were standing by. Samah heard an old woman asking the police officers why they let the soldier assault civilians and his cool reply was, "The people asked for the army so let them deal with them." For a whole week, *Amn Elmarkazi* officers were in street war with *baltegeya* at Mohamed Mahmoud Street, defending the Ministry of Interior. Once the army tanks arrived at the scene, they cleared up the street within an hour by building a thick tall wall made of cement blocks. Apparently, the army presence drew respect by the people, including *baltegeya*. When protestors moved their protest in front of the ministry of defense, the army pursued the protestors from Abbasiya all the way to Tahrir.

The difference in treatment between police officers and army officers is the root of the problem. The police are favored in treatment, benefits and prestige over the army. The army is therefore envious of the police. Samah knows this personally, as she compares her father and uncle's careers. After the revolution, the aura of the police was shattered and the police held the army accountable. On an institutional level, the police and army never were one hand and Samah does not foresee it changing in the future. However, that might happen on personal basis.

Mediocre Media

In Samah's opinion, the worst media coverage during the revolution was from the Egyptian media, which clearly delivered an incomprehensible picture. Most of the private channels reported the story in an unbiased, calm logic. On the other hand, state television broadcasts were beyond unacceptable, with alleged conspiracy theories obfuscating the truth. Generally, Samah believes that media did not play a role in the revolution, apart from explaining situations to the viewer. Samah thinks that the media failed to deliver on its capacity, as they should have presented solutions, rather than just interviews and discussions. The focus should have been more on digging into the causes of events, and presenting documentaries, rather than intense arguments between polarized views. Samah believes this did not happen due to a lack of understanding of events as they were unfolding. Then there was the fear factor, which crippled reporters, discouraging them from making analyses that they may regret later.

As long as there are no controls and checks on media, the product presented will continue in its mediocre tone. From Samah's viewpoint, she sees that anchors were subjective in their reporting, giving more airtime to views they sympathized with, and less time to the opposing views. This was reflected in the allotted time, the numbers of live telephone calls, and even the anchors' demeanor. None of the channels were presenting proper objective, professional coverage. They were acting the role of the unbiased, however, their intents were well known. The fact that a viewer could tell which side a channel supported is in itself a sign of their failure.

Alaa El Aswany wrote in 2009, "What brings about revolution is awareness of the causes of injustice, so everything that prevents people from being aware of their rights becomes an instrument in the hand of despotism."[105] *One such instrument is media, among others.* After the revolt Egypt enjoys freedom of expression, however Samah vouches that media remains directed. She believes that checks and controls are necessary. This is difficult with the minister of media already biased politically and religiously. Samah has nothing against the ministerial position but he or she needs to be independent.

When the Media City was barricaded by Islamists in March 2013, in an effort to 'cleanse the media', Samah was furious. Media cover reality. If the ruler is just, nothing the media says will sway public opinion. She found accusing the media of corruption, whilst threatening and cursing the people entering and leaving the media city, to be ludicrous.

In Samah's view, the media has an important role to play in rebuilding the trust and rapport between the people and the police. They could fulfil this role by simply not talking about and nitpicking the police's performance. It is due to the immature dealing of the police with the uprising that matters escalated exponentially. *It is important to realize media is a very powerful tool that regimes abuse like in Burma. "Not all the news they published could be relied on...Phone Maw Journal."*[106]

Samah believes January 25 started as an *Intifada* that changed its form into a revolution. It was not a coup d'etat. In her father's point of view, it was chaos, as the revolution had no leader. Her father is certain that *Jihadists* were behind much of the bloodshed on January 28 and February 2, 2011, as well as the prison breaks. Samah personally visited a prison El Marg and from her observations, she is certain that the demise was propelled from outside the prison walls.

Pretend Democracy
President Morsi's democracy was a fake democracy, because if it were real, then the president would not have been scared to address the people at Tahrir as he did at the presidential palace in December 2012. There was segregation between the activists

and the *Ikhwan* in the demonstrations. Opposing views are unable to respect one another and on the contrary, were continuously under attack and criticism. It cannot be a democracy when activists who oppose the President are targets for assaults and fatalities. The perceived unconstitutional committee and its defective constitution were the reasons behind this violence. Samah believes Egypt is facing many issues due to the flawed constitution, like the right of the army and police to vote in elections, and generally the issues relating to women's rights.

Democracy exists where the cultural and educational systems mold the human to accept, tolerate and respect an opposing view. Democracy cannot co-exist with ignorance.

The revolution is far from over and is certainly to continue for some time. So far, it has not succeeded, but has achieved some targets. It is a long bumpy road that needs high doses of patience.

Foresees a Bloodbath

In South Africa, Mandela wrote, "Despite protest and criticism, the Nationalist response was to tighten the screw of repression. A few weeks later, the government introduced the notorious Suppression of Communism Act…Essentially, the bill permitted the government to outlaw any organization and to restrict any individual opposed to its polices."[107] When activists who curse the president are convicted and imprisoned like Ahmed Douma in June 2013, it seems that the Ikhwan regime are viewing opposition similar to old regime in South Africa. It is an oxymoron as in 2015, after the overthrow of President Morsi, Ikhwan are listed as a terrorist organization in Egypt and few other countries.

If things do not change, the future is bleak and dark. Unfortunately, in Samah's view, the only path to a brighter future is a bloody path, as she believes that *Ikhwan* will not cede power otherwise. For the real size and sphere of influence of the ruling party to be apparent, many people need to take to the streets. Clashes are bound to happen, with more bloodshed. In her calculation, Islamists will never exceed a minority of fifteen million Egyptians. The opposition is not any better than the ruling party is. For Egypt to have a better future, new players need to dominate the scene, with all current players completely exiting the stage.

Samah despises *Ikhwan*, as she views them as hypocrites who are only concerned with their group's interests. Their policies are far from what Islam sets, although their campaigns clearly manipulate the vote for Islam as the selling line; dismissive of the fact that lairs are far from Muslims.

After the Second Revolution

In Samah's view, the January 25 revolution was clearly a revolt against a blatantly corrupt regime, whereas with June 30, 2013 matters are very mixed. She is certain that former President Morsi created divisions in Egyptian society, that have never existed before, and failed to improve anything in society. Although she is for the people revolting, she has her fears that Egypt may return to a police state once again, with the military back in the scene.

Media is clearly playing an instrumental role in shaping events on the ground, with CNN and Jazeera taking a clear-cut pro-*Ikhwan* position. It is too early to judge the political scene, as events and information are unfolding rapidly. Nevertheless, from the onset Egypt seems to be fighting a media battle; whether it was a people's revolution or a soft coup. The media is a big player in the political scene, when it reports what is happening. However, as it omits pieces of the story, it does not report all that is taking place, falling short in reporting the full truth. It will take a long time for media to reform, but Samah believes it will, eventually.

Samah was among many Egyptians who signed *Tamarod* calling for early presidential elections. She joined swarms of people on June 30, demanding the ousting of President Morsi, and again in July 26, 2013 delegating the army to tackle terrorism. However, Samah was saddened at the bloody way in which the police dispersed the Islamist vigils. Samah has no idea what the future holds, but she is certain that Egypt is back to ground zero, if not worse.

"In every drama there has to be an antagonist and a protagonist, and if the antagonist is not there the press will find and build one."[108] *Samah agrees with this statement by Martin Luther King. Media viewers need to be wary of this.*

PART IV

The Others

"Nobody can go back and start a new beginning,
But anyone can start today and make a new ending."
Maria Robinson

CHAPTER 17

Raving Rhetoric

"All this - all that 'great critique' to use the language of the Chinese revolutionaries, and it is essentially negative — helped to convey a new vision, a vision of politics that was trying to wrench itself" Alain Badiou[109]

Among the several meetings I had, I met with Nadia Abou El Magd, a journalist whom I asked to get me in contact with a former member of the former ruling National Democratic Party. I needed someone who would be willing to talk about the revolution. She recommended Gehad Auda, who has written several books. Dr. Auda was very welcoming, and we met for the first time at one of his favorite locations, the Diwan bookstore in Zamalek on March 17, 2012.

Multiple Hats

He is a tall well-built man with a rounded waistline, clean-shaven with a distinctive deep, husky voice, with some white hair, and he wears eyeglasses. Professor Gehad Auda was born on May 17, 1954 in Giza. His father, Abdel Malek Auda, was a professor of political science at Cairo University. His mother was an Arabic language teacher for high school students. Like many sons, Gehad wanted to follow the footsteps of his father, and studied Political Science at Cairo University, earning a Bachelor's degree in 1975. What drew Gehad to this field was philosophy and law, in addition to his political activism while he was a student. Gehad embarked onto the field of politics when he joined the *elShabab*, a state youth organization during the Nasser era.

Due to his father's career, Gehad lived in the United States intermittently for most of the 70's and '80's. Gehad accepted two scholarships in American Studies in '79 and comparative politics in '80. In 1983, a committee selected him to be amongst the top twenty of the brightest students in political science from all over the country.

After completing the scholarships, Gehad returned to Egypt in 1984, during which time he re-joined the Center for Strategic Studies at Al Ahram Institution, from which he had been on study leave since 1979. One day he noticed an opening for a full time professor and he enthusiastically applied. After a lengthy assessment by The Permanent Committee of Political Science, in 1996, Gehad embarked on his academic career. He became a Professor at Helwan University, located South of Cairo, and was the head of the department, and deputy dean for some time. Late in 2013, Gehad was appointed as head of faculty of political science at Beni Suef University.

For the past eighteen years of his academic career, Gehad specialized in foreign and defense policies, and continued his academic interests in Israeli politics, Islamic studies and Islamic groups, as well as strategic perspectives. The latter is the ability to estimate national risks, threats and opportunities during crisis.

Failure of Education

Gehad describes the educational system in Egypt as a 'total failure,' as there is no system. When the system is absent, reform can never be the solution. The seeds had been sown since the days of Gamal Abdel Nasser. It is very difficult to change an old-fashioned mentality. Moreover, in Egypt there are two separate and peculiar ministries; the ministry of higher education and the ministry of education. From Gehad's vantage point, he believes each ministry is working independently, resulting in two disconnected educational systems. In other countries, one ministry handles all aspects of education, delivering a sound, comprehensive curriculum that builds student knowledge. He believes that planning is the issue, not budgeting.

Curriculum does not change in Egypt, but is added upon year after year, leaving students overwhelmed with a heavy curriculum that leaves feeble room for knowledge and understanding. Due to the continuous additions, the curriculum has become inconsistent and deformed. The system is unidentifiable, though it seems familiar. Any good student is not the product of the education system, but rather, the product of independent efforts or chance.

Any educational system is established to prepare its students for life in general, and specifically for the job market upon graduation. The Egyptian system fails to prepare the student for both life and work. The educational system is disconnected from the market, failing to envision the future market needs. The market needs segmentation and needs must be clearly defined. Colleges built were based on mass education requirements, stemming from social pressures rather than market needs. The disconnection between the market and education is irrational, and cannot be sustainable.

When it comes to the educational system, one must not talk about a priority, which assumes there is a skeletal structure in place. In the case of Egypt there is no skeleton, and the system needs to be established. The solution is not in defining what domain is more important than the other. The whole system is extinct, and urgently needs redrawing. Like an old building with weak foundations and leaking roofs, it needs to be completely demolished and built from scratch.

The Ruling Party

Besides his academic career, Gehad embarked on a political career with the ruling party in 1994, in the era of President Mubarak. Gehad co-opted into establishing a political training program and system for the party members in Cairo. The objective of the program was to link the members to reality, thereby improving their performance, starting at the bottom of the pyramid and slowly working upwards. Due to the bureaucracy of the National Democratic Party (NDP), this initiative was defeated and discontinued sometime in 2000. The project created a big problem, as the rationale of the program membership was perceived to be in contradiction with the party's feudalistic policy. Gehad ended up with a promotion within the party, to the central level, and hence he was no longer responsible for this project, as it became beneath his jurisdiction. In other words, the party diplomatically brushed him aside, but he could not complain as it was in the form of a promotion. However, his new job was void, rendering him incapable of effecting change and innovation.

After his discontinued project, Gehad had arrived to the conclusion that bottom up reform is idealistic and unrealistic as it is theoretical and impractical. When one reforms a structure, there must be a starting point. The starting point is either from the lower or upper half of the echelon. After this experience, feeling a bit let down, Gehad left the party for a while, to focus on his academic career.

In 2002, the new era was born wherein it was rumored that the former president's son, Gamal, was being groomed for the presidency. The new era encompassed the new thought that set the stage for Gamal Mubarak to embark on an ambitious political career, with many expecting him to be the future president after his father ends his term and retires.

Gehad re-joined the political committee in the NDP in 2004, after his hiatus, summoned for his diverse experience. The committee Gehad joined was called 'Egypt and the World', which covered diplomatic and strategic ties between Egypt and other countries. It was considered 'la crème,' but not as significantly powerful as the economic committee. It was a prestigious position but not very effective.

Advocating Liberalism

By 2006, Gehad was evolving into a nonconformist voice within the party, and soon after, the party sidelined him once again. However, this time he remained a member of the party, until the revolution transpired. Gehad is a man who cannot understand emotions, let alone describe them. Hence, he is unable to express feelings about the party. Many Egyptians talk about the party in an idealistic way, as if it were independent of the ruling system. He argues, however, that it is clearly a function of the political system, making it a dependent variable. Is it possible that if a country changes its political system, then automatically the parties would also change?

For the last five years before the revolution, Gehad was actively voicing the need for liberalism. During this period, Gehad became a dissident, as he was calling for liberalism and not democracy within the system. When he wrote a book about liberal beliefs, it rocked the boat and possibly was among the reasons he became unpopular. Unfortunately, the Egyptian political mindset viewed liberalism as the enemy of nationalism and hence, somehow, treasonous. This way of thinking about liberalism has been instilled into Egypt's socialist political system since the days of the late President Nasser.

In Gehad's view, the Egyptian revolution was calling for liberal democracy with a civic state as its basic building block. Liberalism focuses on individual rights, whereas democracy is an organizational order that allows government rotation among different parties in line with a time framework and rules, defined in a constitution. A nation can be democratic but lack liberalism, for instance. That is the case with Israel. Liberalism is an ideology different from democracy, mainly concerned with individualism, enterprises and the free market. Israel has a strong democratic culture but is feeble on the liberal end. In the past, when West Germany existed, the political system was based on social democracy, but not really on a liberal ethos.

Gehad believes that Egypt's greatest pitfall is that it does not recall history critically and hence, lacks intellect and critical thinking, which perfectly fits in with the authoritarian style of thinking and culture. *This Orwellian mindset was referred to as 'Newspeak' in 1984 about which Syme said, "Don't you see that the whole aim of Newspeak is to narrow the range of thought?"*[10]Egyptians, certainly have narrow and short ranges of thought. Whether brought upon by themselves or by the political system is another matter.

Gehad has extensively studied Islamic groups, becoming an expert on the subject and even publishing works on them. Egyptian authorities have been internally fighting a war with the Islamic groups. This war lasted around two decades. Egyptians are living in a hallucinatory memory where they recall twenty years of corruption. Gehad challenges that skewed memory by asking, "Where is it?" With the lack of critical thinking, the Egyptian tends to forget history and is actually selective on what he or she prefers to recall, leaving Egypt worse off, all doomed to a state of non-learning. This is why Egypt is making the same mistakes as it did in the past. As had become apparent after the Nasser era, the welfare state was inefficient. Mubarak ushered in an open door policy, that moved away from the welfare core. Yet in 2011, the revolution called for the reinstatement of the welfare state with the continuous demand of 'bread, social equality and dignity'. Egyptians are not trying to understand critically what is happening but rather are gagging and silencing the understanding much like Orwell's 'Newspeak'.

The National Democratic Party (NDP) was supporting democracy theoretically, but practically it reeked of feudalism, clearly not advocating a liberal political economy. Like an octopus, the NDP had several arms. There were *Salafists,* although their original teachings were to abstain from politics. They were born at the hands of the NDP and *Amn Eldawla* (State Security). They are not a new group, but most people recently became aware of their existence. There was a tug of war between two arms of the party; the conservative religious and nationalists one on one hand, and the few liberals on the other hand. The *Salafi* and *Ikhwan* wings are strong and well rooted in the rural governorates. There were several wings: a modernist faction, a pro Nasser faction, a state bureaucracy and liberals, the latter being the smallest wing. The liberals within the party were themselves divided, the larger portion promoting economic liberalism in line with World Bank standards and a smaller segment, to whom Gehad belonged, who believed political liberalism to be a socioeconomic corrective mechanism. The difference is that the bigger liberal faction wanted to liberalize the economy first, but Gehad aimed at liberalizing authority first. The party, regardless of the various segments, was against any corrective mechanisms; this political stand was reflected publicly in the belief amongst the people that the party was corrupt. This public image was imprinted and nothing could ever erase it; as the popular saying goes, first impressions are difficult to change. Under Mubarak, *Amn Eldawla* imprisoned but did not torture *Ikhwan.* Gehad pointed out that they have had seats at the parliament since 1984. What the media and the party reported –usually loaded with political rhetoric- and what the reality of politics was, are two altogether different matters.

Reform and Corruption Inseparable

Scientifically, there is no reform without corruption. Gehad cites historical proof, with the *Meiji* restoration in Japan 1868 to 1915, which gave birth to the modern Japanese state. Another such example was during the New Deal from 1933 to 1936 in the United States under President Franklin D. Roosevelt, after the Great Depression, where government focused on the 3R's: Relief, Recovery and Reform. The third example is that of the British civil war. After the execution of King Charles I, Oliver

Cromwell established the Commonwealth in 1648, which required reform. All these countries brought about reform while corruption existed.

Gehad asserts that there can be neither political nor economic reform, without political or economic corruption. The question that needs addressing, is how to bring about reform while reducing corruption. That is why Gehad thought authority should be liberalized first, as it would minimize corruption and pave way for a state of law and justice. Liberalizing the economy first would lead to a volcanic eruption, like January 25, 2011. Corruption needs to exist in order to achieve reforms; however, the trick is to find the right formula for the co-existence of the two. They are twin integral dynamics, meaning they need integration and mutual inclusivity. However, they were mutually exclusive. Reform by definition is reformulating an existing community, which requires shaking of rules, and it is during this time of instability that people jump at the opportunity to take advantage of the situation, paving the road for corruption. Gehad advocates for reform that starves corruption ideally rather than feeds it.

The issue that faced the old *nizam* was its separation of the two roads, reform and corruption, whereby they ceased to operate as a twin integral dynamic. Those two roads sometimes ran parallel and at other times, they overlapped, creating clashes, which the newspapers jumped at. With this setup, progress and accountability were not apparent. Reform was underway, based on scientific methods that should have brought about apparent change. On the other hand, the capitalists were not very bright, as they were not able to surf the wave of reform. Instead, they were drowned by the wave of corruption. Autocratic rule was beneficial in some ways as the different parties were immersed in their own issues, leaving the bigger, pressing issues to the ruling elite. Gehad believes that the origin of the revolution was the lack of compounding effect within the reform, and its necessary companion, corruption. Reform was neither correcting nor eliminating corruption under Mubarak's regime, but rather encouraging it.

Deep State

The Mubarak regime came to be termed 'the deep state' as a reflection of the vast security state, a state within a state. The reform plan served the interests of authoritarianism that was deeply rooted in the deep state. The giant national security and the bureaucratic apparatus permitted the coexistence of reform, and corruption without a compound effect, as that would have threatened the powers of the security state. There are two goals in the political realm. The security apparatus had no problems as long as there were two separate blocks in constant conflict, that helped maintain the status quo of the *ancien regime*. However, if the two waves were compounded it would mean the beginning of a new regime, and a different balance of power, independent of the Egyptian deep state. The new regime would be capable of checking and correcting itself.

According to Dr. Gehad, the security apparatus plays a fundamental role in preserving the public order. However, in Egypt their role is beyond this, as they played a fundamental role in securing the autocratic rule. A new regime would have changed the role of security from controlling the public order, to its basic function of preserving public order. In reality, who would give up his power? *As Martin Luther King rightly wrote, "Lamentably, it is an historic fact that privileged groups seldom give up their privileges voluntarily."*[111] *The deep state is not ready to give up its grip on Egypt. The ever-arching question is, will it ever be ready? Is it in the interest of Egypt that it gives up its grip?*

In Egypt, the security and national monitoring system is elaborate, consisting of twelve organizations, which is one of the reasons that Egypt is commonly described as 'deep state'. The security environment failed to stabilize order with these two dynamics of reform and corruption playing separately. Putting it differently, the antithesis of reform is corruption. The theory assumes, for synthesis to take place, the two dynamics should blend, producing a new child, and a new regime would be born. *Gehad heartily laughed at his child simile.* However, the synthesis never came about, guaranteeing the continuation of the deep security state. In his view, the revolution came about due to the inability of the security apparatus to maintain the proper balance between corruption and reform. In addition to this, there was the grave miscalculation of members of the governing elite, like Ahmed Ezz, a steel tycoon and former senior member of the National Democratic Party, NDP. Ezz was sentenced to 7 years in prison after the revolution, convicted of money laundering. Gehad believes no revolution happens without the strategic elite's serious miscalculation. *This lack of synthesis brought about leaks in the house, which represents the deep state, "There is a Burmese saying to the effect that if the roof is not sound the whole house becomes vulnerable to leaks."*[112]

Faltering Bygones
During his work with *Hezb Alwatani*, NDP, Gehad was countering the *Salafi* wing, armed with his secular voice. One of his main roles was to integrate Christians into the political arena. Due to the obnoxious hatred towards Christians, the percentage of Christians in the party was almost non-existent. Gehad believes that Egypt suffers from genuine problems between Muslims and Christians that started in 1952. After the 1952 revolution, which overthrew the monarchy, the problem became dormant or as the saying goes 'let bygones be bygones'. There was a very strange agreement and love affair between the Church and Nasser. Although Nasser confiscated land from property owners to give to farmers and many property owners were Christians, the Christians, strangely, genuinely love Gamal Abdel Nasser.

Digging deeper, one can understand this seemingly strange, sadistic love. The Egyptian Jewish minority used to be concentrated in the areas of Azbakia, El Daher, Abbasiyah and certain districts of Alexandria. In the nineteenth century, Christians were treated as third class citizens after the Jews, Greeks and Armenians. However, after Abdel Nasser extradited the Jews from Egypt in 1956, Christians automatically moved up to second class and hence their unfaltering support for President Abdel Nasser came about, despite his unpopular land reform. This religious strife was reborn after Israel defeated Egypt in 1967, leaving Egyptians devastated. They sought something to fall back on in order to reassert solidarity, maintain faith and hope. During this difficult period, most Egyptians sought refuge in their religion and therefore Muslims and Christians sealed their religious divisions.

Weak Political Party

The political party is not equivalent to the government. *Hezb Alwatani* (NDP) was designed as a tool for the government. Despite popular perception, the party was weak. The executive wing in Egypt controls and governs the affairs of the country, whereas the NDP has always been merely the appendix. This appendix was called upon when the government needed popular mobilization to demonstrate support and fulfill its policy. The constitution is crystal clear, where the political party has limited power versus the government; they are not on equal footing. The relationship between the executive power and political parties depends on the design of the constitution. In Egypt, the political party has a secondary role in the political theatre. This design was inherited from Gamal Abdel Nasser and will be similar in any authoritarian regime, where the privacy and superiority of the executive, over the political party, is cherished and maintained at all costs. This design is not based on whether the country is a republic or a monarchy or whether it is a presidential or parliamentary system. It is an original part of the political culture.

The power structure in Egypt is hierarchal with the president and the executive authority on top of the pyramid, followed by the legislative and judicial bodies at the same level then the political party and finally the civil society. The president is the head of the state, who appoints his ministers. The governorates are under the domain of the executive power. During his work with the party, Gehad worked on the constitutional committee, which gave the judiciary some form of independence. However, it made the president the head of the judicial body. *Gehad broke into hysterical laughter as* placing the president at the head of the judicial committee automatically wiped out its independence, and it turned into a democratic masquerade. To seal the package, the *ancien regime* gave the head of the Appeal Court and the Constitutional Court the power to contradict each other, and the president appointed both members. Selection criteria was based on seniority, not on merit or experience.

Noticeably, most positions in the country were appointed, and those elected ran through rigged elections. Gehad recalls one time when some members of parliament wanted to argue with the president over the issue of the election of leaders. Former President Mubarak laughingly said, "Don't say that, you are appointed." Gehad critically said, "False conscience actually made them believe they were elected, forgetting that they were just appointed." Formally, members of parliament were elected, but in reality they are selected to run, therefore, the elections are essentially fixed, another masquerade.

Ugly Duckling

During his days in the National Democratic Party, Gehad became frustrated with his inability to influence the public. Misgivings always clouded the statements of the political party. Small segments of the party were preaching democracy, secularism and liberalism, which were impossible under the current authoritarian policy. Gehad never was a member of parliament. Generally, he felt he was a disowned child, the ugly duckling of the party while it was officially in power, and even afterwards.

On several occasions, Gehad was nominated for senior positions within the university and the National Democratic Party (NDP) but never once did he obtain the position. Despite his lack of popularity within the NDP, Gehad seemed relatively known to the public, as on many occasions people on the street would point at Gehad, recognizing him as a National Democratic Party member.

Gehad had direct contact with Gamal Mubarak, and judged him as a regular man from a few encounters they had at the party. He even wrote a book about Gamal, and his likely role as an emerging civilian leader. Gehad noticed that Gamal listened and talked sparingly. Gehad dared to think that Gamal might function and work as a vehicle for restoring a civil secular state after autocratic Mubarak.

Internal War

Former President Hosni Mubarak is at another level completely from his son, when it comes to a question of personality. Mubarak was a very powerful man. Gehad deeply respects the former President or *rayees*, and is undisturbed by how the media tarnished the former *rayees'* reputation; his respect is unflinching. One cannot imagine the incredible feat of leading a security state. Gehad talks about history objectively looking at the state of the country at the time when Mubarak became president. It was after former President Anwar El Sadat's army officers assassinated him in 1981 under the instructions of Islamic groups. Mubarak himself managed to avoid the bullets during Sadat's assassination. Not only was this high treason, it also indicated the daunting disarray within the army ranks that identified the nation's president as the enemy of the state! Three or four days after the assassination there was an attempt at a *coup d'état* in Assiut. At such a critical crossroads as Egypt was facing, the transfer of power to the Vice President Mubarak was crucial for the stability of the country. The Islamic Groups had a wide network spanning from Assiut, deep in the South of Egypt all the way to Alexandria, in Northern Egypt. These groups believed violence was a legitimate path to achieving their objectives.

President Mubarak was faced with a situation soaked in distrust; he could not leave any stone unturned. As mentioned earlier, it took twenty years of an internal war with these Islamic groups, until this state extinguished the movement. This explains the Islamic groups' deep animosity towards former President Hosni Mubarak, which was essentially due to this long lasting feud with them. *Ikhwan* and the *Gamat Islamiya* epistemologically were branches of the same tree, but with different practices and approaches. *Ikhwan* are cleverer, and sly.

Nonetheless, this was not the reason behind the emergency law, which was in place due to the internal war. The *Gamat Islamiya* wanted to kill former President Mubarak and change the regime into Islamic one. *Al Qaeda* partially funded Islamic terrorism in Egypt and shared a common outlook with them, but not necessarily a common thinking; they were from the same tree but different branches. The 2011 revolution-cum-coup has ushered in their long enduring dream of Islamist rule. *Will Egyptians with the running of time, rediscover and reawaken civil conscious and continue a civil revolt all over Egypt? Alternatively, is civilian rule simply not destined for Egyptians?*

Former President Mubarak managed to maintain the internal coherence of the Egyptian security state while a major threat to national security lied within its borders from Israel, Libya, Sudan and Hamas. One should not judge the man based on his wife and his son, but on his own deeds. Gehad does not understand what is meant when people talk of Mubarak being corrupt. He asks, what do people expect? Any security state is by definition corrupt, as they rule with financial incentives and suppression. There goes a popular saying, *"seif al moaz wa zhahaby"* which means the choice is between the sword that is capable of killing and the gold, it is up to the individual to decide. If he chooses the gold, then he needs to accept the regime's rule. The former president has fat bank accounts in his name, but Gehad is certain he does not have control over them. This was the case with Presidents Gamal Abdel Nasser and Hosni Mubarak. In Gehad's opinion, prosecution cannot bring any legal case against either of them due to overseas accounts.

Egypt was in a state of constant fight against an enemy, whether real or imagined. This concept referred to in an Orwellian theory about authoritarian regimes manipulating the war against the enemy as a justification for their autocracy. *George Orwell portrayed in 1984 with the broadcast vilification of Emmanuel Golstein as the enemy of the people as "he was the primal traitor... he was advocating freedom of speech, freedom of press, the freedom of assembly, freedom of thought, he was crying hysterically that the revolution had been betrayed.*"[113] *This resonates distressingly with the opposition's accusations against Ikhwan in Egypt after taking power. Yet again, it echoes with Ikhwan's accusations against the supporters of the military after the ouster of President Morsi.*

The Raving Fallacy
Gehad was in between the regime and the state, shouldering interests for both. He does not consider himself part of the *ancien regime*. Gehad challenges the public opinion about the grooming of Gamal to be the President by simply saying, "Plan! Show me where the plan is!" Gehad believes that President Mubarak would have run for president for his fifth term, not his son, if the revolution had not taken place.

If President Mubarak wanted Gamal appointed to any key position, he would have done so. To be qualified for the position of the presidency in Egyptian political culture one should rise through the executive branch. Gehad believes if Mubarak wanted Gamal on his side he would have appointed him within the executive power, for instance, as minister of youth. In reality, this never happened. Mubarak did not want his son to run for presidency, contrary to popular opinion. Gehad recalls that when people questioned former President Mubarak about this theory, he clearly stated that he did not want his son to die.

The golden road to the presidency is not through being a member of a political party that stands on the lower base of the pyramid, lacking power. How could Gamal have jumped from National Democratic Party member to president? The stairway has many levels prior to the tip, the president. According to Gehad, the theory that Mubarak wanted his son to take over the presidency, is complete humbug fantasy. There was a segment of the ruling party, which advocated the continuation of Gamal's policies and his role. Gamal was involved in the economic and social sectors of the country and far less in real politics. The raving inheritance theory, Gehad believes, was dispersed into the public as a high-level political game, which he refrained from explaining about at the time. However, a few months later he elaborated that this theory was an essential base in building a distorted image of the regime, basically promoted by the army and in turn it served the opponents of the regime. It paved the road to vilifying the regime, preparing for a revolutionary atmosphere wherein the army guaranteed the security, and state remained unaccountable, unlike what Gamal intended.

Revolution Phases
Opposition to the *ancien regime* was clear since 2004. In 2008, the protests at Mahala were the first serious signal of the imminent revolution and constituted its first phase. Between the two rounds of the parliamentary elections in late 2010, Gehad predicted

Egypt was entering a coup d'état phase. At the run-off, Gehad wrote in the Dostour newspaper, announcing the end of the experimental restrictive democracy and the demise of the *Hezb Elwatany* (NDP). While Gehad was far sighted and saw the party dig its own grave, the National Democratic Party announced its victory, and were basking in the limelight of their parliamentary sweep. Gehad predicted a coup, "It was obvious a coup was going to happen; it was being written on the wall." Little did the members understand that it was going to be the last election their party will enter for a while.

When the Tunisian revolution transpired, Gehad told his colleagues at the party that it was a revolution based on social mobilization. He predicted that Egypt was susceptible to a similar civil revolution. The revolution came about because of mistakes by the strategic elite. How did events start on January 25? It was a demonstration that took place in agreement between *Dakhleyah* and the April 6 Movement, where they were supposed to protest, and return to their homes at the end of the day.

The protesters were mainly classy bourgeoisie—high and upper middle class- pleasantly scented, walking in a great civil demonstration. Around 4pm that afternoon, a door of opportunity opened. Other groups saw the golden chance to jump over this unprecedented demonstration. *Ikhwan* wanted to play a role; their youth joined that afternoon although officially they were asked not to demonstrate. Another group that infiltrated the crowds was Leon Trotsky supporters, communists - he was a leading figure of the Russian Revolution in 1917 who advocated the concept of a permanent revolution such that the state is continuously radicalized and the world revolution pursued. Among the various players on the field were anarchists, who believed the state should end. Destroying all institutes was their prime aim. *There was a melting pot of different ideologies attracted by the promise of Tahrir, freedom.*

A new phase of the revolution had commenced as *Amn Eldawla*, and the police drenched the protestors with water hoses and muffled them by volleys of tear gas. In the evening of January 27, 2011, new waves of protestors swept the streets, many from the middle class – middle strata of the middle class and the lower middle class- joined forces. The protest base was widening. Gehad views the violation of public property on January 28, as an act of betrayal towards the state. It was treason. *Hezb Elwatani* headquarters and the police stations all across the country were set ablaze, while massive numbers of prisoners escaped. These acts of treason occurred with the increasing incoherence and ineffectiveness of the police force, which unceremoniously departed the scene. By nightfall, the military mobilized on the main streets, and the former President Mubarak addressed the Egyptians for the first time since the crisis unfolded. The tone of delivery was somehow relaxed, which provoked the protestors. Matters could have ended swiftly had he addressed the initial non-radical, demands of the people.

The third wave of the revolution demonstrated the lack of intelligence and subsequent failed rhetoric on the part of the NDP members, with the pivotal, bloody confrontation on February 2. The objective of this attack was to turn the scene from a revolutionary one, as by that time this was in full swing, to a revolt, and hence losing credibility. However, this operation failed dramatically and backfired, positioning the revolutionaries under the spotlight as victims, attracting compassion. This third wave sparked aggressive revolutionary demands, an unwavering outcry to overthrow the president. A national cry was launched, a new government led by Ahmed Shafik formed a National Committee to investigate the second and third of February, behind the scene and the scene itself. Ibrahim Kamel, among other NDP leading capitalist members, was accused of financing the attack. Ahmed Ezz was not behind it. However, all the accused were exonerated. Two years later, new evidence is slowly emerging, indicating that *Ikhwan* might have been the main player behind what happened on February 2 and 3, 2011. Originally, Gehad thought NDP were behind the attacks but later changed his opinion based on testimony of two NDP members, that *Ikhwan* orchestrated the attacks the evening of February 2 while NDP drove the assault the morning of the same day.

Observing

The first five days of the revolution, Gehad stayed at home, like many Egyptians. Gehad was at his Agouza home with his son Marwan, a university student watching television. At the time, his wife, Moshira, was delivering her thesis for the doctorate program and his daughter, Mariam, a graduate student, was in Holland. Occasionally Gehad conducted telephone interviews to comment on the fluid political situation. Unlike his father, Marwan was politically passive, but participated in the civilian checkpoints, excited and proud that he was playing a role.

BBC television station summoned Gehad twice for interviews at nighttime at Agouza. It was not easy, due to the enforced curfew, as the car required a permit to move after the curfew. Agouza is a quiet residential area located in Giza, on the western banks of the Nile River. Most neighbors know each other and therefore, the community did not witness any violence during the eighteen days. The streets were quite deserted, and almost every five minutes, the car was stopped at a civilian checkpoint before passing. Normally it would have taken a couple of minutes by car, but with the checkpoints and the interrogation, it took around twenty minutes to arrive at the BBC Station.

A young civilian said, "Who are you? Where are you coming from? Where are you going?"

Gehad said, "I am Professor Gehad Auda of Helwan University on my way to BBC station for a televised interview," while showing him his personal ID.

Another man checked the boot and gave a nod allowing the car to pass.

Amsterdam Trip

Gehad had booked a flight for January 30, 2011 before the revolution took place, to accompany his wife and daughter in Holland. Gehad stuck to the plan, and left to Holland. The airport was packed with many foreigners fleeing to their native countries, and Egyptians seeking asylum in other countries. Even though Gehad felt satisfied that his prophesy had materialized, he was saddened to see the exodus of expatriates and compatriots. The timing of the flight changed with all the turmoil at the airport, as many passengers were requesting to travel without any booking. The ticket was originally a direct flight from Cairo to Amsterdam, which the airline cancelled. Gehad managed to find a seat on a flight from Cairo to Hamburg, and a train from Hamburg to Amsterdam.

The worst part of this commotion was that Gehad was unable to contact his wife to inform her of the changes in his flight, as mobiles were not operating. Gehad tried to anticipate what his wife would do and vice versa. Gehad does not know Dutch and by mistake, he disembarked in an earlier train station. When Gehad disembarked he did not find himself at Amsterdam, as there are many stations names that start with Amsterdam but are at different areas, clearly confusing him. He managed to get in touch with his daughter, when he bought a cellular line at Hamburg, as his Egyptian phone network did not have roaming. She informed him at which station to disembark. Foreign language aside, the emotional pressure he felt with the turmoil at the airport and in Egypt had kicked in. *For a man who does not relate well with emotions, you can imagine his state.*

Gehad had to figure out once more, which train he should take. This second time, he did not pay for the ticket. The scheduled arrival time of the train was 10:30 am at Amsterdam, where his wife was patiently waiting. But Gehad did not arrive. His wife was at a loss, thinking 'Why did Gehad not arrive? Where could he be?' Gehad finally arrived at the train station at 11:30 am, and was eager to find his wife. Gehad figured his wife, Moshira, might have asked the information desk at the station and hence went there and surely, he found his wife standing there in tears. Gehad embraced his wife and explained his little adventure on the earlier stop. She was amazed that Gehad was actually in front of her. Her imagination had run wild, with all the uncertainty the revolution brought. Moshira was at a complete loss during that hour of waiting; she did not know what to do, or how to explain to her children that their father was missing. She was relieved to see him and hold him.

While in Amsterdam, Gehad, burdened by the events back in Egypt, checked the news whenever he could. He sensed the end was imminent. It was coincidence that his planned return flight to Cairo was on February 11. Actually, on the airplane, all the passengers were informed about the vice president's announcement. Gehad looked around at the passengers and could see the men and women having difficulty in believing. It was a state of shock. The Egyptians were wary of each other, as they were not sure if the passengers were happy or sad. The mood, suspended in midair just like the airplane, with everone waiting to read the reactions of Egyptians upon landing. Two hours after the announcement, the flight arrived, at eight in the evening. Gehad called one of his friends to get an update, and he confirmed the breaking news. The three-decade long reign of President Mubarak was over and a long chapter in Egypt's history was finished. Gehad was certainly worried, expecting social turmoil and ensuing chaos.

The curfew was still in effect and Gehad's flight arrived after the curfew so he needed to return to his home while avoiding the checkpoints on the main roads. Gehad briefed a taxi driver to drive through the side roads. The driver was very effective, as they did not meet any marches or crowds, although, the main streets were packed with Egyptians celebrating the end of the Mubarak's era. Gehad asked him what fare he would want, and he gave him the amount gladly as he arrived home.

Returning the Treasure
After the third and final speech of Mubarak, things appeared to be over. The game was over. The former President handed the trophy to the army who honored him in the first place. This move did not invalidate the revolution's reality. It was not a radical young officer's military coup but rather, a handing over of power, or, a returning of power to its source. Gehad compares it to someone who, entrusted with a treasure and if he needs to leave it, he will return the treasure to whoever entrusted him with it in the first place. In his opinion, it only made sense that Mubarak returned the Egyptian treasure to the army.

Nonetheless, not all things are mutually exclusive; labeling it as either a revolution or a *coup d'etat* are not the only options. Matters are not unitary; either black or white, there is grey as well. This was the predicament. Gehad had predicted that Mubarak would hand over his reigns to the army institution, and his prophesy had materialized. Gehad supports a civilian revolution. The Egyptian revolution, in his view, was neither a political nor a social revolution. The main objectives were to increase personal freedom and equal rights, which define a civic revolution in general. Gehad has been advocating these rights with his support of liberalism while he was working at the NDP, but with no avail.

Multiple things happened simultaneously in Egypt in 2011. A civil revolution-cum-coup took place; it was a special type of coup, not a radical or Latin American type coup, In addition to widespread social disturbance in the form of demonstrations and strikes demanding better pay, there was, not in the least, the powerful silent majority. All these variables were in motion, at some times intersecting and other times not.

Constitutional Blunder

Gehad's support of the revolution wavered until March 2011, with the constitutional referendum that swelled the wave for the religious tide. For starters, the committee that proposed the changes in the constitution, mostly consisting of members affiliated with *Ikhwan*, were not legal experts, with the exception of maybe two. From that moment, Gehad visualized the concept of counter-revolution; those who wanted the old system upheld. The civic revolution was overthrown at this stage, ephemerally lasting around 6 weeks, like an untimely plucked rose that has withered away rapidly. It was no longer a civil revolution, but took another rhetorical façade, namely a 'religious' one. Gehad believes the stereotype bandied around, that the main concerns of *Ikhwan* were centered around the confining of the role of women to the home, limiting their political role. *However, many Ikhwan women work.* Unlike common *Ikhwan* rhetoric, he believes they want women to resume the role of subservience as second-class citizens. Take for instance, the fact that no woman can be an *Imam Kobra* (senior clerk status); she can, however, be *Imam Soughra*, a junior clerk status, but needs male supervision. The *Salafists* are concerned with growing beards for police officers and installing general system for monitoring the behavior of the people according to the *Salafi* preaching. In Gehad's view, the authoritarian system in Egypt is not going to change and is steadfast. There will be no checks and balances on the Egyptian political scene. Gehad believes the first step should have been the constitution, followed by elections. Therefore, he voted no in the referendum, along with almost 23% of voters.

During the revolution, the former NDP building was torched; the party dismantled and was replaced by nine different political parties. Many members dispersed their forces and joined existing parties like *Ikhwan* and *Wafd*, but none of them invited Gehad to join them. He was still the ugly duckling after the party dismantled.

For a country to have a sound system of checks and balances, a fundamental assumption is that there are existing, qualified political forces, on an almost equal footing. Since Egypt does not have two qualified political forces, which would carry out the checks and balances? Unfortunately, this system is not in place in the parliament. On the one hand, the government is not checking and balancing affairs with the parliament. On the other hand, the legal system and courts each play an independent role. For such a system to exist, certain constitutional frames and constitutional rules are required. As for the new 2013 constitution, it has the base to develop coherent political policy, ensuring women an equal footing to men.

The new Islamist constitution post-revolution confirmed the original position, however Gehad doubted that it would see the light of day, with an expected court ruling on the legitimacy of the constitutional assembly that was scheduled for a hearing on December 2, 2012 at the Supreme Constitutional Court. *However, despite its flaws, the Islamist-led constitution passed on December 2012 amidst legal issues, violence and bloodshed. The court was never able to adjourn due to the Islamist stand off for weeks in December 2012.*

The government most often appoints the people who write the constitution. The selections are qualitatively different from the governmental appointments to parliament, as they come from a different pool, credentials and imperatives. According to the temporary constitutional declaration issued by the Supreme Council of Armed Forces, SCAF, it states that the election of members who write the constitution needs to take place. Heedless, the predominately *Ikhwan* parliament in 2011 interpreted the article to fit its liking, and selected the members. Some may deduce that the parliament, or the dominating Islamist parties, wrote the constitution, as they selected the members.

The hierarchical power structure design changed with the 2012 Islamist constitution, wherein the executive branch of government maintained its primacy, the legislative was given more weight, and the judiciary stayed as is. In other words, the leveling increased.

The 2013 constitutional committee is attempting to cleanse the articles from the *Ikhwanisation,* to establish some form of modern state that may eventually usher in civilian rule. For the army it is important to establish Egypt as a modern state, not liberal and not civilian. At best, conditioned civilian rule may preside. As Egypt is not yet a civil society, the definition of its citizens will continue to be vague, complicated by restrictions imposed by the references to *Sharia.*

Deceiving Appearances

The manner in which the presidential elections took place has left the revolutionary atmosphere opaque, untouched and hence, instability persists. Added to this is President Morsi's style of running the country, and the opposition's response. Uncertainty has become the norm, making it difficult to understand the unfolding events, hence leaving the future unpredictable. For instance, it is not clear why President Morsi issued the highly controversial constitutional declaration in November 2012. In early 2013, Egypt was in chaos but not anarchy, with a functioning state and government, though showing increasing weakness. This is a phase of internal war. Once the situation reaches that of a totally failed state, a civil war will unfold, and hence Egypt will be in anarchy. Will Egypt reach civil war?

Political propaganda is one thing, and the political reality is another, with political rhetoric in between. Propaganda and rhetoric are means to obscure the reality at any given time, let alone at times of turmoil. In any revolution, there is a difference between the transformed picture, which brought about revolution, and the reality. *Machiavelli touched on this in Prince when he wrote, "Everyone sees what you appear to be, few experience what you really are."*[114]

Things are mysterious and hidden, awaiting revelation. What appears to be real is not actually the reality. The transformed picture usually sticks to the reputation. Gehad has lived in France and has studied the French revolution. Several times the French have discovered new facts about the first revolution, which contradicted the previously established discourse. Egyptians misunderstand the process of writing history. They do not distinguish between history and historic writing. History is a continuous process with several versions and as time progresses, more information is discovered and hence, history is perpetually re-written. Until today, there are valid questions about the role of *Ikhwan* during 1952 revolution that Abdel Nasser spearheaded. When all the dust has settled, historians formulate a proper perspective and reading.

You cannot write history while it is still fluid and revolutionary. If history is happening now how can you know the real role of *Ikhwan*? How did *Ikhwan* leaders like Mohamed Morsi, elected president of Egypt, and Essam El Erian, escape from prison directly to Tahrir square? There are conflicting reports about how General Mohamed El-Batran was shot dead at El-Kat prison in Qulabuiya. Some claim that police killed him, and others that prisoners killed him. One cannot judge if these stories are true or not. Many situations remain unclear, including the murder of Khaled Said, the bombing of the All Saints Church, the bloodshed at Mohamed Mahmoud Street, and Maspero, where atrocious crimes were committed, among others. History is derived from facts and not emotions. Egyptians need to be wary, as projected facts are not always the reality.

Short-Lived Law
The Egyptian law itself is legally unsound. Since 1952, Egypt has been lacking proper laws, and essentially the laws that rule the lawmakers were altered and manipulated, to benefit the authorities. Civil and criminal laws need radical rewriting in a proper, sound manner in order to uphold full individual justice according to universal rights. It is possible for civil and administrative tribunals to pass a legal judgment against

you while you are unaware. Outrageous as it may seem, it is possible to raise a lawsuit in a court in Tanta, north of Cairo, while the defendant is completely unaware, and once they are sentenced officers would come to arrest him or her in Cairo.

Justice is unlikely to prevail since the current laws are not legally sound. Justice is consequential. Gehad questions if any real democracy exists the world over, and hence foresees that Egypt will not be any different from the democratically advanced countries. *Rousseau touched on this observation, "If we take the term in the strict sense, there never has been a real democracy, and there never will be."*[115] Gehad chose to start his chapter in the book with this quote, "All this - all that 'great critique' to use the language of the Chinese revolutionaries, and it is essentially negative – helped to convey a new vision, a vision of politics that was trying to wrench itself." *Alain Badiou analyzed democracy highlighting all its faults and Gehad sees the Egyptian revolution falling into the glorious traps of utopian democracy, blinded to the defects.*

In order to predict where Egypt is going, one must ask where Egypt is coming from. Egypt will witness slight improvements in life, but nothing dramatic. The differences are unquantified, as they are minor. Corruption based on what? What is the definition of corruption? Corruption within the state is a legal question that only law can define. Gehad is optimistic that the laws in Egypt will one day be legally sound. One of biggest problems Egypt is facing is not the relativity of law: what is legal and what is not legal, but that the law is so short-lived that it is dangerous. Take for instance, back in the 1980's, currency traders were pursued and their trade was made illegal, while today they constitute the legal elite of the financial society.

However, with the growing, raving winds of Islamists, Egypt might never see the light of day and the law will never become sound. One can never know what tomorrow holds. Things can change suddenly and there are no guarantees who the next ruling elite will be.

Machiavelli wrote, "Revolution (left or right) will fail if it does not develop majority political support within democratic institutions."[116] *This is the fallback of the civic revolution, where the revolutionaries failed to gain popular support as was proven during the constitutional referendum, parliamentary elections in 2011 and yet again in the presidential elections in 2012. Moreover, institutions in Egypt have a long road ahead before transforming into democratic bodies.*

Paradigm Shift
The Turkish revolution that dissolved the Ottoman Empire in 1922 is a classic military/national model of a revolution. Gehad believes the Arab world is trying to follow suit and specifically, Egypt has been trying to mimic Ataturk's era and more

recently Erdogan's. The American and British models of civic revolutions did not seduce Egyptian political culture. These models created the notion of *magna carta* with the rise of civic constitutional culture and hence, they set up the public order. However, Gehad believes the Egyptian revolution shows more cultural affinity with the model of the French revolution than a social revolution.

Over the past twenty months, Gehad has not changed his mind, however, his understanding of affairs has deepened. The crisis facing the ruling regime, he had conceptualized as a long-term crisis. What has happened in Egypt requires Egyptians to become aware and thoroughly think of the events with a critical mind. The Egyptian revolution is an example of a civic revolution hijacked - by the Islamists in collaboration and the consent of the Supreme Council of the Armed Forces, SCAF. Usually any Islamic movement has been either traditional, or reformist, or radical. According to Gehad's understanding, an Islamic movement is unable to be revolutionary. Previously, Islamic movements had a small social base but today, *Ikhwan* are championing a false consciously social movement. *Ikhwan* are speaking in revolutionary language, which is unprecedented.

The dichotomy after the 2011 revolution was clear-cut with the left liberal revolutionary wing opposing the right wing, represented by the Islamic decadent conservatives. Over the course of President Morsi's rule, the polarization heightened.

Ikhwan and other Islamic movements are perceived as conservative. Even Hassan El Banna, the founder of *Ikhwan* in 1928, was clearly against revolutions. In Egypt, *Ikhwan* adopted and co-opted the slogans of the left liberals as if their own. *Ikhwan* created a political party after the revolution and called it 'Justice and Freedom Party' that could be attributed to traditional Turkey, or more likely, their exposure to communism while in prison and the liberals during the revolution.

The pressing question that baffles Gehad is: how did *Ikhwan* start speaking revolutionary rhetoric? He understands how they reached this position but is still not clear on how its usage will unravel. President Morsi talks as if he was the revolutionary president and that the revolution was Islamic. Muslim Shiites have advocated revolutionary Islam, but *Ikhwan* are Muslim *Sunnis*, which is a different sect. Gehad points out that rhetoric usually contains the truth partially, but not completely.

Gehad thinks that the explanation behind this fundamental paradigm shift within *Ikhwan* is due to the suppression by the *ancien regime*. It led them to the use of radical terms. *Ikhwan* have reached total denial with regard to modern life; a belief that society is infidel in its entirety referred to as *Takfeer*. What is the nature of this

Islamic revolution that *Ikhwan* are championing? "A spectre is haunting Europe - the spectre of Communism" is the powerful opening of the Communist Manifesto[117] which resonates across continents and time. As Gehad points out, "a spectre is haunting," the spectre of Islamism post the Arab Spring in Egypt and in fact the Middle East. Will this Islamism be moderate or radical? Will it prevail?

Amongst the failure of the revolution is the people's inability to grasp the meaning of the change within *Ikhwan*. This change has yet to transcend to the new, higher level. Until today the liberal socialists view *Ikhwan* using the old conservative lens, trapped like hostages within this lens and unable to understand the change. *Ikhwan* however, have been changing from the inside, with the birth of a new civil wing composed of young critical minds, while still sustaining its conservative wing. *It is still unclear how and what shape will Ikhwan turn into, will the change be a mutation or a metamorphosis? Will it invite support or opposition?*

With the radical atmosphere that erupted in Egyptian society, by May 2013, Egypt had 5544 recorded protests in five months, higher than any other country, based on the Democratic Indicator issued by Center of International Development. This revolutionary fervor requires time to settle and eventually, usher and pave the roads of security. The problem facing Egypt is the suspended atmosphere that is very slow in settling. Gehad predicts at least another two to three years of uncertainty and friction.

Egypt is facing three big issues; firstly, a political crisis in formulating the political community; secondly, a political crisis in formulating the political structure, and thirdly, a political crisis in redirecting the security apparatus. These three crises are simultaneous and complex, leaving Egypt in an undesirable situation. Moreover, the leadership is not innovative enough to overstep these hurdles and international ties bind the administration. Abdel Nasser was able to close down the radical atmosphere by his innovative policy of neutrality. He swiftly implemented agricultural reform and was capable of controlling his more liberal minded military commanders. After crossing over these hurdles, the presidential elections in 1956 went smoothly, as opposition was confined and subdued. *Is General Sisi planning something similar with the upcoming elections in 2014?*

New Middle East Order
Back in 1916 in the Sykes-Picot Agreement, France and Britain set forth a plan, dividing their sphere of influence in Asia Minor after defeating the Ottoman Empire in World War I. Gehad's reading behind this agreement is that it was made to make the Near East the home of the minorities, including Jews. It was the seed to implanting a Jewish state in Palestine, namely Israel. Gamal Abdel Nasser attempted

to dismantle the Sykes-Picot Agreement by uniting the Arab world under the Islamic umbrella, however, he failed, as the agreement, almost a century later, is still intact.

Gehad has a theory about the new order that is formulating in the Middle East. Another attempt to readdress this agreement has been tackled by President Obama who is trying to change the formula to set up a rule of majorities in the Middle East. For instance, the Shiites are ruling Iraq after pushing the Sunnis, the minority, to the periphery. By default, once the majority rules a state, the minority are automatically marginalized and no longer protected. Iraq, Syria, Gaza and Egypt witnessed the persecution and murder of Christian minorities. The American strategy was immersed in their assumption that with the majority in power, the Americans would have broader influence. When the minorities ruled, conflicts were common, providing excuse for European interference. For America to have the upper hand, it has paved the way for a new balance of power with the aid of *Ikhwan* in Egypt, after their sweeping win in 2012.

The story is still in the making and certainly, Gehad believes it involves redrawing of borders, as has happened with the division of Sudan in July 2011. The Americans are seeking sectarian strife in the Middle East, to assert their geo-political control. In Gaza, the Christians were persecuted and finally forced to emigrate. *Ikhwan* are trying to gain this sectarian majority and Gehad sees the constitutional declaration in November 2012 by President Morsi as an example of this strategy. Gehad analyzed the actions of expediting the constitution; after the revolution, Egypt has witnessed a very high level of political participation, and President Morsi was trying to reduce this level. In order to control society, *Ikhwan* need to safeguard the president's decisions by consolidating his powers and erasing the possibility of appeals, subduing resistance and minimizing opposition. *Ikhwanising* the institutes is part of this plan and the only institute which is out of *Ikhwan* control is media, *which was tackled by a physical standoff and campaign of 'cleansing the media' at the Media City in March 2013.* Moreover, *Ikhwan* do not believe in institutions, but only in the Supreme Guide's office as the maestro orchestrating the musicians. Gehad sees that the next step that is needed is for the people to unite with the army against *Ikhwan,* to secure the demands of the civil revolution. Millions of Egyptians placed their trust in the army once again demanding an end to *Ikhwan* rule on June 30, 2013. The failure of *Ikhwan* means that the Sykes Picot agreement is still in place, especially as it seems Syria is standing its ground against the rebels.

Restarting
A little less than three years after the revolution, Gehad has realized there is a genuine problem in the creation of civilian liberal rule in Egypt, as the political culture and mindset is incapable of accepting the civilian notion. It is still tied up with the

expectation of the leader, the Pharaoh, *rayees*. The atmosphere is not yet acclimatized. This infatuation with the leader is possibly one of the many reasons why ousted President Morsi failed with the Egyptian people, as he simply fell short as their leader. *The media tirelessly emphasized that he was the President of his people, rather than all Egyptians. The same phenomenon of the Pharoah can explain why Egyptians are glorifying Generalissmo Sisi, which the media has embraced. It seems to be a pure media game, not simply a political one.*

The army is proposing an institutional reform path and not a secular trajectory. The conflict between the army and the *usuliyeen* (fundamentalists) concerns who would be the captain of the ship. *'Usuliyeen'* means the fundamentals of religion, and is not the same thing as rigidity. Each party has varying priorities. The army is neither a fundamentalist nor a secular institution, unlike in Turkey where the army represented secular thought. In Egypt, the army represented the national streak. Among the problems within the fundamentalists is the rising sectarianism among them.

In Gehad's opinion, Egypt has taken a step back from fascism to authoritarianism, returning to the starting point before the January revolution. The *ancien regime* lacked political intelligence to implement the progressive plans that Gamal Mubarak championed. Gehad believes there was a genuine urge to transform the system to secularism, but uncarefully planned and unsoundly founded. Noble intentions do not suffice to transform a modern state into a liberal secular modern state, as it requires thorough understanding and a comprehensive blueprint. The civilian politicians are unfortunately weak, including *Ikhwan*. Gehad concluded that military politicians are stronger in performance than the current civilian politicians are, such as Gamal Mubarak and Mohamed Morsi. These weaknesses are ethnological and epistemological, dating back years and decades. Egypt is facing a political dilemma in how to establish independent civilian thought and rule, where the thought is the base for the rule and not vice versa.

Second Revolution

The transition from authoritarianism to civilian fascism or civilian liberalism has failed and hence, the decision is to return to merciful authoritarianism. Egyptians stood up against the uncertainty of fascism and opted to call back authoritarianism. In Gehad's view, this represented a new revolution, not a counter-revolution. It is not just a matter of facets or masks, as there is the underlying issue of comprehending civilian rule.

This second revolution reclaimed Egypt and its identity to Egyptians after the nation was threatened by civilian fascism under the Islamist mask, which the media clearly painted, *and opposition readily believed*. *Tamarod* mobilized this people's revolution, supported by the popular current represented in Hamdeen Sabahi, the presidential candidate. Progress cannot always be linearly positive; the second revolution was regressive, wherein Egypt returned to the same position prior to the first revolution on January 25, 2011. June 30 halted the regression after the 2012 presidential elections, whereby Egypt was thrown into a regressive course, where the state was undermined as perceived by the opposition of *Ikhwan*.

The social contract is an abstract concept that is unreal. The Bill of Rights was the outcome of a severe crisis, as it was the only method to unite the different parties. So long as there is a dominant regime then it is unnecessary. The outpour of unity among Egyptians on June 30, 2013 is proof that the people are united; hence, there is no need for a social contract or charter. As it is today, such a contract has not surfaced on the table from either revolutionaries or politicians or media. The social contract is an ideal solution, not proposed by Egyptians, possibly as the political, mental, social and cultural atmosphere is not ready for such an idealistic manifestation of unity.

War on 'Terrorism'

In order to reach a balanced authoritarian regime, the government must combat 'terrorism'. This war on terrorism originated in Egypt. In Gehad's view, the Islamists were groomed by the regime, and the repression was part of the plan to ensure the *ancien regime* remained in power. It is not that repression created these Islamists, but in reality, the regime created its bogeyman and scapegoat under the Islamist facet with the help of the *Dakhleya*. Take for instance Aboud elZomor, the hardline Islamist military man, who was assigned to training, and blessed by the late President Sadat, and in turn assassinated him. Currently, reconciliation is not up for discussion as 'terrorists' are being cleansed, and police and *Ikhwan* have scores to settle. The road ahead is unclear with a temporary president and a temporary supreme guide. Gehad finds it strange that *Ikhwan* opted for impermanent leadership, mimicking the current interim government.

Ikhwan are living through the same dilemma, since 1954, after the defeat that drove them underground. In 2013, *Ikhwan* refused to be driven there again and hence are voicing their presence via high visibility protests covered by the media. *Ikhwan* have separated between the secret work and the Islamic missionary work.

In Gehad's view, it was necessary for the army to call for a delegation to combat 'terrorism' as it signified the size of the revolutionary weight on the political scales. With the influx of people taking to the streets in response to the summoning by the army on June 30 - much greater than the response to revolutionaries, he deduces that the political weight of the army is heavier than that of the revolutionaries. Gehad views it as a defeat for the activists. July 26 then became an agreement between the people and army, excluding the revolutionaries. On June 30, legitimacy split between the revolutionaries and the army to overthrow the President and after July 26, it was solely the army's legitimacy. This was a shrewd move by General Sisi, as he challenged the game theory by changing partners during the race. It gave him a national and international advantage, undermining the claims that a military coup took place.

Egypt went back to the starting point, to merciful authoritarianism. Certainly, only a semblance of democracy is possible without any civilian facet. Gehad predicts that General Sisi will run for upcoming presidential elections and will win.

CHAPTER 18

Deceived Devotee

'You know best the affairs of your worldly life'
"Antoum Aalam be shoun denyakoum"
Prophet Mohamed Peace Be Upon Him

Among the difficult characters to meet was a member of Ikhwan willing to have a heart-to-heart. Heba Labib, my friend, got me in touch with Hanan Magdy who she knows from the Engineers Syndicate and was formerly an Ikhwan sister. We met at the Faculty of Music at Zamalek on Friday May 17, 2013.

Ikhwan Initiation

Her smile emanates love and she likes the color white. She is of average build, and wears eyeglasses. She wears the veil and likes to wear long wide skirts with loose long blouses. Like most Egyptians, she drinks her tea with a lot of sugar. Hanan Magdy was born in Helwan on October 17, 1974. Her father was a manager in a housing company, and her mother a homemaker. Hanan's father idolized Abdel Nasser, placing pictures of the late president in their home. Her father was politically active, even turning one of the rooms in their house into an office for the Socialist Labor party (*Hezb Elamal Eleshtaraki*). Her parents were not very religious from her viewpoint, as her father started praying when he was older, and her mother did not wear the veil. Nonetheless, they taught Hanan ethics and the deep meaning of Islam; no lying, no cheating, no stealing and to love and fear God. Her father was an outspoken man who spoke the truth regarding corruption in a board meeting, that ultimately led to his firing. He raised lawsuits but was unable to get work. With no income, the financial situation forced Hanan's mother to work as a teacher in Saudi Arabia, where she took up the veil and lived alone for two years. Hanan and her sister stayed behind in Cairo with their father. Her mother grew more religious, influenced by living in Saudi Arabia, which trickled onto her family.

Hanan graduated in 1998 from the faculty of engineering, Helwan University, specializing in communications, but never practiced engineering technically. She used her skills, however to present science and engineering in a simple, fun way to children within social activities. She felt that with her dedication she was serving her beloved country. Other female members in *Ikhwan* pursued their careers in various fields whilst participating in *Ikhwan* activities. In 1997 while she was in her senior year, Hanan got married, and today is the proud mother of three children. She only once traveled abroad, to perform the pilgrimage at Mecca, Saudi Arabia. Hanan views her life in two phases: the first twenty years and the second twenty years. During the first phase, Hanan went to a French school, Ecole de la St Famille, run by nuns. She was into sports, and entered handball competitions. She liked to swim and ride bicycles. Her primary school did not have a secondary unit, so she went to a regular Arabic secondary school, which exposed her to a different and new tone of life. Religion in her early years was not central to her life. For instance, she did not fear the afterlife, something she believes she shared with most Egyptians, as very few adopt the proper Islamic behavior.

At her secondary school, one of the teachers talked to the girls about *hijab* (veil), faith and prayers, most of which were new topics to Hanan. She wore the veil when she was fourteen years old. Prophet Mohamed, Peace be upon Him, advised that whoever has a good thought must transmit it within society, and she lives by this. Before embarking on teaching children how to recite the *Quran,* as a young student, Hanan took lessons on the two forms of Quranic recitation in both styles, known as *tarteel* and *tagweed*. She alternated taking and giving lessons. A group of students from her French school started the lessons and eventually Hanan was the only one who stayed committed. Hanan likes to practice what she learns and started to get closer and more committed to *Allah*. Hanan excelled in her assignments, and she generally prospers when she succeeds in her studies and Islam. Hanan took lessons at an Islamic center, which greatly affected her mindset.

At the mosque, Hanan came to learn about the *Ikhwan* organization, through observing a boy who talked to a girl separated by a curtain. This curtain is not essential in the *Ikhwan* ideology, but left to individual interpretation and religious instinct and piety. The girl, whose name was Eman, was a student at the faculty of commerce and was noticeably polite, polished and smelled pleasant. Everything about the girl was appealing to Hanan; her impressive morals and ethics, and the fact that she was raised in a religious house. Hanan visited Eman's house, which had an evidently different aura to her own. Her brother did not see any visiting female friend. Upon entering the house, they removed their shoes to the side, to keep the area clean. This household was the model that *Ikhwan* were hoping their members would attain. Eman always helped Hanan to be a better person and encouraged her to think moderately about matters. Eman, her friend, became the ideal reference that Hanan admired.

In 1993, Eman married and traveled after five years of being both a student and a teacher, leaving a void in *Ikhwan* and a need for replacement. As Hanan was very committed, the *Ikhwan* naturally selected her to be in charge of the mosque; she was around nineteen. Hanan cannot recall an exact date for her initiation, as it happened gradually. Due to security reasons, women unofficially enroll in *Ikhwan*. *Ikhwan* women are referred to as sisters and the men as brothers.

Hanan met a lovely person, Sheikh Ahmed, who was like the Godfather and mentor for her. *Ikhwan* sisters, brothers and other Muslims visited him to listen to his teachings. Hanan attended classes by Sheikh Ahmed, which gave her a deeper solid understanding of Islam and its fairness. This helped safeguard her Islamic principles.

World Caliphate

Hanan admired Imam Hassan El Bana, the founder of *Ikhwan*, who advocated that Muslims must maintain Islam in the center of their lives and not the periphery. He set a curriculum defining the steps *Ikhwan* should take to introduce, through their ideology, how Islam should be central in a Muslim's life. Muslims need to adopt a complete Muslim life following all its principles like honesty, justice and peace; *Ikhwan* commonly refer to this as the "summoning to Islam". Once a Muslim is able to attain complete and central Islamic life and he or she feels able to beckon other Muslims to the same, then that Muslim becomes part of the Brotherhood. Eventually those who are more pious and capable may proceed to summon non-Muslims to Islam. In her opinion, among the mistakes committed was that only *Ikhwan* set up such curriculum, and it was consequently faulty. *Ikhwan* are like a company working with values, principles and rules. In addition, Imam Hassan El Bana set a mission and a vision for his organization. His vision was to reach a World *Caliphate* or a Super Power. Today, the USA is the super power without invading countries in the military sense.

Hanan studied closely, and fully understood the three messages by Imam Hassan El Bana. Hanan perceived a problem within the organization; sometimes its members would quote words without being fully aware of the meaning and depth of those words. For instance, Hanan frequently felt she needed to check her fellow brothers on the meaning of words like the World Caliphate and *Uma* (Islamic nation). Egyptians misunderstood the concept of the *Uma* as an abolishment of borders, *possibly confusing it with the Communist concept of world power. Ikhwan and Communists may share the concept of a World power as a common vision, however, with different ideologies and conceptualization of this power. "The Communists are further reproached with desiring to abolish countries and nationality"*[118] *Ikhwan* was also reproached for having the same intentions, but much of that is based on misconceptions. The Islamic world summoning was across borders, but did not seek to abolish or erase borders.

The curriculum divides the world into individual, family, society, nation and World Caliphate or Empire. Attaining a certain level of maturity is necessary in order to attain World Caliphate. The first individual level is where the Muslim reforms himself and his relation with God, as well as the relationship between him and the people around him so that he becomes an ideal Muslim. Once attained, he could then move onto the next level, which is reforming his family, with the objective of making it an ideal family. Aggregating reformed families would lead to a reformed society, which is the third level. The fundamental shortcoming with this framework is, who defines these ideals, who can judge, and how can a person be allowed to judge another Muslim?

Hanan sat with many brothers and sisters, influencing their understanding of Islam as per the *Ikhwan* curriculum. Among the messages of El Bana was the summoning towards *nour* (light or enlightenment). She would explain Imam Hassan El Bana's definition of *nour*. He defined criteria for the obligations of a Muslim brother. They include being an able entrepreneur, worshiping well, and having a sound *akeeda* (doctrine). Another document he wrote was the twenty *ousoul* (principles). They are core values that would help avoid any fallout between members. His approach was practical, demanding agreement on these principles and flexibility for the brothers on the sub principles. Due to this, it is very difficult for two brothers to dispute. Among the simple misinterpretations by the brothers, is that those twenty principles are meant to unify the brothers only, wherein they intend to unify all Muslims.

Hanan believes one of the reasons why the brothers have kept these values within their inner circle was the intense crackdown by the old Mubarak *nizam*. Authorities cunningly permitted *Ikhwan* to protest only once in a closed area, the stadium, which meant that the brothers were only talking to one another, far away from other Egyptians and society in general. It was a confined, polite protest that did not reach society. The *Ikhwan* would chant and shout but nobody heard them. With this forced atmosphere, *Ikhwan* were living as in a state of *Jihad*, fighting or struggling in the name of God, sacrificing for their cause. But in reality, this consciousness is false. All their efforts were limited to the individual and the family and never to society. What warrior fights a war with himself and his family? It was insane. Hanan believes that the continuous suppression by the Mubarak regime of *Ikhwan* drove them into the closed aloof society. Moreover, how *Ikhwan* focused on this inner circle with continuous self-blame, and self-involvement, made it almost impossible to move out of this closed circle.

The women perceived the men as brothers. Mind you, the mentality in *Ikhwan* is completely different within the group from outside of it, when it comes to the ideal man who places Islam as his central concern. The knight in shining armor is a certain image for any girl, and a very different image for an *Ikhwan* girl. She expects that the 'knight' toils and plays an influential role in his work field, and adheres to the Islamic summoning by holding either the title of *imam or haraky*, (religious leader or activist). The latter is in charge of work that benefits *Ikhwan*. Some men are leaders and others are team players. Among the leaders are those who seek power and its benefits and there are those who are simply talented leaders, not looking for power. He must have his own *werd* (a prayer that consists of a certain part of the Quran and other prayers that a person chooses to do and read daily). He must awaken from his sleep for additional night prayers. *Ikhwan* organized themselves into *osra* (groups that take over the upbringing or discipline), which are led by a *Nakeeb* (tutor or leader).

Within the *Ikhwan* family, among the wife's duties is to remind her husband every day, not to forget God in his work; all his work must be pure. The word *Allah* is part of their daily home life.

Faults

The biggest fault in their approach is that the Muslim will continuously be stuck in reforming the individual, as there is no ideal Muslim and it is almost impossible for a human to reach indefinite *reda* (a state of satisfication and gratefulness for what God has provided). This has trapped the organization at the first level.

Her upbringing has allowed Hanan to have critical thinking and allowed her to see that *Ikhwan* were off course from the original ideology. After the revolution, *Ikhwan* had reached the ideal individual and family, but had not rolled it out onto society. However, they were suddenly in charge of the nation, demonstrating a typical case of biting off more than they can chew.

Unfortunately, *Ikhwan* failed to exert the required effort to interpret the writings of their founder in modern times and accordingly plan the future. Hanan attributes this shortcoming to widespread intellectual laziness. Analysis and strategic thinking is not their cup of tea. Hanan believes what encouraged this is the lack of intellectual curiosity on the economic, political and military fronts by any Islamic philosopher. Discussions are superficial, merely at face value without delving any deeper and lacking critical thinking. With this in mind, when talking about the Egyptian nation, *Ikhwan* spoke superficially, unable to grasp its dimensions. She doubts that they read the history of the political development of a nation, at best only a few might have. Within the Brotherhood, they failed to elaborate that the *Uma* and nation go together and are not mutually exclusive. Despite *Ikhwan* teaching respect of the nation and patriotism to the extent of positioning love of the country as a form of worship, a mutation happened along the way. *Ikhwan* overlooked the nation to achieve the Super Power status. They failed in trying to understand the pillars of a nation and hence, their disastrous failure after winning the elections in 2012.

Ikhwan failed to move out of their inner circle and reform society. All their meetings were among the same brothers and sisters and no mingling took place with non-*Ikhwan* Egyptians. This should have happened back in 2006, where *Ikhwan* should have worked with other organizations; however, that was not implemented. Hanan was among the exceptional sisters who succeeded in integrating in society over six years, as she was among a few others who managed to work on their inner and outer circles in parallel. She noticed that many Egyptians are devout Muslims, work diligently and love God without being *Ikhwan*. Her faith in Egyptians strengthened; she did not feel any difference between her and others.

Integration was hurried. Some people positively responded, like the *Shabab* (youth) who broke away from the *Ikhwan* after the revolution, due to disagreements and due to their point of view falling on deaf ears. Hanan finds losing brothers a loss, after all, human beings work and make mistakes, and should correct their mistakes and go back to work.

Over the years, *Ikhwan* equated three important pillars: *Ikhwan*, Islam and Egypt, which is simply wrong. In other words, they believed that the three had common interests. Some brothers are not significant players outside the organization, but are instrumental inside it. If you remove *Ikhwan* factor from a brother's life, it would mean that his identity shifts and is threatened. The fight becomes over his own individual existence and not over the *Ikhwan*. It became personal. *Rousseau touched on this when he wrote, "As soon as this multitude is so united in one body, it is impossible to offend against one of the members without attacking the body, and still more to offend against the body without the members resenting it."*[119]

Although, Hanan is critical of the faults within the Brotherhood, she is confident that *Ikhwan* have two unfaltering pillars. The first is their ability to emphasize the importance of ethics in all fields as central to the practice of Islam. Piety and ethics go hand in hand. They can serve as an example in various industries; arts, medicine and science, demonstrating the ideal ethics of Muslims in work domains. The other pillar is the genuine desire to free Palestine and Palestinians from occupation. *Ikhwan* do not believe that the state of Israel should exist. They have no issues with Jews, just the Zionist state. Hanan finds it ridiculous when Egyptians question the intentions of *Ikhwan* and even accuse them of being double agents of the American and the Jews.

It is Personal
The reason why Hanan never worked as a communication engineer was her dedication to *Ikhwan*, as she realized that, had she worked, it would have affected her work with the Brotherhood. It was a personal choice and a big sacrifice. She had a dream of achieving the great level within *Ikhwan* that would enable her to preach to Muslims that Islam is central in life, and to summon non-Muslims to Islam. Hanan rebukes the definition of sacrifice, as she should not have made such a choice. Nobody stopped her and asked her what she was doing back in the beginning, when she decided to dedicate her professional life to *Ikhwan* and again recently, when she opted to leave *Ikhwan* as a political party. Within an organization, senior members should keep a watchful eye on dedicated members to retain, coach and mentor them, but nobody questioned Hanan. She believes there are key brothers and sisters that should be convinced to stay their course with *Ikhwan*.

Hanan was the head of *Ikhwan* within Helwan University on a voluntary basis since 1998. She compares herself to a woman who works in a company as a communication engineer. If someone starts attacking the company she works for, she is sure that the woman would defend her company. When it comes to *Ikhwan,* Hanan feels that her existence is based on them, and feels she would die for the Brotherhood. Hanan will not allow someone to attack *Ikhwan,* as they are the base of her existence. It is personal. Involuntarily, a dangerous unification between the brothers and *Ikhwan* transpired.

Former President Mubarak dried up the wells, weakening *Ikhwan*, as they could not bring up new leaders. Leaders are trained in camps and seminars, both of which are not permitted. There were no announced meetings or trips, for fear of arrest. Hence, the trainers themselves were not qualified to train new leaders and therefore the brothers became weak. Although not planned, it was *force majeure*. If they had worked according to their curriculum, *Ikhwan* could have been a force to reckon with today.

Before the revolution, Hanan had signed up on Facebook, where she saw the banner of 'We are Khaled Said' and read about his murder. She felt saddened, but she knew from her father's political work that such torture and killings took place. It was not unheard of. Hanan did not take the calls for revolution seriously, as there was no leader. On January 25, 2011, Hanan attended a meeting with *Ikhwan* in one of their homes. Hanan was in charge of the political committee, studying the models in Turkey and Sudan, intending to prepare the political education of girls within *Ikhwan*. It was her personal initiative.

Role of Women

On paper, there are no restrictions when it comes to *Ikhwan* sisters. In reality, each woman determines her role, which depends on her mentality and her surroundings. The wife heeds to her husband, so if he refused that she works there would be no discussion. There are husbands who refuse to allow their wives to talk to any men, while others may accept. Some men will accept that their wives wear *niqab* (full veil covering her face only revealing the eyes) although it is not part of their beliefs. When it comes to the circumcision of girls, the doctor decides based on the size of the clitoris if she may need to be circumcised, otherwise, she is untouched.

Due to the repression exerted by the Mubarak regime over any opposition, particularly *Ikhwan*, the Brotherhood were forced into becoming a secret society. Hanan was under the impression the office of the Supreme Guide organized matters with great transparency and democracy. However, recently she discovered, as portrayed by the media and the actions on the ground that only four or five leaders have significant influence in *Ikhwan*. These top brothers channel the views of fellow brothers. They may take opinions, but from selected people with limited understanding and knowledge, such that more often than not the brother who may have a different opinion from the senior brother will back down, as he could not possibly understand better than the likes of Mahmoud Ezzat and Khairat El Shater. Automatically the simple-minded *Ikhwan* adopts the opinion of the senior *Ikhwan*. Due to the tight reigns of the leadership, secrecy is the norm, as the plans are contained within those few senior brothers. There is no transparency.

Hanan is annoyed by the unfounded rumors that Iran and Hamas source *Ikhwan*. The Muslim Brotherhood is an international organization. In Egypt, the brothers pay seven percent of their salary to the Brotherhood. Hanan explains the secrecy simply as arrogance, when the public demanded to know its sourcing, they did not oblige.

The revolution was a spark by an ignored generation that had lost hope. They rebelled against the classic, mind your own business upbringing. The youth refused the old imposed *nizam* upon them as it had been on their parents who had acquiesced. *Ikhwan* endorsed this spark, but it was not an Islamic revolution.

Protesting

As Friday 28 unfolded, Hanan pondered the events and she started to take it seriously. She decided to protest independently on the Friday of Anger and she was surprised to see that most of the people she met on the streets were *Ikhwan*. Her husband, also

Ikhwan, told her later that they had received orders to join the protests demanding change. There were *Ikhwan* who joined the revolution during the first days on their own initiative. However, on Friday 28, the actual *Ikhwan* organization officially participated with a good turnout. It was a top down decision.

Hanan left her children at home and joined the protests wholeheartedly, as she saw how Egyptians are inherently good people, denied their fortune by the Mubarak era. She saw theft and lying in the public domain. She started the day with her husband and mid-way each of them parted with friends. Her husband went on alone to Tahrir. She joined a march from Helwan that walked around the district, heading all the way to Tahrir. Hanan stopped a little before Maadi, as it was very tiring. She had met relatives by coincidence and decided to return home that day. Hanan slept until nine in the morning. She woke up, dressed and went to Tahrir, and did not leave until February 11, 2011. Her husband took their tent, and spent Friday night in Tahrir. Her mother was very concerned for her safety. She was surprised to find her mother joining the protest, there to protect her daughter. Hanan's husband left their children with her sister, who had just delivered a baby. Her brother-in-law, who is an *Ikhwan* admirer, joined the protestors. It was like a family reunion at Tahrir. Her husband's siblings, all *Ikhwan*, were also among the camp.

At Tahrir, she saw many *Ikhwan* brothers and sisters, but there were many non-*Ikhwan* protestors as well. *Ikhwan* supported the seed of change that was apparent at Tahrir. They endured until they achieved their objectives and then left, betraying the protestors' unmet objectives. Hanan did not sleep. She often stood behind the platform, where she talked frequently with Dr. Beltagy, a key *Ikhwan* leader. She talked with the protestors, convincing them that no matter what, they should not leave Tahrir. Hanan never bothered to take photographs. She was practicing her missionary role inside the *midan* on her own initiative. Fridays were always the most crowded. Most of the protestors came and left, few camped out.

A few of the *Ikhwan* had a negative impact in Tahrir. For instance, some were segregating protestors, having the women chanting with other women, shouting divisive, pro-Islamist chants.
Hanan said to one of the women, "You should not chant something Islamist, as you will be excluding others."
The woman defiantly replied, "No I will chant Islamist chants."

She saw a few *Ikhwan* sitting secluded from the protestors, passing up on this great opportunity to mingle and break the barriers. This worried Hanan to such an extent that she could not sleep, as she was up and about surveying and talking with protestors and *Ikhwan*. She felt her role was as relevant as the front lines.

Green Branch

Hanan will never forget the fear on February 2, 2011 when the protestors were attacked. She felt death at almost every moment. Hanan felt snipers were always hawking from the rooftops. This might have been a hallucination, but she surely felt watched. Hanan will not forget a young man holding a green branch walking towards the assailants, waving his branch as a sign of peace, fearless of death. The young man was well dressed. She saw a tank behind him and the man was standing alone. At his side were iron fences, and he was boldly facing the assailants. Moments later, he was lying down on the street, still holding the branch to his chest. Hanan imagines he is among the martyrs, but she did not see what happened to him as she ran with her mother, into shelter in a nearby building to hide away from the shots.

While Hanan was running, one of her shoes fell off. She was crying, as she despised the forced dispersal from the *midan*. She took a photograph of the demands of the revolution hanging from a building. She noticed that the woman who was checking ID's of people before entering Tahrir, who Hanan thought was a protestor, was inside the building, laughing with a man, but was unable to hear the conversation. She gathered that the woman must have been an agent of *Amn Eldawla* calling the man in her company, *Pasha*.

Her mother was very scared that something could happen to Hanan, however she was also happy that the people were toppling the old *nizam*. She had also suffered injustices a long time ago, resulting in the untimely dismissal of Hanan's father from his work, and the ensuing financial crunch. Years before these injustices took place, her father had been blacklisted as part of the political prosecution.

In Hanan's view, the mastermind of the attacks on the protestors were the ruling elite who did not want to leave there seat of power, and wanted by any means to vacate Tahrir of the protestors. She rejects completely that *Ikhwan* could have been behind it, and classifies it among the ludicrous lies floating around, along with the claim that *Hamas* or Iran financialy sourced them. It is beyond imagination, as Hanan saw her husband and other *Ikhwan* hurt defending Tahrir. She knows that among their faults, *Ikhwan* are too engrossed in life and cannot imagine them parting it so easily.

Often Hanan ate cheese sandwiches, buying them from a restaurant at Tahrir. For most of her prayers, she could not use water for her ablutions and she would pat her hands on the ground and preform *tetyamem* (ablutions without water). She would wash her face using wet wipes, and used the smelly public toilet at the square once, which ended up blocked, and her husband had to enter and fix it. Sometimes she used the bathroom at the mosque. Another time she used the restroom of some merchants whose apartment was in the same building as their shop.

Hanan met with two of her friends at Tahrir and she realized that each of them had different feelings and personal experiences to hers. She preferred to roam the *midan* on her own, trying to stay away from her fear-stricken mother, who was holding her hand too much.

Hanan remembers an old woman holding a paper with the words 'I regret every moment I was silent' written on it. This sight really moved Hanan, as it wraps up the main problem of the old generation, their silence, that ultimately led to the revolution. One thing that bothered Hanan was a young woman who stayed in a nearby tent with some men. A man kissed her more than once that night. It happened only that night.

Negotiations

While at Tahrir, Hanan learnt new political thoughts that surfaced after *Ikhwan* met with the late Vice President Omar Suleiman. She met people talking about an independent organizational state. Hanan started hearing news about *Ikhwan*, different from her understanding and from what other *Ikhwan* said, that there was an agreement between *Ikhwan* and National security while there were talks between the *Ikhwan* and Supreme Council of the Armed forces. Hanan was shocked when she heard these reports, as she could not believe that her ideal, her beloved organization, could ever play in a puddle of mud. These details were absent from the regular brothers and sisters, as only the leadership knew about them. Hanan understands their justification for these talks, which were not treasonous. She considers it yet another manifestation of weak strategic thinking. It appeared that Egyptian society was not capable of dealing with a scenario like Syria and hence it is unfathomable for *Ikhwan* to keep demanding and pressuring the regime until all demands were fulfilled. It was a possibility that the army could have bombed the protestors and the revolution would have been over before it had begun.

Ikhwan perceived that if the protests persisted, Egypt would have fallen into civil war like in Syria, and they were fully aware that Egyptians were not ready for that. Hence, they decided to negotiate with the old *nizam*, especially as *baltegeya* were infiltrating within the protestors. Hanan felt that the short breathed Egyptians were tired from waiting. *Ikhwan* were not just playing revolutionaries, as they jumped into the political scene, satisfied that Gamal Mubarak would not be running for President. However, Hanan wanted to play revolutionary all the way to attain the demands of the people. She called an *Ikhwan* leader at *Helwan University*, upset. Hanan asked him, "Why did *Ikhwan* leave Tahrir?"
The leader replied, "We rode public transport and have realized that people are not ready to pay a higher price than what they had paid at Tahrir, their patience was running out and we cannot do anything more."

This was their justification. *Ikhwan* perceived that Egyptians were concerned with earning their bread and could be patient in earning their living, but would not accept sacrificing souls, hence their decision that a political solution was preferred. Hanan disagreed with their reasoning, as *Ikhwan* was built on the weakest link in society, the less fortunate, ignorant, and illiterate strata. *Hanan's opinion resonates with what Suu Kyi wrote, "'You can't pick up something and then drop it,' she said, "You have to see it through".*[120]

Many leaders resigned from *Ikhwan* on the local level, like Abdel Meniem Abou El Fotouh and even on the international level. Abou El Fotouh fought the lack of strategic thinking and tried to reform their mentality. For Hanan, it seemed *Ikhwan* had become hopeless with his resignation. One of the leaders in the office of the Supreme Guide criticized an *Ikhwan* sister whose living room was not tidy when he had visited, emphasizing that the first priority for a woman is to ensure her house is clean. Hanan was shocked to hear such stereotypical talk from a senior brother.

Hanan left Tahrir crying and pained, as if her soul was forcefully pulled out of her body, fully understanding the consequence of *Ikhwan* folding. It was as if Egyptians were trying to build on water. It is almost impossible for something solid to endure on moving waters.

Unease

When former President Mubarak stepped down, Hanan was not engrossed in this historic moment as her thoughts concerned with the future. She was scared of what would happen without the president. People around her were celebrating and hugging. She ran to the platform to announce to the people that it was not over, and that they should stay at Tahrir. Her words fell on deaf ears.

Hanan said, "We must not leave Tahrir" and Dr. Beltagy said, "We won't."

Hanan said, "Really?"

Dr. Beltagy said, "Certainly we won't leave."

Dr. Beltagy is one of the senior *Ikhwan* and certainly, he did not keep his word, as he left. The official position of the Brotherhood was that they should leave Tahrir, as they had achieved their objective with the disposal of the president.

Hanan found that the information gathered by *Ikhwan* about Tahrir was haphazard and did not depend on any scientific method. When *Ikhwan* decided to withdraw, they had based it on reports from a few *Ikhwan* stationed around the square to observe and report. Hanan questioned which members they chose to observe and gather intelligence. They may have been rural men who may for instance, judge a man with long hair as an agent. The presented observations led to a misconceived lack of confidence in the protestors and their willingness to sacrifice. In Hanan's view, the distorted picture of the report led to premature withdrawal of *Ikhwan*.

Mutation
Hanan tried putting the pieces of the puzzle together until she saw the big picture. She is certain that *Ikhwan* witnessed some form of intellectual erosion, a paralysis in thought that lead to weakening of the individual body and the entire *Ikhwan* body on the mental and psychological levels. The leadership went bankrupt, lacking input, lacking readings, and hence awareness. It took Hanan around six months after the revolution to gather all the pieces of the *Ikhwan* puzzle and see it whole. Based on this, she sadly concluded that *Ikhwan* had mutated from the original course and diverted from the objectives set by Imam Hassan El Bana. *Ikhwan's* sole purpose is the Islamic mission, embracing all people and not competing with different ideologies. However, they did not stick to this purpose.

She refers to the detrimental referendum in March 2011 where *Ikhwan* lobbied that voting 'yes' would mean the voter would go to heaven and 'no' the voter would go to hell. She rejected this, as *Ikhwan* is not a political party. However, it had metamorphosed into one, with the power vacuum after the ruling National Democratic Party (NDP), was torched and banned. When *Ikhwan* transferred into a political party Hanan refused to fill the application, as she believes that a party is not part of the principles set by the founder. Due to her adamant refusal, she received an ultimatum to fill the application for the creation of the political party, or pay a penalty of one hundred pounds, fourteen dollars. Hanan was furious, as she believed the members should have voted on such a decision and not be financially coerced.

Hanan's husband is a power engineer who works in the cement industry and they actually met via *Ikhwan*. Three people recommended Hanan to her husband when he wanted to get married. Her husband disapproved of many things at Tahrir. He documented his observations and presented them to senior leaders, but there is not much more he can do. Within the organization, there is a hierarchal framework for the channeling of feedback.

Hanan joined demonstrations in front of the *Ikhwan* head office, protesting the disbanding of youth from the organization. That was right after the Mohamed Mahmoud incident in November 2011, where *Ikhwan* forbade brothers and sisters from joining the street war and directly revoking membership of those who disobeyed orders.

Disbanded
Around the time of the Mohamed Mahmoud Street war in November 2011, Hanan participated in a sit-in at the Engineering Syndicate. Hanan's children accompanied

her, playing with their scooter around the building while she set up her own tent in the sit in. She noticed she was the only woman present. She recalls there was tension between *Ikhwan* and *non-Ikhwan* that led to her standing on the platform talking and calming the people. After the attention she got during the sit in, she nominated herself for the elections in the Syndicate. The Syndicate called her later to add her to the coalition list.

At the time, some brothers went to her neighborhood to ask for her and people informed them that Hanan was in the sit-in. At the time, there was another sit-in, at Mohamed Mahmoud, which *Ikhwan* had warned its members that they should avoid. They mistakenly thought Hanan disobeyed the orders and went to the banned sit in. Based on this, her neighborhood chapter, a sister, questioned her 'sisterhood', instilling doubts about Hanan's intentions in the organization. With the changing tides in the country, *Ikhwan* had decided any brother or sister must be one hundred percent loyal, or face disbandment. She also heard that it was said that her attendance was low in the training sessions. Hanan felt embittered, as she had dedicated twenty years of her life, sacrificing an engineering career for the sake of *Ikhwan*. In the end, she felt unsoundly and unfairly plucked. She is not sure what happened, but it seems to her that the accusations were imaginary. Despite her life with *Ikhwan* and in her role in it, she was inexplicably forced to feel guilty. In either case, she faced two difficult choices, 'the better of which was bitter too': to leave *Ikhwan*, or stay with *Ikhwan* but be cut off from society. She opted for the former.

Hanan was personally shocked, and cried rivers over the inexplicable injustice she met. Dr. Beshr and Eng Omar Abdallah, who worked at the Supreme Guide's office, called Hanan, requesting a report on the sit-in. Impressed by her report, as she mentioned the behavior of the brothers, and stated what *Ikhwan* needed to do to change and reach their ideal.
Omar Abdallah said, "Hanan, are you not a sister? Don't you attend sessions?"
Hanan replied, "I attend."
Omar said, "While writing the names, a sister said that you are not a sister. As you want to run in the Syndicate elections and removed your name from nomination list of *Ikhwan*."

Hanan, upset, went to talk to the election specialist.
She asked him, "Why is my name not on the nomination list?"
The electoral specialist replied, "I told them to add your name under the coalition list." Ironically, she ran for the elections as non-*Ikhwan*, and her list won. She works with *Ikhwan* at the Syndicate, but does not attend their organizational meetings. She stopped being as personally involved as before. Hanan was unceremoniously disbanded from *Ikhwan* after her twenty years of voluntary service.

Now being an outsider, she finds the words used by *Ikhwan* strange, like '*halaka*' and '*osra*', (circle and family). They are all exclusive. Feeling immense depression, Hanan decided to take up music. She is taking violin lessons at the Music Faculty at Zamalek, where we met the first time.

Political Islam

Politics is managing the affairs of a country. God sets rules on how to run a country and Islam is clear in defining the manner in which the ruler should treat the ruled. The only religion that delves into such rules is Islam. Islam certainly plays a role in politics, however, it is important that Muslims fully understand these principles. For rules to be applied correctly they need to be approached properly. A wrong approach in implementation, as has already been witnessed, has led to problems and resistance in Egypt, with the *Ikhwan* winning the parliamentary and presidential elections in 2011 and 2012 respectively.

The beauty of Islam is that it defines the framework without getting into the nitty gritty details. For instance, the ruler must rule with justice. Islam helps define what is right and wrong in politics, but does not define how things should run. It is not political Islam to promise and then break the promise, as was done by President Morsi. Rules are clear; there will be no lying and no breaking promises. *Actions speak louder than words, as Machiavelli wrote, "The only sound, sure and enduring methods of defense are those based on your own actions and prowess."*[121] *President Morsi and Ikhwan failed to walk the talk, compromising the first path to democracy in Egypt.*

In the presidential elections, Hanan voted for Abou El Fotouh in the first round and Mohamed Morsi in the run off. Like many other Egyptians, she could not vote for Shafik as she viewed him as a corrupt person from the old *nizam*. Hanan is certain that *Ikhwan* are neither thieves nor traitors. Nevertheless, she admits their thinking is defective. Their exclusion from society has left them estranged in their own country. In all honesty, she believes they need psychological treatment. The solution is for *Ikhwan* to feel safe; then they will compromise. But so long as they feel threatened, the deadlock will continue. Like a hedgehog when it is scared, it uses its spikes to hurt.

Islam is not a separate ideology. It is an all-encompassing ideology, even including liberalism and secularism to a certain extent. Prophet Mohamed Peace be upon Him says, "You know best the affairs of your worldly life," possibly indicating a secular streak. Likewise, one of the *Sahaba*, (companions, of the Prophet) Peace be upon Him said that we were sent to earth in order to lead whom He wills from the worship of man to the worship of God alone. Islam is not a competing ideology, as it includes all ideologies. The similarity between liberalism and *Ikhwan* lies in freedom, in that nobody has the power over an individual with the exception of God. Those who refute the power of God, she considers atheist. In her mind, one should not borrow a concept from abroad like liberalism and simply adopt it locally, as it requires cultural context prior to implementation, to gurantee proper fit.

Media is interested in its own stakes, running a commercial business worth millions. At the time of the revolution, their interest was to be against the revolution and hence the media was anti-revolution in tone and delivery, trying to scare people away from the streets. During the *Ikhwan* rule, it was the media's advantage to stand up against them, as *Ikhwan* did not have power over the reins. There were three main sources of power: *Dakhleya* (ministry of interior), the Supreme Council of the Armed Forces (SCAF), and the combined force of President Morsi and the *Ikhwan*. Power was shared amongst them. Hanan believes neither President Morsi nor the Supreme Guide rule Egypt. Four or five members of the senior *Ikhwan* committee were actually running the country.

The ordinary Egyptian is clueless about the corruption within the ranks of SCAF and has a shiny perception of the army that won the October War with Israel in 1973. However, politicians are aware that the army is running a commercial operation, not merely a military one. The broken trust between the political elite and the army is not easy to overcome. Once the military return to the barracks and are only occupied with securing the country, then the elite will restore trust in the army. It is wrong for the army to be preoccupied with its budget when it should focus on protecting national security and the borders.

From Hanan's point of view, she believes negotiations led to an agreement between the army and *Ikhwan* and that they are friends, not foes. She is sure that the police and the army are not the best of friends.

For the people to trust the police once more, Hanan believes that the police members who committed crimes and extrajudicial punishments must face the guillotine. A healthy spirit needs instilling within the force, far away from the psychopathy and sadism. Hanan does not trust the law, as she believes the law was tailored to the interests of the old *nizam*, and is not rendering justice for all; the system frequently acquits thieves, and murderers.

Marin Luther King said, "Human beings with all their faults and strengths constitute the mechanism of a social movement. They must make mistakes and learn from them, make more mistakes and learn anew. They must taste defeat as well as success, and discover how to live with each."[122] *Unfortunately, Ikhwan have failed to accept defeat and to live with other humans who are non-Ikhwan.*

The only way for *Ikhwan* to gain the trust of the people is through transparency. They need to admit that they are unqualified to rule the country alone and initiate an essential coalition government.

There is no religious strife in the general tide; however, there is ignorance that can occasionally spark unrest. The *ancien regime* manipulated this to serve its agenda.

Egyptians can only achieve democracy if they read about what it entails and understand its full dimensions; then the dream of democracy can materialize. Without grasping its meaning, it will never be a reality. Hanan is clueless on where Egypt is heading. The January 2011 events were an attempt at a revolution, that led to complete chaos. The revolution is continuing but in another guise. Hanan has faith that the revolution will not fail, but it will certainly be lengthy. One thing she is certain of is that no ruling regime will oppress the new generation. They simply will not accept what their parents had silently endured.

Black and White Portrait

The controversial constitutional declaration which President Morsi issued in November 2012 was based on misinformation and misunderstanding of the Egyptian people. *Ikhwan*'s perception was wrong and hence their ensuing judgment was wrong, just as their decision to leave Tahrir in February 2011 was wrong. Mohamed Hamed, former MP and opposition figure, confessed his intention to storm into the presidential palace with the intent of ousting President Morsi, and creating a Presidential Council with the blessing of the Church and *AlAzhar*. Hence, *Ikhwan* sent men to beat the protestors who they assumed supported Hamed's idea. Again, the misunderstood scene was viewed as a simple black and white portrait, with Hamed's supporters and Morsi supporters. As a result, a terrorist act was committed based on a demented mentality that sees the world in purely black and white.

Hanan cannot perceive the downfall of *Ikhwan*, as she is convinced that the young men who believe their ideology will not let it wither and they will fight for it. *Ikhwan* will not be extinct; however, their trajectory is modified. Ideas never die, and Hanan believes the idea of *Ikhwan* is amongst those eternal ideas, the idea that Islam has to be central in all Muslims' life. *Peter Hain said in his book about Mandela that the ideas of political prisoners, "would never die."*[123] *Hanan's view agrees with this statement; no matter how many Ikhwan are killed or imprisoned their idea will live through generations.*

Hanan went through a nervous breakdown when in August 2013, police attacked her friends and colleagues at *Rabaa Adawiya* and at *Nahdah*, protests she did not participate in. Hanan was against many *Ikhwan* policies and could not support their suppression and violence. She considered herself a member of the opposition but independent, as she could not find herself standing against *Ikhwan* due to differences in opinion. She assured me that they were unarmed peaceful protesters, whom the police violently attacked. It was brutal injustice and heavy-handed oppression of the opposition. As Ann Suu Kyi wisely wrote, *"To oppress the opposition is to assault the very foundation of democracy."*[124]

"History consists of a series of swindles, in which the masses are first lured into revolt by the promise of Utopia, and then, when they have done their job, enslaved over again by new masters."[125] *George Orwell predicted that all revolutions would end up with a new dictator that promises a utopia but ends up even worse than the previous dictator, as depicted in* Animal Farm. *Therefore, in Egypt, a possible argument is that Morsi replaced Mubarak as dictator or Pharaoh, making Mubarak look innocent in comparison. On July 3, 2013, the army heeded the request of the people and ousted President Morsi. Has this revolution or coup, ushered back the old dictator?*

AFTERWORD

"You have your way. I have my way. As for the right way, the correct way, and the only way, it does not exist." Friedrich Nietzsche.

Educated Mind

A striking quote I heard was from Khaled Sharkawi, one of the expatriate Egyptian men I had interviewed but not featured in this book. When I asked him which opening quote represents his viewpoint, he quickly quoted Aristotle, "It is the mark of an educated mind to be able to entertain a thought without accepting it."

I hope you have entertained the thoughts of these eighteen Egyptians without necessarily accepting them. My wish is that these stories help you to see the various points of view of Egyptians about the revolution and the subsequent chain of events. I believe in order for real progress to materialize, Egyptians need to tolerate different points of view and stop being arrogant, believing that they are always right. I hope and dream for a better Egypt where Egyptians live a decent, respectful, happy, fortunate and healthy life. I dream that all the great Egyptian minds in voluntary exile will happily return to their country, like my dear brothers, Mustafa and Kareem, who remain estranged from Egypt.

Corrupt Cancer

From the different perspectives in the book, you may have observed that many Egyptians are struggling, while others are desperate at the state of the nation. Many times Egyptian society has been described as suffering from advanced corruption, even likening it to a malignant cancer that has spread to all levels, ailing the body, mind and soul of Egypt. More specifically, we have heard the expression frequently that the ancien regime is like a cancer that has spread throughout the country.

Egyptian people felt embittered towards Mubarak's regime as they felt the victims of society were completely ignored and simply not important in the mind of the ruler. This was clearly portrayed in the state policy. The people misdiagnosed the problem by simply ousting the head of the state, believing that this would mean that the government would no longer ignore the people, attributing all the problems to the ousted head. However, they were wrong, as problems stem from deep within the government body and the fabric of society. Matters worsened for all Egyptians. In the subsequent years, considering the cancer analogy, the patient was misdiagnosed, chemotherapy was wasted and failed to tackle the disease.

The problem started with the referendum on an already ousted, hence illegitimate constitution in March 2011. The whole transition under the military failed to meet the demands of the still ignored people. Already continuing on the wrong path, presidential elections took place in 2012, paving the road for Ikhwan to rule. As a result of the widespread prosecution of the opposition under the Mubarak's rule, they were the only organized opposition party. The intermediary government misdiagnosed the problem just as their predecessors had. Not only was all this treatment just futile, but in fact it turned detrimental to the health of the nation as the misdiagnosis actually fed and increased the cancer until it became dangerous and fatally aggressive. It was suicide to keep this regime intact, and the experiment of political Islam rapidly reached a cul-de-sac, dead-end. The Egyptian people decided to abort President Morsi's rule, as Egypt's identity was in danger.

The revolution has exposed the mistakes of all parties, and the one critical mistake of the romantic, idealistic activists was lack of vision; what will happen to Egypt post Mubarak? As Che wrote about Latin American revolutionaries, "But these young insurgents were warriors of the heart, not the head; their plans lacked coherence"[126] Egypt unfortunately failed to avoid this trap.

Call for a Leader and Change

The beauty of the Egyptian revolution is its curse; it miraculously had no one tangible leader. After former President Mubarak stepped down, political parties mushroomed and scampered for power and the bigger slice of the cake. In the process, they lost sight of the general good and focused on individual or ideological gains. Egypt lacks a charismatic morally just leader like Nelson Mandela or Mahatma Gandhi or Martin Luther King Will these tumultuous times bring forth a new, much needed Egyptian savior? Can Egypt have a president outside the military realm? Does Egypt need a leader or an ideology or both to unite its people? Do Egyptians need unity or is it enough for them to learn how to live with one another and accept each other's differences? After the ousting of President Morsi, General Sisi has evolved into the aspired Egyptian leader. In 2013, there were campaigns calling for General Sisi to nominate himself for presidency. Some people find this an issue as yet again, he is a military man; nonetheless this materialized in 2014. President Sisi won the 2014 presidential elections with a landslide victory. The existence of nearly one million voided votes (even more than what the other candidate, Sabahi, actually received), is a clear statement that many people resent another military president and do not believe that the army will ever reform.

When the general called for people to flood the streets of Egypt on July 26, his pictures were distributed and suddenly he became an icon in Egypt, the exaggerated savior of Egyptians from the draconian President Morsi. This appeal bothered many. However, the majority were pleased that he rescued them and willingly bestowed him with the title of Pharaoh, which means god-king. It was no passing phenomenon, as it strengthened over time, clearly depicting Egyptian infatuation with the concept of the ruler, the King, the Pharaoh.

The ailing issue is the complacency and generally lack of executive function among Egyptians. This is apparent in the lack of discipline at work, with keeping time and driving. Their attitude is summarized in these terms: "maalesh, bokra and inshallah" (no worries, tomorrow, and God willing). They have moved from actors to spectators in their own lives, which has affected their productivity and standing in society. For any revolution to succeed, the people and the system need to evolve and there needs to be a paradigm shift. Without this fundamental change in attitudes, behavior and work ethic the demonstrations in 2011 could be termed a revolt and not a revolution. As Martin Luther King said, "A social movement that only moves people is merely a revolt. A movement that changes both people and institutions is a revolution"[127] Although cataclysmic, Egypt had a revolt that is struggling to be a revolution, the right term in reference to January 25, may be a quasi-revolution.

Beside the fundamental building blocks of Egypt, its people, there are many foundations that need urgent reform or even rebuilding, a few of which were emphasized by the different perspectives in this book namely, **justice**, **education**, and **healthcare**.

Justice and judicial reform was one of the initial demands of the protestors when they took to the streets on January 25, 2011. Protestors denoted it in "adala egtemaia" (social equality) and "horeya" (freedom). If a proper justice system is in place where corruption is minimized by a comprehensive system of checks and balances and where equal opportunity is ensured and individual rights and freedom are respected and guaranteed, then envy, anger and resentment will automatically be reduced, subsequently leaving a healthy environment conducive to progress and growth. As Martin Luther King said, "hatred and violence must be cast into the unending limbo if we are to survive."[128]

Education is an essential component of a progressive society. Egypt is plagued by ignorance, illiteracy and a lack of critical thinking skills, even amongst the educated. Egypt needs, no deserves, a high quality education system, a system that encourages and develops students' creativity, critical thinking and true understanding. Teachers need to involve the students and encourage questions, to seek knowledge and a deeper understanding of their world. The free university education introduced in the 1940s is not serving the country well, as for example, many engineers end up working blue-collar jobs simply because they cannot find employment as engineers. Can we consider stopping the subsidizing of university *education for the sake of school education? Moreover, in Egypt, no authority maps the needs of the market against the required number of specialists. For instance, in France, the number of engineers admitted is based on the forecasted needs of the country and not the number of interested students, hence reducing the unemployment. The education quota is planned according to the needs of the nation.*

The government definitely needs to increase the meager seven percent of the national budget dedicated to education, and to focus on the primary and secondary education levels. The powers to be must also improve the teachers' training and increase their compensation, to discourage private lessons and significantly revise the current school curriculum.

*The public **health care** system needs an increased share of the national budget with fair compensation to doctors and nurses. Doctors must be encouraged to work in one hospital or clinic where they have time for consultations, operations, patient follow-up, and research and to attend seminars and conferences. Medical specialization needs focus. For instance, in Egypt, oncologists treat all sorts of cancer whereas in France the oncologist differs depending on the type of cancer.*

Buckminister Fuller said, "You never change things by fighting the existing reality. To change something, build a new model that makes the existing model obsolete." Egypt needs numerous new models, but first Egyptians must realize and accept that the current models are extinct and have conviction that new models are the way forward. Out with the old and in with the new.

Seize the Future
The idea for this book started as a documentation of stories, which is ultimately a part of history. The book has developed into a personal journey of discovery and understanding of my compatriots and my country. Egyptians have changed and they will never be the same again. With all my readings and meetings, I have gathered that the Egyptian system is going through a slow but painful process of change, which I would like to view as healing. Zig Ziglar said, "You must make a 'Choice' to take a 'Chance' or your life will never 'Change.'"

Egypt underwent what Thoreau predicted, "periods of violence and revolution do to peoples...horror of the past takes the place of forgetfulness and the State, set on fire by civil wars, is born again, so to speak, from its ashes, and it takes on anew, fresh from the jaws of death, the vigor of youth."[129] Egyptian youth embody the hope of a new Arab Republic of Egypt. Will the regime learn from its mistakes and pave the way to civil society? Alternatively, will they repeat the same mistakes?

What you dream of you will get, but just believe in your dream and act accordingly. Some may find this nonsense, as the corrupt institutions in the country especially the "ubiquitous state apparatus" [130] *do not appear to reform. On the contrary, they seem to have returned to their old ways from before the January revolt. They may be right, but maybe they are wrong. Just maybe, the few good men inside those institutes will take upon themselves the biggest challenge of reforming their colleagues and their institutions. As Fischer said, "Thoreau believed in the ability of the determined moral minority to correct the evils of the majority."* [131] *Egyptians need to rise above the situation and put their trust in the nation and believe that it will improve for reform to materialize.*

In South Africa, a common crime during the height of Apartheid was 'necklacing' where anyone in Black South African communities suspected of being an Apartheid spy would have a gasoline soaked tire put around their neck, and the tire would be ignited. The perpetrator of this terrible act would watch his victim burn into ashes and hope that the act served as a warning to anyone else who thought of betraying the community to the Apartheid Police. Despite this and other heinous crimes against humanity, which apartheid brought forth, South Africans rose to a higher level and turned a new chapter in their history. They heeded the late Nelson Mandela when he said, "We can forgive but we can never forget" [132]

When will Egyptians reach reconciliation with the nizam and move forward? Will Egypt witness the creation of a true civil society? Will Egypt be able to develop capable civil rulers? When will Egyptians accept Ikhwan as part of Egyptian society? Why did Ikhwan not work with the opposition towards a better future for all Egyptians? When will feloul, activists and Ikhwan recognize and reconcile their mistakes and strive to build a better Egypt with all Egyptians? Can Egyptians move forward from this exaggerated demon-like Ikhwan monster? Is it right to consider all Ikhwan brothers and sisters as terrorists? It is a fact, that Ikhwan committed huge mistakes, some possibly even crimes and treason, but is ostracizing them the only way? Is it proper to bring up our children demonizing anyone related to Ikhwan? Egyptians are capable of forgiving and moving ahead. The core of a true Muslim society and value system is having a tolerant society, apparently a long road ahead for Egypt. Impartial justice is essential to whoever breaks the law. Moreover, if justice fails in this life, if Egyptians are really the most pious people on this earth as per the Gallup survey, they surely know that the Almighty God will render justice on Judgment Day.

The scholar in Candide summed up part of the situation in Egypt when he said, "I find that all goes wrong with us, and that no one knows his place in society or his proper employment…our time is spent in pointless quarrels…In fact, it is perpetual civil war." [133] *When will Egyptians realize this and stop the pointless quarrels trying to prove who is right?*

Free Minds

The late Egyptian President Gamal Abdel Nasser rightly said, "La yomken algaaea algahel an yakoun huran fey ekhteratehoho." (It is impossible that the hungry ignorant man be free in his choices). Democracy can never be a one size fits all countries. Is democracy the ideal fit for Egypt? Whoever said that democracy and a military president are mutually exclusive? Let me remind you that the United States, the mother of democracy, has had over twenty-six presidents who have served in the military ranks at one point in their lives, out of the fifty so presidents. So why is it blasphemous to have a military president in a developing country like Egypt?

Not many people will agree with me, but over my long journey compiling this book and talking to Egyptians from all sorts of walks in life, I am at ease when I say that Egyptians cannot be tangibly free until they free their minds. Mandela said, "I wanted to be free so I let it go." This is what Egyptians need to do to move on. "Those who see liberty as the freedom to do what they please will not be able to govern themselves"[134] Egyptians sadly and clearly misunderstood freedom. Free minds must be wary of the worldly matters, if not literally, then at least independent in thinking. Egyptian men and women must make informed and rational decisions determining what they want their future to be and who they want to represent them without simple manipulation and directing.

Each country requires a different set of solutions that considers its history, society, culture, literacy, economy, politics and so many other factors. This is why democracy cannot always be the solution to all countries. Maybe a semblance of democracy for one country, an almost democracy for another, and maybe no democracy for another. I agree with Thoreau when he said, "If we take the term in the strict sense, there never has been a real democracy, and there never will be"[135] So far, in Egypt, the road to democracy has become a zero–sum game for the Egyptian people. The polarized scene between the Islamists led by Ikhwan and the military with the activists played as if muppets, while the people pay the price and no Realpolitik in the midst. Group interests are outweighing and outmaneuvering national interests.

Despite the Egyptian plight, the glass is half-full. Though freedom is not complete, it is not extinct. Take for instance the case of military-ruled Burma that had minor freedoms. Burmese were not free socially as to visit or spend the night at friends or families, "their presence has to be reported to the local Law and Order Restoration Council (LORC) before nine o'clock in the evening...." "Form 10 is the list of all the members of a family"[136] Therefore, if authorities had found a person not in the Form 10 at night, the guest and the host would have gotten into trouble with authorities. Promoting political parties was not a freedom; "it was announced that no party signboards should be put up in offices at the village and ward level. The reason given was that a multiplicity of party signboards in

362

small villages and wards would lead to clashes among members of the respective parties. "[137] *Things may have changed in Burma.*

Egyptians seeking the ideal democracy need to look around all developing countries. They should not refer to what takes place in mature democracies, but look at countries with similar military dominance. Once they do that, I believe they will see the glass half-full as Egypt has more freedoms than Burma as sited above. They should also refer to mature democracies, but need to be realistic as Egypt will not be a mature democracy overnight. This is the fruit of years of hard work and a key prerequisite is to have free minds. Egyptians need to free their minds - not only the illiterate, but perhaps more so, many of the literate who judge, are intolerant and stereotype, erasing any education they may have received.

The January revolt has led some individuals to want to be their best, to become better citizens. I have always wanted to write, but never actually came around to it. This revolt has inspired so many other Egyptians too, as is apparent in the new wave of music, art, movies, sport, literature, science, entrepreneurs among others. Nevertheless, for the revolt to reap its fruits the people must change, specifically their values. Actually, Egypt needs a cultural revolution, not in the form of protests but revolutionary change in the culture in terms of values, behavior and beliefs. As Martin Luther King said, "we as a nation must undergo a radical revolution of values"[138] Egyptians need to learn to respect, tolerate and accept differences. For a society to be balanced and healthy it needs the richness of diversity and inclusivity, the young and the old, the men and the women, the conservative and the liberal, the moderate and the extremist, the abled and differently abled. The Muslim and the Christian, the educated and the non-educated, the civilian and the military, the lawmaker and the law enforcer, the blue collar and the white collar, are all important for Egyptian society. Everyone has a positive role to play in building a better future for our children. Each role will have a different path to follow.

As Friedrich Nietzsche said, "You have your way. I have my way. As for the right way, the correct way, and the only way, it does not exist." May Egypt tread a good way, whatever that may be, a way that will ensure bread, freedom and social equality, whatever form of government the future may hold.

"When the power of love overcomes the love of power, the world will know peace."
Jimi Hendrix

363

GLOSSARY

Abaya: loose robes

Ahkam: theological rules

Akrab: The Arabic word for Scoprion, a maximum-security prison inside the Tora prison complex

Al Jihad: Strife in general, usually used in a religious context

al-Ahram newspaper: *The most prominent quasi governmental newspaper*

Amn el Dawla: State security

Amn Elmarkazi: Central Security forces; The Egyptian anti-riot police

Amn El Watani: National Security

Azan: The call to prayer

Baladi bread: local flat bread made of whole-wheat flour

Baltegeya: thugs

Calipha: The Caliph; an Islamic political leader. A position that is no longer officially in existence

El Midan: The square

El share'a: Theological law

Feloul: Literally remnants; a term used to refer to supporters of the Mubarak regime

Fitna: sedition

Foul: fava beans

Gaber Ibn Hayan: The popular name for the state security premises on Giza on Gaber Ibn Hayan St.

Galabeya: Traditional robes. The name applies to both the female and male versions of them although they differ greatly

Gamaat Al Jihad Al Islamiya: An Egyptian Islamist armed group active since the late 1970s and under embargo by the United Nations for its affiliation with Al- Qaeda. It is responsible among other things for the assassination of former Egyptian president Sadat refered in the book in abbreviation as Al Gamaa

Ghawghaa: mobs

Hadith: The tradition and sayings of the prophet Mohamed

Haga: a title given to women who have completed the pilgrimage but is also often used to address older women in general

Haram: sinful

Hasanat: good deeds

Hezb el Kanaba: Literally the Couch Party symbolizing the silent majority during the revolt.

Hijab: Muslim woman wearing a scarf or viel covering her hair, long sleeve and long skirt or trouser.

Ikhwan: The Muslim Brotherhood

Imam: Leader of prayer and generally a title given to influential Islamic figures of theological background

Jihadist activists: activists, sometimes armed, belonging to Al Jihad and other militant Islamic movements

Itihadiyah Palace: The presidential palace

Khemar: A long veil reaching to the waist or beyond

Koshari: An Egyptian cheap and popular dish of rice, lentils and pasta with various sauces

Maghreb: sunset

Masalan: for instance

Milyouneya: 'millions' march; a march that aims at attracting over a million participants

Mogamaa El Tahrir: A building housing many governmental departments that deals directly with citizens

Maghoul: unknown

Mokhabarat: The intelligence

Nahda: The name given to President Morsi and Ikhwan's political program

Nassara: Nazarites the name given by Islamists to Christians meaning the followers of Jesus of Nazareth

Maalesh: Its ok; I am sorry in a laid-back way

Niqab: full-face veil

Nizam: Regime

Nokhba: The elite; mainly used in association with the intellectual elite

Ousar: families; the name given to the units or cells of the Muslim Brotherhood that have a role indoctrination

Pasha: A rank given to some men of the aristocracy and members of the top level of government officials and members of society during the royal era. After the cancelation of ranks with the end of the monarchy it started being used on a haphazard basis to indicate someone is talking to a person they perceive as higher in rank.

Rabaa: A square in Cairo where the opponents to the removal of President Morsi, many of them Muslim Brotherhood members, staged a sit in that was finally dispersed by the Egyptian forces causing a large number of casualties

Rayees: Chief, usually meaning the president

Salafists: People adhering to the Salafi ideology that takes the early Islamic period as their reference

Sayedna: Our master; a title given to the early companions of the prophet Mohamed

Intifada: uprising
Selah el eshara: Signal Corps
Shaab: people
Shabab: youth
Shehada: Testimony, in either court or speech or the proclamation of faith by a Muslim
Shoura: Consultation; Shura Council, is the upper house of parliament
Soul: lieutenant
Taher: Pure, often used in the religious sense
Tala' el Fatah: Vanguards of the Conquest; an offshoot from Al Jihad movement in the early 1990 that folded in under Al Jihad again later
Tahrir: Liberation, Tahrir Square is where the main events of the 2011 revolution took place in Cairo
Tamarod: A political campaign aimed at registering opposition to President Morsi to force him to call early presidential elections
Tashreefa: Literally the ceremonial procession; a popular name for the reception of prisoners in prison, which include physical assaults
SheikhAl Azhar: Highest-ranking Islamic clergyman in Egypt
Thawragy: revolutionary
Tekdeer: to make someone miserable
Tora: A prison complex that include many several prisons inside its walls
Wahhabism: A fundamentalist Islamic ideology that originated with the thought of Saudi militant Mohamed Ibn Abdel Wahab
Wasta: nepotism
Zebiba: scar on the forehead or leg from prostration during prayer
Zohr: noon

SUGGESTED SIMILAR READINGS

1. Rising from Tahrir by Hoda Rashad,
2. Liberation Square by Ashraf Khalil.
3. 18 Days in Tahrir: Stories from Egypt's Revolution by Hatem Rushdy
4. L'Egypte de Tahrir: Anatomie d'une revolution by Claude Guibal and Tangi Salaun
5. The Instigators by David Wolman.
6. Alaa Aswany, On The State of Egypt.
7. Cairo: My City, Our Revolution by Ahdaf Soueif.
8. Revolution 2.0: The Power of the People is Greater than the People in Power: A Memoir by Wael Ghonim.

Suggested Related Readings

1. The Long Walk to Freedom, Nelson Mandela
2. Gandhi: The Life and Message for the World, By Louis Fischer
3. The Autobiography of Martin Luther King, Jr edited by ClayBorne Carson
4. Mandela by Peter Hain
5. Animal Farm: A Fairy Story, George Orwell
6. 1984, George Orwell
7. Utopia, Thomas Moore
8. The Communist Manifesto, Karl Marx and Frederick Engels
9. The Prince, Machiavelli
10. Candide, Voltaire
11. The Social Contract or Principles of Political Right, Jean Jacques Rousseau
12. The Lady and The Peacock: The Life of Aung San Suu Kyi of Burma by Peter Popham
13. Letters from Burma, Ann San Suu Kyi
14. Che's Afterlife The Legacy of an Image by Michael Casey

ABOUT THE AUTHOR

Nadine Moussa is an Egyptian who had the privilege of growing up in several countries in Africa, Europe and the Middle East within the realms of the diplomatic community which her father was amongst. With the constant traveling, Nadine was exposed and open to new cultures, religions and languages, thirsty to learn more, happy to settle in new homes and countries and always eager for new learning and adventure.

Curious bookworm and ardent learner, Nadine was inspired to read by her late grandmother who was an avid reader frequently visiting the library where Nadine accompanied her on many days. She studied English Literature and European History during high school at Sierra Leone and later Business Administration and Philosophy at the American University in Cairo. Her intellect inspired by great legendary leaders like Gandhi, Nelson Mandela and Martin Luther King.

She is a critical, curious, logical, receptive, respected, responsible woman who seeks for all individuals respect, chance to be listened and understood. She is a liberal open-minded woman yet conservative and value driven. She is a fighter for justice and equality for all humans. She is a change agent, inspiring others to be the change they want. Her challenging career in marketing and business excellence and development sharpened her insight and innovation. The revolution, however, awoke her true inner fire, her passion for writing and her curiosity to understand.

Nadine lives in Giza with her husband and two sons.

About the Editors

Nada is an American with Egyptian and Syrian origins. Nada's experience is an eclectic mix of international development work with a focus on early childhood projects. Nada has worked for a number of prestigious international organizations. Currently she is living and working in New York.

Nermin Serhan is an Egyptian writer and editor since 1993.

Dominique lives in Johannesburg, South Africa with her two children, where she tutors English and Math, writes magazine articles, and edits everything from MBA dissertations to books. Her passion for language and appreciation of diversity in culture has given her a unique perspective that allows her the ability to appreciate the diversity that binds us together, and sets us apart.

About the Illustrator

Yasser Gaessa is an Egyptian painter, cartoonist and writer since 1992.

ENDNOTES

1   1984 George Orwell
2   Cairo My City, Our Revolution, Ahdaf Soueif, 2012
3   Long Walk To Freedom The Autobiography of Nelson Mandela
4   Alaa Aswany, On The State of Egypt.
5   The Cairo Review of Global Affairs. Special Report: Arab Revolution
6   Peace be Upon him is a small prayer or address that Muslims traditionally say
    when mentioning the Prophet Mohamed
7   The Autobiography of Martin Luther King, Jr edited by ClayBorne Carson
8   My City, Our Revolution, Ahdaf Seouif.
9   Animal Farm, George Orwell
10 https://www.youtube.com/watch?v=9oIFEyGS6wQ
11 The Autobiography of Martin Luther King, Jr edited by ClayBorne Carson
12 The Autobiography of Martin Luther King, Jr edited by ClayBorne Carson
13 https://www.youtube.com/watch?v=v_Pazrk7C3c
14 Voltaire, Candide
15 Thomas Moore, Utopia.
16 Autobiography of Martin Luther King, Jr. edited by Clayborne Carson.
17 https://www.youtube.com/watch?v=kWr6MypZ-JU
18 Candide, Voltaire.
19 The Communist Manifesto, Karl Marx and Frederick Engels.
20 The Autobiography of Martin Luther King, Jr edited by ClayBorne Carson.
21 The Prince, Machiavelli.
22 1984, George Orwell.
23 A.Yusuf Ali, Tranlation and Commentary of Quran.
24 The Holy Qur-an, English translation of the meanings and Commentary.
    Revised and Edited by The Presidency of Islamic Researches, IFTA
25 The Autobiography of Martin Luther King, Jr. edited by Clayborne Carson.
26 Interview part 1 http://www.youtube.com/watch?v=-o3EKhugaJQ
    Interview part 2 http://www.youtube.com/watch?v=v-OcuTypFwQ
27 A.Yusuf Ali, Tranlation and Commentary of Quran.
28 The Autobiography of Martin Luther King, Jr. edited by Clayborne Carson.

29 A.Yusuf Ali, Tranlation and Commentary of Quran.
30 The Social Contract or Principles of Political Right, Jean Jacques Rousseau.
31 The Autobiography of Martin Luther King, Jr. edited by Clayborne Carson.
32 https://youtu.be/7vprfST-PiM
33 Mandela by Peter Hain, 2010.
34 Gandhi: The Life and Message for the World, Louis Fischer.
35 Che's AfterLife: The Legacy of an Image by Michael Casey.
36 Mandela by Peter Hain, 2010.
37 The Cairo Review of Global Affairs, Special Report: Arab Revolution.
38 Gandhi: The Life and Message for the World, Louis Fischer.
39 The Autobiography of Martin Luther King, Jr. edited by Clayborne Carson.
40 The Cairo Review of Global Affairs, Special Report: Arab Revolution.
41 Gandhi: The Life and Message for the World, Louis Fischer.
42 Gandhi: The Life and Message for the World, Louis Fischer.
43 The Prince, Machiavelli.
44 The Prince, Machiavelli.
45 The Cairo Review of Global Affairs, Special Report: Arab Revolution.
46 Che's AfterLife: The Legacy of an Image by Michael Casey.
47 The Cairo Review of Global Affairs. Special Report: Arab Revolution
48 http://youtu.be/EAhmuVDy9tw and http://youtu.be/imvws8H09uw
49 Index Mundi 2012
50 The Autobiography of Martin Luther King, Jr edited by ClayBorne Carson.
51 The Autobiography of Martin Luther King, Jr edited by ClayBorne Carson.
52 Lady and The Peacock. The Life of Aung San Suu Kyi of Burma by Peter Popham.
53 The Autobiography of Martin Luther King, Jr edited by ClayBorne Carson.
54 Che's Afterlife The Legacy of an Image by Michael Casey
55 Egypt Independent, "Egypt stifles traditionally tolerated Salafi outlerts ahead of polls', by Noha El Hennawy, 26 October, 2010.
56 The Autobiography of Martin Luther King, Jr. edited by Clayborne Carson.
57 http://en.wikipedia.org/wiki/Demographics_of_Egypt
58 The Autobiography of Martin Luther King, Jr. edited by Clayborne Carson.
59 http://www.youtube.com/watch?v=_SsccRkLLzU
60 Thomas Moore, Utopia.
61 Thomas Moore, Utopia.
62 The Prince, Machiavelli.
63 George Orwell, Animal Farm: A Fairy Story.
64 The Holy Qur-an, English translation of the meanings and Commentary. Revised and Edited by The Presidency of Islamic Researches, IFTA
65 The Autobiography of Martin Luther King, Jr. edited by Clayborne Carson.
66 The Autobiography of Martin Luther King, Jr. edited by Clayborne Carson.

67 The Autobiography of Martin Luther King, Jr. edited by Clayborne Carson.

68 Bible, Dar El Ketab AlMokadas.

69 Bible, Dar El Ketab AlMokadas.

70 The Autobiography of Martin Luther King, Jr. edited by Clayborne Carson.

71 George Orwell, Animal Farm: A Fairy Story.

72 The Autobiography of Martin Luther King, Jr. edited by Clayborne Carson.

73 George Orwell, Animal Farm: A Fairy Story.

74 George Orwell, Animal Farm: A Fairy Story

75 The Prince, Machiavelli.

76 The Autobiography of Martin Luther King, Jr. edited by Clayborne Carson.

77 Mandela by Peter Hain, 2010.

78 https://www.youtube.com/watch?v=KsK0Yqiyjrs
    https://www.youtube.com/watch?v=UyIRd5TmLLI

79 The Lady and The Peacock. The Life of Aung San Suu Kyi of Burma by Peter Popham.

80 http://english.ahram.org.eg/NewsContentP/1/6372/Egypt/Egypt-Police-officer-shoots-microbus-driver-in-Cai.aspx this link is from the quasi official newpaper Al Ahram and clearly states that the police officer shot the driver. Despite not interfering in the testimony of any person featured in the book it is worth mentioning that all accounts of the incident clearly states that the officer had and used a handgun

81 https://www.google.com.eg/search?q=%D8%A3%D8%B4%D8%B1%D9%81+%D8%A7%D9%84%D8%B3%D8%AC%D9%8A%D9%86%D9%8A+%D8%A7%D9%84%D9%85%D8%B9%D8%A7%D8%AF%D9%8A&client=firefox-b&biw=1366&bih=657&tbm=vid&source=lnms&sa=X&ved=0ahUKEwiImYnHhLnNAhVBAxoKHUXzA68Q_AUICigD&dpr=1

82 Gandhi: The Life and Message for the World by Louis Fischer

83 Prince by Machiavelli.

84 Utopia by Thomas Moore.

85 The Social Contract or Principles of Political Right, Jean Jacques Rousseau.

86 The Holy Quran, English translation of the meanings and Commentary. Revised and Edited by The Presidency of Islamic Researches, IFTA

87 The Communist Manifesto Karl Marx and Frederick Engels

88 The Autobiography of Martin Luther King, Jr edited by ClayBorne Carson

89 Alaa Al Aswany On The State of Egypt.

90 The Autobiography of Martin Luther King, Jr edited by ClayBorne Carson

91 The Autobiography of Martin Luther King, Jr edited by ClayBorne Carson

92 The Holy Quran-an, English translation of the meanings and Commentary. Revised and Edited by The Presidency of Islamic Researches, IFTA

93 The Holy Quran-an, English translation of the meanings and Commentary. Revised and Edited by The Presidency of Islamic Researches, IFTA

94   The Holy Quran-an, English translation of the meanings and Commentary. Revised and Edited by The Presidency of Islamic Researches, IFTA

95   The Holy Quran-an, English translation of the meanings and Commentary. Revised and Edited by The Presidency of Islamic Researches, IFTA

96   The Lady and The Peacock: The Life of Aung San Suu Kyi of Burma by Peter Popham.

97   Cairo My City, Our Revolution, AhdafSoueif

98   Cairo My City, Our Revolution, AhdafSoueif

99   Machiavelli, The Prince

100 Machiavelli, The Prince.

101 The Prince, Machiavelli

102 The Autobiography of Martin Luther King, Jr edited by ClayBorne Carson, pg 268.

103 Machiavelli, The Prince

104 Long Walk to Freedom, Nelson Mandela.

105 On the State of Egypt, Alaa Al Aswany.

106 The Lady and The Peacock. The Life of Aung San Suu Kyi of Burma by Peter Popham

107 Long Walk to Freedom, Nelson Mandela.

108 The Autobiography of Martin Luther King, Jr edited by ClayBorne Carson

109 The Communist Hypothesis, Alain Badiou p 56

110 1984, George Orwell.

111 The Autobiography of Martin Luther King, Jr edited by ClayBorne Carson.

112 Letters from Burma, Ann San Suu Kyi.

113 1984, George Orwell

114 The Prince, Machiavelli.

115 The Social Contract or Principles of Political Right, Jean Jacques Rousseau.

116 The Prince, Machiavelli.

117 The Communist Manifesto, Hegel and Marx

118 The Communist Manifesto, Karl Marx and Frederick Engels

119 The Social Contract or Principles of Political Right, Jean Jacques Rousseau.

120 The Lady and The Peacock: The Life of Aung San Suu Kyi of Burma by Peter Popham

121 Machiavelli, The Prince

122 The Autobiography of Martin Luther King, Jr edited by ClayBorne Carson

123 Mandela by Peter Hain in 2010.

124 Ann San Suu Kyi Letters from Burma

125 Brodie's Notes on George Orwell's Animal Farm.

126 Che's Afterlife The Legacy of an Image by Michael Casey.

127 The Autobiography of Martin Luther King, Jr edited by ClayBorne Carson.

128 The Autobiography of Martin Luther King, Jr edited by ClayBorne Carson.

129 The Social Contract or Principles of Political Right, Jean Jacques Rousseau.

130 Mandela by Peter Hain in 2010.

131 Gandhi: The Life and Message for the World, By Louis Fischer

132 The Long Walk to Freedom, Nelson Mandela

133 Voltaire, Candide.

134 http://www.abuddhistlibrary.com/Buddhism/B%20-%20Theravada/Teachers/Ven%20Payutto/Buddhist%20Solutions%20for%20the%20%20Twenty-First%20Century/The%20Making%20of%20Democracy.htm

135 The Social Contract or Principles of Political Right, Jean Jacques Rousseau.

136 Ann San Suu Kyi Letters from Burma.

137 Ann San Suu Kyi Letters from Burma.
http://www.abuddhistlibrary.com/Buddhism/B%20-%20Theravada/Teachers/Ven%20Payutto/Buddhist%20Solutions%20for%20the%20%20Twenty-First%20Century/The%20Making%20of%20Democracy.htm

138 The Autobiography of Martin Luther King, Jr edited by ClayBorne Carson.

Printed in the United States
By Bookmasters